PERSPECTIVES *on*

AMERICAN

FOREIGN POLICY

PERSPECTIVES *on* AMERICAN FOREIGN POLICY

Readings and Cases

BRUCE W. JENTLESON

Duke University

W · W · NORTON & COMPANY   NEW YORK · LONDON

150182

The text of this book is composed in Minion
with the Display set in Bauer Bodoni and PSpire.
Composition by PennSet, Inc., Bloomsburg, PA
Manufacturing by The Courier Companies, Inc.

Acknowledgments and copyright continue on p. 325
which serves as a continuation of the copyright page.

Library of Congress-in-Publication Data

Perspectives on American foreign policy: readings and cases / Bruce W. Jentleson, editor.
    p. cm.
    Includes bibliographical references.
    ISBN 0-393-97564-9 (pbk.)
    1. United States—Foreign relations. 2. United States—Foreign relations—Case studies.
I. Jentleson, Bruce W., 1951–

E183.7.P496 2000
327.73—dc21   99-056471
    ISBN 0-393-97564-9 (pbk.)

W. W. Norton & Company, Inc., 500 Fifth Avenue, New York, NY 10110
http://www.wwnorton.com

W. W. Norton & Company Ltd., 10 Coptic Street, London WC1A 1PU
1 2 3 4 5 6 7 8 9 0

Contents

Preface

No textbook can delve into as much depth as the author would like. In the trade-off between scope of coverage and depth of discussion and analysis, the former needs to take priority given the principal purposes texts serve. This is why supplemental books of readings are of such value. They provide the articles, case studies, and other readings that more fully develop key theories, concepts, histories, and policies introduced in the text, and they also more extensively explore major scholarly and policy debates. Teaching utility is especially great when text and reader are crafted for genuine complementarity.

This is the relationship we intend between this book, *Perspectives on American Foreign Policy: Readings and Cases*, and the text, *American Foreign Policy: The Dynamics of Choice in the 21st Century*. The chapter structure is identical in both; "Reader icons" in the margins of the text refer the student to the pertinent supplemental reading, either article **1.1** or case study **CS2** .

The articles (Chapters 1, 3, 4, 9, and 10) are drawn from major journal articles and book chapters, classics in the field as well as important new perspectives, reprinted and abridged with permission. Authors include Inis Claude, Francis Fukuyama, Ole Holsti, Samuel Huntington, George Kennan ("Mr. X"), Henry Kissinger, Walter LaFeber, Edward Mansfield and Jack Snyder, Hans Morgenthau, and other eminent scholars and experienced policy-makers.

The case studies are abridged from longer versions written as part of the Kennedy School of Government Case Program. Each case study is illustrative of the key themes and concepts for its corresponding chapter: the South Africa anti-apartheid economic sanctions as bringing out the domestic politics of U.S. foreign policy (Chapter 2), key decisions on the Vietnam War as crucial to understanding a fundamental set of lessons and legacies of the

Cold War (Chapter 5), the 1995 Dayton Accords ending the Bosnia war as an example of the U.S. role as peace broker (Chapter 7), and the 1990–91 Persian Gulf crisis as demonstrating both the scope and the limits of American power (Chapter 8).

Thanks go to many members of the team who also were crucial to the text: Roby Harrington, for his clear conception from the outset of the value of the combination of text and reader; Sarah Caldwell and Rob Whiteside, for their steady and thorough roles in administering and developing the project; Sarah Johnson, for unflappable research assistance, no matter how many tasks small and large kept coming.

BWJ

1 The Strategic Context: Foreign Policy Strategy and the Essence of Choice

"The national interest": All of us have heard it preached. Many of us may have done some of the preaching ourselves—that American foreign policy must be made in the name of the national interest. To be sure, no one would argue with the proposition that following the "national interest" is the essence of the choices to be made in a nation's foreign policy. But defining what the national interest is and then developing policies for achieving it have rarely been as easy or self-evident as such invocations would imply.

The framework developed in *American Foreign Policy: The Dynamics of Choice in the 21st Century* frames the analysis of the U.S. national interest in terms of four core goals: power, peace, prosperity, and principles. The articles in this chapter are representative of each of the four corresponding "schools" of international relations theory.

Hans Morgenthau is widely regarded as one of the intellectual founding fathers of Realism and is the author of the classic statement that "statesmen think and act in terms of interest defined as power." This reading, "The Mainspring of American Foreign Policy," is drawn from his book *In Defense of the National Interest*. It makes a strong case for why power needs to be the priority goal for U.S. foreign policy, the essential basis for defining the national interest.

While in a sense all four of the national interest objectives are about peace, in this particular notion of the national interest we have in mind two main types of foreign policy. One is building international organizations and institutions as mechanisms for managing even if not eliminating power politics. The other is the "peace broker" role the United States has played, historically as well as in the contemporary world, in wars and conflicts to which it has not been a direct party. The excerpt here from Inis Claude's

1

Swords into Plowshares: The Problems and Prospects of International Organization principally addresses the former.

Among the theories that stress prosperity and the economic motivations driving U.S. foreign policy are some that take a benign view ("general welfarism") and others that portray the United States as an imperialistic power. As Gabriel Kolko sees it, in his *The Roots of American Foreign Policy,* "to understand the unique economic interests and aspirations of the United States in the world, and the degree to which it benefits or loses within the existing distribution and structure of power and the world economy, is to define a crucial basis for comprehending as well as predicting its role overseas."

The fourth core goal involves the values, ideals, and beliefs that the United States has claimed to stand for in the world. This emphasis on principles is most evident in theories of democratic idealism. Such theories argue both that the United States should make its principles a defining feature of its national interest, and that the diplomatic record shows that American foreign policy largely has lived up to this standard. Tony Smith's book *America's Mission: The United States and the Worldwide Struggle for Democracy in the Twentieth Century* exemplifies these arguments.

 *Power*

HANS J. MORGENTHAU
The Mainsprings of American Foreign Policy

Wherever American foreign policy has operated, political thought has been divorced from political action. Even where our long-range policies reflect faithfully, as they do in the Americas and in Europe, the true interests of the United States, we think about them in terms that have at best but a tenuous connection with the actual character of the policies pursued. We have acted on the international scene, as all nations must, in power-political terms; but we have tended to conceive of our actions in non-political, moralistic terms. This aversion to seeing problems of international politics as they are, and the inclination to view them in non-political and moralistic terms, can be attributed both to certain misunderstood peculiarities of the American experience in foreign affairs and to the general climate of opinion in the Western world during the better part of the nineteenth and the first decades of the twentieth centuries. Three of these peculiarities of the American experience stand out: the uniqueness of the American experiment; the actual isolation, during the nineteenth century, of the United States from the centers of world conflict; and the humanitarian pacifism and anti-imperialism of American ideology.

∗ ∗ ∗

∗ ∗ ∗ [W]hile the foreign policy of the United States was forced, by circumstance if not by choice, to employ the methods, shoulder the commitments, seek the objectives, and run the risks, from which it had thought itself permanently exempt, American political thought continued to uphold that exemption at least as an ideal. And that ideal was supposed to be only temporarily beyond the reach of the American people, because of the wickedness and stupidity of either American or, preferably, foreign statesmen. In one sense, this ideal of a free, peaceful, and prosperous world, from which popular government had forever banished power politics, was a natural out-

From *In Defense of the National Interest* (New York: Alfred A. Knopf, 1951), chapters 1 and 8.

growth of the American experience. In another sense, this ideal expressed in a particularly eloquent and consistent fashion the general philosophy that dominated the Western world during the better part of the nineteenth century. This philosophy rests on two basic propositions: that the struggle for power on the international scene is a mere accident of history, naturally associated with non-democratic government and therefore destined to disappear with the triumph of democracy throughout the world; and that, in consequence, conflicts between democratic and non-democratic nations must be primarily conceived not as struggles for mutual advantage in terms of power but as fights between good and evil, which can only end with the complete triumph of good, and with evil wiped off the face of the earth.

* * *

The fundamental error that has thwarted American foreign policy in thought and action is the antithesis of national interest and moral principles. The equation of political moralizing with morality and of political realism with immorality is itself untenable. The choice is not between moral principles and the national interest, devoid of moral dignity, but between one set of moral principles divorced from political reality, and another set of moral principles derived from political reality.

The moralistic detractors of the national interest are guilty of both intellectual error and moral perversion. The nature of the intellectual error must be obvious from what has been said thus far, as it is from the record of history: a foreign policy guided by moral abstractions, without consideration of the national interest, is bound to fail; for it accepts a standard of action alien to the nature of the action itself. All the successful statesmen of modern times from Richelieu to Churchill have made the national interest the ultimate standard of their policies, and none of the great moralists in international affairs has attained his goals.

The perversion of the moralizing approach to foreign policy is threefold. That approach operates with a false concept of morality, developed by national societies but unsuited to the conditions of international society. In the process of its realization, it is bound to destroy the very moral values it sets out to promote. Finally, it is derived from a false antithesis between morality and power politics, thus arrogating to itself all moral values and placing the stigma of immorality upon the theory and practice of power politics.

There is a profound and neglected truth hidden in Hobbes's extreme dictum that the state creates morality as well as law and that there is neither morality nor law outside the state. Universal moral principles, such as justice or equality, are capable of guiding political action only to the extent that they have been given concrete content and have been related to political situations by society. What justice means in the United States can within wide limits be objectively ascertained; for interests and convictions, experiences of life and institutionalized traditions have in large measure created a consensus concerning what justice means under the conditions of American society. No such consensus exists in the relations between nations. For above the national societies there exists no international society so integrated as to be able to define for them the concrete meaning of justice or equality, as national societies do for their individual members. In consequence, the appeal to moral principles by the representative of a nation vis-à-vis another nation signifies something fundamentally different from a verbally identical appeal made by an individual in his relations to another individual member of the same national society. The appeal to moral principles in the international sphere has no concrete universal meaning. It is either so vague as to have no concrete meaning that could provide rational guidance for political action, or it will be nothing but the reflection of the moral preconceptions of a particular nation and will by that same token be unable to gain the universal recognition it pretends to deserve.

Whenever the appeal to moral principles provides guidance for political action in international affairs, it destroys the very moral principles it intends to realize. It can do so in three different ways. Universal moral principles can serve as a mere pretext for the pursuit of national policies. In other words, they fulfill the functions of those ideological rationalizations and justifications to which we have referred before. They are mere means to the ends of national policies, bestowing upon the national interest the false dignity of universal moral principles. The performance of such a function is hypocrisy and abuse and carries a negative moral connotation.

The appeal to moral principles may also guide political action to that political failure which we have mentioned above. The extreme instance of political failure on the international plane is national suicide. It may well be said that a foreign policy guided by universal moral principles, by definition relegating the national interest to the background, is under contemporary conditions of foreign policy and warfare a policy of national suicide, actual or potential. Within a national society the individual can at times afford, and may even be required, to subordinate his interests and even to sacrifice his very existence to a supra-individual moral principle—for in national societies such principles exist, capable of providing concrete standards for individual action. What is more important still, national societies take it upon themselves within certain limits to protect and promote the interests of the individual and, in particular, to guard his existence against violent attack. National societies of this kind can exist and fulfill their functions only if their individual members are willing to subordinate their individual interests in a certain measure to the common good of society. Altruism and self-sacrifice are in that measure morally required.

The mutual relations of national societies are fundamentally different. These relations are not controlled by universal moral principles concrete enough to guide the political actions of individual nations. What again is more important, no agency is able to promote and protect the interests of individual nations and to guard their existence—and that is emphatically true of the great powers—but the individual nations themselves. To ask, then, a nation to embark upon altruistic policies oblivious of the national interest is really to ask something immoral. For such disregard of the individual interest, on the part of nations as of individuals, can be morally justified only by the existence of social institutions, the embodiment of concrete moral principles, which are able to do what otherwise the individual would have to do. In the absence of such institutions it would be both foolish and morally wrong to ask a nation to forego its national interests not for the good of a society with a superior moral claim but for a chimera. Morally speaking, national egotism is not the same as individual egotism because the functions of the international society are not identical with those of a national society.

The immorality of a politically effective appeal to moral abstractions in foreign policy is consummated in the contemporary phenomenon of the moral crusade. The crusading moralist, unable in the absence of an integrated national society to transcend the limits of national moral values and political interests, identifies the national interest with the manifestation of moral principles, which is, as we have seen, the typical function of ideology. Yet the crusader goes one step farther. He projects the national moral standards onto the international scene not only with the legitimate claim of reflecting the national interest, but with the politically and morally unfounded claim of providing moral standards for all mankind to conform to in concrete political action. Through the intermediary of the universal moral appeal the national and the universal interest become one and the same thing. What is good for the crusading country is by definition good for all mankind, and if the rest of mankind refuses to accept such claims to universal recognition, it must be converted with fire and sword.

There is already an inkling of this ultimate degeneration of international moralism in Wilson's crusade to make the world safe for democracy. We see it in full bloom in the universal aspirations of Bolshevism. Yet to the extent that the West, too, is persuaded that it has a holy mission, in the name of whatever moral principle, first to save the world and then to remake it, it has itself fallen victim to the moral disease of the crusading spirit in politics. If that disease should become general, as well it might, the age of political moralizing would issue in one or a series of religious world wars. The fanaticism of political religions would, then, justify all those abominations unknown to less moralistic but more politically-minded ages and for which in times past the fanaticism of other-worldly religions provided a convenient cloak.

In order to understand fully what these intellectual and moral aberrations of a moralizing in foreign policy imply, and how the moral and political problems to which that philosophy has given rise can be solved, we must recall that from the day of Machiavelli onward the controversy has been fought on the assumption that there was morality on one side and immorality on the other. Yet the antithesis that equates political moralizing with morality and political realism with immorality is erroneous.

We have already pointed out that it is a political necessity for the individual members of the international society to take care of their own national interests, and that there can be no moral duty to neglect them. Self-preservation both for the individual and for societies is, however, not only a biological and psychological necessity but, in the absence of an overriding moral obligation, a moral duty as well. In the absence of an integrated international society, the attainment of a modicum of order and the realization of a minimum of moral values are predicated upon the existence of national communities capable of preserving order and realizing moral values within the limits of their power.

It is obvious that such a state of affairs falls far short of that order and realized morality to which we are accustomed in national societies. The only relevant question is, however, what the practical alternative is to these imperfections of an international society that is based upon the national interests of its component parts. The attainable alternative is not a higher morality realized through the application of universal moral principles, but moral deterioration through either political failure or the fanaticism of political crusades. The juxtaposition of the morality of political moralism and the immorality of the national interest is mistaken. It presents a false concept of morality, developed by national societies but unsuited to the conditions of international society. It is bound to destroy the very moral values it aims to foster. Hence, the antithesis between moral principles and the national interest is not only intellectually mistaken but also morally pernicious. A foreign policy derived from the national interest is in fact morally superior to a foreign policy inspired by universal moral principles. Albert Sorel, the Anglophobe historian of the French Revolution, summarized well the real antithesis when he said in grudging admiration of Castlereagh:

> He piqued himself on principles to which he held with an unshakable constancy, which in actual affairs could not be distinguished from obstinacy; but these principles were in no degree abstract or speculative, but were all embraced in one alone, the supremacy of English interests; they all proceeded from this high reason of state.

In our time the United States is groping toward a reason of state of its own—one that expresses our national interest. The history of American foreign policy since the end of the Second World War is the story of the encounter of the American mind with a new political world. That mind was weakened in its understanding of foreign policy by half a century of ever more complete intoxication with moral abstractions. Even a mind less weakened would have found it hard to face with adequate understanding and successful action the unprecedented novelty and magnitude of the new political world. American foreign policy in that period presents itself as a slow, painful, and incomplete process of emancipation from deeply ingrained error, and of rediscovery of long-forgotten truths.

* * *

Forget and Remember!

Forget *the sentimental notion that foreign policy is a struggle between virtue and vice, with virtue bound to win.*

Forget *the utopian notion that a brave new world without power politics will follow the unconditional surrender of wicked nations.*

Forget *the crusading notion that any nation, however virtuous and powerful, can have the mission to make the world over in its own image.*

Remember *that the golden age of isolated normalcy is gone forever and that no effort, however great, and no action, however radical, will bring it back.*

Remember *that diplomacy without power is feeble, and power without diplomacy is destructive and blind.*

Remember *that no nation's power is without limits, and hence that its policies must respect the power and interests of others.*

Remember *that the American people have shown throughout their history that they are able to face the truth and act upon it with courage and resourcefulness in war, with common sense and moral determination in peace.*

And, above all, remember always that it is not only a political necessity but also a moral duty for a nation to follow in its dealings with other nations but one guiding star, one standard for thought, one rule for action:

The National Interest.

1.2 *Peace*

INIS L. CLAUDE, JR.

International Organization and World Order

"One World" is in some respects an ideal and an aspiration, born of modern interpretations of ancient moral insights and of rational estimates of the requirements for human survival; it is in other respects a pressing reality, an actual condition of mankind, produced by a century of change that has tied all the peoples of the earth together in an unprecedented intimacy of contact, interdependence of welfare, and mutuality of vulnerability. Whether or not we obey the religious injunction to behave like brothers, or attain the ethical objective of a peaceful world community, we human beings cannot escape the hard fact that all of us are, as John Donne put it, "involved in Mankinde." Given the existence of One World defined as a set of objective conditions, disaster may be the price of failure to achieve One World defined in terms of a moral and political ideal.

Sincere and sensible men may differ as to how much and what kind of world unity is possible and desirable, how it can or should be achieved, and how quickly it is likely to be or ought to be attempted. * * *

* * * However, we are not simply confronted with a debate about hypothetical possibilities for the future. The growing complexity of international relations has already produced international organizations; the world is engaged in the process of organizing. This process has a past which is not very long, as historians measure time, but which is nonetheless significant. It has a present which is confused and troubled, but which is not for that reason less important as an object of study. And, it may be confidently asserted, if man has a future, so has the process of international organization.

* * *

In functional terms, the process of international organization has brought greater progress toward a governed world than has been generally recognized, and certainly more than is acknowledged by those who adhere to the

From *Swords into Plowshares: The Problems and Progress of International Organization*, 4th ed. (New York: Random House, 1984), introduction and chapter 19.

doctrinaire view that government and anarchy are the two halves of an absolute either-or formula.

The last century, and particularly the last generation, has been an era of continuous development of patterns and techniques for managing the business of the international community. The old story of the sociological lag emphasizes the important truth that mankind has far to go, but it tends to obscure the fact that we are living in a period of adventurous experiment and flourishing inventiveness in the field of international relations. The creation of such institutional innovations as the general international organization, the international secretariat, the international conference of the parliamentary type, the international field commission for investigation and supervision, the peace-keeping force, the international technical assistance mission, the multilateral defense machinery of the NATO type, and the supranational functional agency of the kind recently developed in the European Community testifies to the significance of that fact. Moreover, fruitful improvisation is being increasingly supplemented by more systematic activities. The invention of invention is not exclusively a phenomenon of the scientific world; the international community is now equipped as never before with the analytical tools, professional staff, and organizational framework for designing and instituting new instruments to meet its needs.

The achievements of international organization include notable gains in the field of noncoercive regulatory devices. The agencies of the United Nations system exercise substantial influence and control—in short, *power* —over the behavior of states through the exploitation of a variety of methods: consultation and advice; inquiry, debate, and criticism of both public and private varieties; examination of reports and conduct of inspections; granting and withdrawal of subsidies and other forms of assistance; and recommendation followed by evaluation of response to this sort of pressure and possibly by insistent reiteration.

International institutions provide, above all, opportunities for states, singly and collectively, to influence each other. The facilities that they offer and the processes that they set in motion make it possible for states to exercise power in new ways, to utilize capabilities that have never before counted for much in international relations. Such factors as voting power, parliamentary skill, persuasiveness in debate, capacity to influence the content and ordering of agenda, and ability to affect the definition of issues and the wording of proposals become important elements of political power in international organizations. These agencies have not, of course, rendered the conventional varieties of power irrelevant to international relations, nor have they made these new varieties decisive, but they have significantly expanded the list of resources and methods available to states for affecting the policies and actions of other states.

International organization has made no such significant progress, nor has it demonstrated great promise, in the realm of coercive control of state behavior. True, the League engaged in a half-hearted effort to suppress Italian aggression in Ethiopia, and the United Nations sponsored the mobilization of collective resistance to Communist attack upon South Korea, with successful if not satisfactory results. More recently, the United Nations has attempted to use diplomatic and economic sanctions as instruments for breaking down the resistance of white-dominated regimes in Southern Africa, most notably that of Rhodesia, to demands for fundamental alteration of the racial and colonial status quo. At the regional level, the Organization of American States has shown some capacity for organized coercive activity against aberrant members. Nevertheless, international coercion of states determined to pursue their objectives or defend their policies by all necessary means, including the use of force, has not become, in any general sense, a reliable expectation or even a meaningful possibility. The United Nations has offered states no substitute for their own strength or that of allies as a resource for deterring or defeating their enemies. It is not, in reality or in evident potentiality, a synthetic superpower, able to protect all states by subduing any assailant. Its major contribution to the security of its members must be a product of its eligibility to serve as a neutral element in international relations, a kind of collective Switzerland, helping states to avoid clashes that their prudence commands them to avoid. While it cannot fight its members' battles for them, it can reinforce their efforts to remain at peace.

The primary resources for regulation of state behavior which have been discovered and developed by the League and the United Nations fall into the category of persuasion and influence rather than edict and compulsion. The question of the implications to be drawn from this factual situation is of central importance for the evaluation of international organization.

The simplest and perhaps the most tempting response is to conclude that international organization offers no real antidote to global disorder. To say that it relies primarily upon regulatory devices that are noncoercive in character is to admit that it is doomed to ineffectuality. Hence, no reasonable man can avoid making a choice between two conclusions: either that statesmen should give up the illusion that a governed world is possible, and settle down to the serious business of power politics, or that leaders and peoples should recognize the imperativeness of making the jump to a genuine world federation. What is not tenable is the assumption that international organization makes sense for a world in which power is the fundamental reality. The only meaningful alternatives are the mobilization of power behind national interest, or the concentration of power in support of the law of a global government.

This response reveals a curiously narrow conception of the means by which government performs regulatory functions, and, in its world federalist version, an extraordinarily broad view of the regulatory potency of the coercive instruments associated with governments. The truth is that all governments rely heavily—and that the most desirable and durable governments rely predominantly—upon noncoercive methods for producing and maintaining social order. To say that international organization has distinguished itself most notably by creating a record of persistence, flexibility, and ingenuity in the development and exploitation of devices for inducing compliance by consent rather than compulsion is not to say that it has proved absolutely either the impossibility or the indispensability of creating a world government. Rather, it is to say that some of the basic means for governing the world have been evolved and are being utilized with increasing effectiveness by agencies that do not conform to theoretical models of governmental institutions. It is surprising how many estimable people, who would recoil with horror at the thought of a purely coercive government in the United States and insist with intelligent understanding that a decent political order in the nation must rest upon processes of inducement and adjustment rather than upon sheer force, seem to picture government solely in terms of a policeman beating criminals into submission when they shift their attention to the international scene. People are being governed at other times than when they cower before a policeman or languish in prison cells. Nations are being governed at other times than when they are being prohibited, restrained, and compelled.

The obvious answer is that noncoercive techniques of social regulation are not enough, either within a nation or among the nations; a system of international organization which must rely almost wholly upon an ability to induce compliance, unsupported by a reserve capacity to command and compel obedience, is not simply an incompletely equipped agency of world order but a fatally defective one.

This observation applies equally to a system which possesses the power to enforce without the capacity to persuade. The experience of governments makes it clear that recognition of the indispensability of force must be qualified by awareness both of its inherent inadequacy and of its limited attainability. Power is not enough, and there cannot in fact be enough power to guarantee against breaches of the peace. The project of endowing a world government with sufficient power to prevent disorder is not only dangerous, but it is ultimately infeasible. Only in a thoroughly atomistic society is there a real possibility that threats to order can be put down by coercion without results that amount to a disruption of social order. Such societies exist only in the minds of theorists and in the objectives of totalitarian dictators. In the real world, national societies are characterized by a pluralism that can never be entirely ground down even by the most determined dictator, and the international society exhibits a pluralistic nature so striking that virtually all world governmentalists defer to it by advancing proposals for global federation rather than unitary government. To admit this is in fact to concede that governmental coercion cannot keep the civil peace; it can at best win the civil war. * * *

* * * [W]hat the United Nations most needs for the purpose of helping to create a meaningful world community is not new instruments of coercion, but precisely the variety of tools for doing useful work in the world which

it has been busily shaping. In these terms, a world that has recently devoted itself to creating and setting into operation an unprecedentedly elaborate system of international service agencies is to be credited with making an intelligent approach to peace. It is conceivable that the development of a public service corps is a more essential contribution to the creation of a community fit for law and order than the establishment of a police force.

In short, the conception of government as an agency that maintains order simply by commanding and compelling, prohibiting and punishing, has little relevance to a pluralistic national society and still less to a global society chiefly characterized by the depth of its divisions, the simplicity of its pluralistic pattern, and the underdevelopment of its capacity to superimpose a universal allegiance upon national loyalties. Given this kind of international community, the realization of the theoretical ideal of subjecting the world to unchallengeable authority would require the creation of an inordinately powerful world government; the fulfillment of the practical task of maintaining order in such a world involves the assiduous application of methods of compromise and adjustment. Here is a real paradox: the international community is so deficient in consensual foundations that it must theoretically be held together more by force than by consent, but it is marked by such decentralization of the resources of political and physical power that it must in practice be managed by agencies, whether they be called instruments of international organization or of world federation, that operate more by persuasion than by coercion. In the world as it is, there is no real alternative to efforts to achieve regulation of state behavior by noncoercive methods, and no more appropriate collective task than the provision of international services which may ultimately prove conducive to the breaking down of those features of the community structure which make reliance upon consent rather than coercion at once so necessary and so precarious. The regulatory methods and functional emphases of international organization may not conform to the image of government concocted by those who are impatient to abolish the problem of war by creating an entity which can, by definition, knock any and all national heads together, but they do correspond closely to the actual approach to the problem of maintaining order in a pluralistic society that the federal government of the United States has found essential. It is less significant that international organization is not a federal world government than that it is engaged in the effort to do the sort of thing that must be done, by the sort of method that can be used, to produce the sort of community that can, with proper management, sustain a peaceful existence.

Government, in the functional sense, is a relative matter, not an either-or proposition. The standard contrast between the state of affairs within national states and among them, which pictures domestic relationships as governed and international relationships as anarchic, has never been fully valid. Today, we must note with dismay that domestic affairs are all too often marked by the disorderliness usually associated with the international sphere, but we can also note with hope that international affairs are increasingly taking on some of the characteristics usually associated with the intranational domain. The domesticating of international relations is being promoted by international agencies. The development of a bureaucratic and a parliamentary apparatus, the inauguration of organs for central planning, the evolution of the sense of collective responsibility for the general welfare and of mechanisms and techniques for undertaking the tasks implied by that sense, the formalization of methods for the definition and legitimization of principles of public policy and community standards of behavior, and the development of institutionalized arrangements for the interplay of political interests—all these are aspects of that continuing process. The meaningful question is not whether the world has "a government," but how much governance is in evidence, how much effective governing is taking place. The answer is that the world has more government than some states, though less than most and less than it needs. The experiment of governing the world is now in operation, and the task of making the world governable is already being undertaken.

International organization has not been unaffected by the urge to solve the problem of world order by developing potentialities of coercion; recurrent expressions of interest in collective security and in the concept of an international military force testify to this point. Nevertheless, in actual operation, international organization reveals a fundamental commitment to the proposition that the nature of international society makes the preservation of peace dependent upon the stimulation of voluntary cooperation, the mobilization of moral restraint, the enlightenment of national self-interest, and the development of mutual understanding. The most urgent question of our time is not how to escape from the necessity of relying upon such methods as these, but how to make that necessity more tolerable. It is doubtful that the cause of world order is better served by agitated obsession with the danger that the essential consent of states to accept restraint and responsibility may not be forthcoming, than by constructive devotion to the task of developing more effective means for inducing that consent.

The Prospects of International Organization

To say that international organization does not represent a fundamentally mistaken approach to the problem of world order is not to assert that it is destined to succeed. The tough reality of the national divisions of world society makes the quest for agreed solutions of international problems a necessary enterprise, but the conflicting interests and purposes of national entities also make that quest a difficult one. Mankind is blessed by no cosmic guarantee that all its problems are soluble and all its dangers are avoidable.

The danger of violent conflict among states possessing vast power is the overwhelming reality of our time. Only the coldest of comfort is to be derived from the observation that the existence of this danger is attributable to the nature of the international community rather than to the nature of the international architecture contrived in 1945. In this situation, it is all too clear that the United Nations can offer no guarantee of peace and security; at best, it can facilitate the balancing of power against power, and mobilize the resources of political adjustment. In the long run, international organization may transform the working of the multi-state system. In the short run, it is inevitably more affected by the circumstances of international relations than effective in altering those circumstances.

There can be no guarantee that international machinery will in fact be utilized for the high purposes to which it may be formally dedicated. The establishment of an international organization does not involve the creation of an autonomous will, inexorably set upon the pursuit of the ideal of peace in a prescribed manner. Rather, it involves the creation of a mechanism to be placed at the disposal of states, which may use it for whatever purposes their agreements or their disagreements dictate. In practice, international organization may serve as the institutional framework for the joint exploration of approaches to peace, but it is also capable of serving as an arena for the conduct of international political warfare, or as an instrument for the advancement of the political objectives of a particular state or group of states.

International organization does not emancipate the world from dependence upon the quality of its statesmanship. Structural apparatus cannot generate its own supply of political decency, discretion, wisdom, and moderation. In the final analysis, both the possibilities and the limitations of international organization are set by political forces operative within and among member states. The deficiencies of the United Nations indicate a greater need for review and revision of national policies than of the Charter itself.

The most casual observer of the international scene can see that the problem of world order has not been solved. The most careful student of international organization can see that no world-saving miracles have been wrought, no infallible formula for solution of fundamental problems has been drafted, and no glorious certainty of a brave new world has been projected before the troubled eyes of modern man. But there is more to be seen than unsolved problems, unresolved conflicts, and unparalleled dangers of chaos and destruction. Fallibility is not the same as futility; limited achievement is not the same as unlimited failure; danger is not the same as doom.

The development of international organization represents both a realistic response to the requirements of doing national business in an increasingly complex international setting and an idealistic attempt to modify the operation of the multi-state system so as to make civilized living possible in an increasingly interdependent world. For better or for worse, the world has abjured the Hobbesian solution of throwing up hastily contrived institutional structures resting upon nothing more substantial than desperate fear of mutual destruction, adopting instead the Ciceronian ideal of establishing institutions of common life upon the limited but solid foundations of *consensus juris* and *utilitatis communione*. The builders of international organization have on occasion overestimated the extent of international agreement upon fundamental issues of right and justice and international preparedness to sustain joint approaches to mutual advantage, but they have not subordinated considerations of foundational adequacy to conceptions of architectural grandeur.

* * *

The world is not only developing a more sophisticated conception of its problems, but it is also beginning to recognize that global problems require global solutions. International organization is something more than a gathering of national governments; it is, in a very rudimentary sense, an expression of the concept that there is an international community which bears responsibility for dealing with matters that refuse to be confined within national boundaries. Statesmen assemble at the United Nations to promote the interests of their national constituencies, but they cannot altogether escape the tendency to feel that they compose a collective body whose constituency is mankind. The international community has become a little bit more than a dream of idealists. There is a limited sense in which it is meaningful to speak of a United Nations which imposes a principle of international accountability upon its member states, asserts its jurisdiction in areas previously encompassed by the functional boundaries of sovereignty, and assumes responsibility for doing as much of what must be done as can be done, on behalf of humanity.

The long-range effects of international organization upon the multi-state system cannot be confidently predicted. It may be regarded as a process of evolutionary unification; yet, it functions now to support the fragmentation of empires into groups of newly independent states. It may be regarded as a process of gradual replacement of national governments as the major agencies for the management of human affairs; yet, it operates now less to deprive governments of their domestic functions than to assist them in acquiring the competence to do their jobs more effectively. It may be regarded as a process leading to the eventual transcendence of the multi-state system; yet, its immediate function is to reform and supplement the system, so as to make the maintenance of legal, political, and administrative pluralism compatible with the requirements of an interdependent world.

It is perhaps necessary to stress again the distinction between international *organizations* and international *organization*. Particular organizations may be nothing more than playthings of power politics and handmaidens of national ambitions. But international organization, considered as an historical process, represents a secular trend toward the systematic development of an enterprising quest for political means of making the world safe for human habitation. It may fail, and peter out ignominiously. But if it maintains the momentum that it has built up in the twentieth century, it may yet effect a transformation of human relationships on this planet which will at some indeterminate point justify the assertion that the world has come to be governed—that mankind has become a community capable of sustaining order, promoting justice, and establishing the conditions of that good life which Aristotle took to be the supreme aim of politics.

# 1.3 *Prosperity*

Gabriel Kolko

The United States and World Economic Power

* * *

To understand the unique economic interests and aspirations of the United States in the world, and the degree to which it benefits or loses within the existing distribution and structure of power and the world economy, is to define a crucial basis for comprehending as well as predicting its role overseas. * * *

* * *

The United States and Raw Materials

The role of raw materials is qualitative rather than merely quantitative, and neither volume nor price can measure their ultimate significance and consequences. The economies and technologies of the advanced industrial nations, the United States in particular, are so intricate that the removal of even a small part, as in a watch, can stop the mechanism. The steel industry must add approximately thirteen pounds of manganese to each ton of steel, and though the weight and value of the increase is a tiny fraction of the total, a modern diversified steel industry *must* have manganese. The same analogy is true of the entire relationship between the industrial and so-called developing nations: The nations of the Third World may be poor, but in the last analysis the industrial world needs their resources more than these nations need the West, for poverty is nothing new to peasantry cut off from export sectors, and trading with industrial states has not ended their subsistence living standards. In case of a total rupture between the industrial and supplier nations, it is the population of the industrial world that proportionately will suffer the most.

* * *

From *The Roots of American Foreign Policy* (Boston: Beacon Press, 1969), chapter 3.

18

It is extraordinarily difficult to estimate the potential role and value of these scarce minerals to the United States, but certain approximate definitions are quite sufficient to make the point that the future of American economic power is too deeply involved for this nation to permit the rest of the world to take its own political and revolutionary course in a manner that imperils the American freedom to use them. Suffice it to say, the ultimate significance of the importation of certain critical raw materials is not their cost to American business but rather the end value of the industries that *must* employ these materials, even in small quantities, or pass out of existence. And in the larger sense, confident access to raw materials is a necessary precondition for industrial expansion into new or existing fields of technology, without the fear of limiting shortages which the United States' sole reliance on its national resources would entail. Intangibly, it is really the political and psychological assurance of total freedom of development of national economic power that is vital to American economic growth. Beyond this, United States profits abroad are made on overseas investments in local export industries, giving the Americans the profits of the suppliers as well as the consumer. An isolated America would lose all this, and much more.

* * *

World Trade and World Misery

If the postwar experience is any indication, the nonsocialist developing nations have precious little reason to hope that they can terminate the vast misery of their masses. For in reality the industrialized nations have increased their advantages over them in the world economy by almost any standard one might care to use.

The terms of trade—the unit value or cost of goods a region imports compared to its exports—have consistently disfavored the developing nations since 1958, ignoring altogether the fact that the world prices of raw materials prior to that time were never a measure of equity. Using 1958 as a base year, by 1966 the value of the exports of developing areas had fallen to 97, those of the industrial nations had risen to 104. Using the most extreme example of this shift, from 1954 to 1962 the terms of trade deteriorated 38 percent against the developing nations, for an income loss in 1962 of about $11 billion, or 30 percent more than the financial aid the Third World received that year. Even during 1961–66, when the terms of trade remained almost constant, their loss in potential income was $13.4 billion, wiping away 38 percent of the income from official foreign aid plans of every sort.

* * *

In fact, whether intended or otherwise, low prices and economic stagnation in the Third World directly benefit the industrialized nations. Should the developing nations ever industrialize to the extent that they begin consuming a significant portion of their own oil and mineral output, they would reduce the available supply to the United States and prices would rise. And there has never been any question that conservative American studies of the subject have treated the inability of the Third World to industrialize seriously as a cause for optimism in raw materials planning. Their optimism is fully warranted, since nations dependent on the world market for the capital to industrialize are unlikely to succeed, for when prices of raw materials are high they tend to concentrate on selling more raw materials, and when prices are low their earnings are insufficient to raise capital for diversification. The United States especially gears its investments, private and public, to increasing the output of exportable minerals and agricultural commodities, instead of balanced economic development. With relatively high capital-labor intensive investment and feeding transport facilities to port areas rather than to the population, such investments hardly scratch the living standards of the great majority of the local peasantry or make possible the large increases in agricultural output that are a precondition of a sustained industrial expansion. * * *

American Tools for Success

The United States' vast expansion in its agricultural exports, and the billions of dollars of lost income to the Third World, reveals the success of the brilliant American synthesis of aid, pressure, and exclusion that is the main characteristic of its foreign economic diplomacy.

The United States is the world's leading state trader, even though it has consistently attacked this principle when other industrial nations used it to advance their own neocolonial export positions. Official American agricultural export subsidy programs involved $3 billion annually in 1957 and 1967, with sums approaching that amount in the interim years. Most of these subsidized exports went to developing nations, often, as in the case of India, in return for vital concessions that aided America's industry, just as agricultural exports aided its big commercial farmers.

Given United States exclusion of many cheaper, freely exportable goods and commodities, and its opposition to higher prices for Third World exports, one can only regard the foreign aid program as a subsidy to American farmers and industry rather than as a gesture of concern for the world's poor. Between 1948 and 1958 ships sailing under the American flag carried 57 percent of the foreign aid despatched from the United States, and Americans owned many of the other vessels flying foreign flags. The United States required aid recipients to spend 68 percent of the aid program expenditures during that period in the United States; American-controlled Middle Eastern oil absorbing part of the remainder. By 1965 over one-third of United States exports to developing countries, which now absorbed nearly one-third of

American exports, were directly financed on a tied basis. There were few humanitarian reasons for exporting vast amounts of cotton abroad under these programs, and in fact cheaper cotton was usually available to developing nations from other Third World countries. In reality, the American program cut into intra-Third World trade on behalf of a standing United States policy to maintain a "fair historical share" of the world cotton market for the United States, a figure somewhere around five million bales a year and in no sense a standard of equity.[1]

* * *

United States Investment and Trade

* * *

American foreign investments are unusually parasitic, not merely in the manner in which they use a minimum amount of dollars to mobilize maximum foreign resources, but also because of the United States crucial position in the world raw-materials price structure both as consumer and exporter. This is especially true in the developing regions, where extractive industries and cheap labor result in the smallest permanent foreign contributions to national wealth. In Latin America in 1957, for example, 36 percent of United States manufacturing investments, as opposed to 56 percent in Europe and 78 percent in Canada, went for plant and equipment. And wages as a percentage of operating costs in United States manufacturing investments are far lower in Third World nations than Europe or Canada.[2]

* * *

Seen in this light, United States foreign aid has been a tool for penetrating and making lucrative the Third World in particular and the entire nonsocialist world in general. The small price for saving European capitalism made possible later vast dividends, the expansion of American capitalism, and ever greater power and profits. It is this broader capability eventually to expand and realize the ultimate potential of a region that we must recall when short-term cost accounting and a narrow view make costly American commitments to a nation or region inexplicable. Quite apart from profits on investments, during 1950–60 the United States allocated $27.3 billion in nonmilitary grants, including the agricultural disposal program. During that same period it exported $166 billion in goods on a commercial basis, and imported materials essential to the very operation of the American economy.[3] It is these vast flows of goods, profits, and wealth that set the fundamental context for the implementation and direction of United States foreign policy in the world.

The United States and the Price of Stability

Under conditions in which the United States has been the major beneficiary of a world economy geared to serve it, the continued, invariable American opposition to basic innovations and reforms in world economic relations is entirely predictable. Not merely resistance to stabilizing commodity and price agreements, or non-tied grants and loans, but to every imperatively needed structural change has characterized United States policy toward the Third World. In short, the United States is today the bastion of the *ancien regime*, of stagnation and continued poverty for the Third World.

* * *

Invariably, this meant opening the doors of developing nations to American investments and the support for pliable *comprador* elements wherever they could be found, in the belief, to cite Secretary of Treasury George M. Humphrey, that "There are hundreds of energetic people in the world who are better equipped than governments ever can be to risk huge sums in search, exploration, and development wherever the laws of the country will give them half a chance."[4]

The implications of such a policy were great, requiring intervention to save American investors and friendly conservative governments, and above all the maximization of raw materials production for export to the fluctuating world market. "Our purpose," Percy W. Bidwell wrote in his studies for the Council on Foreign Relations, "should be to encourage the expansion of low-cost production and to make sure that neither nationalistic policies nor Communist influences deny American industries access on reasonable terms to the basic materials necessary to the continued growth of the American economy."[5] Hence nationalism and modest but genuine reform were quite as great an enemy as bolshevism. This meant that via diplomatic pressures and contingent loans and aid the United States engaged in what Eugene Black has called "development diplomacy" throughout the world, a strategy that attempts to show that "The desire for autarky will not be tempered until there is more awareness of how, by underemphasizing exports, the leaders of these nations are prolonging the poverty of their people."[6] That fluctuating raw materials prices and immense foreign profits were crucial handicaps to the problems of development was of no consequence, since the primary objective of the United States was to serve its own interests.

The advancement of American capitalism and an open field for development in the Third World were the guiding principles of American diplomacy, both on the part of government and business leaders. This has required, in turn, specific opposition to every measure likely to alleviate Third World misery at the expense of the industrial nations. * * *

* * *

* * * The numerous American interventions to protect its investors throughout the world, and the United States ability to use foreign aid and loans as a lever to extract required conformity and concessions, have been more significant as a measure of its practice. The instances of this are too plentiful to detail here, but the remarkable relationship between American complaints on this score and the demise of objectionable local political leaders deserves more than passing reference.

* * *

In today's context, we should regard United States political and strategic intervention as a rational overhead charge for its present and future freedom to act and expand. One must also point out that however high that cost may appear today, in the history of United States diplomacy specific American economic interests in a country or region have often defined the national interest on the assumption that the nation can identify its welfare with the profits of some of its citizens—whether in oil, cotton, or bananas. The costs to the state as a whole are less consequential than the desires and profits of specific class strata and their need to operate everywhere in a manner that, collectively, brings vast prosperity to the United States and its rulers.

Today it is a fact that capitalism in one country is a long-term physical and economic impossibility without a drastic shift in the distribution of the world's income. Isolated, the United States would face those domestic backlogged economic and social problems and weaknesses it has deferred confronting for over two decades, and its disappearing strength in a global context would soon open the door to the internal dynamics which might jeopardize the very existence of liberal corporate capitalism at home. * * *

The existing global political and economic structure, with all its stagnation and misery, has not only brought the United States billions but has made possible, above all, a vast power that requires total world economic integration not on the basis of equality but of domination. And to preserve this form of world is vital to the men who run the American economy and politics at the highest levels. * * *

NOTES

1. Department of Agriculture, *Handbook of Agricultural Charts*, 42, 48; U.S. Congress, Joint Economic Committee, *Hearings, Outlook for United States Balance of Payments*. 87:2. December 1962 (Washington, 1963), 63; Department of State, *United States Economy and the Mutual*

Security Program, 66, 80; Committee on Foreign Relations, *United States-Latin American Relations*, 445, 455; National Export Expansion Council, "Report of Task Force 1 . . . ," 10; National Export Expansion Council, *Trade and Investment in Developing Countries* (Washington, April 3, 1967), 11.

2. Department of Commerce, *U.S. Business Investments*, 43, 65–66; *The Economist*, July 10, 1965, 167; Allan W. Johnstone, *United States Direct Investment in France* (Cambridge, 1965), 48–49; *Le Monde*, January 14–15, July 23, 1968; *Wall Street Journal*, December 12, 1967; Committee on Foreign Relations, *United States–Latin American Relations*, 338; *New York Times*, April 16, 1968.

3. Department of Commerce, *Balance of Payments*, 120, 150–51.

4. George M. Humphrey to Paul G. Hoffman, March 26, 1957, Eisenhower Papers, OF116-B.

5. Percy W. Bidwell, "Raw Materials and National Policy," *Foreign Affairs*, XXXVII (October 1958), 153.

6. Eugene R. Black, *The Diplomacy of Economic Development* (Cambridge, 1960), 53.

Principles

Tony Smith

The United States and the Global Struggle for Democracy

If the United States had never existed, what would be the status in world affairs of democracy today? Would its forces based in France, Britain, the Low Countries, and Scandinavia have survived the assaults of fascism and communism, or would one of these rival forms of mass political mobilization have instead emerged triumphant at the end of the twentieth century?

The answer is self-evident: we can have no confidence that, without the United States, democracy would have survived. To be sure, London prepared the way for Washington in charting the course of liberal internationalism; and the United States was slow to leave isolationism after 1939, while the Red Army deserves primary praise for the defeat of Nazi Germany. Yet it is difficult to escape the conclusion that since World War I, the fortunes of democracy worldwide have largely depended on American power.

The decisive period of the century, so far as the eventual fate of democracy was concerned, came with the defeat of fascism in 1945 and the American-sponsored conversion of Germany and Japan to democracy and a much greater degree of economic liberalism. Here were the glory days of American liberal democratic internationalism (and not the 1980s, however remarkable that decade, as some believe). American leadership of the international economy—thanks to the institutions created at Bretton Woods in 1944, its strong backing for European integration with the Marshall Plan in 1947 and support for the Schuman Plan thereafter, the formation of NATO in 1949, the stability of Japanese political institutions after 1947 and that country's economic dynamism after 1950 (both dependent in good measure on American power)—created the economic, cultural, military, and political momentum that enabled liberal democracy to triumph over Soviet communism. Except perhaps for NATO, all of these developments were the

From *America's Mission: The United States and the Worldwide Struggle for Democracy in the 20th Century* (Princeton: Princeton University Press, 1994), chapter 1 and appendix.

product of the tenets of thinking first brought together in modern form by Woodrow Wilson, before being adapted to the world of the 1940s by the Roosevelt and Truman administrations.

In the moment of triumph, it should not be forgotten that for most of this century, the faith in the future expansion of democracy that had marked progressive thinking in Europe and America at the turn of the century seemed exceedingly naive. By the 1930s, democracy appeared to many to be unable to provide the unity and direction of its totalitarian rivals. Indeed, again in the 1970s, there was a resurgence of literature predicting democracy's imminent demise: its materialism, its individualism, its proceduralism (that is, the elaborate set of rules and institutions needed to make it function), its tolerance, not to say its permissiveness—the list could be extended indefinitely—seemed to deprive it of the toughness and confidence necessary to survive in a harsh world of belligerent, ideologically driven fascist and communist states.

Fascism was essentially undone by its militarism and its racism; Soviet communism by its overcentralized economic planning and its failure to provide a political apparatus capable of dealing with the tensions of nationalism not only within the Soviet empire but inside the Soviet Union itself. By contrast, however varied the forms of government may be that rightly call themselves democratic, they have demonstrated a relative ability to accommodate class, gender, and ethnic diversity domestically through complicated institutional forms centering on competitive party systems and representative governments. As importantly, the democracies have shown an ability to cooperate internationally with one another through a variety of regimes managing the complex issues of their interdependence, despite the centrifugal force of rival state interests and nationalism. Hence, at the end of the twentieth century, democracy is unparalleled for its political flexibility, stability, legitimacy, and ability to cooperate internationally.

* * *

The most important statement on the uniqueness of American liberalism remains Alexis de Toqueville's *Democracy in America* published in 1835 (a second volume appeared in 1840). Commenting that the United States was "born free," that "the social state of the Americans is eminently democratic . . . even the seeds of aristocracy were never planted," Toqueville continues:

> There society acts by and for itself. There are no authorities except within itself; one can hardly meet anybody who would dare to conceive, much less to suggest, seeking power elsewhere. The people take part in the making of the laws by choosing the lawgivers, and they share in their application by electing the agents of the executive power; one might say that they govern themselves, so feeble and restricted is the part left to the administration, so vividly is that administration aware of its popular origin, and obedient to the fount of power. The people

reign over the American political world as God rules over the universe. It is the cause and the end of all things; everything rises out of it and is absorbed back into it.[1]

Toqueville was correct to see how democratic the United States was by contrast with other countries in the 1830s, for with Andrew Jackson's election in 1828 it could rightfully call itself the first modern democracy. Yet it should be recalled that at the time of American independence there were property qualifications for the vote and that certain religious denominations, as well as women and slaves, were disfranchised. Had Toqueville arrived a decade earlier, his account might not have been so perspicacious.

* * *

It is inevitable that the meaning of liberal democracy in domestic American life should deeply mark the conduct of its foreign policy. When their policy intends to promote democracy abroad, Americans rather naturally tend to think in terms of a weak state relative to society. The result for others is a paradoxical form of "conservative radicalism": radical in that for many countries, democracy has meant an abrupt and basic political change away from the narrow-based authoritarian governments with which these people are familiar; conservative in that in fundamental ways, the Americans have not meant to disturb the traditional social power relations based on property ownership.

Here was the genius, and also the tragedy, of the American sponsorship of democracy abroad: it was genuinely innovative politically, but it was not profoundly upsetting socioeconomically. The genius of the approach was that it could be attractive to established elites abroad (provided that they had the wit to try to adapt), for whatever the hazards of introducing democracy, it promised to modernize and stabilize those regimes that could reform enough to be called democratic. The tragedy, especially in lands that were predominantly agrarian, was that these political changes (where they were accepted) were often not enough to create the cultural, economic, and social circumstances that could reinforce a democratic political order. As a result, American efforts either failed completely (as in Central America and the Caribbean during Wilson's presidency) or created narrowly based and highly corrupt elitist forms of democracy (as in the Philippines or more recently in the Dominican Republic).

It was different when the United States occupied Japan and Germany to promote democracy in 1945. But the men and women who undertook this mission were not liberal democrats of the traditional American sort. Instead, many of them were New Dealers, for whom the prerequisites of democracy included strong labor unions, land reform, welfare legislation, notions of racial equality, and government intervention in the economy. Moreover, they had the good fortune to be working with societies that already had centralized political institutions, diversified industrial economies, and (at least in Germany) many convinced democrats awaiting deliverance from fascism and communism alike. The Americans who conceived of the Alliance for Progress in Latin America were for the most part cut of the same cloth as the New Dealers. But their power in Latin America was not nearly so great as their predecessors' had been in Germany and Japan, and the socioeconomic structures of South and Central America lacked the inherent advantages for democratizers that the former fascist powers possessed. Hence the Alliance's failure.

This New Deal outlook was not typical of the Americans who took the Philippines in 1898 or who were in power under what was deservedly called the "progressive" presidency of Woodrow Wilson. These Franklin Roosevelt Democrats were also different from liberal reformers like Jimmy Carter, who favored a strictly human-rights approach to democratization. The most interesting contrast comes with Ronald Reagan, however, whose insistence on the contribution free markets could make to democratic government shared with the New Dealers the notion that political life depends in good measure on the structure of power socioeconomically (even if the two approaches differed on the need for governmental regulation and social redistribution).

As these cases suggest, American liberal democratic internationalism varied in its agenda over time. The continuity was such, however, that we can speak of a tradition in American foreign policy, one with an agenda for action abroad tied to a firm notion of the national interest that was to have momentous consequences for world affairs in the twentieth century.

* * *

In different countries, American influence has counted in different ways. For example, Czechs and Slovaks today often gratefully acknowledge the American contribution to the establishment of their democracy in 1918–9 and consider Woodrow Wilson to be virtually a founding father of their republic. Nevertheless, Czechoslovak democracy during the interwar period was almost entirely the doing of its own people. So too, Germany might well have become a democracy even without the American occupation after 1945, though the character of its political order without Allied supervision might have made it less liberal than it is today, and the pace of European economic integration might have been altogether slower, with dramatic consequences for political stability on the continent. By contrast, Japanese democracy bears a more indelible American mark due to General Douglas MacArthur's assertive role in the establishment of its postwar order.

When we turn to the pre-industrial world, the impact of American policy changes dramatically. Thus, the Philippines is a fragile democracy, the American-inspired political institutions not having resolved fundamental issues of class power in this predominately agrarian country. So too in Latin

America, the American contribution to democracy has been problematic, as in the case of Chile, or decidedly negative, as in Guatemala or in the Dominican Republic (before 1978, when for the first time a positive intervention occurred). Indeed, whatever its intentions, American policy on balance may have done substantially more to shore up dictatorships in the region than to advance the cause of democracy: the emergence of the Somoza and Trujillo tyrannies as the fruits of American interventions beginning with Wilson illustrates this clearly.

However, country studies alone do not tell us enough. After both the First and Second world wars, and again today in the aftermath of the cold war, America has formulated frameworks for world order in which the promotion of democracy played a conspicuous role. The emphasis on global security, the world market, and international law and organizations figure prominently alongside the call for national, democratic self-determination. The administrations of Wilson, Roosevelt, Truman, and Reagan emerge as particularly important in this context, where the focus is on the ability of democratic countries to cooperate internationally.

Historical watersheds, such as we are now passing through, are moments when the study of the past is especially invigorating. The past is now securely the past: the actors and the consequences of their policies have less claim on the present and so can be studied with some dispassion. Simultaneously, the present is in search of its future and must take stock of how it arrived at its current position. * * *

As Americans ponder the challenges of world affairs at the end of the cold war, they may think back to other times when Washington's decisions were critical: not only to the end of the world wars in 1918 and 1945, but to the end of the Spanish-American War in 1898 and the Civil War in 1865 as well. What they will find is that in the aftermath of victory, Washington determined to win the peace by promoting a concept of national security calling ultimately for democratic government among those with whom the United States would work most closely.

Just how to achieve this end was never a clear matter, to be sure. As the North debated what to do with its victory over the South in 1865, so in 1898 American leaders were somewhat unsure what to do with their new role in the Far East and the Caribbean. The national debate in 1918–9 over Wilson's vision of a "peace without victory" so as "to make the world safe for democracy" was likewise raucous and uncertain. Only in the 1940s, in its planning for the postwar order, did Washington appear relatively clear in its thinking (and here too there were debates, contradictions, improvisations, and accidents aplenty as policy was made). Thus, when President Clinton, like Presidents Bush and Reagan before him, speaks of his conviction that no feature of U.S. foreign policy is more critical at the end of the cold war than helping the democratic forces in Russia, he may often be at a loss on how best to proceed. But he is articulating his concerns for peace in a recognizable way that stretches back across the generations, to American leaders in other times who have speculated on what to do in the aftermath of victory and who rightly concluded that the answer consisted in promoting the fortunes of democracy for others for the sake of American national security.

* * *

International Relations Theory: The Realist Tradition

Realism holds that the major actors in world affairs are states, and that their actions will primarily be based on calculations having to do with their power relative to that of other states. Given the anarchy of the international order, war is an ever-present possibility; hence, the first duty of states is to ensure their own survival by evaluating the needs of the national security. From this perspective, *world order* may be understood as any stable distribution of power that inhibits war, while the term *the balance of power* can be used to refer to those configurations of states—whether in multipolar, bipolar, or hegemonic systems—that achieve this end.

Realists hold that their insights have been true of the human condition since time immemorial. A line they often quote comes from Thucydides' *History of the Peloponnesian War* written in the fifth century B.C.: "What made war inevitable was the growth of Athenian power and the fear which this aroused in Sparta." Or again, they cite as timeless a phrase from Machiavelli's *The Prince*, written in the sixteenth century:

> A man who wishes to make a profession of goodness in everything must necessarily come to grief among the many who are not good. Therefore, it is necessary for a prince, who wishes to maintain himself, to learn how not to be good and to use this knowledge or not to use it, according to the necessity of the case.

To bring the lessons up to date, realists may cite Henry Kissinger's hardnosed affirmation on the first page of *A World Restored*:

> Those ages which in retrospect seem most peaceful were least in search of peace. Those whose quest for it seems unending appear least able to achieve tranquillity. Whenever peace—conceived as the avoidance of war—has been the primary objective of a power or a group of powers, the international system has been at the mercy of the most ruthless member of the international community.

Based on their conviction that it is states that matter in world affairs, and that the primary focus of the state's considerations will be rational assessments of how to optimize its power position given the shape of the international system, realists' principal concerns are matters of military strategy and diplomatic negotiations as well as the logic of state action in terms of the existing configuration of power internationally.

* * *

While the value of realism's insights should not be doubted, its recommendations come at a price. Its very analytical sharpness has led to a disregard for aspects of world affairs whose importance is devalued by its paradigm: for example, the study of international law and ethics.

* * *

By the same token that it discounts ethics and the role of the irrational in world affairs, realism likewise accords little importance to the domestic base of the state in its concern to explain the pattern of international relations. Hence, the tremendous change in the structure of domestic politics that has swept over the world in the last two centuries with the rise of nationalism and corresponding changes in the structure of the state * * * would necessarily be of no more than secondary interest to realists, any more than such issues as whether a country were capitalist or Christian would matter.

* * * [T]he realists' rejection of the appeal of liberal democratic internationalism undermined their ability to comprehend international relations in this century. Lacking a theory of domestic politics, realism could not perceive the stakes involved in world affairs with the rise of mass-based states. They therefore could not appreciate the importance of the efforts to remake Japan and Germany domestically after the war, the practical seriousness of Kennedy's Alliance for Progress in the early 1960s, the political dynamic of European integration long sponsored by the United States, the depth of the appeal generated by Carter's human rights campaign in the late 1970s, or the political effectiveness of the enduring claims of Wilsonianism put forth by Reagan in the 1980s. Nor did their own paradigm save many realists from supporting American involvement in Vietnam or backing the shah, for they were quite able to argue "realistically" that the loss of these countries to movements hostile to the United States compromised the basic tenets of containment and so should be resisted for the sake of national security.

NOTES

1. Alexis De Toqueville, *Democracy in America* (Harper and Row, 1966), pt. 1, chaps. 2–3. For a modern restatement of Toqueville's insistence on American egalitarianism, see Gordon S. Wood, *The Radicalism of the American Revolution* (Knopf, 1992).

CHAPTER 2

The Domestic Context: Foreign Policy Politics and the Process of Choice

Whereas foreign policy strategy is the essence of choice, establishing the goals to be achieved and forging the policies that are the optimal means for achieving them, foreign policy politics are the process of choice, the making of foreign policy through the political institutions and amid the societal influences of the American political system. The old adage that "politics stops at the water's edge" is more myth than reality, as we discuss at the very outset of Chapter 2 in *American Foreign Policy: Dynamics of Choice*. Consensus has been less the norm than conflict has, and not just in recent years but at many times in the history of U.S. foreign policy.

This chapter features the first of our case studies, *The United States and South Africa: The Anti-apartheid Sanctions Debate of 1985 (with 1986 Postscript)*. This case both was important in its own right and is of great teaching value because of the ways in which it illustrates broader patterns and dynamics of foreign policy politics. All five major sets of actors—the president and the Congress and the "Pennsylvania Avenue diplomacy" that marks (and often mars) their interbranch relationship; the policy- and decision-making processes within the executive branch; the pressures brought to bear by major interest groups; the impact of the news media; and the nature of public opinion and its influence—played key roles in the South Africa sanctions case.

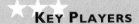

KEY PLAYERS

United States

President Ronald Reagan

Chester Crocker, Assistant Secretary of State for African Affairs

Senator Richard Lugar (R-Ind.), Chairman, Senate Foreign Relations Committee

Congressman William Gray (D-Pa.), sponsor of key House sanctions bill

Randall Robinson, Executive Director, TransAfrica

South Africa

President P. W. Botha

Bishop Desmond S. Tutu, 1984 Nobel Peace Prize laureate

Nelson Mandela, leader of the African National Congress (ANC) and political prisoner

BACKGROUND
KEY DATES AND EVENTS

1948	Afrikaner Party comes to power and imposes "apartheid," a policy of strict racial segregation and inequality favoring the white minority and repressing the black majority.
1960	Wave of anti-apartheid protests culminates in Sharpeville massacre where 69 black protesters killed by police. South African government bans the African National Congress (ANC), the leading black African political movement.
1962	Nelson Mandela, ANC leader, arrested. Jailed as political prisoner until 1990.
1976	Series of protests in Soweto township and elsewhere in South Africa against government's efforts to require Afrikaner language in schools instead of English, giving rise to Black Consciousness Movement. Over 500 killed.
1977	Steve Biko, prominent black African leader, tortured and killed in police custody.
1977	United Nations imposes mandatory arms embargo against South Africa.
1977	Sullivan Principles established. Named for African-American Reverend Leon Sullivan, these call for U.S. companies with investments in South Africa to pledge to nonsegregation in the workplace, equal pay and equal employment. Are voluntary, not mandatory.
1978	P. W. Botha elected prime minister of South Africa. Repeals some apartheid laws but largely minor ones, keeping basic system in place.
1984	Limited constitutional reform granting some political rights to "Coloreds" (mixed race) but still not blacks. Sets off a new wave of anti-apartheid protests, which Botha government meets with crackdown and violence.
Thanksgiving Day 1984	First major protest at South African embassy in Washington, D.C., led by Randall Robinson and Reverend Jesse Jackson.

CS2 *Foreign Policy Politics Case Study*

The United States and South Africa:
The Anti-apartheid Sanctions Debate of 1985
(with 1986 Postscript)

Introduction

During President Ronald Reagan's first term in office, the United States policy of "constructive engagement" toward South Africa was a matter of acute concern to a small cadre of political activists, but it was not a high priority either for Congress generally, or for the White House. Although liberal House Democrats periodically introduced legislation intended to toughen US policy toward the controversial white regime, their efforts were handily deflected by more mainstream and conservative lawmakers.

Late in 1984, however—shortly before Reagan's landslide re-election victory—violent confrontations erupted between South African security forces and black demonstrators, marking the worst violence since the bloody "Soweto uprising" of 1976. After the election, national television news programs continued to feature the South African riots, sparking a chain of events that catapulted the nation's South Africa policy into the public spotlight and onto the 1985 congressional agenda. To the administration's surprise, a bill to impose sanctions on South Africa sailed through the House with bipartisan support the next summer while a milder version won approval in the Republican-controlled Senate. By the end of July, a conference committee had succeeded in hammering out a compromise bill, and it looked as though both the House and Senate were prepared to override a presidential veto if necessary. As one magazine reported, the "Republican migration" from an anti- to a pro-sanctions position that summer "turned into a stampede with Republican lawmakers scrambling all over one another to show that they were not 'soft on South Africa.' "[1] In the end, the president managed to forestall passage of sanctions legislation only by an eleventh-hour

This case was written by Pamela Varley for Gregory Treverton, a senior research associate at the Kennedy School of Government's Center for Science and International Affairs and a senior fellow at the Council on Foreign Relations. It was funded by a grant from the Pew Charitable Trusts and prepared in association with the University of Pittsburgh Graduate School of Public and International Affairs to develop teaching cases in international negotiations.

decision to issue an "executive order" closely mirroring the House/Senate compromise bill. What's more, the 1985 debate paved the way for a 1986 showdown between the Hill and the White House that ended with Congress overriding a presidential veto to enact a more extensive sanctions bill; this marked the first congressional override of the president on a major foreign policy issue since the 1973 War Powers Act.

Although the legislative outcome was more dramatic in 1986, the significant shift of ground within Congress occurred the year before. Some observers even argue that the high water mark for Republican support of sanctions came in the summer of 1985; even with the passage of the 1986 bill, a Republican backlash against the sanctions approach was beginning, and by the fall of 1988, the South African sanctions debate was once again dividing along party lines. What happened, then, in 1984 and 1985 to raise the stakes of the South Africa question for US lawmakers? How did the administration's policy wind up on a collision course with events in southern Africa and on the American domestic political scene? And how did the imposition of sanctions on South Africa move from a marginal cause supported by churches and certain political liberals, to a mainstream movement, supported by some of the most conservative Republicans in Congress?

Background

* * *

Race relations in South Africa. The evidence of racial inequality was legion in South Africa during the early 1980s. It was a nation where only 16 percent of the population was white, yet where whites monopolized political, economic, and military power. Blacks—72 percent of the population, and the most disenfranchised of South Africa's non-white population*—were not permitted to vote, and virtually every aspect of their lives—where they lived, where and how they travelled, where they worked, how much they earned, how they were educated, and what kind of medical care they received—was controlled by the white minority and was vastly inferior to what was available to white South Africans. Whites controlled two thirds of the disposable income in the country. They also laid claim to two thirds of the land in the country, relegating the last third to non-whites and game park animals.[2]

Apartheid, the policy of South Africa since the Afrikaner National Party came to power in 1948, means "separatehood."[3] It was a policy enshrined in the nation's constitution and justified as a system designed to preserve

---

*   South Africa also had a mixed race population of 9 percent, and an Asian population of 3 percent. These racial groups were somewhat better off than blacks but much worse off than whites.

the cultural integrity of each racial and ethnic group within South Africa. This was the underlying notion behind the practice of rounding up blacks, removing them from areas designated white, and depositing them in ten desolate, undeveloped "homelands," where they were expected to establish their own nations and eventually move to a system of self-rule. (By the mid-1980s, four of these homelands had been granted "independence" by the South African government, but none was recognized by any other nation in the world.) Most black South African leaders expressed a flat rejection of this elaborate expatriation scheme, but for the most part, the Afrikaners, backed by their powerful military establishment, were able to make it stick.

What complicated the pristine simplicity of the original apartheid vision, however, was the fact that economically, blacks and whites needed each other. Whites needed black laborers, and blacks, who suffered tremendous unemployment, needed jobs, since the homelands offered no possibility of economic self-sufficiency. Thus, in reality, whites were not able simply to jettison blacks into the netherworld of rural South Africa. What arose instead was a tortuously complex, highly regulated system of migrant labor, under which many black families lived in the homelands while family breadwinners lived miles away in black townships outside South Africa's urban centers, perhaps visiting their families once a year. Blacks were permitted to live in the townships only if they had an approved governmental "pass." Hundreds of thousands of blacks were arrested for pass law violations each year.

Black opposition to the Afrikaner government and its policies had periodically erupted and been squelched ever since the 1940s, but became more militant in the 1960s and 1970s. The largest opposition groups—the African National Congress (ANC) and the Pan African Congress (PAC) were banned in 1960 in the wake of the "Sharpeville massacre," where 69 blacks had died when police opened fire on a crowd demonstrating against the pass laws. A number of opposition leaders—including the popular Nelson Mandela—were jailed shortly thereafter.

* * *

US Policy in the Region

* * *

Up until the mid-1980s, the United States had taken a few actions to express its disapproval of South Africa's repressive apartheid system. During the Kennedy administration in 1963, the US imposed an arms embargo on South Africa and in 1977, under the Carter administration, joined the UN arms embargo. In 1978, the US government barred US exports to the South African military, police, or apartheid enforcing agencies of the government. * * *

* * *

Indeed, the US position was marked by ambivalence. At the same time that the government criticized apartheid, the US worked closely with Pretoria in failed efforts to usher less radical factions to power in Angola, Zimbabwe, and Namibia. One journalistic investigator, Andrew Cockburn, reported in December 1984 that there were also extensive covert intelligence ties between the US and South Africa—a charge denied by the Defense Department.

For the American private sector, meanwhile, lucrative financial dealings with South Africa burgeoned during the 1960s and 70s.[4] By the early 1980s, some 350 US firms had operations in South Africa, including 57 of the Fortune 100 companies. US investment in South Africa—estimated at $2.5 billion—accounted for 18 percent of South Africa's foreign investment. And US banks had supplied private firms in South Africa with about $7.5 billion in loans.

In addition, the US was South Africa's primary trading partner, supplying 15 percent of South Africa's imports. All in all, US companies in South Africa provided the country with 70 percent of its computer equipment, 45 percent of its oil, and 33 percent of its cars. Eight percent of American imports came from South Africa, including, in 1983, more than 75 percent of the United States' supply of chromium—vital in making stainless steel and aircraft engines—and two thirds of US platinum—used in catalytic converters and in the manufacture of fertilizer, explosives and purified glass. In 1984, the US purchased $485 million in Krugerrands and $140 million in diamonds. The US imported shellfish, steel, coal, apples, peaches, and uranium from South Africa. There was also a healthy exchange of people between the two countries. Some 70,000 US visitors went to South Africa each year, and in 1983, 47,250 South Africans—including 9000 businessmen—visited the US.

* * *

Chester Crocker and the Tenets of "Constructive Engagement"

* * *

When Ronald Reagan took the reins of government in January 1981, he delegated formulation of his South Africa policy to the State Department and his newly appointed assistant secretary for African affairs, Chester Crocker. * * *

* * *

At about the same time Crocker was tapped for the State Department post, he published a widely read essay in the Winter 1980–81 issue of the professional journal *Foreign Affairs*, in which he laid out criticisms of US policy toward South Africa under the Nixon/Ford and Carter administrations and made a case for his own approach, which he christened "constructive engagement."

* * *

In terms of diplomatic strategy, Crocker believed that the best way to maximize US influence was to stop excoriating the government of South Africa, and instead establish quiet, friendly relations with the white Afrikaner leadership. By this, he noted, he did not mean completely normalized relations; he believed the US should continue to respect the UN arms embargo on South Africa, for instance, and should continue to refuse use of South African defense facilities. But in general, Crocker wrote, "Constructive engagement does not mean waging economic warfare against the Republic; nor does it mean erecting foolish pinpricks that only erode the American position in South African and world markets." Crocker has consistently argued that sanctions tend to be "a generalized blunderbuss which hurts everybody and hurts nobody."

* * *

Late 1984: South Africa in the Spotlight

Rebellion and Repression in South Africa

Racial violence within South Africa—relatively quiescent during Crocker's first four years—suddenly exploded in the fall of 1984, ignited by the adoption of a new constitution in South Africa which extended limited rights to Asians and persons of mixed race, but gave no representation to the country's black majority. This step received qualified praise from the US administration, which saw it as a move in the right direction, albeit flawed in the sense that it re-codified the exclusion of blacks from the system.

Within South Africa, however, the new constitution provoked outrage. Elections for the two new non-white Parliamentary chambers, held August 22 and 28, generated rallies and protests as demonstrators urged the eligible voters to boycott the election. Police arrested about 20 prominent non-white opponents on the eve of the first election which led to increasingly heated demonstrations. A bomb exploded in a government building on August 24 and again on September 3—the day the new constitution officially took effect. The same day, 14 blacks were killed during riots and police counterattacks in five black townships outside Johannesburg. The following day, in a precedent-setting move, the South African government called in army units to keep the peace in one black township and the death toll rose to 29. By mid November, the violence had claimed the lives of 160 South Africans, all but one of them black.

Across the US, several things conspired to increase media coverage of turmoil in South Africa. One was vivid television footage of the violence in that country, including scenes of South African police using guns, whips, and tear gas against poor angry young blacks armed primarily with stones. The media focused further attention on South Africa after the October announcement that South Africa's Anglican Bishop Desmond M. Tutu, a prominent and eloquent advocate of peaceful change, had been chosen to receive the 1984 Nobel Peace Prize. Tutu was touring the United States at the time, criticizing Reagan's policy of "constructive engagement" as "immoral, evil, and totally unChristian" and urging the US to apply significant political and diplomatic pressure on South Africa.

* * *

TransAfrica Takes Action

In the midst of the publicity, a fairly low-profile black foreign policy organization called TransAfrica suddenly took the spotlight. In early November, according to Cecelie Counts Blakey, former coordinator of the organization's Free South Africa Movement, TransAfrica's chairman of the board—Richard Gordon Hatcher, mayor of Gary, Indiana—telephoned the agency's director, Randall Robinson, to ask what the organization was doing about the situation in South Africa. Robinson replied that TransAfrica was engaged in its usual lobbying activity—calling the State Department to demand action, writing letters to decry the situation and the American response to it. Hatcher urged more dramatic action. The situation in South Africa had grown extreme, and demanded a strong response, he argued.

At that point, says Blakey, Robinson began to consider orchestrating an act of civil disobedience to dramatize the plight of South African blacks. He discussed the idea with other black leaders and anti-apartheid groups to see whether they would support this kind of direct action. In mid November, Robinson and other leaders agreed upon the plan: On Thanksgiving Eve, while demonstrators outside the embassy protested the detention of 13 South African labor leaders, four respected black leaders—TransAfrica's Robinson, DC Delegate Walter E. Fauntroy, Mary Frances Berry of the US Civil Rights Commission, and Georgetown law professor Eleanor Holmes Norton, former chair of the Equal Employment Opportunities Commission—met with South African Ambassador Bernardus G. Fourie and two of his aides at the embassy. An hour into the meeting, Norton excused herself and told the 30 demonstrators outside that the other three were not going to leave the embassy voluntarily. The ambassador learned this news himself when he received a call from a reporter asking what he was doing about the "sit-in" inside his embassy. The three visitors confirmed that they did not intend to leave, and at that point, the ambassador called the US Secret Service and had them arrested and removed from the embassy in handcuffs. (He later likened this and future acts of deliberate trespassing to the occupation of the US embassy in Tehran in 1979–80.[5])

Robinson, Fauntroy, and Berry spent the night in jail, which generated healthy, though still not overwhelming, press interest. The *Washington Post* ran a small story on page one, and some local television stations carried it as well. Two days later, Robinson announced that the protests marked the start of a "Free South Africa Movement":

> The action already taken and those planned have been arrived at reluctantly. But the circumstances in South Africa and the support of this country have demonstrated that a direct action is necessary, meaning any measure that will focus American attention to this problem and cultivate an American understanding and sympathy for those who suffer much in South Africa.

"Black leadership," he added, "has reached a point where it is willing to return to those measures that produced results in the past."[6]

Meanwhile, leaders of TransAfrica's nascent Free South Africa Movement spent Thanksgiving weekend making phone calls to see whether they could drum up support to hold late afternoon protests for a week, with three prominent individuals arrested each day. They succeeded, and by the end of the week, TransAfrica had begun receiving calls from major and minor celebrities requesting to be arrested as part of the civil disobedience demonstrations. Buoyed by the show of interest, the organization decided it could keep the effort going for a second week. After a month of daily demonstrations and arrests, it was clear to the organizers that the project had taken off. By mid December, the string of "celebrity arrests" included 15 members of Congress. The protests were to continue for a year, with groups from around the country making the pilgrimage to Washington, DC to submit themselves for arrest. * * *

Critics, on the other hand, charged that the Free South Africa Movement was a political ploy on the part of black leaders to revive "a moribund civil rights movement"[7]—a charge sharply denied by leaders of the movement.* Blakey says that TransAfrica deliberately worked with a wide array of ethnic, church, and labor groups from across the country—in part to keep the protests from being perceived as a "black" issue. * * *

---

* In retrospect, one longtime black political activist told the *New York Times* that—as a side benefit—the Free South Africa Movement did represent a milestone for blacks in the US, however: "This is the first time you have had a black-led movement on a foreign policy issue where whites have accepted the black position. It is the first time that black women have participated equally in the planning, and it is the first black movement in which the black church has not played the leadership role." (September 15, 1985)

Warning Signs from Congress

The enormous public attention focused on the South Africa issue in the fall meant that the average citizen was gaining an unprecedented awareness of South Africa. Before September of 1984, noted Hazel Ross-Robinson, foreign policy adviser to staunch apartheid critic Rep. William Gray III (D-Pa.), "People didn't even understand that South Africa was a country. They thought it was a region." This newfound public interest in South Africa, coupled with the fact that their own colleagues were submitting themselves to arrest to protest apartheid, began to jostle Republican legislators from their "constructive engagement" moorings by late November.

The Kassebaum/Lugar letter. On November 30, Sen. Richard Lugar (R-Ind.), the newly designated chair of the Senate Foreign Relations Committee, and Sen. Nancy Landon Kassebaum (R-Kan.), chair of the Senate's African Affairs Subcommittee, sent a letter to Ronald Reagan. Lugar, who called himself as "a skeptical supporter of the Reagan policy of constructive engagement in 1981 and 1982," later wrote that in their letter, he and Kassebaum "urged the President to conduct a major review of the South African policy, in part because of its implications for the country and for the Republican Party." The two senators had hoped that "addressing a letter to the President and citing his role as the Republican Party leader would channel the message to the White House political staff," according to Lugar. Instead, however, the letter wound up on the desk of a middle-rank State Department official. "I have often wondered," Lugar mused, "how different would have been the outcome had that letter received more of the President's attention."[8]

COS throws down the gauntlet. On December 4, a group of 35 House Republicans caused a more dramatic ruckus by publicly and dramatically parting ways with the administration's constructive engagement policy. In an effort orchestrated by the so-called "young turk" Republicans in the Conservative Opportunity Society (COS), the lawmakers signed an open letter to the South African ambassador, threatening to impose sanctions on his country "unless certain economic and civil rights guarantees for all persons are in place." The move, led by Robert S. Walker (R-Pa.), Vin Weber (R-Minn.), and Newt Gingrich (R-Ga.), was in keeping with the spirit of the Opportunity Society—a loosely organized group of 20 to 25 congressmen who wanted to broaden the popular base of the Republican Party and were willing to buck the party's conventional wisdom to do so. * * *

"South Africa has been able to depend on conservatives in the United States . . . to treat them with benign neglect," said Weber, who swiftly emerged as the principal spokesman for the group. "We served notice that, with the emerging generation of conservative leadership, that is not going to be the case."[9] * * *

"When the letter came out, it created a tremendous amount of stir," says Paul Guppy, legislative assistant to Robert Walker for foreign affairs.

Traditional and right-wing conservatives excoriated the group for being "up-pity" (*National Review*) and supporting the "lynch mobs of the left" (*Human Events*), and they branded the initiative shamelessly opportunistic.[10] Looking back, says Crocker, "What it showed was that in fact, that domestic politics is king when it comes to foreign policy action of the Congress."

> Some of the people involved—the Conservative Opportunists—have said so. They want to make it clear that for them, they want to see a Republican Party that is a place where black Americans feel welcome. And that the way to do that is to adopt a posture on South Africa.

Right-wing critics of the COS also argued that by backing away from South Africa, the "young turks" were effectively ceding US influence in the entire southern African region to the Soviet Union. As Howard Phillips, chair of the influential Conservative Caucus Foundation, put it, "It's not just a black/white issue. It's red versus red, white, and blue." In general, COS members were strongly anti-communist and continued to join the American Right in such causes, for instance, as supporting the UNITA in-surgency against Angola's Marxist government. But Weber argued that the case of South Africa was different: "We can't hold back because of South Africa's strategic importance. We are heading toward the bloodiest race bat-tle in the history of the world, and if that happens, our strategic interests are doomed."[11] * * *

Symbolically, the letter was "the watershed event" of the sanctions debate in the eyes of one South African embassy source: "It opened the process up to a bipartisan coalition." In fact, this act of mutiny was to mark the start of a steadily widening gulf dividing Republicans on the South Africa ques-tion.

That same week, there were two more small ripples on the congressional front. On December 4, Bishop Tutu addressed the House Foreign Affairs Subcommittee on Africa and received a rare standing ovation led by Howard Wolpe (D-Mich.), chair of the panel and longtime critic of Pretoria. At about the same time, a group of 35 House and Senate members signed a letter urging Ronald Reagan to meet with Tutu personally.

The administration's response. The administration did not totally ignore this string of warning shots from Congress, but its response was decidedly understated. The president did meet with Tutu on December 7. (At that meeting, the president assured the South African bishop that there had been "sizable progress in South Africa because of US policy"; Tutu responded that any such gains "have not been things that the victims of apartheid would be able to say they have perceived."[12]) Three days later, in a speech honoring International Human Rights Day, Reagan referred to "our con-cerns and our grief over the human and spiritual costs of apartheid," language which represented a departure from the State Department's con-tinuing defense of Pretoria for improving the position of South African blacks.

But beyond these gestures, the administration did little. The White House response to the Kassebaum/Lugar letter was pro forma, and the administration did not respond to the COS legislators at all. As Weber later told the *Wall Street Journal*, "There was no active attempt to discourage us. In fact, we felt almost a subtle approval of what we were doing."[13]

State of Affairs in Congress

Though Congress approached the problem of the US's South Africa policy with special vigor in 1985, the topic was not altogether new—especially for a crew of liberal congressional representatives—most notably William Gray, Stephen Solarz, Howard Wolpe, and the members of the Congressional Black Caucus—who had taken a keen interest in South Africa for years. * * *

* * *

Sanctions legislation had been proposed in every session of Congress since the spring of 1978. * * *

The Role of Richard Lugar

From the start, Richard Lugar made it clear that he planned to take up the South Africa question in his committee. "I had hoped to make the Senate Foreign Relations Committee the forum for national debate on how best to bring pressure on the dominant white government of South Africa to speed the end of apartheid and to open negotiations with black South Africans on a structure for democratic government," he writes in his 1988 book, *Letters to the Next President*.[14]

There were a number of reasons why Lugar is thought to have taken on the South Africa issue. For one, the apartheid debate had drawn fresh attention to some of the United States' own racial tensions. *Washington Post* columnist Courtland Milloy reported in December that at one point, a white person had driven by a South African embassy demonstration "wearing a Rebel hat and carrying a sign that read, 'Hang in there, Pretoria.'" Milloy wrote: "It's not just about South Africa. What's happening over there has been going on for years. It's about America too, and the insulting manner in which the Stars and Stripes have been waved in the name of racism." Milloy quoted a remark from Rep. Parren Mitchell (D-Md.): "People are seeing the way Reagan supports the white South Africans, and the way he treats blacks here and are beginning to make a connection between the two."[15]

In fact, liberal critics had long charged that the president and his judicial appointees were "rolling back the clock" on civil rights, opposing the extension of the 1965 Voting Rights Act, for instance, supporting tax credits for private school tuition, and defending the right of private colleges to exclude blacks. One South African embassy source argues that the apartheid controversy would never have mushroomed the way it did had the administration not been perceived as having a poor track record domestically on civil rights. As it was, he adds, the entire issue became a "litmus test" for senators and congressional representatives on where they stood on domestic race relations.

Lugar knew his Republican colleagues felt themselves to be under fire. What's more, the terms of 22 Republican senators were due to expire the following year, and some of them were feeling vulnerable on the South Africa issue. One Senate staff aide told the *Washington Post*, "For most Republicans, the administration's policy provides no political cover."[16]

Lugar also aspired to prove himself a strong and able leader within the Senate. The Foreign Relations Committee was, however, comprised of nine Republicans—ranging widely in philosophy from arch-conservative Jesse Helms to relatively liberal Charles Mathias Jr. (R-Md.)—and eight liberal Democrats, who tended to act quite cohesively. The net result was a committee that tended to be more liberal than the Senate as a whole, and was fully capable of passing some kind of legislation—with or without Lugar's help.

* * *

At the same time, Senate Democrats knew that adopting a stiff sanctions bill at the committee level—only to have it die on the Senate floor—would accomplish little. Any sanctions bill would ultimately have far greater chance of success if Lugar—who was fairly representative of mainstream Republican opinion in the Senate—supported it. In this sense, the senator from Indiana found himself well-positioned to take a leadership role on the matter.

Discussing US Policy Toward South Africa

During the spring of 1985, the House and Senate held a number of hearings to discuss US policy toward South Africa. During those hearings, members of the committee heard from their congressional colleagues, from Chester Crocker, and from an assortment of pro- and anti-sanctions lobbyists. The discussion ranged from generalized comments about constructive engagement, to the efficacy and appropriateness of imposing sanctions on South Africa, to a debate over specific measures under Senate consideration.

Inside and outside the Senate hearings, the major charge leveled against constructive engagement was that Crocker's strategy had accomplished nothing—that, in reality, the administration's policy amounted to nothing more than "a wicked wink at the evils of apartheid."[17] * * *

* * *

* * * In terms of the internal race relations of South Africa, the State Department pointed to a number of improvements as evidence of the South African government's gradual reform effort: the integration of some hotels, restaurants, parks, libraries, theaters, sports facilities; the integration of some athletic teams; the permission granted blacks to form and bargain in trade unions; the suspension of forced relocations of blacks from white urban areas; the abolition of laws forbidding marriage between the races and forbidding people of different races to belong to the same political party.

Liberal critics, however, argued that these reforms of so-called "petty apartheid" were insubstantial, and had nothing to do with the central problem of a small white minority ruling a large black majority, which was permitted no voice. As Randall Robinson testified before the Senate Foreign Relations Committee on May 22, "[U]ntil we respond to that, we are doing nothing but moving the deck chairs on the Titanic." In addition, liberals charged, there was a healthy supply of evidence indicating that race relations were worsening rather than improving. * * *

* * * In addition to the criticism for not having "done" anything. Crocker was subject to criticism over the tone and emphasis of his diplomatic strategy. During Reagan's first term, the US had extended a number of friendly and concrete overtures to the South African government. US export restrictions of the Carter era were eased, and there were increases in computer sales to the government, and of aircraft and nonlethal items to the military and police. There was increased cooperation over nuclear power, and training in the US for South African naval personnel. The US voted in favor of a crucial International Monetary Fund loan to South Africa, and vetoed a UN Security Council resolution condemning South Africa's 1981 invasion of Angola.

And, according to plan, there was a dramatic reduction of anti-apartheid rhetoric from Reagan's State Department. Even when the department did issue a rebuke of a South African action, the words were decidedly measured. One Hill staffer complained that fleets of bureaucrats labored over whether a State Department press release should say that the US "regretted," "deplored," or "lamented" a given incident. These subtleties, he argues, were "lost on the rest of us: You should have a balanced *policy*, but *each statement* should not be balanced. It sounds like you're making excuses."

* * *

Debating Sanctions

The role of the South African economy. In the debate over imposing sanctions on South Africa, there were several basic areas of disagreement. Most fundamentally, there was disagreement over whether a healthy and booming South African economy would serve as the "engine" of race reform, or whether it would further entrench the ruling white minority. Helen Suzman, a member of P. W. Botha's liberal Parliamentary opposition, argued the former case: "The steady upward movement into skilled occupations by blacks eventually [will give] blacks the muscle with which to make demands for shifts in power and privilege, backed up by the force of black urbanization."[18] * * *

Liberal critics, however, disputed this claim. *Washington Post* correspondent Glenn Frankel wrote that "Capitalism and apartheid have been co-existing however uneasily, for 36 years—since the National Party came to power—and both seem to be more flexible and accommodating than their theorists would allow."[19] In a letter to the *Washington Post*, Howard Wolpe wrote, "This old argument, that somehow economic and social change lead inexorably to political liberalization and to democratization, is more than just an unproven assumption; it is blatantly false. We only have to look at the experience of Nazi Germany, Stalinist Russia, Fascist Italy, Communist Poland—indeed, to the experience of South Africa itself—to see the fallacy of such a thesis. In all of these instances, there has been progressive industrialization, economic, and social change—and greater repression."[20]

The role of American investment in South Africa. There was parallel debate over the role of American business presence in South Africa—whether it was, in the words of black activist Winnie Mandela, "a shoulder to the wheel, moving apartheid forward,"[21] or whether it was a powerful force for race reform, providing better wages, training, housing and employment opportunities for blacks than would otherwise be available. Randall Robinson argued that less than one percent of the South African black work force—66,000 people—was employed by American firms, so that the impact of US firms in bettering the lives of individual blacks in the country was minimal.

* * *

Paul Murphy countered that an American business presence in South Africa had a positive effect in the society far beyond the number of actual citizens these businesses employed. * * *

In addition, he argued that, with American business leadership, South African businesses had become a major force for reform within the country.

Would sanctions hurt blacks? Overlapping the question of whether an American business presence was helpful or hurtful to apartheid was the question of whether sanctions might end up hurting blacks. Opponents of sanctions pointed to a 1984 survey conducted by Lawrence Schlemmer of the University of Natal Centre for Applied Social Sciences that indicated that of 550 black factory workers polled, only 25 percent favored sanctions such as a trade boycott or withdrawal of US investment. Sanctions opponents also argued that hurting the South African economy meant hurting the economies of all the struggling countries of southern Africa, which were highly dependent on South Africa.

While acknowledging that some blacks might be affected by US disinvestment, sanctions proponents questioned the legitimacy of the Schlemmer study, which, they noted, had been funded in part by the US government. A Gallup poll taken during the summer of 1985 found that of 400 blacks interviewed, 75 percent supported the notion of economic sanctions.[22] In addition, Robinson noted that the leaders of the black-ruled nations in southern Africa, as well as many prominent black South African leaders, advocated a strategy of US economic pressure. * * *

Would sanctions work at all? Opponents of sanctions questioned whether such measures would be effective—especially in the case of a country like South Africa with a diverse and basically healthy economy. * * *

"We should not discount the perverse results of existing sanctions," stated Crocker at an April 24 Senate hearing. "To the contrary, in South Africa's case, sanctions or the threat of them, have encouraged that country to become one of the developing world's largest arms producers and to have one of the most effective coal gasification programs. . . . South Africa today is far more self-sufficient than it was ten years ago, in part because of both sanctions and the threat of sanctions." In addition, sanctions opponents argued that if the US companies sold their assets, they would probably be bought up swiftly by the Western Europeans and the Japanese, at bargain basement prices, so that the South Africans would not feel the effects of the sanctions at all, and the only people to be hurt would be Americans.

Sanctions proponents, however, noted that some of the same people who questioned the effectiveness of sanctions in the case of South Africa strongly supported them in the case of some 20 communist countries. During one Foreign Relations Committee hearing, Senator Alan Cranston (D-Calif.) quoted a remark made by Secretary of State George Shultz with respect to the Nicaragua sanctions—that "there is a sense or a feeling that, regardless of the effect, certain types of relationships with countries we think are doing a lot of damage are undesirable." Cranston suggested that such reasoning was certainly appropriate in the South Africa case. And Stephen Solarz argued to the *Washington Post*, "Can anyone seriously doubt that it is far worse to live today as a black man or woman in South Africa than as an opponent of the Sandinistas in Nicaragua?"[23]

Crocker countered this argument before the Senate Foreign Relations Committee, saying that the Nicaraguan case was significantly different from that of South Africa, both because of US security concerns in the case of Central America, and because sanctions were more likely to be effective there: "The South African economy is something like 30 times the size of Nicaragua's and has vast international trading relationships, and in fact a bigger economy than a number of our NATO allies. It has options."

* * *

US strategic interests. One argument, voiced in other forums by the American Right, received little attention in the hearings—namely, the question of whether the US should be willing to jeopardize its alliance with South Africa, however morally reprehensible, if that meant risking the long-term loss of influence in the larger region of southern Africa. * * *

Sanctions proponents tended to dismiss this argument—to argue, in fact, that the US would have less influence in the long run if it aligned itself with the ruling white minority, alienating the black majority which was sure to take power in South Africa sooner or later. But opponents of sanctions worried that, absent a strong US alliance with South Africa, sea travel around the Cape of Good Hope in South Africa might be impeded. In addition, there was a concern over whether, by pursuing a policy of estranged relations, the US might forfeit access to certain valuable minerals—the most critical of which was chromium, available only in southern Africa or the Soviet Union.

Spring/Summer 1985: Amassing a Bill

Action in the House

The dramatic COS letter of December, and the possibility of Republican support for sanctions, led William Gray to approach Robert Walker early in 1985 in an effort to forge a bipartisan coalition to back a sanctions initiative, but the legislators were unable to reach agreement. Instead, Walker, Weber, and Gingrich introduced their own broad-brushed bill in March, which they called the "International Human Dignity and Opportunity Act of 1985." This bill, primarily aimed at communist countries, would have imposed loan restrictions on countries involved in international terrorism or drug trafficking, and would have denied most-favored nation status to countries that limited emigration or censored the press. The sole provision aimed at South Africa was a section that prohibited federal contracts or federal economic assistance to any companies, domestic or foreign, which had operations in South Africa and did not implement the Sullivan Principles.

The COS bill was one of some 20 anti-apartheid bills introduced in Congress that spring. Meanwhile, the House Democrats teamed up with their counterparts in the Senate to introduce jointly the Anti-Apartheid Act of 1985 (HR 1460 and S635) on March 7. This bill, sponsored by Gray in the House and Kennedy in the Senate, became the point of departure for discussion in the House and a focus of discussion in the Senate as well. The bill proposed to ban new bank loans to the South African government, and prohibit sales to the government of computer equipment intended for enforcement of apartheid. The measure would have barred US citizens from purchasing gold Krugerrands and would also have prohibited new investment in South Africa by any US firms. These last two sanctions might be postponed, under the terms of the bill, if the South African government took a series of eight significant steps to dismantle apartheid.

* * *

* * * The COS bill did not receive serious consideration in the House. The Gray bill, on the other hand, sailed through the House Foreign Affairs Committee by a vote of 29 to 6 on May 2, with support from four of the ten Republicans on the committee. The full House began to work on the measure on May 21. By margins of two to one, the congressional represen- tatives deflected seven different attempts by Republicans to soften the bill and two Democratic attempts to toughen it. The House did approve one amendment introduced by John Conyers Jr. (D-Mich.), which barred the sale of any nuclear technology or equipment to South Africa, and, on June 5, approved the amended bill by a vote of 295 (including 56 Repub- licans) to 127 (including 6 Democrats). * * *

* * *

Action in the Senate

* * * The Foreign Relations Committee began its work on March 27, when its members voted 16 to 1 to approve a bill sponsored by Mathias, S998, that threatened the imposition of economic sanctions on South Africa in two years time if no "significant progress" had been made to end apartheid. Lugar, Mathias, and Majority Leader Robert Dole (R-Kan.) then agreed to sponsor jointly a slightly altered version of the bill—S995—introduced on April 24. * * * S995 included the withdrawal of government support to those US businesses operating in South Africa but not adopting the Sullivan Principles, as well as financial assistance to black students and businesses. Like the Mathias original, it proposed further sanctions in two years if no significant progress had been made to end apartheid. Lugar was quick to dissociate this bill from efforts aimed at US disinvestment: "In drafting my 1985 legislation, I concluded that strong encouragement should be given to American businesses to stay and to grow in South Africa. . . . The most progressive and constructive forces in South Africa are American and South African business leaders."[24]

At the same time that he introduced this bill, however, Lugar signalled his willingness to consider a stronger measure. On April 26, two Republican senators not on the Foreign Relations Committee—freshman Senator Mitch McConnell (R-Ky.) and veteran William V. Roth Jr. (R-Del.)—introduced a somewhat tougher sanctions bill. Foreign Relations Committee member Christopher J. Dodd (D-Conn.) agreed to co-sponsor the McConnell-Roth bill if the two agreed to add certain provisions. * * * They agreed. During the ensuing debate in the committee, Lugar recalls, "it became clear that I would have to accept [the] three [most important] economic sanctions" in the McConnell-Roth-Dodd bill: A ban on computer sales to the South

African government; a ban on new bank loans to the government, with the exception of educational, housing, or health facilities which are nondiscriminatory; and prohibition of nuclear cooperation with South Africa unless South Africa signed the nuclear non-proliferation treaty. On June 4, the Foreign Relations Committee voted 12 to 5 to adopt the McConnell-Roth-Dodd bill. By a vote of 16 to 1, the new measure was attached to S995, the Lugar-Mathias-Dole bill.

The full Senate began to consider the new measure July 10. Lugar maneuvered between efforts of arch conservative senators—led by Jesse Helms (R-N.C.)—to delay and weaken the measure and efforts of Democrats to expand the sanctions. Helms' goal at that point was to use the filibuster as a bargaining chit. "My purpose," he told the *Washington Post*, "was to prevent, if I could, loading the Senate bill with the kind of garbage Senator Kennedy and others were promoting."[25] According to the *Post*, the Democrats agreed to withhold further amendments to prevent another filibuster. As one aide to a liberal senator pointedly remarked, "You could say Helms was the chief architect of the way it came out."[26] After what Lugar called "a long and contentious day of debate," the Senate approved the bill 80 to 12 on July 11, marking the first time the Senate had ever gone on the record in favor of sanctions against South Africa.

In the end, the main differences between the House and Senate bills were these: the House version banned new US investments in South Africa and prohibited the import of Krugerrands. The Senate bill did neither of these things, but did require the president to recommend the imposition of some kind of political or economic sanctions within 18 months if no significant progress had been made to end apartheid.

According to a July 13, 1985 *National Journal* story, the White House did not mount an all-out effort to defeat the bill during this period. Says a former member of the State Department's Congressional Affairs division, "There was a lot of feeling in the administration that the Senate wouldn't pass a bill." Staff members who had regular contact with the Hill were convinced that some kind of bill would pass, the staffer added. "But I don't think people in the White House really believed it."

* * *

For the last two weeks of July, Lugar worked hard to win support for the Senate bill in the House, to avoid taking the bill to a conference committee. His efforts to win House support for the milder bill were undermined, however, when on July 20, for the first time in 25 years, South African President P. W. Botha declared a sweeping state of emergency across many areas of South Africa. This decree gave police and military personnel "virtually unlimited powers in the designated areas to search and seize property without warrants, and arrest without formal charge and hold indefinitely without access to lawyers anyone deemed a threat to public safety. The security forces can also seal off any of the areas, impose curfews, and censor all news from the specified locations."[27] Within three days, more than 400 people—mostly black—had reportedly been detained by South African authorities. On July 24, France announced a suspension of new investment in South Africa and recalled its ambassador in protest to the South African crackdown. The administration's response to the state of emergency was mild—winning no hearts among congressional liberals. The State Department issued a statement that read in part, "We are deeply troubled by the ongoing unrest in South Africa. . . . The situation has deteriorated to the point that the South African government felt compelled to institute new measures. We hope sincerely that the unrest will abate rapidly, permitting the South African government to remove these measures and get on with the urgent business of reform."[28] On July 26, the United States—joined by Great Britain—vetoed a UN Security Council resolution threatening to impose mandatory sanctions against South Africa. The US abstained on—but did, however, permit to pass—a resolution which urged nations to enact sanctions voluntarily.

The Conference Committee

Lugar finally gave in on July 26, and appointed Senate members to a conference committee, which he convened on July 31.* That same day, the South African government imposed tight restrictions on funerals for blacks killed in civil unrest, which had been one of the few remaining lawful forms of assembly for blacks. By this point, more than 600 South Africans had been killed in the violence since September—all but two of them black.

The chief item of contention within the conference committee was whether or not the final bill would include either the no-new-investment clause or the Krugerrand ban, both of which were included in the House bill. Lugar was particularly adamant in opposing the no-new-investment clause. From the Democrats' point of view—if they were going to allow the

---

* Also on the 31st, a rumor—later confirmed—began to circulate that the Chase Manhattan Bank was about to stop making loans to the South African private sector, and to refuse to allow South African debtors to "roll over" their current debts. Chase had only about $400 million out in loans to South Africa at that point, but because of its prestige, other banks were expected to follow suit. Overnight, the value of the South African rand plummeted 10 percent, and continued to fall throughout the month of August, as American banks, one after another, refused to roll over short-term loans. Crocker would later remark: "That was a very important decision. The marketplace was making a judgment which is the way it should be, rather than the government intervening to politicize those judgments by saying. 'One sovereign country is going to punish another.' It's much better to have the private sector say, 'That's not a place where we have the confidence we had six months ago.' It's a cleaner message, it's a purer message, and it's actually more credible."

no-new-investment item to be removed from the bill, as Lugar insisted—they at least wanted it added to the list of suggested sanctions to be imposed later unless Pretoria made significant progress in ending apartheid. "That was an important negotiating point," recalls one Democratic staffer. During the conference committee discussion, Lugar, along with Mathias and Kassebaum, finally agreed to include the Krugerrand ban in the conference committee report. The report also included a provision urging the president to impose a new economic or political sanction against South Africa after 12 months if the government had not taken one of the eight steps identified in the House bill to end apartheid, and to add an additional sanction for each successive 12-month period in which no significant progress was made.

The next day, the House approved the conference committee bill 380 to 48—reflecting a much higher margin of support among Republicans than the vote of June 5. Howard Phillips of the Conservative Caucus Foundation attributes a "50 to 60" vote shift among Republicans to the decision of Rep. Jack Kemp—who had voted against the House bill on June 5—to switch sides and support the conference committee report. Kemp—a populist conservative leader in the House, known for a sensitivity to race unusual among Republican lawmakers—had not taken a leading role either in supporting or opposing sanctions, but he was a personal friend of Rep. Gray's and had associated himself with Gray's remarks about South Africa during the 1983–84 sanctions debate. When he voted in favor of the conference committee report, and other Republicans followed suit, Howard Phillips and other staunch sanctions opponents were incensed; they threatened to undermine Kemp's 1988 presidential bid: "Jack Kemp has badly damaged his presidential prospects by being to the left of George Bush on this issue," Phillips told the *Washington Post*.[29]

The conference report was briefly considered by the Senate also on August 1, where Lugar reportedly "abandoned his customarily bland speaking style and made an emotional, armwaving plea to his colleagues," but the Senate debate was ultimately postponed until after the August recess when Senate conservatives—led by Jesse Helms (R-N.C.) and Malcolm Wallop (R-Wyo.)—threatened to filibuster the bill.

Behind the Scenes

In retrospect, some Republicans on the Hill believe that the 1985–86 Republican defection from "constructive engagement" had less to do with a rejection of the theoretical tenets of the approach, and more to do with a frustration at the way the State Department had implemented and explained the policy. "There was a growing sense, as the administration moved into its second term, of a policy not well-articulated and not having much effect," says Al Lehn, national security adviser to Sen. Dole. "I think it was more frustration at the absence of a clearly articulated policy than criticism of an existing policy."

* * *

Crocker's mainstream conservative critics tend to stress problems with his "political skills"—both abroad, represented in his failure to retain meaningful contacts with black South African leaders, and at home. Says one long-time Africa observer:

> A political figure has got to work the political scene. You have to work the Hill. You've also got to work the press. The people working on South Africa policy did neither. To me, that's a self-inflicted wound.

* * *

The strained relations with Congress played out in a number of ways. One was that Crocker and his team tended to dismiss the suggestions made by senators, congressional representatives, and staff specialists on the Hill, which served to ruffle some influential feathers. Says one Hill source, "It was an attitude of—really, Congress doesn't know that much. And that gets felt—first on the staff level because there is more day to day contact."

Another complaint held that Crocker bucked the time-honored convention that senators were a species higher on the food chain than assistant secretaries and thus to be accorded a certain level of deference. During one Senate hearing, Crocker infuriated Sen. Sarbanes by suggesting that "the South African question today in this country has become for some the moral equivalent of a free lunch," which led Sarbanes to retort, "You are sitting there, I am beginning to think, in total isolation from what is going on around you."[30] According to another story, a senator asked to meet with Crocker and he sent back word that he would prefer to meet with a group of senators so as to avoid wasting his time. "To me, that's arrogance," says one Senate aide.

Perhaps most damaging, Crocker neither consulted much with Congress, nor kept legislators well-informed of his activities. "Crocker plays the constructive engagement game like solitaire," one side to a House Republican complained to the *Wall Street Journal*.[31] * * *

"The Hill likes to be talked to candidly," agrees Christenson. "Sharing confidence with people is a big part of establishing power." In addition, consulting with members of Congress tends to make them feel more invested in the policy at hand, he adds. "You've got to build up a reserve of good will to draw upon if you run into trouble. There's an old political saw: 'If you're not on board for takeoff, you don't get on board for the crash landing.' "

August 1985: A Strange Interlude

The State of US–South African Relations

From Crocker's point of view, relations between the US and South Africa had reached their lowest point since Ronald Reagan had come to office—not because of unrest in South Africa, which, Crocker says, did not in itself "create an issue in terms of foreign policy." And certainly not because of the congressional sanctions debate: "I say this, and I mean this, and I'm quite happy to be quoted saying it: The issue of sanctions has always been a side show." Rather, it was because of South Africa's recent conduct in the region. * * *

Then, within the next two months, "South Africa launched an operation in northern Angola, and they launched a cross-border attack in Botswana. That was what triggered us pulling our ambassador out for a period of seven months," he says. "I can't underscore enough the importance of the Botswana raid."

The Vienna Meeting

About two months later, the South African government made an "urgent" request to meet with a US delegation secretly in Vienna to discuss some "new ideas." The August 8–9 session—with the US team led by National Security Adviser Robert McFarlane and a South African team led by South African Foreign Minister "Pik" Botha—was the first high-level meeting between the two governments since Crocker's visit in March. At the meeting, says Crocker, it was "pretty obvious" that the South Africans "were trying to figure out where there was a basis to move forward in our relationship." * * *

The South African delegation had arrived, meanwhile, full of news about some important domestic reforms under serious consideration. According to a South African embassy source, "Pik" Botha brought with him to Vienna an approved draft of a speech the South African president was scheduled to deliver to his party on August 15. The address was to include some relatively dramatic steps: to create a single South African nation with common citizenship for all people regardless of race; to halt development of the black "homelands" and perhaps to reintegrate the four existing homelands back into South Africa; to develop some kind of "power-sharing" scheme with blacks which would fall short of majority rule, but would allow for more black control at the regional level. Also up for discussion, Botha indicated, were the ideas of inviting South African leaders of all races together to draw up a new constitution, to consider abolition of "influx controls" for blacks, and to consider releasing ANC leader Nelson Mandela from jail.[32]

* * *

In fact, the August 15 speech was a tremendous disappointment to US officials. The South African president struck a defiant—even bellicose— tone, announcing none of the predicted reforms. Botha explicitly rejected the principle of one man, one vote in any unitary system of South African government, as well as the idea of creating a fourth chamber of Parliament for blacks. ("I am not prepared to lead white South Africans and other minority groups on a road to abdication and suicide," he said.) In addition, he pointedly attacked efforts at "coercion" from abroad and talked ominously of South Africa "crossing the Rubicon" in its dealings with the rest of the world: "We have never given in to outside demands and we are not about to do so. South Africa's problems will be solved by South Africans and not by foreigners," he said, adding. "The tragedy is that a hostile press and agitation from abroad have acted as an encouragement to the military revolutionaries in South Africa to continue with their violence and intimidation."

Stunned and appalled, the administration nonetheless bravely attempted to paint the address in a positive light. Reagan and McFarlane publicly called the speech an "important statement," but reports circulated that McFarlane was "upset" at the address, and had asserted that there was "nothing in it." The next day, administration spokespersons conceded that they were "disappointed" by the lack of major concessions, but urged that the address be understood in the context of South Africa's polarized domestic political situation. Crocker said that the speech was "written in the code language of another culture" and suggested that the government was more reform-minded than a literal reading of the address would indicate.

* * *

Indeed, the speech provoked an immediate, indignant response from many members of Congress. "P. W. Botha has dashed all real hope that the South African government is ready to change its racist ways," Kennedy declared.[33] "It led to a lot of crowing on the American left, and a lot of further hype by the American media," Crocker says. But it had "a number of [other] consequences" as well, he continues. People "less acquainted with the issue" began to understand "how difficult it was to move the issue," for one thing. Perhaps the most dramatic consequence, Crocker says, was the reaction of a number of banks in the wake of the speech to cease making loans to the South African private sector.

From the standpoint of the Reagan administration, vis-a-vis the spectre of a congressional sanctions bill, the speech represented another nail in the coffin. As syndicated columnists Rowland Evans and Robert Novak wrote:

If this much-advertised speech in Durban had lived up to its billing, Reagan might have been able to send the sanctions bill back to Congress with a soft veto message. He could have said the path to ending apartheid does not lie through the minefield of punitive legislation. Indeed, if Botha's reform plan had found support from credible black leaders in South Africa, the president might conceivably have been able to get the Senate bill withdrawn.[34]

Two more incidents embarrassing to many Republican lawmakers occurred in close succession during the next few days. On August 21, Rev. Jerry Falwell—just back from a six-day visit to South Africa—excoriated Nobel Prize winner Bishop Tutu for being a "phony"—a charge which provoked a reaction of outrage from much of the press and public. A few days later, on August 26, Reagan "inexplicably ignored staff advice" according to Lugar, by granting an interview to an Atlanta radio station in which he declared that the South Africans "have eliminated the segregation that we once had in our own country."[35] Reagan's aides were quick to explain that the president's meaning had been misunderstood, that, in fact, the president understood that South Africa still had a long way to go in rectifying apartheid. Still, in an atmosphere of heightened scrutiny, the gaffe further undermined the credibility of the administration's policy.

Resolving the Standoff

By early September, although the president continued publicly to oppose sanctions, he stopped short of promising to veto Congress's sanctions bill. A source in the Senate pointedly told the *New York Times*, "The president will have to decide who's more important, Dick Lugar or Chester Crocker."[36]

For some time, in fact, lower level State Department officials had been convinced that sanctions were inevitable and had been trying to persuade the powers-that-be in the State Department that the best strategy was to work with Congress in order to have some influence in framing the bill. But, according to one State Department official, Crocker and officials all the way up to the president himself remained adamantly opposed. In part, this may have been because several of Reagan's close personal associates—including his influential communications director Patrick Buchanan—were set against sanctions. Others in the White House, however—including McFarlane and Chief of Staff Don Regan—had shifted on the issue, and urged the president to take action to avoid a veto override, which they feared would jeopardize a number of important items on the president's fall legislative agenda.

In the end, Reagan took their advice. On September 4, Lugar recalls, Shultz called him by phone to hear him out once again on the South African question. And "once again," Lugar says, "I stressed the importance of President Reagan's willingness to sign the bill and to assert his foreign policy leadership. Our country could speak with one voice followed by unified action."[37]

Three days later, on the Saturday before the Senate was scheduled to take up the matter, Shultz and Crocker arrived at Lugar's office at 4 p.m. with a proposed "executive order"—drafted by a fleet of State Department staffers working round the clock—which mirrored the conference committee bill in many respects, and which the president was prepared to issue. As Lugar remembers it, Shultz turned to him and said, "This is your bill in executive order form."[38]

Dubbing the new US policy "active constructive engagement," Ronald Reagan signed the order during a nationally televised speech just five hours before the Senate was scheduled to take a key vote on "cloture" (ending the Senate filibuster, which would have allowed the Senate to vote on the conference committee bill). At the same time, he returned Ambassador Herman Nickel back to South Africa.

Reagan's order was immediately criticized as weak by anti-apartheid activists. Rep. William Gray called the order "full of loopholes," noting that the ban on importation of Krugerrands was subject to the uncertain approval of GATT—an international trade organization—and that the ban on bank loans could be exempted if the loans were deemed to "improve the welfare or expand the opportunities" of blacks and non-white minorities—language vague enough to justify any number of endeavors.[39] Bishop Tutu dismissed the order as "not even a flea bite."[40]

"I too wished the president had simply agreed to sign our bill," Lugar remembers. "But that was not going to happen," and at that point, Lugar was not inclined to fight the president on the matter. * * *

What's more, if the conference committee report passed the Senate, the president would likely veto it, presenting "a tough choice for all Republican senators on a vote to override the veto." Therefore, Lugar and Dole agreed "that we should declare victory"—and stop the Senate from enacting the conference committee report. "No one wanted to go out and overturn a presidential veto if we could avoid it," says Al Lehn, adviser to Dole. But as Lugar and Dole were well aware, "convincing our colleagues in the Senate . . . would not be easy." According to Lugar:

> Most had spent the 5-week recess explaining why they opposed the president's views on South Africa, and now we wanted them to applaud his new action.[41]

The Senate Democrats, meanwhile, were determined to seek a vote on the conference committee report, and nearly succeeded in an effort to end the filibuster on September 9. The stakes rose, as Reagan personally telephoned Republican senators to ask that they defeat the motion for cloture, while 11 members of the Congressional Black Caucus took the unprecedented action of entering the Senate chamber and talking to members of the all-white Senate, urging them to vote for cloture. In the vote that day, the Senate was just three votes shy of the 60 necessary to end the filibuster, but the Democrats were still pushing, and it looked as though a re-vote within the next few days had a chance of succeeding. "The issue now was one of partisan control," Lugar recalled. "Which party controlled the Senate agenda?"[42] Republicans charged their Democratic colleagues with playing a game of pure politics, trying to push the original bill for the sole reason of embarrassing the president.

On September 12, Dole conferred with Lugar and the Senate parliamentarian to discuss a procedural ploy. Under the Senate's rules of order, the senators were precluded from consideration of any piece of legislation not physically present. In addition, the rules stipulated that the chair of the committee with jurisdiction over a conference report had the right to do what he liked with the report. Upon hearing that, Dole picked up the bill and handed it to Lugar. Lugar "tucked the bill into my coat pocket and walked to the fourth floor of the Capitol for another meeting."[43]

When Kennedy asked to take up the South Africa bill, Dole informed him that the document had been removed from the chamber, and that no action could be taken upon it. Kennedy was furious, and charged Lugar with "trickery beneath the dignity of the Senate." Lugar remembers:

> While Kennedy fulminated, [Sen. Robert C.] Byrd [D-W.Va.] argued that even though I was within my rights, he hoped I would reconsider and bring back the bill. Several days later, he led a three-hour chorus of Democratic senators denouncing my activity on the Senate floor.[44]

In addition, Democratic staffers from the House as well as the Senate picketed the Senate to register their disapproval with signs demanding that Lugar "let the captive bill go."

Lugar held firm, and his tactic succeeded, but with some cost in terms of his good relations with the Senate Democrats. "Lugar played along with us, and then went back—reneged on the deal," says one House staffer. "I thought it was really a betrayal. The House people compromised in the conference, because they thought Lugar was sincere. And then Lugar was really getting off the boat and playing ball with the administration." (On the other hand, argues one Republican staffer, the Democrats could have pushed the matter if they had really wanted to—for instance, by offering the sanctions language as an amendment to another bill.)

Whether the final outcome represented triumph or defeat for the administration was a matter of debate. In a sense, the administration had squirmed out of a tight spot. "They saw that they could get away a little cheaply," says Weissman of the House Subcommittee on African Affairs. "They could say the Krugerrand thing was symbolic instead of real and punitive. They were still against *punitive* sanctions."

Still—even though the executive order was not all that the liberals wanted on the issue—it marked "a decisive shift in the South Africa policy debate," according to Finnegan, "from *whether* sanctions were effective to *which* sanctions were most effective. The executive order had been the least humiliating alternative of the several that the White House faced in early September, yet it repudiated constructive engagement as emphatically as any act of Congress could."[45]

Postscript 1986: Comprehensive Anti-apartheid Act Passed by Congress over Reagan Veto

Seeking to re-open the sanctions issue, in May 1986 Democrats in the House introduced a new bill calling for more extensive sanctions. The bill was approved on the floor with an amendment sponsored by Rep. Ronald Dellums (D-Ca.) not only prohibiting new investments by American companies in South Africa but also requiring disinvestment (i.e., selling off of existing investments).

The Senate then passed its own bill that went further than the 1985 Reagan executive order but not as far as the House bill. Senator Lugar kept the coalition together amidst opposition to any sanctions bill from conservatives like Senator Helms and pressure from liberals like Senator Kennedy for making the bill as tough as the House one.

Largely on the basis of a commitment by Senator Lugar to stand by the bill even if President Reagan vetoed it, House Democratic leaders agreed to bypass the negotiations of a conference committee and accept the Senate version of the bill. Reagan did veto the bill. And by votes of 313–83 in the House and 78–21 in the Senate, well beyond the necessary 2/3 majorities, the veto was overriden and the Comprehensive Anti-Apartheid Sanctions Act became law.

This was the first time since 1973 and President Richard Nixon's veto of the War Powers Resolution that a presidential veto on a foreign policy issue had been overriden by Congress. Political forces overwhelmingly were on the side of sanctions. Anti-apartheid activism was strong enough at both the national and local levels to outweigh anti-sanctions business pressures. More and more state and local governments kept passing their own versions of sanctions, through their procurement laws and pensions funds and prohibitions on purchases from and investments in American companies doing business with South Africa. Public opinion polls showed a majority in favor of sanctions. And the South African government continued its violent tactics, of which television news and newspapers kept the American public informed.

NOTES

1. Finnegan, William, "Coming Apart Over Apartheid: The Story Behind the Republicans' Split on South Africa," *Mother Jones*, April/May 1986.

2. Joseph Lelyveld, *Move Your Shadow: South Africa, Black and White* (New York: Penguin Books, 1985), p. 43.
3. Lelyveid, p. 26.
4. The following information about: US/South Africa financial ties comes from two sources: a background note on South Africa printed in the October 1985 issue of the Department of State Bulletin, and a January 28, 1985 *Washington Post* article written by Rick Atkinson.
5. *Washington Post*, December 6, 1984.
6. *Washington Post*, November 24, 1985.
7. *National Journal*, February 16, 1985.
8. Lugar, Richard, *Letters to the Next President* (New York: Simon and Schuster, 1988), pp. 212–213.
9. *Washington Post*, December 6, 1984.
10. *New Republic*, May 20, 1985.
11. *Washington Post*, December 11, 1984.
12. *Congressional Quarterly*, March 9, 1985.
13. *Wall Street Journal*, August 23, 1985.
14. Lugar, p. 213.
15. *Washington Post*, December 6, 1984.
16. *Washington Post*, May 15, 1985.
17. *Washington Post*, September 20, 1985.
18. *Washington Post*, December 9, 1984.
19. *Washington Post*, December 9, 1984.
20. *Washington Post*, June 15, 1985.
21. *Washington Post*, January 17, 1985.
22. *Washington Post*, September 8, 1985.
23. *Washington Post*, May 15, 1985.
24. Lugar, p. 217.
25. *Washington Post*, July 12, 1985.
26. *Washington Post*, July 12, 1985.
27. *Washington Post*, June 21, 1985.
28. *Washington Post*, July 21, 1985.
29. *Washington Post*, August 22, 1985.
30. Senate Foreign Relations Committee hearing, May 2, 1985.
31. *Wall Street Journal*, August 23, 1985.
32. *Newsweek*, August 19, 1985.
33. *Washington Post*, August 16, 1985.
34. *Evans and Novak*, August 23, 1985.
35. Lugar, p. 220.
36. *New York Times*, August 17, 1985.
37. Lugar, p. 220.
38. Lugar, p. 220.
39. *Congressional Quarterly*, September 14, 1985.
40. *Washington Post*, September 10, 1985.

41. Lugar, p. 221.
42. Lugar, p. 222.
43. Lugar, p. 222.
44. Lugar, p. 223.
45. *Mother Jones*, April/May 1986 (emphasis added).

3 The Historical Context: Great Debates in American Foreign Policy, 1789–1945

"The Past is Prologue": the words are inscribed on the base of the National Archives in Washington, D.C. For all the ways that today's world is new and different, there is much to be learned from history. The particular choices being debated for U.S. foreign policy in the twenty-first century clearly differ in many ways from past agendas. But for all the changes, we still wrestle with many of the same core questions of foreign policy strategy and foreign policy politics that have been debated over the course of American history. The readings in this chapter explore further three of the historical "great debates" discussed in the main text.

The isolationism vs. internationalism debate, over whether the United States should seek to minimize its involvement in world affairs or take a more activist role, has recurred time and again. The first reading, drawn from Henry Kissinger's *Diplomacy*, examines the political constraints President Franklin D. Roosevelt had to grapple with in trying to shake the United States out of its 1930s isolationism amidst the rise of Adolf Hitler and Nazism in Europe and of Japanese imperialism and aggression in Asia. Congress had passed a bevy of isolationist legislation, and the American public was having difficulty seeing the connection between what was happening "over there" and the U.S. national interest.

The excerpt from Robert Osgood's classic book, *Ideals and Self Interest in America's Foreign Relations*, deals with World War I and President Woodrow Wilson. Wilson is the president most often associated with the democratic idealist tradition in U.S. foreign policy, its aspirations as well as its internal tensions. The decision to go to war in Europe for the first time in U.S. history, and the vision for the postwar peace toward which Wilson sought to lead both the world and his own country, were as Osgood observes, "a highly significant context of events in which to examine the real conditions for reconciling national self-interest with universal ideals."

While lagging in the attention it gets from some historians, the late nineteenth century and the Spanish-American War are stressed by others as a crucial defining period in American foreign policy. It is with this focus that Walter LaFeber makes the case for how the United States sought to forge its own "new empire." This expansionism was driven largely by the economic forces of capitalists seeking new markets for exports, new opportunities for investments, and cheap supplies of raw materials—i.e., prosperity more than power or peace and especially more than principles.

3.1 *Isolationism vs. Internationalism*

HENRY KISSINGER

Franklin D. Roosevelt and the Coming of World War II

For contemporary political leaders governing by public opinion polls, Roosevelt's role in moving his isolationist people toward participation in the war serves as an object lesson on the scope of leadership in a democracy. Sooner or later, the threat to the European balance of power would have forced the United States to intervene in order to stop Germany's drive for world domination. The sheer, and growing, strength of America was bound to propel it eventually into the center of the international arena. That this happened with such speed and so decisively was the achievement of Franklin Delano Roosevelt.

All great leaders walk alone. Their singularity springs from their ability to discern challenges that are not yet apparent to their contemporaries. Roosevelt took an isolationist people into a war between countries whose conflicts had only a few years earlier been widely considered inconsistent with American values and irrelevant to American security. After 1940, Roosevelt convinced the Congress, which had overwhelmingly passed a series of Neutrality Acts just a few years before, to authorize ever-increasing American assistance to Great Britain, stopping just short of outright belligerency and occasionally even crossing that line. Finally, Japan's attack on Pearl Harbor removed America's last hesitations. Roosevelt was able to persuade a society which had for two centuries treasured its invulnerability of the dire perils of an Axis victory. And he saw to it that, this time, America's involvement would mark a first step toward permanent international engagement. During the war, his leadership held the alliance together and shaped the multilateral institutions which continue to serve the international community to this day.

No president, with the possible exception of Abraham Lincoln, has made a more decisive difference in American history. Roosevelt took the oath of office at a time of national uncertainty, when America's faith in the New

---

From *Diplomacy* (New York: Simon and Schuster, 1994), chapter 15.

World's infinite capacity for progress had been severely shaken by the Great Depression. All around him, democracies seemed to be faltering and anti-democratic governments on both the Left and the Right were gaining ground.

* * *

America's journey from involvement in the First World War to active participation in the Second proved to be a long one—interrupted as it was by the nation's about-face to isolationism. The depth of America's revulsion toward international affairs illustrates the magnitude of Roosevelt achievement. A brief sketch of the historical backdrop against which Roosevelt conducted his policies is therefore necessary.

In the 1920s, America's mood was ambivalent, oscillating between a willingness to assert principles of universal applicability and a need to justify them on behalf of an isolationist foreign policy. Americans took to reciting the traditional themes of their foreign policy with even greater emphasis: the uniqueness of America's mission as the exemplar of liberty, the moral superiority of democratic foreign policy, the seamless relationship between personal and international morality, the importance of open diplomacy, and the replacement of the balance of power by international consensus as expressed in the League of Nations.

All of these presumably universal principles were enlisted on behalf of American isolationism. Americans were still incapable of believing that anything outside the Western Hemisphere could possibly affect their security. The America of the 1920s and 1930s rejected even its own doctrine of collective security lest it lead to involvement in the quarrels of distant, bellicose societies. The provisions of the Treaty of Versailles were interpreted as vindictive, and reparations as self-defeating. When the French occupied the Ruhr, America used the occasion to withdraw its remaining occupying forces from the Rhineland. That Wilsonian exceptionalism had established criteria no international order could fulfill, made disillusionment a part of its very essence.

Disillusionment with the results of the war erased to a considerable extent the distinctions between the internationalists and the isolationists. Not even the most liberal internationalists any longer discerned an American interest in sustaining a flawed postwar settlement. No significant group had a good word to say about the balance of power. What passed for internationalism was being identified with membership in the League of Nations rather than with day-to-day participation in international diplomacy. And even the most dedicated internationalists insisted that the Monroe Doctrine superseded the League of Nations, and recoiled before the idea of America's joining League enforcement measures, even economic ones.

* * *

The Kellogg-Briand Pact * * * turned into another example of America's tendency to treat principles as self-implementing. Although American leaders enthusiastically proclaimed the historic nature of the treaty because sixty-two nations had renounced war as an instrument of national policy, they adamantly refused to endorse any machinery for applying it, much less for enforcing it. President Calvin Coolidge, waxing effusive before the Congress in December 1928, asserted: "Observance of this Covenant . . . promises more for the peace of the world than any other agreement ever negotiated among the nations."[1]

Yet how was this utopia to be achieved? Coolidge's passionate defense of the Kellogg-Briand Pact spurred internationalists and supporters of the League to argue, quite reasonably, that, war having been outlawed, the concept of neutrality had lost all meaning. In their view, since the League had been designed to identify aggressors, the international community was obliged to punish them appropriately. "Does anyone believe," asked one of the proponents of this view, "that the aggressive designs of Mussolini could be checked merely by the good faith of the Italian people and the power of public opinion?"[2]

The prescience of this question did not enhance its acceptability. Even while the treaty bearing his name was still in the process of being debated, Secretary of State Kellogg, in an address before the Council on Foreign Relations, stressed that force would never be used to elicit compliance. Reliance on force, he argued, would turn what had been intended as a long stride toward peace into precisely the sort of military alliance that was so in need of being abolished. * * *

To prevent America from once again being lured into war, the Congress passed three so-called Neutrality Acts between 1935 and 1937. Prompted by the Nye Report, these laws prohibited loans and any other financial assistance to belligerents (whatever the cause of war) and imposed an arms embargo on all parties (regardless of who the victim was). Purchases of nonmilitary goods for cash were allowed only if they were transported in non-American ships.[3] The Congress was not abjuring profits so much as it was rejecting risks. As the aggressors bestrode Europe, America abolished the distinction between aggressor and victim by legislating a single set of restrictions on both.

* * *

After his landslide electoral victory of 1936, Roosevelt went far beyond the existing framework. In fact, he demonstrated that, though preoccupied with the Depression, he had grasped the essence of the dictators' challenge better than any European leader except Churchill. At first, he sought merely to enunciate America's moral commitment to the cause of the democracies. Roosevelt began this educational process with the so-called Quarantine Speech, which he delivered in Chicago on October 5, 1937. It was his first warning to America of the approaching peril, and his first public statement that America might have to assume some responsibilities with respect to it. Japan's renewed military aggression in China, coupled with the previous year's announcement of the Berlin-Rome Axis, provided the backdrop, giving Roosevelt's concerns a global dimension:

> The peace, the freedom and the security of ninety percent of the population of the world is being jeopardized by the remaining ten percent who are threatening a breakdown of all international order and law. . . . It seems to be unfortunately true that the epidemic of world lawlessness is spreading. When an epidemic of physical disease starts to spread, the community approves and joins in a quarantine of the patients in order to protect the health of the community against the spread of the disease.[4]

Roosevelt was careful not to spell out what he meant by "quarantine" and what, if any, specific measures he might have in mind. Had the speech implied any kind of action, it would have been inconsistent with the Neutrality Acts, which the Congress had overwhelmingly approved and the President had recently signed.

Not surprisingly, the Quarantine Speech was attacked by isolationists, who demanded clarification of the President's intentions. They argued passionately that the distinction between "peace-loving" and "warlike" nations implied an American value judgment which, in turn, would lead to the abandonment of the policy of nonintervention, to which both Roosevelt and the Congress had pledged themselves. Two years later, Roosevelt described the uproar that resulted from the speech as follows: "Unfortunately, this suggestion fell upon deaf ears—even hostile and resentful ears. . . . It was hailed as war mongering; it was condemned as attempted intervention in foreign affairs; it was even ridiculed as a nervous search 'under the bed' for dangers of war which did not exist."[5]

Roosevelt could have ended the controversy by simply denying the intentions being ascribed to him. Yet, despite the critical onslaught, Roosevelt spoke ambiguously enough at a news conference to keep open the option of collective defense of some kind. According to the journalistic practice of the day, the President always met with the press off-the-record, which meant that he could neither be quoted nor identified, and these rules were respected.

* * *

Munich seems to have been the turning point which impelled Roosevelt to align America with the European democracies, at first politically but gradually materially as well. From then on, his commitment to thwarting the dictators was inexorable, culminating three years later in America's entry into a second world war. The interplay between leaders and their publics in a democracy is always complex. A leader who confines himself to the experience of his people in a period of upheaval purchases temporary popularity at the price of condemnation by posterity, whose claims he is neglecting. A leader who gets too far ahead of his society will become irrelevant. A great leader must be an educator, bridging the gap between his visions and the familiar. But he must also be willing to walk alone to enable his society to follow the path he has selected.

There is inevitably in every great leader an element of guile which simplifies, sometimes the objectives, sometimes the magnitude, of the task. But his ultimate test is whether he incarnates the truth of his society's values and the essence of its challenges. These qualities Roosevelt possessed to an unusual degree. He deeply believed in America; he was convinced that Nazism was both evil and a threat to American security, and he was extraordinarily guileful. And he was prepared to shoulder the burden of lonely decisions. Like a tightrope walker, he had to move, step by careful, anguishing step, across the chasm between his goal and his society's reality in demonstrating to it that the far shore was in fact safer than the familiar promontory.

On October 26, 1938, less than four weeks after the Munich Pact, Roosevelt returned to the theme of his Quarantine Speech. In a radio address to the Herald-Tribune Forum, he warned against unnamed but easily identifiable aggressors whose "national policy adopts as a deliberate instrument the threat of war."[6] Next, while upholding disarmament in principle, Roosevelt also called for strengthening America's defenses:

> . . . we have consistently pointed out that neither we, nor any nation, will accept disarmament while neighbor nations arm to the teeth. If there is not general disarmament, we ourselves must continue to arm. It is a step we do not like to take, and do not wish to take. But, until there is general abandonment of weapons capable of aggression, ordinary rules of national prudence and common sense require that we be prepared.[7]

In secret, Roosevelt went much further. At the end of October 1938, in separate conversations with the British air minister and also with a personal friend of Prime Minister Neville Chamberlain, he put forward a project designed to circumvent the Neutrality Acts. Proposing an outright evasion of legislation he had only recently signed, Roosevelt suggested setting up British and French airplane-assembly plants in Canada, near the American border. The United States would supply all the components, leaving only the final assembly to Great Britain and France. This arrangement would technically permit the project to stay within the letter of the Neutrality Acts, presumably on the ground that the component parts were civilian goods. Roosevelt told Chamberlain's emissary that, "in the event of war with the dictators, he had the industrial resources of the American nation behind him."[8]

Roosevelt's scheme for helping the democracies restore their air power collapsed, as it was bound to, if only because of the sheer logistical impossibility of undertaking an effort on such a scale in secret. But from then on, Roosevelt's support for Britain and France was limited only when the Congress and public opinion could neither be circumvented nor overcome.

* * *

Isolationists observing Roosevelt's actions were deeply disturbed. In February 1939, before the outbreak of the war, Senator Arthur Vandenberg had eloquently put forward the isolationist case:

> True, we do live in a foreshortened world in which, compared with Washington's day, time and space are relatively annihilated. But I still thank God for two insulating oceans; and even though they be foreshortened, they are still our supreme benediction if they be widely and prudently used. . . .
>
> We all have our sympathies and our natural emotions in behalf of the victims of national or international outrage all around the globe; but we are not, we cannot be, the world's protector or the world's policeman.[9]

When, in response to the German invasion of Poland, Great Britain declared war on September 3, 1939, Roosevelt had no choice but to invoke the Neutrality Acts. At the same time, he moved rapidly to modify the legislation to permit Great Britain and France to purchase American arms. * * *

* * * Roosevelt had for many months been acting on the premise that America might have to enter the war. In September 1940, he had devised an ingenious arrangement to give Great Britain fifty allegedly over-age destroyers in exchange for the right to set up American bases on eight British possessions, from Newfoundland to the South American mainland. Winston Churchill later called it a "decidedly unneutral act," for the destroyers were far more important to Great Britain than the bases were to America. Most of them were quite remote from any conceivable theater of operations, and some even duplicated existing American bases. More than anything, the destroyer deal represented a pretext based on a legal opinion by Roosevelt's own appointee, Attorney General Francis Biddle—hardly an objective observer.

Roosevelt sought neither Congressional approval nor modification of the Neutrality Acts for his destroyer-for-bases deal. Nor was he challenged, as inconceivable as that seems in the light of contemporary practice. It was the measure of Roosevelt's concern about a possible Nazi victory and of his commitment to bolstering British morale, that he took this step as a presidential election campaign was just beginning. (It was fortunate for Great Britain and for the cause of American unity that the foreign policy views of his opponent, Wendell Willkie, were not significantly different from Roosevelt's.)

Concurrently, Roosevelt vastly increased the American defense budget and, in 1940, induced the Congress to introduce peacetime conscription. So strong was lingering isolationist sentiment that conscription was renewed by only one vote in the House of Representatives in the summer of 1941, less than four months before the outbreak of the war.

∗　∗　∗

Few American presidents have been as sensitive and perspicacious as Franklin Delano Roosevelt was in his grasp of the psychology of his people. Roosevelt understood that only a threat to their security could motivate them to support military preparedness. But to take them into a war, he knew he needed to appeal to their idealism in much the same way that Wilson had. In Roosevelt's view, America's security needs might well be met by control of the Atlantic, but its war aims required some vision of a new world order. Thus "balance of power" was not a term ever found in Roosevelt's pronouncements, except when he used it disparagingly. What he sought was to bring about a world community compatible with America's democratic and social ideals as the best guarantee of peace.

In this atmosphere, the president of a technically neutral United States and Great Britain's quintessential wartime leader, Winston Churchill, met in August 1941 on a cruiser off the coast of Newfoundland. Great Britain's position had improved somewhat when Hitler invaded the Soviet Union in June, but England was far from assured of victory. Nevertheless, the joint statement these two leaders issued reflected not a statement of traditional war aims but the design of a totally new world bearing America's imprimatur. The Atlantic Charter proclaimed a set of "common principles" on which the President and Prime Minister based "their hopes for a better future for the world."[10] These principles enlarged upon Roosevelt's original Four Freedoms by incorporating equal access to raw materials and cooperative efforts to improve social conditions around the world.

∗　∗　∗

When the Atlantic Charter was proclaimed, German armies were approaching Moscow and Japanese forces were preparing to move into Southeast Asia. Churchill was above all concerned with removing the obstacles to America's participation in the war. For he understood very well that, by itself, Great Britain would not be able to achieve a decisive victory, even with Soviet participation in the war and American material support. In addition, the Soviet Union might collapse and some compromise between Hitler and Stalin was always a possibility, threatening Great Britain with renewed isolation. Churchill saw no point in debating postwar structure before he could even be certain that there would be one.

In September 1941, the United States crossed the line into belligerency. Roosevelt's order that the position of German submarines be reported to the British Navy had made it inevitable that, sooner or later, some clash would occur. On September 4, 1941, the American destroyer *Greer* was torpedoed while signaling the location of a German submarine to British airplanes. On September 11, without describing the circumstances, Roosevelt denounced German "piracy." Comparing German submarines to a rattle-snake coiled to strike, he ordered the United States Navy to sink "on sight" any German or Italian submarines discovered in the previously established American defense area extending all the way to Iceland. To all practical purposes, America was at war on the sea with the Axis powers.[11]

Simultaneously, Roosevelt took up the challenge of Japan. In response to Japan's occupation of Indochina in July 1941, he abrogated America's commercial treaty with Japan, forbade the sale of scrap metal to it, and encouraged the Dutch government-in-exile to stop oil exports to Japan from the Dutch East Indies (present-day Indonesia). These pressures led to ne-gotiations with Japan, which began in October 1941. Roosevelt instructed the American negotiators to demand that Japan relinquish all of its con-quests, including Manchuria, by invoking America's previous refusal to "rec-ognize" these acts.

Roosevelt must have known that there was no possibility that Japan would accept. On December 7, 1941, following the pattern of the Russo-Japanese War, Japan launched a surprise attack on Pearl Harbor and de-stroyed a significant part of America's Pacific fleet. On December 11, Hitler honored his treaty with Tokyo by declaring war on the United States. Why Hitler thus freed Roosevelt to concentrate America's war effort on the coun-try Roosevelt had always considered to be the principal enemy has never been satisfactorily explained.

America's entry into the war marked the culmination of a great and daring leader's extraordinary diplomatic enterprise. In less than three years, Roosevelt had taken his staunchly isolationist people into a global war. As late as May 1940, 64 percent of Americans had considered the preservation of peace more important than the defeat of the Nazis. Eighteen months later, in December 1941, just before the attack on Pearl Harbor, the pro-portions had been reversed—only 32 percent favored peace over preventing triumph.[12]

Roosevelt had achieved his goal patiently and inexorably, educating his people one step at a time about the necessities before them. His audiences filtered his words through their own preconceptions and did not always understand that his ultimate destination was war, though they could not have doubted that it was confrontation. In fact, Roosevelt was not so much bent on war as on defeating the Nazis; it was simply that, as time passed, the Nazis could only be defeated if America entered the war.

That their entry into the war should have seemed so sudden to the American people was due to three factors: Americans had had no experience with going to war for security concerns outside the Western Hemisphere; many believed that the European democracies could prevail on their own, while few understood the nature of the diplomacy that had preceded Japan's attack on Pearl Harbor or Hitler's rash declaration of war on the United

States. It was a measure of the United States' deep-seated isolationism that it had to be bombed at Pearl Harbor before it would enter the war in the Pacific; and that, in Europe, it was Hitler who would ultimately declare war on the United States rather than the other way around.

By initiating hostilities, the Axis powers had solved Roosevelt's lingering dilemma about how to move the American people into the war. Had Japan focused its attack on Southeast Asia and Hitler not declared war against the United States, Roosevelt's task of steering his people toward his views would have been much more complicated. In light of Roosevelt's proclaimed moral and strategic convictions, there can be little doubt that, in the end, he would have somehow managed to enlist America in the struggle he considered so decisive to both the future of freedom and to American security.

Subsequent generations of Americans have placed a greater premium on total candor by their chief executive. Yet, like Lincoln, Roosevelt sensed that the survival of his country and its values was at stake, and that history itself would hold him responsible for the results of his solitary initiatives. And, as was the case with Lincoln, it is a measure of the debt free peoples owe to Franklin Delano Roosevelt that the wisdom of his solitary passage is now, quite simply, taken for granted.

NOTES

1. Selig Adler, *The Isolationist Impulse, Its Twentieth-Century Reaction* (New York: Free Press; London: Collier-Macmillan, 1957), p. 214.
2. Quoted in *ibid.*, p. 216.
3. Ruhl J. Bartlett, ed., *The Record of American Diplomacy* (New York: Alfred A. Knopf, 1956), pp. 572–77. The First Neutrality Act, signed by FDR on August 31, 1935: arms embargo; Americans not permitted to travel on ships of belligerents. The Second Neutrality Act, signed by FDR on February 29, 1936 (a week before the reoccupation of the Rhineland on March 7): extended the First Act through May 1, 1936, and added a prohibition against loans or credits to belligerents. The Third Neutrality Act, signed by FDR on May 1, 1937: extended previous acts due to expire at midnight plus "cash and carry" provisions for certain nonmilitary goods.
4. Address in Chicago, October 5, 1937, in Roosevelt, *Public Papers* (New York: Macmillan Co., 1941), 1937 vol., p. 410.
5. *Ibid.*, 1939 vol., Introduction by FDR, p. xxviii.
6. Radio address to the Herald-Tribune Forum, October 26, 1938, in Roosevelt, *Public Papers*, 1938 vol., p. 564.
7. *Ibid.*, p. 565.
8. Donald Cameron Watt, *How War Came: The Immediate Origins of the Second World War, 1938–1939* (London: William Heinemann, 1989), p. 130.
9. Vandenberg speech in the Senate, "It Is Not Cowardice to Think of

America First," February 27, 1939, in *Vital Speeches of the Day*, vol. v, no. 12 (April 1, 1939), pp. 356–57.

10. The Atlantic Charter: Official Statement on Meeting Between the President and Prime Minister Churchill, August 14, 1941, in Roosevelt, *Public Papers*, 1941 vol., p. 314.

11. Fireside Chat to the Nation, September 11, 1941, in *ibid.*, pp. 384–92.

12. Adler, *Isolationist Impulse*, p. 257.

3.2 *Democratic Idealism*

ROBERT E. OSGOOD
World War I and Woodrow Wilson

World War I is a crucial period in the evolution of America's attitude toward international relations. It provides a highly significant context of events in which to examine the real conditions for reconciling national self-interest with universal ideals.

* * *

The practical demands of national self-interest were further obscured by the exacerbation of an underlying temperamental and ideological conflict, personified in the antipathy of Theodore Roosevelt toward Woodrow Wilson, between those most conscious of the imperatives of power and those most anxious to subordinate national egoism to universal moral values. This conflict was suspended momentarily in the common embrace of a new crusade, but, as in 1898, it flared up with increasing heat as the issues of war aims and the peace settlement arose. Largely because the circumstances of the war failed to provide the incentive for subjecting either militant or pacific sentiments to the test of expediency, the deep-rooted struggle for public opinion between the Rooseveltians and the Wilsonians, instead of bringing about a fusion of realism with idealism, actually exacerbated their dissociation.

As it was, neither the egoistic nor the idealistic motives which led the United States to intervene in the European contest were sufficiently rooted in a consciousness of compelling self-interest to sustain beyond victory the break with the nation's pacific ideals and its traditional sense of self-interest in isolation. This fact was concealed during the period of American intervention by the nation's preoccupation with the overriding object of victory and by President Wilson's success in reconciling even the tenderest consciences to warfare through the identification of intervention with America's altruistic mission. However, when victory was achieved, altruism collapsed,

From *Ideals and Self-interest in America's Foreign Relations: The Great Transformation of the 20th Century* (Chicago: University of Chicago Press, 1953), part II.

75

and the nation reverted to its normal isolationist behavior in the society of nations. Those with the greatest inhibitions toward intervention became impatient with the frustration of their proportionately lofty expectations; the most militant interventionists became apprehensive lest idealism get out of hand and hamstring the nation's power of independent action; and with the immediate object of winning the war removed, the nation as a whole relaxed its moral muscles and began comparing the human and material sacrifices of war with its meager rewards, both tangible and spiritual.

* * *

Wilson's Indifference Toward Power and Strategy

Before the war in Europe broke out Wilson had demonstrated, especially in his policy toward Latin America, his profound dedication to America's mission of bringing constitutional and democratic liberty, universal peace, and the Golden Rule to all the peoples of the world. He had proclaimed that Americans were placed on earth as mankind's shining example of the subordination of material and national interests to the highest moral values and the service of humanity. By 1914 Wilson had formulated and had begun to put into practice certain ideal principles of American foreign policy. On the other hand, he had given very little thought to problems of national security and the exigencies of power politics. And as for the balance of power, he abhorred it as a tool of militarists and despots.

* * *

After the first half-year of the war Wilson steadfastly maintained that, no matter which side won, the warring nations of the world would be so utterly exhausted that, for a generation at least, they could not possibly threaten the United States, even economically; but that, on the contrary, they would desperately need America's healing influence.[1]

Those who had direct access to the President during the neutrality years have testified to their inability to impress upon him the gravity of the German threat. Thus Secretary of State Robert Lansing in a memorandum to himself early in the summer of 1916 expressed his amazement at Wilson's inability to grasp the real issues of the war: "That German imperialistic ambitions threaten free institutions everywhere apparently has not sunk very deeply into his mind. For six months I have talked about the struggle between Autocracy and Democracy, but do not see that I have made any great impression."[2]

Actually, Wilson was impressed by the struggle between autocracy and democracy; and, eventually, in his War Message he placed American might on the side of democracy; but, far from implying the preservation of a balance of power, as Lansing hoped, Wilson's pronouncement heralded the death of this iniquitous system and the birth of a new order in international relations, in which power politics and the pursuit of selfish national interests would be supplanted by the higher moral standards of personal conduct. In fact, Wilson's conception of foreign relations was remarkable not so much for its neglect of the problems of power as for its conscious subordination of national expediency to ideal goals. Above all, he coveted for America the distinction of a nation transcending its own selfish interests and dedicated in altruistic service to humanity.

* * *

Wilson's Ideal of Neutrality

From the moment President Wilson learned of the outbreak of war in Europe he looked to America to exemplify that self-control and dispassionate idealism which he believed was indispensable for the fulfilment of her historic mission to serve humanity. As the German Army advanced through neutralized Luxemburg he told newspaper correspondents, "I want to have the pride of feeling that America, if nobody else, has her self-possession and stands ready with calmness of thought and steadiness of purpose to help the rest of the world."[3] It was in response to this aspiration, as well as to America's traditional policy toward European belligerents and to the overwhelming weight of public opinion, that he issued a proclamation on August 4, explicitly stating the duties imposed upon Americans as citizens of a neutral nation.[4] Two weeks later he evoked the full measure of self-possession implied in this proclamation by asking Americans not only to observe their legal obligations but to "act and speak in the true spirit of neutrality, which is the spirit of impartiality and fairness and friendliness to all concerned."

> My thought is of America. . . . She should show herself in this time of peculiar trial a Nation fit beyond others to exhibit the fine poise of undisturbed judgment, the dignity of self-control, the efficiency of dispassionate action; a Nation . . . which keeps herself fit and free to do what is honest and disinterested and truly serviceable for the peace of the world.[5]

* * *

President Wilson's more bellicose critics denounced his position on neutrality as a transparent rationalization of timidity and moral myopia, but in Wilson's mind neutrality did not mean simply keeping out of trouble; it meant self-control and service to humanity. As he said in this same message, America's purpose in staying out of the war was to bring peace to the belligerents, for this was a war "whose very existence affords us opportunities of friendship and disinterested service which should make us ashamed of any thought of hostility or fearful preparation for trouble." America, he declared, had been "raised up" to "exemplify the counsels of peace."

* * *

Compared to the goal of world peace and democracy, national self-interest seemed an ignoble consideration. Wilson may have entertained some vague apprehensions of the practical effect of a German victory upon America's strategic position in the world, but these apprehensions were insignificant when measured against his concern for America's moral position. In Wilson's philosophy it was the things of the spirit that counted, and how could America serve as an impartial peacemaker if she placed her own self-interest above the interests of mankind and adopted national expediency rather than Humanity as her guide? Wilson was determined that Americans should not lose sight of their mission in the world by abandoning their self-composure and falling victim to the alarms of German peril sounded by the jingoes and militarists. Americans were different; they created their nation, not to serve themselves, but to serve mankind.

* * *

America's Goal: World Peace

Behind [Colonel Edward] House's famous peace mission in 1916 there was a background of Wilson's growing interest in the bases of a just and lasting peace. During the autumn of 1915 his ideas on this subject matured to the stage of specific provisions, including a league of nations. In January, 1915, as a first step toward permanent peace, he sent House to sound out the belligerents concerning American mediation. House's mission failed, but Wilson continued to ponder the bases of peace. Throughout 1915 his interest in world organization increased, along with the growing concern of a large body of highly educated Americans with such projects as the League to Enforce Peace. He rejected House's advice that the United States discard its neutrality and throw its whole weight behind a demand for a just peace based on a world league; but during the fall of 1915 he did decide that the nation should become a partner in an organization for world peace, and to that end he encouraged House and Sir Edward Grey to develop their ideas on the subject of the formation of a league after the war.

* * *

Wilson had long been convinced of the interdependence of the peoples of the world. Now, for the first time, he clearly challenged America's political isolation and acknowledged the revolutionary character of the movement for a league to enforce peace. "We are participants, whether we would or not, in the life of the world. The interests of all nations are our own also. . . . What affects mankind is inevitably our affair as well as the affair of the nations of Europe and Asia." But Wilson was referring to moral interdependence, not strategic interdependence. America's mission was conceived in altruism, not self-interest. Americans, he said, wanted to end the war because it affected their rights and interests, but they approached the task of establishing permanent peace as an opportunity to replace the selfish struggle among nations and the balance-of-power system with a "new and more wholesome diplomacy," as an opportunity to realize among nations the same standards of honor and morality that were demanded of individuals. He expected an association of nations to come about as a great moral awakening rather than as a response to new conditions of national security. The war had disclosed "a great moral necessity," but he said nothing about strategic necessity.

As for America's part in bringing about an association of nations, in Wilson's view she remained an impartial, magnanimous bystander, ready to apply her moral weight to the service of humanity whenever the warring nations were willing to accept it. With the "causes" and "objects" of the war she had no concern. "We have nothing material of any kind to ask for ourselves, and are quite aware that we are in no sense or degree parties to the present quarrel. Our interest is only in peace and its future guarantees." This principle of disinterested service to the cause of world peace dominated Wilson's foreign policy thereafter.

Wilson's determination to keep the nation out of war in order that it might fulfill its mission was symbolized by the Democratic campaign slogan "He Kept Us out of War." With this slogan still ringing in his ears the President entered upon one final desperate effort to achieve its implied promise. On December 18, 1916, he sent identical notes to the belligerents asking them to state the terms upon which they would be willing to stop fighting.[6] While his advisers were urging him to align the country on the side of the democracies, and while Roosevelt was fairly apoplectic over his refusal to abandon neutrality, Wilson was more soberly resolute than ever in his determination to refrain from moral judgments that might distract the nation from its goal of impartial mediation. Thus he pointed out in his note that "the objects which the statesmen of the belligerents on both sides have in mind in this war are virtually the same, as stated in general terms to their own people and to the world." America, he said, had no interest in the outcome of the war except the achievement of these objects, including a league of nations "to insure peace and justice throughout the world." But Americans were interested in the immediate ending of the war "lest it should presently be too late to accomplish the greater things which lie beyond its conclusion, lest the situation of neutral nations be rendered altogether intolerable, and lest, more than all, an injury be done civilization itself which can never be . . . repaired."

* * *

Intervention

On January 31, 1917, the foundation of American neutrality collapsed, for on that date the German government announced that U-boat commanders would henceforth sink all ships—neutrals included—within the war zone. Before the American government had extracted the *Sussex* pledge it had unequivocally stated, "Unless the Imperial Government should now immediately declare and effect an abandonment of its present methods of submarine warfare against passenger and freight-carrying vessels, the Government of the United States can have no choice but to sever diplomatic relations."[7] It was evident that the government could not now consistently or honorably avoid carrying out this threat. Reluctantly, Wilson returned to his dogged defense of American rights. On February 3 he told Congress that the nation was severing relations with Germany. The American people wellnigh unanimously supported him. On February 26, 1917, he asked Congress for authority to provide arms for American merchantment. The House passed a bill for this purpose, but eleven Senators, whom Wilson branded as "a little group of wilful men," filibustered it to death. Wilson found authority to arm American vessels anyhow, and it then became just a question of time before a German submarine commander would commit an "overt act" that would bring the United States into the war. A number of such acts occurred before the middle of March. By March 21 Wilson had finally made the fateful decision to ask Congress to declare that a state of war existed.

To the last, Wilson was oppressed by the thought of taking America into war. He could find no solace in the ecstasy of patriotism. His bellicosity was too refined. He had reached his decision simply because he could find no alternative. In his final reckoning with the logic of strict accountability, which he had constantly feared but which he was powerless to escape, there is an element of the high tragedy that befalls men who, due to the inevitable choices dictated by their nature, become the victims of events beyond their control.

However, if Wilson could finally choose no other course but intervention, he would, at least, lead America into war upon the highest possible moral ground: the service of others. He had always believed in a holy war to vindicate spiritual conceptions and set men free. For a man with his strong emotional and intellectual revulsion toward international conflict, war had to be holy in order to be justifiable. Wilson was following a higher consistency than his opposition to war when he based his War Message of April 2 on the very principles for which he had sought to keep America a disinterested bystander.[8]

> I have exactly the same things in mind now that I had in mind when I addressed the Senate on the twenty-second of January last; the same that I had

in mind when I addressed Congress on the third of February and on the twenty-sixth of February. Our object now, as then, is to vindicate the principles of peace and justice in the life of the world as against selfish and autocratic power and to set up amongst the really free and self-governed peoples of the world such a concert of purpose and of action as will henceforth insure the observance of those principles.

He explained that America had taken up arms as a last resort. "We enter this war only where we are clearly forced into it because there are no other means of defending our rights." And he reviewed the events on the high seas that made neutrality untenable, also mentioning the spies and "criminal intrigues" which Germany had set loose upon the nation. But it was not just American rights which he was considering; it was the fundamental rights of all peoples. "The present German submarine warfare against commerce is a warfare against mankind. It is a war against all nations. . . . The challenge is to all mankind."

Wilson further generalized America's cause by presenting it as the cause of democracy against autocracy. He said that only an autocratic government, in which the moral voice of the people was suppressed, could perpetrate such crimes against international law and humanity. He avowed that neutrality was no longer feasible or desirable where peace and freedom of peoples were menaced by autocratic government. Therefore, the only remedy was a peace founded upon a concert among democratic nations.

Some Realists had been saying the same thing ever since the *Lusitania* sank; however, when they talked about autocracy, they referred not only to the principle of autocracy but to the fact of German military power; when they talked about democracy, they were thinking not only of the ideal but, in particular, of the mutual political interests of Great Britain and the United States; and when they talked about a concert among democratic nations, they did not anticipate the end of power politics but rather the beginning of a larger political arrangement, through which America could secure its power and its vital interests. But Wilson was bound to dwell upon the spiritual aspects of America's cause, simply because he believed that it was the things of the spirit that gave the American mission its power. He was bound to stress the democratic basis of a concert of nations, because he believed, "Only free peoples can hold their purpose and their honor steady to a common end and prefer the interests of mankind to any narrow interest of their own."

Wilson would not taint America's mission with the suggestion of self-interest, for he believed that only in proportion as the nation was disinterested could it serve the rest of the world. Therefore, he declared that Americans sought nothing material for themselves. They would fight only for the ultimate peace and liberation of others. Nor would he have the nation forsake that magnanimity and self-control which it had exemplified during the trials of neutrality. He pleaded that the war be conducted without rancor

toward the German people. America would fight only the selfish and irre-
sponsible German leaders. It would fight only for the privilege of all men,
including Germans, to be free. "The world must be made safe for democracy. Its peace must be planted upon the tested foundations of political
liberty."

Concluding his address, in solemn tones Wilson spoke again of the reluctance with which he had reached his fateful decision.

> But the right is more precious than peace, and we shall fight for the things
> which we have always carried nearest our hearts—for democracy, for the rights
> and liberties of small nations, for a universal dominion of right by such a concert
> of free peoples as shall bring peace and safety to all nations and make the world
> itself at last free. To such a task we can dedicate our lives and our fortunes,
> everything that we are and everything that we have, with the pride of those who
> know that the day has come when America is privileged to spend her blood and
> her might for the principles that gave her birth and happiness and the peace
> which she has treasured. God helping her, she can do no other.

Amid the orgy of rejoicing and congratulation that followed this pronouncement, Wilson stood pale and silent. He later remarked to his secretary, Tumulty, "My message today was a message of death for our young
men. How strange it seems to applaud that."[9] Only a holy war could vindicate a message so elevated and yet so tragic.

∗ ∗ ∗

The Egoistic Defection From Wilson's Program

Woodrow Wilson viewed the making of peace as a fulfilment of the purpose
for which America had waged war, and he relied upon the common people
of America, with their tremendous resources of idealism, to support his
plans for peace with the same zeal they had spent upon war. On the day of
the Armistice, November 11, 1918, he told a joint session of Congress that
victory was no mere military decision, no mere relief from the trials of war,
but a divine vindication of universal principles and a call to greater duties
ahead.[10] Two days before he sailed for the Paris peace conference he proclaimed the continuation in peace of America's disinterested service to humanity during war: "We are about to give order and organization to this
peace not only for ourselves but for the other peoples of the world as well,
so far as they will suffer us to serve them. It is international justice that we
seek, not domestic safety merely."[11]

Wilson forgot—if, indeed, he ever realized it—that America, as a whole,
had not entered the war in the spirit of altruism; that there was implicit in
American intervention no acceptance of revolutionary international commitments; that the nation's war-born enthusiasm for a world made safe for
democracy and the end of all wars gained a good part of its inspiration from

a simple desire to lick the Hun and stay out of future trouble. However fervent America's belief in the righteousness of its cause may have been, the general approval of Wilson's war aims implied no eagerness to sacrifice traditional modes of national conduct for the sake of other nations and peoples.

Nevertheless, one cannot deny that the American people had come to believe that their war was a crusade for a freer, more democratic, and more peaceful world. This vague aspiration would somehow have to be fulfilled in order to justify the sacrifices of war. For by the time the German Army was defeated, the principal reasons which had justified intervention in April, 1917—the maintenance of neutral rights and the vindication of national honor—had all but disappeared from popular discussion. The war had been fought for a different set of reasons from those that had led to intervention; and these reasons, however imperfectly conceived, raised expectations of a nature that could not be satisfied by mere military victory.

Wilson counted upon the fundamental altruism of the people to bridge the gap between the League and tradition. But with the strongest basis for popular idealism removed by victory, it seems likely that only some persuasive appeal to fundamental national self-interest could have sustained America's crusade into the period of peacemaking. Yet Wilson, by his very nature, could appeal only for an even greater subordination of self-interest to moral principle.

Wilson insisted that the League of Nations was pre-eminently a moral conception, an organization to turn the "searching light of conscience" upon wrong and aggression wherever it might be contemplated.[12] It followed from his faith in the moral sense of the masses that the American people were bound to embrace this plan once they understood its lofty nature. Therefore, he expounded its transcendent idealism in the confidence that Americans would prefer the interests of mankind to all other interests. While this approach made American membership in an international league seem less and less compelling to the great body of Americans as war-born idealism subsided, it positively assured a mounting hostility toward the project on the part of Realistic national egoists like Roosevelt and Lodge.

Although Wilson was not ignorant of the practical national advantages to be gained through membership in a league, his whole nature rebelled at a frank acknowledgment of expediency as a basis for national action. He preferred to emphasize the universal moral principles that bound men together as human beings rather than the fine adjustments of self-interest among nations, which might disintegrate into violent jealousies with a slight change of circumstance. Consequently, he presented the League as a substitute for the balance-of-power system, not as a supplementation or extension of it. As he told an English audience on December 30, "If the future had nothing for us but a new attempt to keep the world at a right poise by a balance of power, the United States would take no interest, because she will join no combination of power which is not the combination of all of us."[13]

Roosevelt, on the other hand, took just the opposite view. In his opinion it was folly to join a concert of nations that did not reflect the actual power situation. As far as he was concerned, both practical and idealistic considerations pointed to the wisdom of an Anglo-American alliance. On November 19 he wrote Arthur Lee that he had become more convinced than ever that "there should be the closest alliance between the British Empire and the United States."[14] To George Haven Putnam, who had solicited his membership in the English-Speaking Union, he wrote,

> I regard the British Navy as probably the most potent instrumentality for peace in the world. . . . Moreover, I am now prepared to say what five years ago I would not have said. I think the time has come when the United States and the British Empire can agree to a universal arbitration treaty.[15]

In one of his last editorials Roosevelt declared that he strongly shared the feeling that there should be some kind of international league to prevent a recurrence of war, but he warned his readers not to be deceived by sham idealism, by high-sounding and meaningless phrases, such as those embodied in the Fourteen Points. Let us face the facts, he wrote. The first fact is that nations are not equal. Therefore, let us limit the league to the present Allies and admit others only as their conduct warrants it. Let us specifically reserve certain rights from the jurisdiction of any international body. America should be very careful about promising to interfere with, or on behalf of, "impotent or disorderly nations and peoples outside this league" where they lie "wholly outside our sphere of interest." Roosevelt concluded with a plea for universal military training.[16]

Actually, Roosevelt's conception of a peace settlement as one phase of a continuing accommodation of power was as remote from the popular view as Wilson's vision of the selfless submerging of national sovereignty in a community of interest. Both views involved a serious break with traditional conceptions of America's relation to world politics. However, in his strong assertion of national prerogatives Roosevelt was joined by parochial nationalists, such as Borah and Beveridge, who were unalterably opposed to all involvements in power politics, including those for limited national ends, on the grounds that nothing that happened overseas could be of enough concern to the United States to warrant contaminating the nation by association with the evil balance-of-power system. While Lodge and Roosevelt had never been opposed to joining an international organization that would redound to the national interest, Beveridge and Borah were convinced, as a matter of principle, that the national interest and membership in a league were mutually contradictory. But, whatever their differences, both groups were agreed that American interests came first; and, if only for this reason, Wilsons' persistent association of the League with altruism proved as repelling to Realistic as to parochial nationalists.

NOTES

1. For example, see Wilson's address at Cincinnati, October 26, 1916, Ray S. Baker and William E. Dodd, *The Public Papers of Woodrow Wilson* (New York, 1927), IV, 377–78.
2. Robert Lansing, *War Memoirs of Robert Lansing* (Indianapolis, 1935), p. 172.
3. *New York Times*, August 4, 1914.
4. *Foreign Relations, 1914, Supplement*, pp. 547–51.
5. Baker and Dodd, *Public Papers*, III, 158–59.
6. *Foreign Relations, 1916, Supplement*, pp. 97–99.
7. Lansing to Gerard, April 18, 1916, *ibid.*, p. 234.
8. Baker and Dodd, *Public Papers*, V, 6–16.
9. Joseph P. Tumulty, *Woodrow Wilson As I Know Him* (New York, 1921), p. 256.
10. Baker and Dodd, *Public Papers*, V, 294–302.
11. Annual message, December 2, 1918, *ibid.*, p. 312.
12. Address at the University of Paris, December 21, 1918, *ibid.*, p. 330.
13. *Ibid.*, pp. 352–53.
14. Roosevelt to Lee, November 19, 1918, in Elting E. Morison, ed., *The Letters of Theodore Roosevelt* (Cambridge, 1951).
15. Roosevelt to Putnam, December, 5, 1918, *ibid*. In reply to Putnam's solicitation, Roosevelt wrote that he was in sympathy with the objects of the English-speaking Union but could not take a position on the board.
16. Theodore Roosevelt, "The League of Nations," *Metropolitan*, XLIX (January, 1919), 9 ff.

3.3 Imperialism

WALTER LAFEBER

The American "New Empire"

Some intellectuals speak only for themselves. Theirs is often the later glory, but seldom the present power. Some, however, speak not only for themselves but for the guiding forces of their society. Discovering such men at crucial junctures in history, if such a discovery can be made, is of importance and value. These figures uncover the premises, reveal the approaches, provide the details, and often coherently arrange the ideas which are implicit in the dominant thought of their time and society.

The ordered, articulate writings of Frederick Jackson Turner, Josiah Strong, Brooks Adams, and Alfred Thayer Mahan typified the expansive tendencies of their generation. Little evidence exists that Turner and Strong directly influenced expansionists in the business community or the State Department during the 1890's, but their writings best exemplify certain beliefs which determined the nature of American foreign policy. Adams and Mahan participated more directly in the shaping of expansionist programs. It is, of course, impossible to estimate the number of Americans who accepted the arguments of these four men. What cannot be controverted is that the writings of these men typified and in some specific instances directly influenced the thought of American policy makers who created the new empire.[1]

Frederick Jackson Turner and the American Frontier

* * *

The importance of the frontier will be associated with the name of Frederick Jackson Turner as long as historians are able to indent footnotes. Yet as Theodore Roosevelt told Turner in a letter of admiration in 1894, "I think you . . . have put into definite shape a good deal of thought which has been floating around rather loosely." As has been amply shown by sev-

---

From *The New Empire: An Interpretation of American Expansion*, 1860–1898 (Ithaca, N.Y.: Cornell University Press, 1963), chapters 2 and 7.

eral scholars, a number of observers warned of the frontier's disappearance and the possible consequences of this disappearance long before Turner's epochal paper. The accelerating communication and transportation revolution, growing agrarian unrest, violent labor strikes, and the problems arising from increasing numbers of immigrants broke upon puzzled and frightened Americans in a relatively short span of time. Many of them clutched the belief of the closing or closed frontier in order to explain their dilemma.[2]

Turner rested the central part of his frontier thesis on the economic power represented by free land. American individualism, nationalism, political institutions, and democracy depended on this power: "So long as free land exists, the opportunity for a competency exists, and economic power secures political power." Stated in these terms, landed expansion became the central factor, the dynamic of American progress. Without the economic power generated by expansion across free lands, American political institutions could stagnate.[3]

Such an analysis could be extremely meaningful to those persons who sought an explanation for the political and social troubles of the period. Few disputed that the social upheavals in both the urban and agrarian areas of the nation stemmed from economic troubles in the international grain markets, from the frequent industrial depressions, or, as the Populists averred, from the failure of the currency to match the pace of ever increasing productivity. This economic interpretation also fitted in nicely with the contemporary measurement of success in terms of material achievement. Perhaps most important, the frontier thesis not only defined the dilemma, but did so in tangible, concrete terms. It offered the hope that Americans could do something about their problems. Given the assumption that expansion across the western frontier explained past American successes, the solution for the present crisis now became apparent: either radically readjust the political institutions to a nonexpanding society or find new areas for expansion. When Americans seized the second alternative, the meaning for foreign policy became apparent—and immense.

With the appearance and definition of the fundamental problems in the 1880's and 1890's, these decades assumed vast importance. They became not a watershed of American history, but *the* watershed. Many writers emphasized the supremely critical nature of the 1890's, but no one did it better than Turner when he penned the dramatic final sentence of his 1893 paper: "And now, four centuries from the discovery of America, at the end of a hundred years of life under the Constitution, the frontier has gone, and with its going has closed the first period of American history." The American West no longer offered a unique escape from the intractable problems of a closed society. As another writer stated it four years after Turner's announcement in Chicago, "we are no longer a country exceptional and apart." History had finally caught up with the United States.[4]

The first solution that came to some minds suggested the opening of new landed frontiers in Latin America or Canada. Yet was further expansion in a landed sense the answer? Top policy makers, as Secretaries of State James G. Blaine, Thomas F. Bayard, and Walter Quintin Gresham, opposed the addition of noncontiguous territory to the Union. Some Americans interpreted the labor violence of 1877, 1886, and 1894 as indications that the federal government could no longer harmonize and control the far-flung reaches of the continental empire. Labor and agrarian groups discovered they could not command the necessary political power to solve their mushrooming problems. The sprouting of such factions as the Molly Maguires, Populists, Eugene Debs' Railroad Union, and several varieties of Socialist parties raised doubts in many minds about the ameliorating and controlling qualities which had formerly been a part of the American system.

* * *

Expansion in the form of trade instead of landed settlement ultimately offered the answer to this dilemma. This solution, embodied in the open-door philosophy of American foreign policy, ameliorated the economic stagnation (which by Turner's reasoning led to the political discontent), but it did not pile new colonial areas on an already overburdened governmental structure. It provided the perfect answer to the problems of the 1890's.

* * *

Alfred Thayer Mahan

* * * The austere, scholarly, arm-chair sailor-turned-prophet constructed a tightly knit historical justification of why and how his country could expand beyond its continental limits.

Mahan grounded his thesis on the central characteristic of the United States of his time: it was an industrial complex which produced, or would soon be capable of producing, vast surpluses. In the first paragraph of his classic, *The Influence of Sea Power upon History, 1660–1783*, Mahan explained how this industrial expansion led to a rivalry for markets and sources of raw materials and would ultimately result in the need for sea power. He summarized his theory in a postulate: "In these three things—production, with the necessity of exchanging products, shipping, whereby the exchange is carried on, and colonies . . .—is to be found the key to much of the history, as well as of the policy, of nations bordering upon the sea." The order is all-important. Production leads to a need for shipping, which in turn creates the need for colonies.[5]

Mahan's neat postulate was peculiarly applicable to his own time, for he clearly understood the United States of the 1890's. His concern, stated in 1890, that ever increasing production would soon make necessary wider trade and markets, anticipated the somber, depression-ridden years of post-1893. Writing three years before Frederick Jackson Turner analyzed the disappearance of the American frontier, Mahan hinted its disappearance and pointed out the implications for America's future economic and political structure. He observed that the policies of the American government since 1865 had been "directed solely to what has been called the first link in the chain which makes sea power." But "the increase of home consumption . . . did not keep up with the increase of forth-putting and facility of distribution offered by steam." The United States would thus have to embark upon a new frontier, for "whether they will or no, Americans must now begin to look outward. The growing production of the country demands it. An increasing volume of public sentiment demands it." The theoretical and actual had met; the productive capacity of the United States, having finally grown too great for its continental container and having lost its landed frontier, had to turn to the sea, its omnipresent frontier. The mercantilists had viewed production as a faculty to be stimulated and consolidated in order to develop its full capabilities of pulling wealth into the country. But Mahan dealt with a productive complex which had been stimulated by the government for years and had been centralized and coordinated by corporate managers. He was now concerned with the problem of keeping this society ongoing without the problems of underemployment and resulting social upheavals.[6]

Reversing the traditional American idea of the oceans as a barrier against European intrigue, Mahan compared the sea to "a great highway; or better, perhaps . . . a wide common, over which men pass in all directions." * * *

* * * To Mahan, William McKinley, Theodore Roosevelt, and Henry Cabot Lodge, colonial possessions, as these men defined such possessions, served as stepping stones to the two great prizes: the Latin-American and Asian markets. This policy much less resembled traditional colonialism than it did the new financial and industrial expansion of the 1850–1914 period. These men did not envision "colonizing" either Latin America or Asia. They did want both to exploit these areas economically and give them (especially Asia) the benefits of western, Christian civilization. To do this, these expansionists needed strategic bases from which shipping lanes and interior interests in Asia and Latin America could be protected.

* * *

The policy makers and other influential Americans who embraced Mahan's teachings made them a central part of the expansionist ideology of the 1890's. Albert Shaw, a close friend of Lodge, Roosevelt, and Mahan, advanced the Captain's ideas through the widely read pages of his newly established *Review of Reviews*. Book reviewers in the most popular periodicals of the day warmly received Mahan's voluminous writings. Theodore Roosevelt, perhaps the most important of these reviewers, emphasized the Captain's basic ideas in the *Atlantic Monthly* and then put these ideas into practice as Assistant Secretary of the Navy in 1897–1898 and later as President. Mahan and Roosevelt were the closest of friends and could often be found in the company of Brooks Adams, John Hay, and Lodge. Congressmen paid homage by plagiarizing not only ideas but phrases and paragraphs from Mahan's works in order to substantiate their own arguments for expansion.[7]

$*$ $*$ $*$

President William McKinley and the Spanish-American War of 1898

$*$ $*$ $*$ The President [McKinley] did not want war; he had been sincere and tireless in his efforts to maintain the peace. By mid-March, however, he was beginning to discover that, although he did not want war, he did want what only a war could provide: the disappearance of the terrible uncertainty in American political and economic life, and a solid basis from which to resume the building of the new American commercial empire. When the President made his demands, therefore, he made the ultimate demands; as far as he was concerned, a six-month period of negotiations would not serve to temper the political and economic problems in the United States, but only exacerbate them.

To say this is to raise another question: why did McKinley arrive at this position during mid-March? What were the factors which limited the President's freedom of choice and policies at this particular time? The standard interpretations of the war's causes emphasize the yellow journals and a belligerent Congress. These were doubtlessly crucial factors in shaping the course of American entry into the conflict, but they must be used carefully. $*$ $*$ $*$

Congress was a hotbed of interventionist sentiment, but then it had been so since 1895. The fact was that Congress had more trouble handling McKinley than the President had handling Congress. The President had no fear of that body. He told Charles Dawes during the critical days of February and March that if Congress tried to adjourn he would call it back into session. McKinley held Congress under control until the last two days of March, when the publication of the "Maine" investigation forced Thomas B. Reed, the passionately antiwar Speaker of the House, to surrender to the onslaughts of the rapidly increasing interventionist forces. As militants in Congress forced the moderates into full retreat, McKinley and Day were waiting in the White House for Spain's reply to the American ultimatum. And after the outbreak on March 31 McKinley reassumed control. On April 5 the Secretary of War, R. A. Alger, assured the President that several important senators had just informed him that "there will be no trouble about holding the Senate." When the President postponed his war message on April 5 in order to grant Fitzhugh Lee's request for more time, prowar congressmen went into a frenzy. During the weekend of April 8 and 9, they condemned the President, ridiculed Reed's impotence to hold back war, and threatened to declare war themselves. In fact, they did nearly everything except disobey McKinley's wishes that nothing be done until the following week. Nothing was done.[8]

When the Senate threatened to overrule the President's orders that the declaration of war not include a recognition of Cuban independence, the White House whipped its supporters into line and forced the Senate to recede from its position. This was an all-out battle between the White House and a strong Senate faction. McKinley triumphed despite extremely strong pressure exerted by sincere American sentiment on behalf of immediate Cuban independence and despite the more crass material interests of the Junta's financial supporters and spokesmen. The President wanted to have a free hand in dealing with Cuba after the war, and Congress granted his wishes. Events on Capitol Hill may have been more colorful than those at the White House, but the latter, not the former, was the center of power in March and April, 1898.

Influences other than the yellow press or congressional belligerence were more important in shaping McKinley's position of April 11. Perhaps most important was the transformation of the opinion of many spokesmen for the business community who had formerly opposed war. If, as one journal declared, the McKinley administration, "more than any that have preceded it, sustains . . . close relations to the business interests of the country," then this change of business sentiment should not be discounted.[9] This transformation brought important financial spokesmen, especially from the Northeast, into much the same position that had long been occupied by prointerventionist business groups and journals in the trans-Appalachian area. McKinley's decision to intervene placated many of the same business spokesmen whom he had satisfied throughout 1897 and January and February of 1898 by his refusal to declare war.

Five factors may be delineated which shaped this interventionist sentiment of the business community. First, some business journals emphasized the material advantages to be gained should Cuba become a part of the world in which the United States would enjoy, in the words of the New York *Commercial Advertiser*, "full freedom of development in the whole world's interest." The *Banker's Magazine* noted that "so many of our citizens are so involved in the commerce and productions of the island, that to protect these interests . . . the United States will have eventually to force the establishment of fair and reasonable government." The material damage suffered by investors in Cuba and by many merchants, manufacturers, exporters, and importers, as, for example, the groups which presented the February 10 petition to McKinley, forced these interests to advocate a solution which could be obtained only through force.[10]

A second reason was the uncertainty that plagued the business community in mid-March. This uncertainty was increased by Proctor's powerful and influential speech and by the news that a Spanish torpedo-boat flotilla was sailing from Cadiz to Cuba. The uncertainty was exemplified by the sudden stagnation of trade on the New York Stock Exchange after March 17. Such an unpredictable economic basis could not provide the spring board for the type of overseas commercial empire that McKinley and numerous business spokesmen envisioned.

Third, by March many businessmen who had deprecated war on the ground that the United States Treasury did not possess adequate gold reserves began to realize that they had been arguing from false assumptions. The heavy exports of 1897 and the discoveries of gold in Alaska and Australia brought the yellow metal into the country in an ever widening stream. Private bankers had been preparing for war since 1897. *Banker's Magazine* summarized these developments: "Therefore, while not desiring war, it is apparent that the country now has an ample coin basis for sustaining the credit operations which a conflict would probably make necessary. In such a crisis the gold standard will prove a bulwark of confidence."[11]

Fourth, antiwar sentiment lost much strength when the nation realized that it had nothing to fear from European intervention on the side of Spain. France and Russia, who were most sympathetic to the Spanish monarchy, were forced to devote their attention to the Far East. Neither of these nations wished to alienate the United States on the Cuban issue. More important, Americans happily realized that they had the support of Great Britain. The *rapprochement* which had occurred since the Venezuelan incident now paid dividends. On an official level, the British Foreign Office assured the State Department that nothing would be accomplished in the way of European intervention unless the United States requested such intervention. The British attitude made it easy for McKinley to deal with a joint European note of April 6 which asked for American moderation toward Spain. The President brushed off the request firmly but politely. On an unofficial level, American periodicals expressed appreciation of the British policy on Cuba, and some of the journals noted that a common Anglo-American approach was also desirable in Asia.[12] The European reaction is interesting insofar as it evinces the continental powers' growing realization that the United States was rapidly becoming a major force in the world. But the European governments set no limits on American dealings with Spain. McKinley could take the initiative and make his demands with little concern for European reactions.

Finally, opposition to war melted away in some degree when the administration began to emphasize that the United States enjoyed military power much superior to that of Spain. One possible reason for McKinley's policies during the first two months of 1898 might have been his fear that the nation was not adequately prepared. As late as the weekend of March 25 the President worried over this inadequacy. But in late February and early March, especially after the $50,000,000 appropriation by Congress, the country's military strength developed rapidly. On March 13 the Philadelphia *Press* proclaimed that American naval power greatly exceeded that of the Spanish forces. By early April those who feared a Spanish bombardment of New York City were in the small minority. More representative were the views of Winthrop Chanler who wrote Lodge that if Spanish troops invaded New York "they would all be absorbed in the population . . . and engaged in selling oranges before they got as far as 14th Street."[13]

As the words of McKinley's war message flew across the wires to Madrid, many business spokesmen who had opposed war had recently changed their minds, American military forces were rapidly growing more powerful, banks and the United States Treasury had secured themselves against the initial shocks of war, and the European powers were divided among themselves and preoccupied in the Far East. Business boomed after McKinley signed the declaration of war. "With a hesitation so slight as to amount almost to indifference," *Bradstreet's* reported on April 30, "the business community, relieved from the tension caused by the incubus of doubt and uncertainty which so long controlled it, has stepped confidently forward to accept the situation confronting it oweing to the changed conditions." "Unfavorable circumstances . . . have hardly excited remark, while the stimulating effects have been so numerous and important as to surprise all but the most optimistic," this journal concluded.[14] A new type of American empire, temporarily clothed in armor, stepped out on the international stage after a half century of preparation to make its claim as one of the great world powers.

＊ ＊ ＊

By 1899 the United States had forged a new empire. American policy makers and businessmen had created it amid much debate and with conscious purpose. The empire progressed from a continental base in 1861 to assured pre-eminence in the Western Hemisphere in 1895. Three years later it was rescued from a growing economic and political dilemma by the declaration of war against Spain. During and after this conflict the empire moved past Hawaii into the Philippines, and, with the issuance of the Open-Door Notes, enunciated its principles in Asia. The movement of this empire could not be hurried. Harrison discovered this to his regret in 1893. But under the impetus of the effects of the industrial revolution and, most important, *because of the implications for foreign policy which policy makers and businessmen believed to be logical corollaries of this economic change,* the new empire reached its climax in the 1890's. At this point those who possessed a sense of historical perspective could pause with Henry Adams and observe that one hundred and fifty years of American history had suddenly fallen into place. Those who preferred to peer into the dim future of the twentieth century could be certain only that the United States now dominated its own hemisphere and, as Seward had so passionately hoped, was entering as a major power into Asia, "the chief theatre of events in the world's great hereafter."

NOTES

1. One of the weakest sections in the history of ideas is the relationship between the new intellectual currents and American overseas expansion during the last half of the nineteenth century. The background and some of the general factors may be found in Alfred Kazin, *On Native Grounds: An Interpretation of Modern American Prose Literature* (Garden City, N.Y., 1942, 1956); Henry Steele Commager, *The American Mind: An Interpretation of American Thought and Character since the 1880's* (New Haven, 1950, 1959); Weinberg, *Manifest Destiny;* Julius W. Pratt, "The Ideology of American Expansion," *Essays in Honor of William E. Dodd . . .* , edited by Avery Craven (Chicago, 1935).

2. See especially Fulmer Mood, "The Concept of the Frontier, 1871–1898," *Agricultural History,* XIX (January, 1945), 24–31; Lee Benson, "The Historical Background of Turner's Frontier Essay," *Agricultural History,* XXV (April, 1951), 59–82; Herman Clarence Nixon, "The Precursors of Turner in the Interpretation of the American Frontier," *South Atlantic Quarterly,* XXVIII (January, 1929), 83–89. For the Roosevelt letter, see *The Letters of Theodore Roosevelt,* selected and edited by Elting E. Morison *et al.* (Cambridge, Mass., 1951), I, 363.

3. Frederick Jackson Turner, *The Frontier in American History* (New York, 1947), 32, 30; see also Per Sveaas Andersen, *Westward Is the Course of Empires: A Study in the Shaping of an American Idea: Frederick Jackson Turner's Frontier* (Oslo, Norway, 1956), 20–21; Henry Nash Smith, *Virgin Land: The American West as Symbol and Myth* (New York, 1959), 240.

4. Turner, *Frontier in American History,* 38; Eugene V. Smalley, "What Are Normal Times?" *The Forum,* XXIII (March, 1897), 98–99; see also Turner, *Frontier in American History,* 311–312. For a brilliant criticism of Turner's closed-space concepts, see James C. Malin, *The Contriving Brain and the Skillful Hand in the United States . . .* (Lawrence, Kan., 1955), the entire essay, but especially ch. xi.

5. A. T. Mahan, *The Influence of Sea Power upon History, 1660–1783* Boston, 1890), 53, 28. This postulate is mentioned two more times in the famous first chapter, pages 70 and 83–84.

6. *Ibid.,* 83–84; Mahan, "A Twentieth-Century Outlook," *The Interest of America in Sea Power,* Present and Future (Boston, 1897), 220–222; Mahan, "The United States Looking Outward," *ibid.,* 21–22. In their work which traces this centralization movement, Thomas C. Cochran and William Miller call the result the "corporate society" (*The Age of Enterprise: A Social History of Industrial America* [New York, 1942], 331).

7. William Livezey, *Mahan on Sea Power* (Norman, Okla., 1947), 116–171; *Congressional Record,* 53rd Cong., 3rd Sess., Feb. 15, 1895, 2249–2250; for Roosevelt's reviews see *Atlantic Monthly,* LXVI (October,

1890), especially 567, and *ibid.*, LXXI (April, 1893), 559; see also Theodore Roosevelt, "The Naval Policy of America as Outlined in Messages of the Presidents of the United States, from the Beginning to the Present Day," *Proceedings of the United States Naval Institute*, XXIII (1897), 509–522; Ralph Dewar Bald, Jr., "The Development of Expansionist Sentiment in the United States, 1885–1895; as Reflected in Periodical Literature" (Unpublished Ph.D. dissertation, University of Pittsburgh, 1953), ch. v.

8. Alger to McKinley, April 5, 1898, McKinley MSS; John L. Offner, "President McKinley and the Origins of the Spanish-American War" (Unpublished Ph.D. dissertation, Pennsylvania State University, 1957), 289–300.

9. Chicago *Times-Herald* quoted in Cincinnati *Commercial Tribune*, Dec. 28, 1897, 6:2. The Chicago paper was particularly close to the administration through its publisher's friendship with McKinley. The publisher was H. H. Kohlsaat. Ernest May remarks, regarding McKinley's antiwar position in 1897 and early 1898, "It was simply out of the question for him [McKinley] to embark on a policy unless virtually certain that Republican businessmen would back him" (*Imperial Democracy: The Emergence of America as a Great Power* [New York, 1961], 118). The same comment doubtlessly applies also to McKinley's actions in March and April.

10. *Commercial Advertiser*, March 10, 1898, 6:3; *Bankers' Magazine*, LVI (April, 1898), 519–520.

11. *Bankers' Magazine*, LVI (March, 1898), 347–348; LVI (April, 1898), 520; Pittsburgh *Press*, April 8, 1898, 4:1; *Commercial and Financial Chronicle*, April 23, 1898, 786.

12. Dugdale, *German Documents*, II, 500–502; Porter to Sherman, April 8, 1898, France, Despatches, and Hay to Sherman, March 26, 28, 29, April 1, Great Britain, Despatches, NA, RG 59; *Public Opinion*, March 24, 1898, 360–361.

13. Margaret Leech, *In The Days of McKinley*, (New York, 1969), 176; Philadelphia *Press*, March 13, 1898, 8:3; Garraty, *Lodge*, 191.

14. *Bradstreet's*, April 9, 1898, 234, also April 30, 1898, 272, 282.

4 *The Cold War in Context: Origins and First Stages*

This chapter examines the origins and first stages of the Cold War, the crucial formative period for U.S. foreign policy for the next forty-plus years.

The sense of these early years as a "golden age" in which bold strategies were set and political consensus prevailed is heartily invoked by Joseph Jones. The very title of his book, *The Fifteen Weeks*, conveys an epochal sense. He recounts "a dazzling process . . . an enduring national conversion to the role of world leadership . . . those fifteen remarkable weeks." The author's role as a speechwriter in the Truman administration provided him with a vantage point that was close enough to the action to make this detailed and inside account possible.

Historians who question the objectivity of such accounts and who more generally attribute at least some of the responsibility for the origins of the Cold War to the United States are known as "revisionists." U.S. Cold War strategy was not just defensive reactions to Soviet aggression and provocations, they argue; the methods may have been less direct and more subtle, but the objective nevertheless was American domination. Melvyn Leffler's article represents some of the main revisionist arguments.

One of the basic Cold War doctrines developed in these early years that would remain at the core of U.S. foreign policy was nuclear deterrence. As the United States thought about its national security in the nuclear age, it was clear that a strong and resilient national defense, while still necessary, no longer was sufficient. A nuclear attack or a crisis that could lead to the use of nuclear weapons had to be deterred before it began. The requisites for nuclear deterrence changed over time, but the basic strategy of preventing a nuclear attack through fear of retaliation stayed the same. Bernard Brodie was one of the leading strategists in developing nuclear deterrence doctrine, and his book *Strategy in the Missile Age*, one of the major works in this field.

No collection of readings on American foreign policy would be complete without the famous "Mr. X" article. No single article has ever had so much influence. George Kennan, the author, was then a highly regarded diplomat whose service in and study of the Soviet Union made him one of the nation's foremost experts on that country. In 1946 while stationed at the U.S. embassy in Moscow, in a cable to the State Department that came to be known as "the long telegram," he stressed the need to shift policy to "contain" Stalin and the Soviets. The *Foreign Affairs* article "Sources of Soviet Conduct" was published a year later under the "Mr. X" pseudonym in order to take Kennan's containment thesis outside classified channels and to a wider political audience.

4.1 *Cold War Consensus*

JOSEPH M. JONES
The "Golden Age"

In Washington

The comfortable, dowdy old structure at Seventeenth Street and Pennsylvania Avenue, known as State, War, and Navy, was soon to lose her distinction as hostess to the Secretary of State and as center of the relations of the United States with the world. War and Navy had abandoned her long ago. Now, in early 1947, the State Department too was leaving her for new quarters, gaudier, more commodious, even air-conditioned, in a questionable part of town. After years of stubborn rearguard resistance to White House encroachments on space, the move was decided—one of George Catlett Marshall's first acts as Secretary of State. Even now files were being packed in Old State and room assignments were being made in New State at Twenty-first Street and Virginia Avenue. But on the gray Friday afternoon of February 21, 1947, Old State, unlike most of her tenants to whom the prospective parting brought anguish and a sense of personal loss, wore her regrets with silence and dignity. There was nothing that afternoon in the cables, or in circulating memoranda, or even in anybody's mind to suggest that the most revolutionary advance in United States foreign policy since 1823 would occur within the next fifteen weeks, and that the last days of State Department tenancy at Seventeenth and Pennsylvania would be a period of intense activity leading to great historical accomplishment.

Mr. Marshall had left his office earlier than usual that afternoon to go to Princeton, New Jersey, where he would the next day attend a celebration of Princeton's Bicentennial, receive a degree of Doctor of Laws, and make his first public address as Secretary of State. He had been gone only a short while when the private secretary to Lord Inverchapel, British Ambassador in Washington, telephoned to request an immediate appointment. As the matter appeared urgent and Secretary Marshall was not expected to return

---

From *The Fifteen Weeks (February 21–June 5, 1947)* (New York: Harcourt, Brace and World, 1955), pp. 3–9, 136–43.

98

to his office until Monday morning, Dean Acheson, Undersecretary of State, was consulted on what to do.

Acheson was reluctant to ask the Secretary to return to his office late Saturday unless it was necessary. Only a month earlier General Marshall had returned from his long and grueling mission to China, to assume immediately the burdens of his new office. In less than two weeks he was to leave for a Conference of Foreign Ministers in Moscow, which would last no one knew how many weeks or months. He deserved, Acheson thought, at least part of a weekend off if it could be managed. Inquiry at the Embassy disclosed that the Ambassador wanted to deliver to the Secretary two notes concerning a decision of the British government to end aid to Greece and Turkey. Acheson therefore arranged that H. M. Sichel, First Secretary of the British Embassy, should at once bring over copies of the notes and discuss them with Loy Henderson, Director of the Office of Near Eastern and African Affairs, and John D. Hickerson, Deputy Director of the Office of European Affairs. Whatever staff work might be required could be started over the weekend, and the Ambassador could call on Secretary Marshall Monday morning, deliver the notes formally, and discuss the problem. Meanwhile the Secretary and the President would be informed.

As Jack Hickerson had another appointment he could not break on short notice, Loy Henderson alone received Mr. Sichel forty-five minutes later. Henderson and Sichel had known each other casually for some time. This day they greeted each other cordially, but there was no preliminary badinage. Sichel drew from his dispatch case copies of two notes and handed them to Henderson, who began to read the note on Greece.

The British government recalled that previous exchanges of views had resulted in the mutual understanding that for military and strategic reasons Greece and Turkey should not be allowed to fall under Soviet control, and mentioned the informal agreement reached between Secretary of State Byrnes and Foreign Minister Bevin in Paris the previous summer that Great Britain would extend chiefly military aid and the United States chiefly economic aid, though the possibility of United States military aid to Greece had not been excluded. Greece was now in most urgent need, and the British government thought it should be decided how much economic aid the United States intended to give and what form it should take.

The Greek economic situation, the note continued, was on the point of collapse. Unless help from the outside was forthcoming there was certain to be widespread starvation and consequent political disturbances.

* * *

The note concerning Turkey was even briefer. The British government recalled that Secretary of State Byrnes had told the British Minister of Defense on October 15, 1946, that the United States would do everything possible to aid Turkey economically and hoped the United Kingdom would furnish military aid. The British government had subsequently studied the Turkish military situation, and the United States and British Embassies in Ankara had studied the economic problems. The British government was of the opinion that it was of the utmost importance for Turkey to maintain its independence, but that in their present state the armed forces could not resist effectively aggression by a first-class power. The Turkish government needed advice on the organization and equipment of the army and aid in procuring the modern weapons decided upon. Great Britain would be unable to provide much equipment for the army; it could help with the navy and air force if financial arrangements could be made.

Turkey needed to carry on a program of economic development, which would improve the military situation, and needed at the same time to re-equip its army. Turkey could do one or the other with its own resources, but not both. Great Britain was unable to offer further financial assistance. The obligation therefore devolved upon the United States or the International Bank. * * *

Sichel had handed over his messages without portentousness or expectation. Henderson wondered, as with mounting excitement he read the two notes, whether Sichel fully appreciated the seriousness and significance of the information he was conveying. Sichel knew very well; his blandness of manner came from his training in the British Diplomatic Service. Moreover he was merely reporting another of the many British withdrawals that were then taking place around the world under the scourge of necessity—India, Burma, Egypt, Palestine—withdrawals that opened vast breaches in the system of political, diplomatic, and military defense by which Britain had for so long maintained a measure of stability in the world. * * *

Reading the messages, Hickerson realized at once, as had Henderson, that Great Britain had within the hour handed the job of world leadership, with all its burdens and all its glory, to the United States. To most people in the United States, Greece and Turkey were only remote places on a map with incidental historical, touristic, or cultural associations, but not to Henderson and Hickerson. They lived daily, hourly—had so lived for several years—with the problems arising out of the crumbling of British power from the Eastern Mediterranean to the South China Sea and the relentless probing and pressing of the Soviet Union into situations of weakness everywhere in Europe and Asia. They were acutely aware of the strategic importance of Greece and Turkey to the security of three continents. The British had borne the chief responsibility for strengthening and sustaining Greece and Turkey and the countries of the Middle East generally. * * *

Now British aid to Greece was to cease within six weeks, and Britain could not be expected to help Turkey carry its increasing burdens. These were the only new facts added to the situation as a consequence of Sichel's call, but they were devastating facts. They meant that the struggle in Greece against Communist domination would be hopeless, and that Turkey's position as a friend of the West, resistant to Soviet pressure, would become untenable.

* * *

That afternoon [February 26] Marshall and Acheson met with President Truman and fully explained the recommendations of the three Departments [State, War, and Navy]. Truman required no convincing. * * * He accepted and approved the joint State-War-Navy recommendations. The problem was not what should be done, but how to get authorizing legislation through Congress. There was no time to be lost, and Marshall would be leaving soon for Moscow. The President decided to invite congressional leaders to the White House the next day to hear Marshall and Acheson put the case and to get their reaction to the proposed program. The White House telephoned the invitations.

That February 27 meeting at the White House is of great importance in this chronicle. Present from Capitol Hill were Senator Vandenberg; Speaker Martin; Representative Sam Rayburn, Democrat, House Minority Leader; Representative Charles A. Eaton, Republican, chairman of the House Committee on Foreign Affairs; Senator Styles Bridges, Republican, chairman of the Senate Appropriations Committee; Senator Tom Connally, ranking Democrat on the Senate Foreign Relations Committee; and Representative Sol Bloom, ranking Democrat on the House Foreign Affairs Committee. Representative John Taber, Republican, chairman of the House Appropriations Committee, was invited but could not attend; nevertheless he hastened to the White House in the afternoon and was informed in detail on what had happened.[1]

At the request of the President, Secretary Marshall led off in the presentation of the problem. In dry and economical terms he gave the congressional leaders the facts about the imminent withdrawal of British support from Greece and Turkey, the situation those countries were left in, vulnerable to Soviet domination, and the recommendations for aid that had been agreed upon the executive branch.

There is no question that the Secretary understood thoroughly the strategic importance of Greece and Turkey, but somehow his summary and cryptic presentation failed to put it across to his listeners. In fact he conveyed the over-all impression that aid should be extended to Greece on grounds of loyalty and humanitarianism, and to Turkey to strengthen Britain's position in the Middle East. This did not go down well with some of the congressional leaders, whose major preoccupation at that moment was reducing aid abroad and taxes at home. Their initial reaction was later described as "rather trivial" and "adverse." The immediate questions asked were: "Isn't this pulling British chestnuts out of the fire?" "What are we letting ourselves in for?" "How much is this going to cost?" Answers only took the discussion farther off the main track.

Things were going very badly indeed, and Acheson was greatly disturbed. Leaning over to Secretary Marshall, who sat beside him, Acheson asked in a low voice, "Is this a private fight or can anyone get into it?" Whereupon Marshall addressed the President and suggested that Acheson had something to say. Acheson was given the floor. Many of the things he said are already known to us, but in view of the impact upon his listeners it is worth following his argument.

In the past eighteen months, Acheson began, the position of the democracies in the world had seriously deteriorated. While Secretary Byrnes and Senator Vandenberg and Senator Connally had gone from conference to conference trying to negotiate peace settlements that would save certain countries of Central Europe from Soviet control, the Soviet Union had been busy elsewhere, and with greater success than was generally realized. It was clear they were making the most persistent and ambitious efforts to encircle Turkey and Germany and thus lay three continents open to Soviet domination.

Acheson described the direct pressures of the Soviet Union on Turkey during the preceding year and a half for territorial cessions and for military and naval bases in the Turkish Straits that would mean the end of Turkish independence. These had been accompanied, he said, by a vicious and prolonged propaganda campaign and, more important, by encircling movements aimed at Iran and Greece. The Turks, with British and American diplomatic support, had stood firm against Soviet pressures, and the move against Iran had for the time being failed. Now Communist pressure was concentrated on Greece, and there was every likelihood that unless Greece received prompt and large-scale aid from the outside the Communists would succeed in seizing control. Reports from Greece indicated that complete collapse might occur within a matter of weeks.

The Russians had any number of bets, Acheson went on. If they won any one of them, they won all. If they could seize control of Turkey, they would almost inevitably extend their control over Greece and Iran. If they controlled Greece, Turkey would sooner or later succumb, with or without a war, and then Iran. If they dominated Italy, where Communist pressures were increasing, they could probably take Greece, Turkey, and the Middle East. Their aim, Acheson emphasized, was control of the eastern Mediterranean and the Middle East. From there the possibilities for penetration of South Asia and Africa were limitless.

As for Europe, Acheson continued, it was clear that the Soviet Union, employing the instruments of Communist infiltration and subversion, was trying to complete the encirclement of Germany. In France, with four Communists in the Cabinet, one of them Minister of Defense, with Communists controlling the largest trade union and infiltrating government offices, factories, and the armed services, with nearly a third of the electorate voting Communist, and with economic conditions worsening, the Russians could pull the plug any time they chose. In Italy a similar if less immediately dangerous situation existed, but it was growing worse. In Hungary and Austria the Communists were tightening the noose on democratic governments.

If Greece and the eastern Mediterranean should fall to Soviet control, the material and psychological effects in the countries that were so precariously maintaining their freedoms and democratic institutions would be devastating, and probably conclusive.

It had been remarked, Acheson observed, that in aiding Greece and Turkey we would only be "pulling British chestnuts out of the fire." Britain's world power was shattered, he said, just as was that of every other democratic country except the United States. Great Britain was in grave financial trouble. He mentioned the two recent White Papers and their dark outlook for national survival, and explained that for financial reasons Britain was now obliged to withdraw troops and economic support from still other positions upon which her world power was based.

Only two great powers remained in the world, Acheson continued, the United States and the Soviet Union. We had arrived at a situation unparalleled since ancient times. Not since Rome and Carthage had there been such a polarization of power on this earth. Moreover the two great powers were divided by an unbridgeable ideological chasm. For us, democracy and individual liberty were basic; for them, dictatorship and absolute conformity. And it was clear that the Soviet Union was aggressive and expanding. For the United States to take steps to strengthen countries threatened with Soviet aggression or Communist subversion was not to pull British chestnuts out of the fire; it was to protect the security of the United States—it was to protect freedom itself. For if the Soviet Union succeeded in extending its control over two-thirds of the world's surface and three-fourths of its population, there could be no security for the United States, and freedom anywhere in the world would have only a poor chance of survival. The proposed aid to Greece and Turkey was not therefore a matter of bailing out the British, or even of responding on humanitarian grounds to the need of a loyal ally. It was a matter of building our own security and safeguarding freedom by strengthening free peoples against Communist aggression and subversion. We had the choice, he concluded, of acting with energy to meet this situation or of losing by default.

Acheson had abandoned the manner of a judge and for ten or fifteen minutes had spoken as a fervent advocate. When he finished a profound silence ensued that lasted perhaps ten seconds. It was broken by the voice of Senator Vandenberg. Slowly and with gravity, Vandenberg said that he had been greatly impressed, even shaken, by what he had heard. It was clear that the country was faced by an extremely serious situation, of which aid to Greece and Turkey, although of great importance, was only a part. He felt that it was absolutely necessary that any request of Congress for funds and authority to aid Greece and Turkey should be accompanied by a message to Congress, and an explanation to the American people, in which the grim facts of the larger situation should be laid publicly on the line as they had been at their meeting there that day.

The President went around the circle, inviting the comments of everyone present. Not one registered opposition. Not one asked trivial questions or raised side issues. All had apparently been deeply impressed. Vandenberg wrote some time later that no commitments were made at this meeting. That is true. None had been asked. But the very definite impression was gained, and was conveyed to the State Department staff the next day as a working hypothesis, that the congressional leaders would support whatever measures were necessary to save Greece and Turkey, *on the condition*, made by Senator Vandenberg and supported by others present, that the President should, in a message to Congress and in a radio address to the American people, explain the issue in the same frank terms and broad context in which it had been laid before them. * * *

The question has often been raised as to why the matter of aid to Greece and Turkey was presented to Congress and the American people enveloped in a statement of global policy that picked up the ideological challenge of communism. The February 27 meeting at the White House holds part of the answer. The explicit reaction of all in the government, from the President down, who were concerned with the decision to aid Greece and Turkey was that a historical turning point had been reached, that the United States must now stand forth as leader of the free world in place of the flagging British and use its power directly and vigorously to strengthen free nations. But there is a great difference between thinking or determining this and announcing it as the policy of the United States to a questionable Congress and an apathetic electorate. Because of the searing political lessons of the previous twenty-eight years, beginning with rejection of membership in the League of Nations and continuing through the isolationism of the twenties, the neutrality of the thirties, and the reaction against President Roosevelt's "quarantine" speech in Chicago in October 1937, the cautious, limited, backdoor approach to involvement in world affairs had become almost a reflex in successive administrations, notwithstanding support of the United Nations and vigorous participation in the negotiation of peace treaties. At the meeting with congressional leaders Acheson discovered that he had to pull out all the stops and speak in the frankest, boldest, widest terms to attract their support for a matter which in parliamentary democracies without a tradition of isolationism would have been undertaken quietly and without fanfare. This time the frank and bold approach, far from shocking congressional leaders into timorousness, paid off. They were deeply impressed and felt that on that basis they could go before their constituents. It was Vandenberg's "condition" that made it possible, even necessary, to launch the global policy that broke through the remaining barriers of American isolationism.

* * *

This sudden spark set off a dazzling process which within fifteen weeks laid the basis for a complete conversion of American foreign policy and of the attitudes of the American people toward the world. It was clear to many at the time that an enduring national conversion to the role of world leadership was taking place. It is even clearer now. This is * * * a story of American democracy working at its finest, with the executive branch of the government operating far beyond the normal boundaries of timidity and politics, the Congress beyond usual partisanship, and the American people as a whole beyond selfishness and complacency. All three faced the facts of international life fearlessly and without sentimentality, made identifiable contributions to the development of a new American foreign policy, and worked together to accomplish a national acceptance of world responsibility.

NOTES

1. Senator Taft was not invited, an error that Senator Vandenburg pointed out to President Truman the next day in a brief note: "If another congressional conference on any matter of *fundamental* and *far-reaching* importance (as yesterday), I respectfully suggest that the representation of the congressional majority include Senator Taft because of his position as chairman of the Republican Senate Policy Committee." Taft was thereafter invited; notably, he attended the second meeting on the Greece-Turkey subject at the White House on March 10.

4.2 *Cold War Revisionist Critique*

Melvyn P. Leffler

The American Conception of National Security and the Beginnings of the Cold War, 1945–48

* * *

In an interview with Henry Kissinger in 1978 on "The Lessons of the Past," Walter Laqueur observed that during the Second World War "few if any people thought . . . of the structure of peace that would follow the war except perhaps in the most general terms of friendship, mutual trust, and the other noble sentiments mentioned in wartime programmatic speeches about the United Nations and related topics." Kissinger concurred, noting that no statesman, except perhaps Winston Churchill, "gave any attention to what would happen after the war." Americans, Kissinger stressed, "were determined that we were going to base the postwar period on good faith and getting along with everybody."[1]

That two such astute and knowledgeable observers of international politics were so uninformed about American planning at the end of the Second World War is testimony to the enduring mythology of American idealism and innocence in the world of *realpolitik.* * * * American assessments of the Soviet threat were less a consequence of expanding Soviet military capabilities and of Soviet diplomatic demands than a result of growing apprehension about the vulnerability of American strategic and economic interests in a world of unprecedented turmoil and upheaval. Viewed from this perspective, the Cold War assumed many of its most enduring characteristics during 1947–8, when American officials sought to cope with an array of challenges by implementing their own concepts of national security.

American officials first began to think seriously about the nation's postwar security during 1943–4. Military planners devised elaborate plans for an overseas base system. These bases were defined as the nation's strategic fron-

From *American Historical Review* 89 (April 1984).

tier. Beyond this frontier the United States would be able to use force to counter any threats or frustrate any overt acts of aggression. Within the strategic frontier, American military predominance had to remain inviolate. These plans received President Franklin D. Roosevelt's endorsement in early 1944.[2]

Two strategic considerations influenced the development of an overseas base system. The first was the need for defense in depth. Since attacks against the United States could emanate only from Europe and Asia, the Joint Chiefs of Staff concluded as early as November 1943 that the United States must encircle the western hemisphere with a defensive ring of outlying bases. In the Pacific this ring had to include the Aleutians, the Philippines, Okinawa, and the former Japanese mandates.[3] In the Atlantic, strategic planners maintained that their minimum requirements included a West African zone, with primary bases in the Azores or Canary Islands. The object of these defensive bases was to enable the United States to possess complete control of the Atlantic and Pacific oceans and keep hostile powers far from American territory.[4]

Defense in depth was especially important in light of the Pearl Harbor experience, the advance of technology, and the development of the atomic bomb. According to the Joint Chiefs of Staff, "Experience in the recent war demonstrated conclusively that the . . . farther away from our own vital areas we can hold our enemy through the possession of advanced bases . . . the greater are our chances of surviving successfully an attack by atomic weapons and of destroying the enemy which employs them against us." Believing that atomic weapons would increase the incentive to aggression by enhancing the advantage of surprise, military planners never ceased to extol the utility of forward bases from which American aircraft could seek to intercept attacks against the United States.[5]

The second strategic consideration that influenced the plan for a comprehensive overseas base system was the need to project American power quickly and effectively against any potential adversary. In conducting an overall examination of requirements for base rights in September 1945, the Joint War Plans Committee stressed that the Second World War demonstrated that the United States had to be able to take "timely" offensive action against the adversary's capacity and will to wage war. The basic strategic concept underlying all American war plans called for an air offensive against a prospective enemy from overseas bases. Delays in the development of the B-36, the first intercontinental bomber, only accentuated the need for these bases.[6]

* * *

The need to predominate throughout the western hemisphere was not a result of deteriorating Soviet-American relations but a natural evolution of the Monroe Doctrine, accentuated by Axis aggression and new technological imperatives.[7] Patterson, Forrestal, and Army Chief of Staff Dwight D. Eisenhower initially were impelled less by reports of Soviet espionage, propaganda, and infiltration in Latin America than by accounts of British efforts to sell cruisers and aircraft to Chile and Ecuador; Swedish sales of antiaircraft artillery to Argentina; and French offers to build cruisers and destroyers for both Argentina and Brazil.[8] To foreclose all foreign influence and to ensure US strategic hegemony, military officers and the civilian Secretaries of the War and Navy Departments argued for an extensive system of US bases, expansion of commercial airline facilities throughout Latin America, negotiation of a regional defense pact, curtailment of all foreign military aid and foreign military sales, training of Latin American military officers in the United States, outfitting of Latin American armies with US military equipment, and implementation of a comprehensive military assistance program.[9]

$$* \quad * \quad *$$

From the closing days of the Second World War, American defense officials believed that they could not allow any prospective adversary to control the Eurasian land mass. This was the lesson taught by two world wars. Strategic thinkers and military analysts insisted that any power or powers attempting to dominate Eurasia must be regarded as potentially hostile to the United States.[10] Their acute awareness of the importance of Eurasia made Marshall, Thomas Handy, George A. Lincoln, and other officers wary of the expansion of Soviet influence there. While acknowledging that the increase in Soviet power stemmed primarily from the defeat of Germany and Japan, postwar assessments of the Joint Chiefs of Staff emphasized the importance of deterring further Soviet aggrandizement in Eurasia.[11] Concern over the consequences of Russian domination of Eurasia helps explain why in July 1945 the joint chiefs decided to oppose a Soviet request for bases in the Dardanelles; why during March and April 1946 they supported a firm stand against Russia in Iran, Turkey, and Tripolitania, and why in the summer of 1946 Clark Clifford and George Elsey, two White House aides, argued that Soviet incorporation of any parts of Western Europe, the Middle East, China, or Japan into a Communist orbit was incompatible with American national security.[12]

Economic considerations also made defense officials determined to retain American access to Eurasia as well as to deny Soviet predominance over it. Stimson, Patterson, McCloy, and Assistant Secretary Howard C. Peterson agreed with Forrestal that long-term American prosperity required open markets, unhindered access to raw materials, and the rehabilitation of much—if not all—of Eurasia along liberal capitalist lines. In late 1944 and 1945, Stimson protested the prospective industrial emasculation of Germany, lest it undermine American economic well-being, set back recovery throughout Europe, and unleash forces of anarchy and revolution. Stimson and his subordinates in the Operations Division of the army also worried that the spread of Soviet power in Northeast Asia would constrain the functioning of the free enterprise system and jeopardize American economic interests. A report prepared by the staff of the Moscow embassy and revised in mid-1946 by Ambassador (and former General) Walter Bedell Smith emphasized that "Soviet power is by nature so jealous that it has already operated to segregate from world economy almost all of the areas in which it has been established." Therefore, Forrestal and the navy sought to contain Soviet influence in the Near East and to retain American access to Middle East oil; Patterson and the War Department focused on preventing famine in occupied areas and resuscitating trade.[13] But American economic interests in Eurasia were not limited to Western Europe, Germany, and the Middle East. Military planners and intelligence officers in both the army and navy expressed considerable interest in the raw materials of Southeast Asia, wanted to maintain access to those resources, and sought to deny them to a prospective enemy.[14]

✳ ✳ ✳

American defense officials, military analysts, and intelligence officers were extremely sensitive to the political ferment, social turmoil, and economic upheaval throughout postwar Europe and Asia. In their initial postwar studies, the Joint Chiefs of Staff carefully noted the multiplicity of problems that could breed conflict and provide opportunities for Soviet expansion. In the spring of 1946 army planners were keenly aware that conflict was most likely to arise from local disputes (for example, between Italy and Yugoslavia) or from indigenous unrest (for example, in France), perhaps even against the will of Moscow. A key War Department document in April 1946 skirted the issue of Soviet military capabilities and argued that the Soviet Union's strength emanated from totalitarian control over its satellites, from local Communist parties, and from worldwide chaotic political and economic conditions. "The greatest danger to the security of the United States," the CIA concluded in mid-1947, "is the possibility of economic collapse in Western Europe and the consequent accession to power of Communist elements."[15]

During 1946 and 1947, defense officials witnessed a dramatic unravelling of the geopolitical foundations and socioeconomic structure of international affairs. Britain's economic weakness and withdrawal from the eastern Mediterranean, India's independence movement, civil war in China, nationalist insurgencies in Indo-China and the Dutch East Indies, Zionist claims to Palestine and Arab resentment, German and Japanese economic paralysis, Communist inroads in France and Italy—all were ominous developments. Defense officials recognized that the Soviet Union had not created these circumstances but believed that Soviet leaders would exploit them. Should Communists take power, even without direct Russian intervention, the Soviet Union would gain predominant control of the resources of these areas because of the postulated subservience of Communist parties everywhere to the Kremlin. Should nationalist uprisings persist, Communists seize power in underdeveloped countries, or Arabs revolt against American support of a Jewish state, the petroleum and raw materials of critical areas might be denied the West. The imminent possibility existed that, even without Soviet military aggression, the resources of Eurasia could fall under Russian control. With these resources, the Soviet Union would be able to overcome its chronic economic weaknesses, achieve defense in depth, and challenge American power—perhaps even by military force.[16]

In this frightening postwar environment American assessments of Soviet long-term intentions were transformed. Spurred by the "long telegram," written by George F. Kennan, the US chargé d'affaires in Moscow, it soon became commonplace for policy makers, military officials, and intelligence analysts to state that the ultimate aim of Soviet foreign policy was Russian domination of a Communist world.[17] There was, of course, plentiful evidence for this appraisal of Soviet ambitions—the Soviet consolidation of a sphere of influence in Eastern Europe; Soviet violation of the agreement to withdraw troops from Iran; Soviet relinquishment of Japanese arms to the Chinese Communists; the Soviet mode of extracting reparations from the Russian zone in Germany; Soviet diplomatic overtures for bases in the Dardanelles, Tripolitania, and the Dodecanese; Soviet requests for a role in the occupation of Japan; and the Kremlin's renewed emphasis on Marxist-Leninist doctrine, the vulnerability of capitalist economies, and the inevitability of conflict.

Yet these assessments did not seriously grapple with contradictory evidence. They disregarded numerous signs of Soviet weakness, moderation, and circumspection. During 1946 and 1947 intelligence analysts described the withdrawal of Russian troops from northern Norway, Manchuria, Bornholm, and Iran (from the latter under pressure, of course). Numerous intelligence sources reported the reduction of Russian troops in Eastern Europe and the extensive demobilization going on within the Soviet Union. In October 1947 the Joint Intelligence Committee forecast a Soviet army troop strength during 1948 and 1949 of less than 2 million men. Other reports dealt with the inadequacies of Soviet transportation and bridging equipment and the moderation of Soviet military expenditures. And, as already noted, assessments of the Soviet economy revealed persistent problems likely to restrict Soviet adventurism.[18]

Experience suggested that the Soviet Union was by no means uniformly hostile or unwilling to negotiate with the United States. In April 1946 Ambassador Smith reminded the State Department that the Soviet press was not unalterably critical of the United States, that the Russians had withdrawn from Bornholm, that Stalin had given a moderate speech on the United Nations, and that Soviet demobilization continued apace. The next month General Lincoln acknowledged that the Soviets had been willing to make numerous concessions regarding Tripolitania, the Dodecanese, and Italian reparations. In the spring of 1946, General Echols, General Clay, and Secretary Patterson again maintained that the French constituted the major impediment to an agreement on united control of Germany. In early 1947 central intelligence delineated more than a half-dozen instances of Soviet moderation or concessions. In April the Military Intelligence Division noted that the Soviets had limited their involvement in the Middle East, diminished their ideological rhetoric, and given only moderate support to Chinese Communists.[19]

In their overall assessments of Soviet long-term intentions, however, military planners dismissed all evidence of Soviet moderation, circumspection, and restraint. In fact, as 1946 progressed, these planners seemed to spend less time analyzing Soviet intentions and more time estimating Soviet capabilities.[20] They no longer explored ways of accommodating a potential adversary's legitimate strategic requirements or pondered how American initiatives might influence the Soviet Union's definition of its objectives.[21] Information not confirming prevailing assumptions either was ignored in overall assessments of Soviet intentions or was used to illustrate that the Soviets were shifting tactics but not altering objectives. A report from the Joint Chiefs of Staff to the President in July 1946, for example, deleted sections from previous studies that had outlined Soviet weaknesses. A memorandum sent by Secretary Patterson to the President at the same time was designed to answer questions about relations with the Soviet Union "without ambiguity." Truman, Clark Clifford observed many years later, liked things in black and white.[22]

＊　＊　＊

Having conceived of American national security in terms of Western control and of American access to the resources of Eurasia outside the Soviet sphere, American defense officials now considered it imperative to develop American military capabilities to meet a host of contingencies that might emanate from further Soviet encroachments or from indigenous Communist unrest. Such contingencies were sure to arise because American strategy depended so heavily on the rebuilding of Germany and Japan, Russia's traditional enemies, as well as on air power, atomic weapons, and bases on the Soviet periphery. Such contingencies also were predictable because American strategy depended so heavily on the restoration of stability in Eurasia, a situation increasingly unlikely in an era of nationalist turmoil, social unrest, and rising economic expectations. Although the desire of the national military establishment for large increments in defense expenditures did not prevail in the tight budgetary environment and presidential election year of 1948, the mode of thinking about national security that subsequently accelerated the arms race and precipitated military interventionism in Asia was already widespread among defense officials.

The dynamics of the Cold War after 1948 are easier to comprehend when one grasps the breadth of the American conception of national security that had emerged between 1945 and 1948. This conception included a strategic sphere of influence within the western hemisphere, domination of the Atlantic and Pacific oceans, an extensive system of outlying bases to enlarge the strategic frontier and project American power, an even more extensive system of transit rights to facilitate the conversion of commercial air bases to military use, access to the resources and markets of most of Eurasia, denial of those resources to a prospective enemy, and the maintenance of nuclear superiority. Not every one of these ingredients, it must be emphasized, was considered vital. Hence, American officials could acquiesce, however grudgingly, to a Soviet sphere in Eastern Europe and could avoid direct intervention in China. But cumulative challenges to these concepts of national security were certain to provoke a firm American response. This occurred initially in 1947–8 when decisions were made in favor of the Truman Doctrine, the Marshall Plan, military assistance, the Atlantic alliance, and German and Japanese rehabilitation. Soon thereafter, the "loss" of China, the Soviet detonation of an atomic bomb, and the North Korean attack on South Korea intensified the perception of threat to prevailing concepts of national security. The Truman administration responded with military assistance to Southeast Asia, a decision to build the hydrogen bomb, direct military intervention in Korea, a commitment to station troops permanently in Europe, expansion of the American alliance system, and a massive rearmament program in the United States. Postulating a long-term Soviet intention to gain world domination, the American conception of national security, based on geopolitical and economic imperatives, could not allow for additional losses in Eurasia, could not risk a challenge to its nuclear supremacy, and could not permit any infringement on its ability to defend in depth or to project American force from areas in close proximity to the Soviet homeland.

To say this, is neither to exculpate the Soviet government for its inhumane treatment of its own citizens nor to suggest that Soviet foreign policy was idle or benign. Indeed, Soviet behavior in Eastern Europe was often deplorable; the Soviets sought opportunities in the Dardanelles, northern Iran, and Manchuria; the Soviets hoped to orient Germany and Austria toward the East; and the Soviets sometimes endeavored to use Communist parties to expand Soviet influence in areas beyond the periphery of Russian military power. But, then again, the Soviet Union had lost 20 million dead during the war, had experienced the destruction of 1,700 towns, 31,000 factories, and 100,000 collective farms, and had witnessed the devastation of the rural economy with the Nazi slaughter of 20 million hogs and 17 million head of cattle. What is remarkable is that after 1946 these monumental losses received so little attention when American defense analysts studied the motives and intentions of Soviet policy; indeed, defense officials did little to analyze the threat perceived by the Soviets. Yet these same officials had absolutely no doubt that the wartime experiences and sacrifices of the United States, though much less devastating than those of Soviet Russia, demonstrated the need for and entitled the United States to oversee the resuscitation of the industrial heartlands of Germany and Japan, establish a viable balance of power in Eurasia, and militarily dominate the Eurasian rimlands, thereby safeguarding American access to raw materials and control over all sea and air approaches to North America.[23]

To suggest a double standard is important only in so far as it raises fundamental questions about the conceptualization and implementation of American national security policy. If Soviet policy was aggressive, bellicose, and ideological, perhaps America's reliance on overseas bases, air power, atomic weapons, military alliances, and the rehabilitation of Germany and Japan was the best course to follow, even if the effect may have been to exacerbate Soviet anxieties and suspicions. But even when one attributes the worst intentions to the Soviet Union, one might still ask whether American presuppositions and apprehensions about the benefits that would accrue to the Soviet Union as a result of Communist (and even revolutionary nationalist) gains anywhere in Eurasia tended to simplify international realities, magnify the breadth of American interests, engender commitments beyond American capabilities, and dissipate the nation's strength and credibility. And, perhaps even more importantly, if Soviet foreign policies tended to be opportunist, reactive, nationalistic, and contradictory, as some recent writers have claimed and as some contemporary analysts suggested, then one might also wonder whether America's own conception of national security tended, perhaps unintentionally, to engender anxieties and to provoke countermeasures from a proud, suspicious, insecure, and cruel government that was at the same time legitimately apprehensive about the long-term implications arising from the rehabilitation of traditional enemies and the development of foreign bases on the periphery of the Soviet homeland. To raise such issues anew seems essential if we are to unravel the complex origins of the Cold War.

* * *

NOTES

1. Henry Kissinger, *For the Record: Selected Statements, 1977–80* (Boston, MA, 1980), 123–4.
2. Plans for America's overseas base system may be found in RG 218, Combined Chiefs of Staff [CCS] series 360 (12–9–42); Joint Strategic Survey Committee [hereafter JSSC], "Air Routes across the Pacific and Air Facilities for International Police Force," March 15, 1943, JSSC 9/1; Joint Chiefs of Staff [JCS], "United States Military Requirements for Air Bases, Facilities, and Operating Rights in Foreign Territories," November 2, 1943, JCS 570/2; Joint War Plans Committee [hereafter

JWPC], "Overall Examination of the United States Requirements for Military Bases," August 25, 1943, JWPC 361/4; and JWPC, "Overall Examination of United States Requirements for Military Bases," September 13, 1945, JWPC 361/5 (revised). For Roosevelt's endorsement, see Roosevelt to the Department of State, January 7, 1944, ibid., JWPC 361/5.

3. JCS, "Strategic Areas and Trusteeships in the Pacific," October 10, 18, 1946, RG 218, ser. CCS 360 (12–9–42), JCS 1619/15, 19; JCS, "United States Military Requirements for Air Bases," November 2, 1943; JCS, "Overall Examination of United States Requirements for Military Bases and Base Rights," October 25, 1945, ibid., JCS 570/40.

4. JCS, "United States Military Requirements for Air Bases," November 2, 1943; JCS, Minutes of the 71st meeting, March 30, 1943, RG 218 ser. CCS 360 (12–9–42); and Joint Planning Staff [hereafter JPS], "Basis for the Formulation of a Post-War Military Policy," August 20, 1945, RG 218, ser. CCS 381 (5–13–45), JPS 633/6.

5. JCS, "Statement of Effect of Atomic Weapons on National Security and Military Organization," March 29, 1946, RG 165, ser. ABC 471.6 Atom (8–17–45), JCS 477/10.

6. For the emphasis on "timely" action, see JWPC, "Overall Examination of Requirements for Military Bases" (revised), September 13, 1945; for the need for advance bases, see JCS, "Strategic Concept and Plan for the Employment of United States Armed Forces," September 19, 1945, RG 218, ser. CCS 381 (5–13–45), JCS 1518. Also see, for the evolution of strategic war plans, many of the materials in RG 218, ser. CCS 381 USSR (3–2–46).

7. This evaluation accords with the views of Chester J. Pach, Jr; see his "The Containment of United States Military Aid to Latin America, 1944–1949," *Diplomatic History*, 6 (1982):232–4.

8. For fears of foreign influence, see, for example, [no signature] "Military Political Cooperation with the Other American Republics," June 24, 1946, RG 18, 092 (International Affairs), box 567; Patterson to the Secretary of State, July 31, 1946, RG 353, SWNCC, box 76; Eisenhower to Patterson, November 26, 1946, RG 107, HCPP, general decimal file, box 1 (top secret); S. J. Chamberlin to Eisenhower, November 26, 1946, ibid.; Minutes of the meeting of the Secretaries of State, War, and Navy, December 11, 1946, ibid., RPPP, safe file, box 3; and Director of Intelligence to Director of P&O, February 26, 1947, RG 319, P&O, 091 France. For reports on Soviet espionage, see, for example, Military Intelligence Service [hereafter MIS], "Soviet-Communist Penetration in Latin America," March 24, 1945, RG 165, OPD 336 (top secret).

9. See, for example, Craig, "Summary," January 5, 1945; JPS, "Military Arrangements Deriving from the Act of Chapultepec Pertaining to Bases," January 14, 1946, RG 218, ser. CCS 092 (9–10–45), JPS 761/3;

Patterson to Byrnes, December 18, 1946; and P&O, "Strategic Importance of Inter-American Military Cooperation" [January 20, 1947].

10. This view was most explicitly presented in an army paper examining the State Department's expostulation of US foreign policy. See S. F. Giffin, "Draft of Proposed Comments for the Assistant Secretary of War on 'Foreign Policy'" [early February 1946], RG 107, HCPP 092 international affairs (classified). The extent to which this concern with Eurasia shaped American military attitudes is illustrated at greater length below. Here I should note that in March 1945 several of the nation's most prominent civilian experts (Frederick S. Dunn, Edward M. Earle, William T. R. Fox, Grayson L. Kirk, David N. Rowe, Harold Sprout, and Arnold Wolfers) prepared a study, "A Security Policy for Postwar America," in which they argued that the United States had to prevent any one power or coalition of powers from gaining control of Eurasia. America could not, they insisted, withstand attack by any power that had first subdued the whole of Europe or of Eurasia; see Frederick S. Dunn *et al.*, "A Security Policy for Postwar America," NHC, SPD, ser. 14, box 194, A1–2.

The postwar concept of Eurasia developed out of the revival of geopolitical thinking in the United States, stimulated by Axis aggression and strategic decisionmaking. See, for example, the reissued work of Sir Halford F. Mackinder: *Democratic Ideals and Reality* (1919; reprint edn, New York, 1942), and "The Round World and the Winning of Peace," *Foreign Affairs*, 21 (1943): 598–605. Mackinder's ideas were modified and widely disseminated in the United States, especially by intellectuals such as Nicholas John Spykman, Hans W. Weigert, Robert Strausz-Hupé, and Isaiah Bowman.

11. For views of influential generals and army planners, see OPD, Memorandum, June 4, 1945, RG 165, OPD 336 (top secret). Also see the plethora of documents from May and June 1945, US Military Academy, West Point, New York [hereafter USMA], George A. Lincoln Papers [hereafter GLP], War Department files. For the JCS studies, see, for example, JPS, "Strategic Concept and Plan for the Employment of United States Armed Forces," September 14, 1945, RG 218, ser. CCS 381 (5-13-45), JPS 744/3; and JCS, "United States Military Policy," September 17, 1945, ibid., JCS 1496/2.

12. For the decision on the Dardanelles, see the attachments to JCS, "United States Policy concerning the Dardanelles and Kiel Canal" [July 1945], RG 218, ser. CCS 092 (7-10-45), JCS 1418/1; for the joint chiefs' position on Iran, Turkey, and Tripolitania, see JCS, "U.S. Security Interests in the Eastern Mediterranean," March 1946, ibid., ser. CCS 092 USSR (3-27-45). JCS 1641 series; and Lincoln, Memorandum for the Record, April 16, 1946, RG 165, ser. ABC 336 Russia (8-22-43); and, for the Clifford memorandum, see Arthur Krock, *Memoirs: Sixty Years on the Firing Line* (New York, 1968), 477–82.

13. Moscow embassy staff, "Russia's International Position at the Close of the War with Germany," enclosed in Smith to Eisenhower, July 12, 1946, Dwight David Eisenhower Library [hereafter DDEL], Dwight David Eisenhower Papers, file 1652, box 101. Also see, for example, Stimson to Roosevelt, September 15, 1944, ML, JFP, box 100; Stimson to Truman, May 16, 1945, HTL, HSTP, PSF, box 157; numerous memoranda, June 1945, USMA, GLP, War Dept files; numerous documents, 1946 and 1947, RG 107, HCPP, 091 Germany (Classified); and Rearmament Subcommittee, Report to the Special Ad Hoc Committee, July 10, 1947, RG 165, ser. ABC 400.336 (3-20-47). For Forrestal's concern with Middle Eastern oil, see, for example, "Notes in Connection with Navy's 'Line' on Foreign Oil" [late 1944 or early 1945], ML, JFP, box 22; Walter Millis (ed.), *The Forrestal Diaries* (New York, 1951), 272, 356–8.

14. Strategy Section, OPD, "Post-War Base Requirements in the Philippines," April 23, 1945, RG 165, OPD 336 (top secret); MID, "Positive US Action Required to Restore Normal Conditions in Southeast Asia," July 3, 1947, RG 319, P&O, 092 (top secret); and Lauris Norstad to the Director of Intelligence, July 10, 1947, ibid.

15. CIA, "Review of the World Situation as It Relates to the Security of the United States," September 26, 1947. Also see, for example, JCS, "Strategic Concept and Plan for the Employment of United States Armed Forces," Appendix A, September 19, 1945; JPS, Minutes of the 249th and 250th meetings; [Giffin (?)] "U.S. Policy with Respect to Russia" [early April 1946], RG 165, ser. ABC 336 (8-22-43); MID, "World Political Developments Affecting the Security of the United States during the Next Ten Years," April 14, 1947, RG 319, P&O, 350.05 (top secret).

16. See, for example, JCS, "Presidential Request for Certain Facts and Information Regarding the Soviet Union," July 25, 1946, RG 218, ser. CCS 092 USSR (3-27-45), JCS 1696; P&O, "Strategic Study of Western and Northern Europe," May 21, 1947, RG 319, P&O, 092 (top secret); and Wooldridge to the General Board, April 30, 1948.

17. For Kennan's "long telegram," see *FRUS, 1946* (Washington, DC, 1970), Vol. 4: 696–709; for ominous interpretations of Soviet intentions and capabilities, also see JCS, "Political Estimate of Soviet Policy for Use in Connection with Military Studies," April 5, 1946, RG 218, ser. CCS 092 USSR (3-27-45), JCS 1641/4; and JCS, "Presidential Request for Certain Facts and Information Regarding the Soviet Union," July 25, 1946.

18. For the withdrawal of Soviet troops, see, for example, MID, "Soviet Intentions and Capabilities in Scandinavia as of 1 July 1946," April 25, 1946, RG 319, P&O, 350.05 (top secret). For reports on reductions of Russian troops in Eastern Europe and demobilization within the

Soviet Union, see MID, "Review of Europe, Russia, and the Middle East," December 26, 1945, RG 165, OPD, 350.05 (top secret); Carl Espe, weekly calculations of Soviet troops, May–September 1946, NHC, SPD, ser. 5, box 106, A8; and JIC, "Soviet Military Objectives and Capabilities," October 27, 1947. For references to Soviet military expenditures, see Patterson to Julius Adler, November 2, 1946, RG 107, RPPP, safe file, box 5; and for the Soviet transport system, see R. F. Ennis, Memorandum for the P&O Division, June 24, 1946, RG 165, ser. ABC 336 (8-22-43); Op-32 to the General Board, April 28, 1948, NHC, General Board 425 (ser. 315).

19. Smith to the Secretary of State, April 11, 1946, RG 165, Records of the Chief of Staff, 091 Russia; and, for Soviet negotiating concessions, see Lincoln, Memorandum for the Chief of Staff, May 20, 1946, USMA; GLP War Dept/files. For the situation in Germany, see OPD and CAD, "Analysis of Certain Political Problems Confronting Military Occupation Authorities in Germany," April 10, 1946, RG 107, HCPP 091 Germany (classified); Patterson to Truman, June 11, 1946, RG 165, Records of the Chief of Staff, 091 Germany. For Clay's references to French obstructionism, see, for example, Smith, *Papers of General Lucius D. Clav.* Vol. 1: 84–5, 88–9, 151–2, 189–90, 212–17, 235–6. For overall intelligence assessments, see Central Intelligence Group [hereafter CIG], "Revised Soviet Tactics in International Affairs," January 6, 1947, HTL, HSTP, PSF, box 254, MID, "World Political Developments Affecting the Security of the United States during the Next Ten Years," April 14, 1947.

20. My assessment is based primarily on my analysis of the materials in RG 218, ser. CCS 092 USSR (3-27-45); ser. CCS 381 USSR (3-2-46); RG 319, P&O, 350.05 (top secret); and NHC, SPD, central files, 1946-8, A8.

21. During 1946 it became a fundamental tenet of American policy makers that Soviet policy objectives were a function of developments within the Soviet Union and not related to American actions. See, for example, Kennan's "long telegram," in *FRUS, 1946*, Vol. 4: 696–709; JCS, "Political Estimate of Soviet Policy," April 5, 1946.

22. Norstad, Memorandum, July 25, 1946, RG 319, P&O, 092 (top secret). For references to shifting tactics and constant objectives, see Vandenberg, Memorandum for the President, September 27, 1946, HTL, HSTP, PSF, box 249; CIG, "Revised Soviet Tactics," January 6, 1947; and, for the JCS report to the President, compare JCS 1696 with JIC 250/12. Both studies may be found in RG 218, ser. CCS 092 USSR (3-27-45). For Clifford's recollection, Clark Clifford, HTL, oral history, 170.

23. For Soviet losses, see Nicholas V. Riasanovsky, *A History of Russia* (3rd edn, New York, 1977), 584–5. While Russian dead totaled almost

20 million and while approximately 25 percent of the reproducible wealth of the Soviet Union was destroyed, American battlefield casualties were 300,000 dead, the index of industrial production in the United States rose from 100 to 196, and the gross national product increased from $91 billion to $166 billion. See Gordon Wright, *The Ordeal of Total War* (New York, 1968), 264–5.

4.3 Nuclear Deterrence Doctrine

BERNARD BRODIE

Strategy in the Missile Age

* * * We shall be talking about the strategy of deterrence of general war, and about the complementary principle of limiting to tolerable proportions whatever conflicts become inevitable. These ideas spring from the conviction that total nuclear war is to be avoided at almost any cost. This follows from the assumption that such a war, even if we were extraordinarily lucky, would be too big, too all-consuming to permit the survival even of those final values, like personal freedom, for which alone one could think of waging it. It need not be certain that it would turn out so badly; it is enough that there is a large chance that it would.

The conceptions of deterrence and of limited war also take account of the fact that the United States is, and has long been, a status quo power. We are uninterested in acquiring new territories or areas of influence or in accepting great hazard in order to rescue or reform those areas of the world which now have political systems radically different from our own. On the other hand, as a status quo power, we are also determined to keep what we have, including existence in a world of which half or more is friendly, or at least not sharply and perennially hostile. In other words, our minimum security objectives include not only our own national independence but also that of many other countries, especially those which cherish democratic political institutions. Among the latter are those nations with which we have a special cultural affinity, that is, the countries of western Europe.

* * *

Deterrence Old and New

Deterrence as an element in national strategy or diplomacy is nothing new. Since the development of nuclear weapons, however, the term has acquired not only a special emphasis but also a distinctive connotation. It is usually

From *Strategy in the Missile Age* (Princeton: Princeton University Press, 1965), chapter 8.

119

the new and distinctive connotation that we have in mind when we speak nowadays of the "strategy of deterrence."

The threat of war, open or implied, has always been an instrument of diplomacy by which one state deterred another from doing something of a military or political nature which the former deemed undesirable. Frequently the threat was completely latent, the position of the monitoring state being so obvious and so strong that no one thought of challenging it. Governments, like individuals, were usually aware of hazard in provoking powerful neighbors and governed themselves accordingly. Because avoidance of wars and even of crises hardly makes good copy for historians, we may infer that the past successes of some nations in deterring unwanted action by others add up to much more than one might gather from a casual reading of history. Nevertheless the large number of wars that have occurred in modern times prove that the threat to use force, even what sometimes looked like superior force, has often failed to deter.

We should notice, however, the positive function played by the failures. The very frequency with which wars occurred contributed importantly to the credibility inherent in any threat. In diplomatic correspondence, the statement that a specified kind of conduct would be deemed "an unfriendly act" was regarded as tantamount to an ultimatum and to be taken without question as seriously intended.

Bluffing, in the sense of deliberately trying to sound more determined or bellicose than one actually felt, was by no means as common a phenomenon in diplomacy as latter-day journalistic interpretations of events would have one believe. In any case, it tended to be confined to the more implicit kinds of threat. In short, the operation of deterrence was dynamic; it acquired relevance and strength from its failures as well as its successes.

Today, however, the policy of deterrence in relation to all-out war is markedly different in several respects. For one thing, it uses a kind of threat which we feel must be absolutely effective, allowing for no breakdowns ever. The sanction is, to say the least, not designed for repeating action. One use of it will be fatally too many. Deterrence now means something as a strategic policy only when we are fairly confident that the retaliatory instrument upon which it relies will not be called upon to function at all. Nevertheless, that instrument has to be maintained at a high pitch of efficiency and readiness and constantly improved, which can be done only at high cost to the community and great dedication on the part of the personnel directly involved. In short, we expect the system to be always ready to spring while going permanently unused. Surely there is something almost unreal about all this.

The Problem of Credibility

The unreality is minimal when we are talking about what we shall henceforward call "*basic deterrence*," that is, deterrence of direct, strategic, nuclear attack upon targets within the home territories of the United States. In that instance there is little or no problem of credibility as concerns our reactions, for the enemy has little reason to doubt that if he strikes us we will try to hit back. But the great and terrible apparatus which we must set up to fulfill our needs for basic deterrence and the state of readiness at which we have to maintain it create a condition of almost embarrassing availability of huge power. The problem of linking this power to a reasonable conception of its utility has thus far proved a considerable strain. * * *

On the other hand, it would be tactically and factually wrong to assure the enemy in advance (as we tend to do by constantly assuring ourselves) that we would in no case move against him until we had already felt some bombs on our cities and airfields. We have, as we have seen, treaty obligations which forbid so far-reaching a commitment to restraint. It is also impossible for us to predict with absolute assurance our own behavior in extremely tense and provocative circumstances. If we make the wrong prediction about ourselves, we encourage the enemy also to make the wrong prediction about us. The outbreak of war in Korea in 1950 followed exactly that pattern. The wrong kind of prediction in this regard might precipitate that total nuclear war which too many persons have lightly concluded is now impossible.

Deterrence Strategy versus Win-the-War Strategies: The Sliding Scale of Deterrence

To return now to the simpler problem of basic deterrence. The capacity to deter is usually confused with the capacity to win a war. At present, capacity to win a total or unrestricted war requires either a decisive and *completely secure* superiority in strategic air power or success in seizing the initiative. Inasmuch as mere superiority in numbers of vehicles looks like a good thing to have anyway, the confusion between deterring and winning has method in it. But deterrence *per se* does not depend on superiority.

* * *

Now that we are in a nuclear age, the potential deterrence value of an admittedly inferior force may be sharply greater than it has ever been before. Let us assume that a menaced small nation could threaten the Soviet Union with only a single thermonuclear bomb, which, however, it could and would certainly deliver on Moscow if attacked. This would be a retaliatory capability sufficient to give the Soviet government pause. Certainly they would not provoke the destruction of Moscow for trivial gains, even if warning enabled the people of the city to save themselves by evacuation or resort to shelters. Naturally, the effect is greater if warning can be ruled out.

Ten such missiles aimed at ten major cities would be even more effective, and fifty aimed at that number of different cities would no doubt work still greater deterrent effect, though of course the cities diminish in size as the number included goes up. However, even when we make allowance for the latter fact, it is a fair surmise that the increase in deterrent effect is less than proportional to the increase in magnitude of potential destruction. We make that surmise on the basis of our everyday experience with human beings and their responses to punishment or deprivation. The human imagination can encompass just so much pain, anguish, or horror. The intrusion of numbers by which to multiply given sums of such feelings is likely to have on the average human mind a rather dull effect—except insofar as the increase in the threatened amount of harm affects the individual's statistical expectation of himself being involved in it.

Governments, it may be suggested, do not think like ordinary human beings, and one has to concede that the *maximum possible deterrence* which can be attained by the threat of retaliatory damage must involve a power which guarantees not only vast losses but also utter defeat. On the other hand, governments, including communistic ones, also comprise human beings, whose departure from the mold of ordinary mortals is not markedly in the direction of greater intellectualism or detachment. It is therefore likely that considerably less retaliatory destruction than that conceived under "maximum possible deterrence" will buy only slightly less deterrence. If we wish to visualize the situation graphically, we will think of a curve of "deterrence effect" in which each unit of additional damage threatened brings progressively diminishing increments of deterrence. Obviously and unfortunately, we lack all the data which would enable us to fill in the values for such a curve and thus to draw it.

If our surmises are in general correct, we are underlining the sharp differences in character between a deterrence capability and strategy on the one hand, and a win-the-war strategy and capability on the other. We have to remember too that since the winning of a war presupposes certain limitations on the quantity of destruction to one's own country and especially to one's population, a win-the-war strategy could quite conceivably be an utter impossibility to a nation striking second, and is by no means guaranteed to a nation striking first. Too much depends on what the other fellow does— how accessible or inaccessible he makes his own retaliatory force and how he makes his attack if he decides to launch one. However much we dislike the thought, a win-the-war strategy may be impossible because of circumstances outside our control.

Lest we conclude from these remarks that we can be content with a modest retaliatory capability—what some have called "minimum deterrence"—we have to mention at once four qualifying considerations, which we shall amplify later: (a) it may require a large force in hand to guarantee even a modest retaliation; (b) deterrence must always be conceived as a relative thing, which is to say it must be adequate to the variable but generally high degree of motivation which the enemy feels for our destruction; (c) if deterrence fails we shall want enough forces to fight a total war effectively; and (d) our retaliatory force must also be capable of striking first, and if it does so its attack had better be, as nearly as possible, overwhelming to the enemy's retaliatory force. Finally, we have to bear in mind that in their responses to threat or menace, people (including heads of government) do not spontaneously act according to a scrupulous weighing of objective facts. Large forces look more impressive than small ones—for reasons which are by no means entirely irrational—and in some circumstances such impressiveness may be important to us. Human beings, differing widely as they do in temperamental and psychic make-up, nevertheless generally have in common the fact that they make their most momentous decisions by what is fundamentally intuition.

*   *   *

The Problem of Guaranteeing Strong Retaliation

It should be obvious that what counts in basic deterrence is not so much the size and efficiency of one's striking force before it is hit as the size and condition to which the enemy thinks he can reduce it by a surprise attack —as well as his confidence in the correctness of his predictions. The degree to which the automaticity of our retaliation has been taken for granted by the public, unfortunately including most leaders of opinion and even military officers, is for those who have any knowledge of the facts both incredible and dangerous. The general idea is that if the enemy hits us, we will kill him.

*   *   *

Deterrence and Armaments Control

We come finally to the question of the political environment favoring the functioning of a deterrence strategy, especially with respect to the much abused and belabored subject of international control of armaments. There is a long and dismal history of confusion and frustration on this subject. Those who have been most passionate in urging disarmament have often refused to look unpleasant facts in the face; on the other hand, the government officials responsible for actual negotiations have usually been extremely rigid in their attitudes, tending to become more preoccupied with winning marginal and ephemeral advantages from the negotiations than in making real progress toward the presumed objective. There has also been confusion concerning both the objective and the degree of risk warranted by that objective.

Here we can take up only the last point. One must first ask what degree of arms control is a reasonable or sensible objective. It seems by now abundantly clear that total nuclear disarmament is not a reasonable objective. Violation would be too easy for the Communists, and the risks to the non-violator would be enormous. But it should also be obvious that the kind of bitter, relentless race in nuclear weapons and missiles that has been going on since the end of World War II has its own intrinsic dangers.

* * *

The kind of measures in which we ought to be especially interested are those which could seriously reduce on all sides the dangers of surprise attack. Such a policy would be entirely compatible with our basic national commitment to a strategy of deterrence. The best way to reduce the danger of surprise attack is to reduce on all sides the incentives to such attack, an end which is furthered by promoting measures that enhance deterrent rather than aggressive posture—where the two can be distinguished, which, if one is looking for the chance to do so, is probably pretty often. It also helps greatly to reduce the danger of accidental outbreak of total war if each side takes it upon itself to do the opposite of "keeping the enemy guessing" concerning its pacific intentions. This is accomplished not through reiterated declaration of pacific intent, which is for this purpose a worn and useless tactic, but through finding procedures where each side can assure the other through the latter's own eyes that deliberate attack is not being prepared against him. * * *

Our over-riding interest, for the enhancement of our deterrence posture, is of course in the security of our own retaliatory force. But that does not mean that we especially desire the other side's retaliatory force to be insecure. If the opponent feels insecure, we suffer the hazard of his being more trigger-happy. * * *

Stability is achieved when each nation believes that the strategic advantage of striking first is overshadowed by the tremendous cost of doing so. If, for example, retaliatory weapons are in the future so well protected that it takes more than one missile to destroy an enemy missile, the chances for stability become quite good. Under such circumstances striking first brings no advantage unless one has enormous numerical superiority. But such a situation is the very opposite of the more familiar one where both sides rely wholly or predominately on unprotected aircraft.

Technological progress could, however, push us rapidly towards a position of almost intolerable mutual menace. Unless something is done politically to alter the environment, each side before many years will have thousands of missiles accurately pointed at targets in the other's territory ready to be fired at a moment's notice. Whether or not we call it "push-button" war is a matter of our taste in phraseology, but there is no use in telling ourselves that the time for it is remote. Well before that time arrives, aircraft depending for their safety on being in the air in time will be operating according to so-called "air-borne alert" and "fail-safe" patterns. Nothing which has any promise of obviating or alleviating the tensions of such situations should be overlooked.

4.4 *The Sources of Containment*

Mr. X [George Kennan]

The Sources of Soviet Conduct

The political personality of Soviet power as we know it today is the product of ideology and circumstances: ideology inherited by the present Soviet leaders from the movement in which they had their political origin, and circumstances of the power which they now have exercised for nearly three decades in Russia. There can be few tasks of psychological analysis more difficult than to try to trace the interaction of these two forces and the relative rôle of each in the determination of official Soviet conduct. * * *

[T]remendous emphasis has been placed on the original Communist thesis of a basic antagonism between the capitalist and Socialist worlds. It is clear, from many indications, that this emphasis is not founded in reality. The real facts concerning it have been confused by the existence abroad of genuine resentment provoked by Soviet philosophy and tactics and occasionally by the existence of great centers of military power, notably the Nazi régime in Germany and the Japanese Government of the late 1930's, which did indeed have aggressive designs against the Soviet Union. But there is ample evidence that the stress laid in Moscow on the menace confronting Soviet society from the world outside its borders is founded not in the realities of foreign antagonism but in the necessity of explaining away the maintenance of dictatorial authority at home.

Now the maintenance of this pattern of Soviet power, namely, the pursuit of unlimited authority domestically, accompanied by the cultivation of the semi-myth of implacable foreign hostility, has gone far to shape the actual machinery of Soviet power as we know it today. Internal organs of administration which did not serve this purpose withered on the vine. Organs which did serve this purpose became vastly swollen. The security of Soviet power came to rest on the iron discipline of the Party, on the severity and ubiquity of the secret police, and on the uncompromising economic monopolism of the state. The "organs of suppression," in which the Soviet leaders had sought security from rival forces, became in large measure the masters of those whom they were designed to serve. Today the major part

---

From *Foreign Affairs*, July 1947.

of the structure of Soviet power is committed to the perfection of the dictatorship and to the maintenance of the concept of Russia as in a state of siege, with the enemy lowering beyond the walls. And the millions of human beings who form that part of the structure of power must defend at all costs this concept of Russia's position, for without it they are themselves superfluous.

As things stand today, the rulers can no longer dream of parting with these organs of suppression. The quest for absolute power, pursued now for nearly three decades with a ruthlessness unparalleled (in scope at least) in modern times, has again produced internally, as it did externally, its own reaction. The excesses of the police apparatus have fanned the potential opposition to the régime into something far greater and more dangerous than it could have been before those excesses began.

But least of all can the rulers dispense with the fiction by which the maintenance of dictatorial power has been defended. For this fiction has been canonized in Soviet philosophy by the excesses already committed in its name; and it is now anchored in the Soviet structure of thought by bonds far greater than those of mere ideology.

II

So much for the historical background. What does it spell in terms of the political personality of Soviet power as we know it today?

Of the original ideology, nothing has been officially junked. Belief is maintained in the basic badness of capitalism, in the inevitability of its destruction, in the obligation of the proletariat to assist in that destruction and to take power into its own hands. But stress has come to be laid primarily on those concepts which relate most specifically to the Soviet regime itself: to its position as the sole truly Socialist régime in a dark and misguided world, and to the relationships of power within it.

The first of these concepts is that of the innate antagonism between capitalism and Socialism. We have seen how deeply that concept has become imbedded in foundations of Soviet power. It has profound implications for Russia's conduct as a member of international society. It means that there can never be on Moscow's side any sincere assumption of a community of aims between the Soviet Union and powers which are regarded as capitalist. It must invariably be assumed in Moscow that the aims of the capitalist world are antagonistic to the Soviet régime, and therefore to the interests of the peoples it controls. If the Soviet Government occasionally sets its signature to documents which would indicate the contrary, this is to be regarded as a tactical manoeuvre permissible in dealing with the enemy (who is without honor) and should be taken in the spirit of *caveat emptor*. Basically, the antagonism remains. It is postulated. And from it flow many of the phenomena which we find disturbing in the Kremlin's conduct of foreign policy: the secretiveness, the lack of frankness, the duplicity, the wary suspiciousness, and the basic unfriendliness of purpose. These phenomena are there to stay, for the foreseeable future. There can be variations of degree and of emphasis. When there is something the Russians want from us, one or the other of these features of their policy may be thrust temporarily into the background; and when that happens there will always be Americans who will leap forward with gleeful announcements that "the Russians have changed," and some who will even try to take credit for having brought about such "changes." But we should not be misled by tactical manœuvres. These characteristics of Soviet policy, like the postulate from which they flow, are basic to the internal nature of Soviet power, and will be with us whether in the foreground or the background, until the internal nature of Soviet power is changed.

* * *

These considerations make Soviet diplomacy at once easier and more difficult to deal with than the diplomacy of individual aggressive leaders like Napoleon and Hitler. On the one hand it is more sensitive to contrary force, more ready to yield on individual sectors of the diplomatic front when that force is felt to be too strong, and thus more rational in the logic and rhetoric of power. On the other hand it cannot be easily defeated or discouraged by a single victory on the part of its opponents. And the patient persistence by which it is animated means that it can be effectively countered not by sporadic acts which represent the momentary whims of democratic opinion but only by intelligent long-range policies on the part of Russia's adversaries—policies no less steady in their purpose, and no less variegated and resourceful in their application, than those of the Soviet Union itself.

In these circumstances it is clear that the main element of any United States policy toward the Soviet Union must be that of a long-term, patient but firm and vigilant containment of Russian expansive tendencies. It is important to note, however, that such a policy has nothing to do with outward histrionics: with threats or blustering or superfluous gestures of outward "toughness." While the Kremlin is basically flexible in its reaction to political realities, it is by no means unamenable to considerations of prestige. Like almost any other government, it can be placed by tactless and threatening gestures in a position where it cannot afford to yield even though this might be dictated by its sense of realism. The Russian leaders are keen judges of human psychology, and as such they are highly conscious that loss of temper and of self-control is never a source of strength in political affairs. They are quick to exploit such evidences of weakness. For these reasons, it is a *sine qua non* of successful dealing with Russia that the foreign government in question should remain at all times cool and collected and that its demands on Russian policy should be put forward in such a manner as to leave the way open for a compliance not too detrimental to Russian prestige.

* * *

IV

It is clear that the United States cannot expect in the foreseeable future to enjoy political intimacy with the Soviet régime. It must continue to regard the Soviet Union as a rival, not a partner, in the political arena. It must continue to expect that Soviet policies will reflect no abstract love of peace and stability, no real faith in the possibility of a permanent happy coexistence of the Socialist and capitalist worlds, but rather a cautious, persistent pressure toward the disruption and weakening of all rival influence and rival power.

Balanced against this are the facts that Russia, as opposed to the western world in general, is still by far the weaker party, that Soviet policy is highly flexible, and that Soviet society may well contain deficiencies which will eventually weaken its own total potential. This would of itself warrant the United States entering with reasonable confidence upon a policy of firm containment, designed to confront the Russians with unalterable counter-force at every point where they show signs of encroaching upon the interests of a peaceful and stable world.

But in actuality the possibilities for American policy are by no means limited to holding the line and hoping for the best. It is entirely possible for the United States to influence by its actions the internal developments, both within Russia and throughout the international Communist movement, by which Russian policy is largely determined. This is not only a question of the modest measure of informational activity which this government can conduct in the Soviet Union and elsewhere, although that, too, is important. It is rather a question of the degree to which the United States can create among the peoples of the world generally the impression of a country which knows what it wants, which is coping successfully with the problems of its internal life and with the responsibilities of a World Power, and which has a spiritual vitality capable of holding its own among the major ideological currents of the time. To the extent that such an impression can be created and maintained, the aims of Russian Communism must appear sterile and quixotic, the hopes and enthusiasm of Moscow's supporters must wane, and added strain must be imposed on the Kremlin's foreign policies. For the palsied decrepitude of the capitalist world is the keystone of Communist philosophy. Even the failure of the United States to experience the early economic depression which the ravens of the Red Square have been predicting with such complacent confidence since hostilities ceased would have deep and important repercussions throughout the Communist world.

By the same token, exhibitions of indecision, disunity and internal disintegration within this country have an exhilarating effect on the whole Communist movement. At each evidence of these tendencies, a thrill of hope and excitement goes through the Communist world; a new jauntiness can be noted in the Moscow tread; new groups of foreign supporters climb on to what they can only view as the band wagon of international politics; and Russian pressure increases all along the line in international affairs.

It would be an exaggeration to say that American behavior unassisted and alone could exercise a power of life and death over the Communist movement and bring about the early fall of Soviet power in Russia. But the United States has it in its power to increase enormously the strains under which Soviet policy must operate, to force upon the Kremlin a far greater degree of moderation and circumspection than it has had to observe in recent years, and in this way to promote tendencies which must eventually find their outlet in either the break-up or the gradual mellowing of Soviet power. For no mystical, Messianic movement—and particularly not that of the Kremlin—can face frustration indefinitely without eventually adjusting itself in one way or another to the logic of that state of affairs.

Thus the decision will really fall in large measure in this country itself. The issue of Soviet-American relations is in essence a test of the over-all worth of the United States as a nation among nations. To avoid destruction the United States need only measure up to its own best traditions and prove itself worthy of preservation as a great nation.

Surely, there was never a fairer test of national quality than this. In the light of these circumstances, the thoughtful observer of Russian-American relations will find no cause for complaint in the Kremlin's challenge to American society. He will rather experience a certain gratitude to a Providence which, by providing the American people with this implacable challenge, has made their entire security as a nation dependent on their pulling themselves together and accepting the responsibilities of moral and political leadership that history plainly intended them to bear.

5 *The Cold War Context: Lessons and Legacies*

The 1960s, '70s, and '80s were turbulent decades for the United States. Foreign policy was not the only reason—the civil rights movement, the counterculture, economic change, and other forces and factors also were at work. But the setbacks, shifts, and shocks endured by American foreign policy clearly were major factors.

The Vietnam War was the most profound setback American foreign policy had suffered since the beginning of the Cold War, if not in its entire history. Many saw it as the first war the United States ever had lost. The reasons why were hotly debated—and still are. But the profundity of the loss as it affected both foreign policy strategy and foreign policy politics was undeniable.

This case study, *Americanizing the Vietnam War*, examines the key decisions in 1965 by President Lyndon B. Johnson and his foreign policy advisers to first commit large numbers of U.S. ground troops to Vietnam. It traces U.S. involvement in Vietnam beginning in the 1950s and through the early 1960s and provides other important background. The focus, though, is on the seminal ground troops decisions, and the who, why, what, and how of the decision process and strategy.

Southeast Asia during the Vietnam War

★ ★ ★
KEY PLAYERS

United States
President Lyndon B. Johnson
Robert S. McNamara, Secretary of Defense
Dean Rusk, Secretary of State
McGeorge Bundy, National Security Adviser
General Earle G. Wheeler, Chairman, Joint Chiefs of Staff
General William Westmoreland, Commander, U.S. troops in Vietnam
George W. Ball, Under Secretary of State
William P. Bundy, Assistant Secretary of State for Asian Affairs
Maxwell D. Taylor, Chairman, Joint Chiefs of Staff, and later U.S.
    Ambassador to South Vietnam
John McNaughton, Assistant Secretary of Defense for Asian Affairs

South Vietnam
Ngo Dinh Diem, President (1955–63)
General Nguyen Khanh, coup leader and President (1964)

North Vietnam
Ho Chi Minh, President and Communist Party leader

BACKGROUND

KEY DATES AND EVENTS

1883   France establishes colonial rule over Vietnam and most of the rest of Southeast Asia, as "French Indochina."

1940   Japan occupies Indochina during World War II.

1941   Ho Chi Minh, nationalist and Communist leader, establishes the Vietminh to fight both the French and the Japanese.

1945   Japan defeated in World War II. Ho declares the independence of Vietnam, but France reasserts its colonial rule. War ensues.

1950   Korean War breaks out. In this context President Truman grants U.S. military aid to French war effort in Vietnam.

1954   Battle of Dienbienphu at which the French are defeated. President Eisenhower considers intervention to aid the French but decides against it.

       Geneva peace conference ends French colonial rule and provides for temporary division between North and South Vietnam, pending nationwide elections; Ho Chi Minh is leader of North Vietnam, Ngo Dinh Diem leader of South Vietnam.

1955   Elections not held, Geneva accords renounced; beginning of U.S. direct involvement in Vietnam.

Cold War Lessons and Legacies Case Study

Americanizing the Vietnam War

In July 1965 President Lyndon B. Johnson completed the process of committing the United States to war in Vietnam. His presidential part in the process had begun three days after the assassination of John F. Kennedy, which followed by three weeks the murder of the South Vietnamese leader, Ngo Dinh Diem. Almost at once Johnson committed himself to far more than his predecessor had bargained for. By late 1963 South Vietnam was entering a period of unremitting instability and vulnerability, periodically seeming about to collapse. In December 1963 the Secretary of Defense, Robert McNamara, returned from a tour of South Vietnam and reported to LBJ: "The situation is very disturbing. Current trends, unless reversed in the next 2–3 months, will lead to neutralization at best and more likely to a Communist-controlled state."[1] Progressively, over the next eighteen months, Johnson heard such warnings. He responded incrementally with increased aid until he crossed the line from "limited partnership" to an Americanized war, accepting for his troops the task of fighting and defeating communist attacks in South Vietnam. This he did without fully acknowledging the change to Congress or public. He thereby launched at once a long war and a credibility gap; three years later these forced him from office.

The moves to war are summarized below.

US and Vietnam in the 1950s

* * * South Vietnam was created in 1954 in the wake of the disastrous attempt by France to retain control of "French Indochina" despite the proclamation from Hanoi of Vietnamese independence in 1945. Franklin Roo-

This case was written by Professor Richard E. Neustadt from a first draft by Philip Bennett under the supervision of Professors Neustadt and May for use at the John F. Kennedy School of Government. Work on this case was made possible by a grant from the National Endowment for the Humanities.

sevelt, leery of the French since their defeat in 1940 and their subsequent abandonment of Indochina to Japan, had intended not to let them back when World War II should end. Truman, however, knowing nothing of this, did not bar their return after Japan's departure. Thereafter, he more or less supported Paris in exchange for French cooperation on the Marshall Plan and NATO.

* * *

Between 1950 and 1954 Washington had supported the French effort in Vietnam with ever-increasing outlays, bearing 40 percent of the war's cost by the end of the Truman administration. This was contemporaneous with the Korean War and the military build-up of NATO. US support had its theoretical base in the "domino theory," the belief that communism, if successful anywhere in Southeast Asia, would leap national boundaries in succession. By light of events in China as well as Korea, and by analogy with Eastern Europe, this had come to be a well-established tenet of American foreign policy. President Eisenhower and his Secretary of State, John Foster Dulles, were vocal adherents of the domino theory, considering the nationalist and Communist leader Ho Chi Minh the conscious instrument of a Sino-Soviet bloc contained on other fronts. Seeing "International Communism" as a unity, they feared that the loss of Indochina to Ho's forces could presage hard blows against a dozen "Free-World" governments elsewhere in Asia.

Eisenhower and his advisers contemplated American military intervention in Vietnam both before and after Dien Bien Phu, but rejected the notion when it became clear that France was not willing to grant independence to the states of Indochina as long as French troops were dying on Vietnamese soil. Besides, in the face of surging anti-war sentiment at home, France would not promise to stay the course until communist forces were crushed. Moreover, Britain, still a nominal world power, refused to join in making any intervention a united effort—a particularly important precondition for Eisenhower and prerequisite, he knew, to bipartisan support in Congress.

Once the Geneva Accord of 1954 brought the immediate military crisis to an end and took France out of play as an Asian colonial power, Eisenhower and Dulles sought to bring American resources and know-how to bear in helping the new southern entity grow into a viable, non-communist country capable of standing as the "cornerstone of the Free World in Southeast Asia."[2]

Diem was the immediate beneficiary of this American interest. A devout Catholic, nationalist, and zealous anti-communist, Diem had gained a following among American leaders while briefly resident in the United States. After his selection as Premier in 1954, his ability to hold on—which exceeded early estimates—won him key American support, despite inefficiency, charges of corruption, and attempted coups against him. As early as

1955, American officials in Saigon were levying harsh criticism against Diem's authoritarian regime, recommending that American aid swing to the opposition. But beneath an overlay of French institutions and a French-speaking elite, the country was a mystery to virtually all Americans. Eisenhower and his advisers could see no stable replacement for Diem, so they stuck with him, prodding and cajoling. By 1961 the Diem regime ranked fifth among recipients of American foreign aid and the American diplomatic mission in Saigon was the largest in the world.[3]

In the late 1950s communist insurgents in South Vietnam known as Viet Cong harassed Diem's countryside; during 1960 a veritable guerrilla war broke out. In addition to receiving direct aid from North Vietnam, the Viet Cong attracted Southerners, non-communists among them, who had suffered from Diem's general anti-communist controls: interference with elections, tight press censorship, restrictions on assembly, arrests without trial, and others. Perhaps inevitably, Diem's government expanded its reprisals against communists to dissidents of other sorts, warming their relations with the Viet Cong while diminishing the base for his own leadership.[4] In addition, discontent among the peasants, disappointed at results of promised land reform, had led by 1960 to a further warming of the climate for the Viet Cong. Mixing appeals with intimidation, the insurgents intensified their efforts to separate the Diem regime from its rural constituency and to profit from the disaffection elsewhere in the system.

The Kennedy Years

Increasing instability in South Vietnam did not at once attract much notice from the Kennedy administration. Initially, the Kennedy regime had trained its sights on meeting communist challenges elsewhere: primarily in Cuba, Berlin, and North Vietnam's neighbor, Laos. Despite widespread acceptance of the domino theory and a voiced enthusiasm for resisting Soviet-backed communist expansion, South Vietnam ranked relatively low on the initial list of Kennedy's most pressing problems abroad.[5] But the Bay of Pigs affair in Cuba, then a stalemate in Berlin (dramatized by the unchallenged Wall), and a decision to negotiate for neutralization in Laos, left the administration looking for a likely place in which to show its firmness to Soviet Premier Khrushchev (who seemed to take Kennedy lightly). Cuba had been bungled, Berlin was a standoff, and landlocked Laos offered a poor target for US efforts—but Vietnam was open to the sea, where Americans moved at will.

By the fall of 1961 the growing Vietnam conflict was identified as a brush fire on the New Frontier [the Kennedy administration's New Deal–like name]. Kennedy's advisers debated how best to put it out. General Maxwell Taylor, Kennedy's own military adviser soon to become chairman of the Joint Chiefs of Staff, and Walt Whitman Rostow, a White House aide soon to be spun off to the State Department, returned from a survey late in 1961 to recommend direct American action, including the use of American troops, contingent on Saigon reforms. Others, like Secretary of State Dean Rusk, cited lack of popular support for the Diem regime and cautioned against a "major additional commitment [of] American prestige to a losing horse."[6] Kennedy chose a middle road. The United States would enter into "limited partnership" with the Diem regime: American presence in Vietnam would be substantially increased, but its role would be limited to training and non-combat support for Vietnamese troops; meanwhile, pressure would be put on Diem for reforms to improve the national morale and strengthen the war effort. (This did not, however, extend to making aid contingent on such reforms.) By combining a hard line against Ho with nominal toughness toward Diem, Kennedy hoped to tamp the conflict down after a moderate American involvement—which excluded combat troops. Those he ruled out.[7]

For a year and a half this seemed to work, at least from the distance of Washington. Thereafter appearances altered. In 1962 and 1963 encouraging statistics and reports were sent from Saigon. For many months the level of perceived problems was low, both at the Pentagon and in the media. Accordingly, it was low at the White House. Confronted by more pressing matters, Kennedy gave South Vietnam only occasional attention. By late spring 1963, however, it became apparent even in Washington that "limited partnership" was achieving very limited results. American military assistance to South Vietnam had doubled in 1961 and 1962; the number of American "advisers" there had increased from 692 when Kennedy took office to almost 16,000. Still, Diem proved unable to solve his own political problems or to organize the Army of the Republic of Vietnam (ARVN) into an effective fighting unit. Moreover, plans to block the source of the insurgency by relocating portions of the peasantry into "strategic hamlets" had been a spectacular failure. In the countryside thousands of peasants had been forcibly removed from their homes to no avail. Guerrillas flourished. Although American advisers remained generally optimistic, they were uncertain which strategy would best help the ARVN beat the Viet Cong back and ultimately win.

Then, in May 1963, Diem's repression of a Buddhist uprising in Saigon, followed by continued, spectacular, often televised unrest during the summer, prompted some American officials to consider him a greater obstacle to victory than the Viet Cong. American public reaction was also severe, spurred by the callous comments of Diem's sister-in-law, then touring the United States. When a group of ARVN officers approached the American Embassy with plans for a coup against Diem, members of the Kennedy administration, including the President himself, gave a measure of approval (over military opposition). The United States would not take part in any attempted coup d'etat, but it would not deny recognition or aid to the government that emerged. Reviewing these instructions Kennedy expressed displeasure, but he did not withdraw them. In any event, the coup never materialized, and JFK turned instead to try to force reforms on Diem by cutting economic aid. This signal of Washington's dissatisfaction was read closely in Saigon. On November 1 a different set of officers staged a successful coup and killed Diem in the process, to Kennedy's horror. Three weeks later, Kennedy was assassinated.

The American commitments made to Diem since 1954 were automatically transferred to his successors. There are signs that Kennedy himself, his influential brother Robert, and his personal adviser Theodore Sorensen were shocked by Diem's demise into some thoughts of reassessment. But by December 1963 these three had vanished from the foreign-policy inner circle.

New President—Growing Crisis

Lyndon Johnson confronted a situation in Vietnam more imminently threatening than any faced by either Kennedy or Eisenhower. Although, as Vice President, Johnson had personally opposed Diem's ouster, Kennedy's acquiescence seemed to obligate his successor to ensure survival for the government eventuating from the coup. But the stable coalition some Americans had envisioned from a military takeover failed to develop. In late January 1964 a group of young military officers, led by General Nguyen Khanh, overthrew the ineffectual junta that had replaced Diem, becoming only the most influential of many rival factions vying for control of the country. South Vietnam was torn by discontent. As putting down strikes and demonstrations became the primary occupation of the government, the prosecution of the war almost halted. Without a strong, united government behind it, the ARVN was increasingly vulnerable to organized assaults from the Viet Cong. American intelligence warned Johnson that unless the Khanh government rose to the challenge immediately, South Vietnam had "at best, an even chance of withstanding the insurgency menace during the next few weeks or months."[8]

The President was faced with a cruel choice. If Khanh failed, Johnson could let South Vietnam go neutralist or communist or both in turn; alternatively he could intervene directly, taking the United States to war.[9] In 1964 LBJ was willing neither to sanction the first nor to do the second, so he refused to make the choice. Despite the pessimism of advisers—and despite Khanh's fall—he stuck to that refusal for more than a year.

During 1964 Johnson hoped to complete an effective presidential transition, tactfully guiding the nation, binding wounds, healing scars, "let us continue"—with concrete accomplishments—while charting his own path to election in November. When it came to domestic tasks like these, no one could have been better qualified than LBJ. During a quarter century in Congress he had become legendary as a skilled political entrepreneur. Elected to the House of Representatives in 1936, he had been an enthusiast for the New Deal of his personal hero, Franklin Roosevelt. In 1948 Johnson moved to the Senate; within five years he was Democratic leader. In the Senate he developed renowned powers of persuasion, becoming the most powerful majority leader in a generation. As President he was eager to apply his legislative skills to a program of social reform outshining Roosevelt's. When Johnson was elected to the presidency by a landslide in November 1964, he moved confidently and swiftly to mobilize support for legislation launching his pledged "Great Society." That had been his dominant objective through the year.

* * *

LBJ was the first President to enter office facing nomination and election during his initial year. This seemed to him no time to either "lose" a country or to "start" a war. In 1964 he temporized, doing nothing on Vietnam that he could put off. Meanwhile, his inherited advisers planned and worried.

Chief among Johnson's advisers were the Secretaries of Defense and State. Defense Secretary McNamara became, for a time, especially close. A systematic analyst, yet fast on his feet, full of energy and confidence, loyal to a fault, the former president of the Ford Motor Company was, according to Johnson, "invaluable."[10] In 1961 McNamara had played a significant part in formulating the increased American commitment to Saigon. In 1964 he saw himself as duty-bound to help Johnson make good on it. So did his soft-spoken and more cautious colleague, Secretary of State Dean Rusk. Rusk knew something of East Asia, having been an Army officer in Burma during World War II and Truman's Assistant Secretary of State for the Far East during the Korean War. Rusk knew the arguments against American participation in another land war on the Asian mainland, and in 1961 had expressed doubts about increased involvement in Vietnam. However, once American prestige was committed, Rusk took success as mandatory and became South Vietnam's unwavering supporter. Rusk saw its problems as more military than political; accordingly he tended to defer to Pentagon opinion.[11] In the fall of 1950 Rusk had underestimated the potential of the Chinese communists: in 1964, and after, he articulated China's menace to the peace of all its smaller Asian neighbors. The Secretary of State was no less dutiful than was his colleague at Defense; and unlike McNamara, Rusk received more deference from Johnson than from Kennedy.

In 1964 the international situation, as these advisers saw it, offered compelling arguments for a strong showing by the United States in Southeast Asia. State and Defense officials were concerned by what they saw as growing instability throughout the Third World where, American intelligence warned, "revolution and disorder" were becoming "epidemic." Anti-American rioting in Panama suggested an unravelling of ties between the United States and parts of Latin America, possibly opening opportunities for Cuba's Fidel Castro. Southeast Asia seemed in dire disarray. The Viet Cong made daily advances. Cambodia's Prince Sihanouk rebuffed American aid and declared his neutrality in the Vietnam conflict. Indonesia had been drawing closer to Communist China (PRC) and now threatened the Western government of Malaysia. Washington officials grew especially concerned that a belligerent PRC would exploit the turmoil in its neighborhood and move to control all the Southeast Asian states. Fear of Chinese intervention matched desire to provide the Soviets a clear sign of American resolve; together these seemed to raise the stakes in Vietnam.[12] Only a little was known of the Sino-Soviet split, by hindsight a dominant fact, but to some it suggested *increased* Chinese aggressiveness.

During the early months of 1964, American officials frequently addressed the international implications of the conflict in Vietnam. Rusk wrote in the *State Department Bulletin* that to withdraw from Vietnam "would mean not only grievous losses to the free world in Southeast and Southern Asia but a drastic loss of confidence in the will and capacity of the free world to oppose aggression."[13] Rusk now saw Vietnam as a critical turning point in the struggle to arrest communist expansionism. He wrote, "If Hanoi and Peiping prevail in Vietnam in this key test of the new Communist tactics of 'wars of national liberation,' then the Communists will use this technique with growing frequency elsewhere in Asia, Africa and Latin America."[14] In private, Rusk asserted to a French diplomat that whether the United States was meeting communist advances in Europe, Latin America, or Southeast Asia, it was "all part of the same struggle."[15]

The most definitive official statement at this time of Saigon's importance to the United States was National Security Action Memorandum (NSAM) 288. Approved by Johnson early in 1964, it expounded the domino theory.

> We seek an independent and non-Communist South Vietnam. . . .

> Unless we can achieve this objective in South Vietnam, almost all of Southeast Asia will probably fall under Communist dominance (all of Vietnam, Laos, and Cambodia), accommodate to Communism so as to remove effective U.S. and anti-Communist influence (Burma), or fall under the domination of forces not now explicitly Communist but likely to become so (Indochina taking over Malaysia). Thailand might hold for a period without help, but would be under great pressure. Even the Philippines would become shaky, and the threat to India on the West, Australia and New Zealand to the South, and Taiwan, Korea, and Japan to the North and East would be greatly increased.[16]

And reinforcing Rusk, the "impact of a Communist South Vietnam [would be felt] not only in Asia, but in the rest of the world, where the South Vietnam conflict is regarded as a test case of U.S. capacity to help a nation meet a Communist 'war of liberation.' "[17]

Nevertheless, "the Vietnamese must win their own fight," and the United States must aid its ally "by means short of the unqualified use of U.S. combat forces."[18] NSAM 288's specific recommendations concentrated on strengthening the internal situation in South Vietnam, boosting the Khanh regime and the ARVN with increased material assistance, and still more American training.

A major criticism of NSAM 288 came from the Joint Chiefs of Staff (JCS). They felt it did not authorize the military the means to achieve its goals. In a memorandum to their civilian colleagues, the JSC doubted that "the recommended program in itself will be sufficient to turn the tide against the Viet Cong in SVN [South Vietnam] without positive [military] action . . . against the Hanoi government at an early date."[19] Urging their addressees to "put aside many of the self-imposed restrictions which now limit our efforts" and to "undertake a much higher level of activity," the JCS argued,

> In a broader sense, the failure of our program in South Vietnam would have heavy influence on the judgment of Burma, India, Indonesia, Malaysia, Japan, Taiwan, the Republic of Korea, and the Republic of the Philippines with respect to U.S. durability, resolution, and trustworthiness. Finally, this being the first real test of our determination to defeat the Communist wars of national liberation formula, it is not unreasonable to conclude that there would be a corresponding unfavorable effect upon our image in Africa and in Latin America.[20]

But in 1964 Johnson would not sanction anything that made the war overtly Washington's instead of Saigon's. He emphatically agreed that Vietnam was a big test of American resolve to prevent communist aggression, but he hoped to prove it by again increasing economic and advisory support for ARVN. He suspected that a demonstration of his military power might cause hostile international reactions.[21] He foresaw that US troops in combat could cost him credit, politically, at home. And he agreed with NcNamara that introduction of American troops would have an "adverse psychological impact" on the South Vietnamese, undercutting their initiative while encouraging the Khanh regime to shove its massive domestic burden onto American shoulders. Johnson, therefore, set aside the criticism from the chiefs.[22]

The President summed up his policy for the election year: "to do more of the same and to do it more efficiently and effectively."[23] He supported McNamara's recommendation to pay for augmentation of South Vietnam's military and civilian services. He also instructed American advisers to develop plans to coordinate increased counterinsurgency and the pacification operations in the South.[24] A new "clear and hold" strategy was designed to enable the South Vietnamese Army to systematically recover insurgent areas and replace the Viet Cong with effective government. Washington increased the number of American advisers from 16,300 to 23,000 and allocated an additional $50 million to support the new efforts.[25] To give vitality to these initiatives, General William Westmoreland, a tough veteran of World War II and Korea, was promoted from deputy to commander of US military forces in Vietnam. That April Johnson cabled Ambassador Henry Cabot Lodge, "As far as I'm concerned, you must have whatever you need to help the Vietnamese do the job, and I assure you that I will act at once to eliminate obstacles or restraints wherever they appear."[26] In midsummer 1964, seeking still more vitality, Johnson replaced Lodge with JCS Chairman Taylor.

Success for American policy as it then stood depended on the ability of Khanh's regime to secure loyalty and support internally. Khanh responded warmly to American encouragement, working up ambitious plans to bring his government to the communities. But many of his programs never went beyond the planning stage. South Vietnam's "National Mobilization Plan" fell behind schedule almost immediately. American financial assistance failed to filter down to the local level, where it was most needed. From late spring into July student unrest at Hué, Danang, and Saigon combined with renewed fighting between Catholic and Buddhist political sects to increase domestic instability. In the countryside the Viet Cong showed themselves more firmly entrenched than had been anticipated.[27] Meanwhile, the ARVN desertion rate climbed. In July American opposition to a planned coup barely saved the Khanh regime. In August Ambassador Taylor reported, "The best thing that can be said about the Khanh government is that it has lasted six months and has about a 50-50 chance of lasting out the year. . . ."[28]

The Tonkin Gulf Resolution

By summer 1964 the remedies prescribed in NSAM 288 were all proving inadequate. Johnson's advisers began to consider more forceful measures to arrest Saigon's decline. General Khanh promoted his own solution: his army would "march North," undoing the Viet Cong by dealing with their North Vietnamese sponsors.[29] Although Ambassador Taylor warned Khanh that he would find no support in Washington for such a venture, many officials there began, like Khanh, to look North for a key of some sort to Saigon's stability and progress in the war.

As early as May the Joint Chiefs had urged "air strikes against the North" in order to "help convince NVN [North Vietnam] . . . that it is in its own self-interest to desist from its aggressive policies."[30] The chiefs were initially alone among Johnson's close advisers to propose overt military pressure on the North, but they led a gradual drift of opinion. Throughout the spring and summer State and Defense analysts engaged in long planning sessions to draw up contingency programs for graduated overt action. William P. Bundy, former assistant secretary of defense and now assistant secretary of state, prepared a paper on how to secure a congressional resolution in support of such action.[31] Various "scenarios" were worked out whereby Johnson, after securing congressional approval, would authorize air strikes against specific, North Vietnamese targets. Still, Rusk and McNamara, joined by LBJ, opposed all such scenarios; they remained concerned by weakness in the Saigon regime, and they, especially Johnson, also thought about reactions from Americans on numbers of domestic fronts, not least the election.

But in early August 1964 a series of unexpected incidents prompted the administration to make use of some of its previous planning. On the morning of August 1 the destroyer USS *Maddox* was intercepted and attacked unsuccessfully by three North Vietnamese torpedo boats while it was conducting electronic espionage in the Gulf of Tonkin off the coast of North Vietnam. * * *

                                   * * *

Immediately after the Tonkin Gulf incidents, LBJ sought passage of a congressional resolution granting him authority to take "all necessary measures to repel any armed attack against the forces of the United States and to prevent further aggression."[32] This was not then intended to give Johnson a blank check to escalate the war in any way he subsequently chose, and Congress did not take it so. Like the retaliatory strikes, it was designed primarily to demonstrate to North Vietnam (and the Chinese and Russians) that Washington was certain to support its words with actions.[33] Johnson believed firmly that Hanoi and the others needed such a demonstration. The day after the second attack (or whatever it was) in the Gulf of Tonkin, he offered an analogy drawn from the rise of Nazism in the 1930s to explain the importance of keeping North Vietnam firmly in check. "Aggression— deliberate, willful and systematic aggression—has unmasked its face to the entire world," the President declared to an audience at Syracuse University. "The world remembers—the world must never forget—that aggression unchallenged is aggression unleashed."[34]

Congress remembered, or at least concurred. Briefed on the proposed resolution the evening of August 4, the leadership lined up behind the President. The "Tonkin Gulf Resolution" went through Congress in two days, voted by the Senate 88 to 2 and winning unanimous approval in the House, August 7. Public opinion also rallied to the President. A Louis Harris survey taken before the raids of August 5 showed 58 percent disagreement with Johnson's handling of Vietnam ("hawks" and "doves" combined); now 72 percent approved.[35]

During those months Johnson did not sanction additional reprisals or attacks against North Vietnam. But the internal political stability of South Vietnam sank to new lows. Washington watched anxiously to see if Saigon could survive another battle with itself. In August Khanh was deposed after huge demonstrations when, in the wake of the Tonkin Gulf raids, he attempted to assume dictatorial powers. His resignation was followed by further rioting and near anarchy in Saigon. Buddhist and Catholic sects erupted into open warfare. While a civilian government labored to clear a path through the debris of the Khanh regime, the Viet Cong continued to operate virtually undisturbed. In October American intelligence reported that troop infiltration from North Vietnam was steadily increasing.

While the disarray in South Vietnam continued, the American election approached. Campaigning against bellicose proposals from his Republican opponent, Barry Goldwater—who had been nailed to the wall for brandishing nuclear weapons—Johnson hailed the virtues of a moderate approach. "We seek no wider war," he said repeatedly in speeches, and "let Asian boys fight Asians."[36] Meanwhile Washington officialdom, remote from the campaign, neared a consensus on the need for limited air strikes against North Vietnam.

In November 1964 Johnson was elected with the largest popular majority a candidate for President had ever won. The sweep produced as a bonus more than forty additional House Democrats, diminishing the power of the old Republican-Southern Democratic coalition and paving the way for the Great Society. The Senate gained more Democrats as well, including the late President's brother, Robert Kennedy, the former Attorney General. In the previous administration RFK had been intimate with McNamara and Taylor, cold to LBJ; Johnson now evidently feared that the freshman senator from New York might rise and charge betrayal of his brother if Saigon should fall.

Inching Toward Escalation

Immediately after the election a National Security Council Working Group on South Vietnam and Southeast Asia, composed of representatives from State, Defense, the Joint Chiefs of Staff, and the Central Intelligence Agency, convened to draw up alternative courses of action for consideration by the President and his key advisers. With the election out of the way, the group anticipated major policy decisions by the end of the month. In this they underestimated LBJ's reluctance to erase the limits set by NSAM 288. His speeches had been more than campaign rhetoric to him.

Before the group began its work, its chairman, William Bundy, noted, "We believe it is essential to the interests of the free world that South Vietnam not be permitted to fall under communist control."[37] The Working Group restated three basic factors which it felt underscored the American commitment to South Vietnam:

a. The general principle of helping countries that try to defend their own freedom against communist subversion and attack.
b. The specific consequences of communist control of South Vietnam and Laos for the security of, successively, Cambodia, Thailand (most seriously), Malaysia, and the Philippines—and resultant increases in the threat to India and . . . to [other nations in Asia].
c. South Vietnam, and to a lesser extent, Laos, as test cases of communist "wars of national liberation" world-wide.[38]

The Working Group agreed that a demonstration of American military power had become a necessary element of these objectives. Ironically, unchecked deterioration of the government of South Vietnam had reinforced

American officialdom's belief that the United States must (could) prevent Saigon's collapse. Opinion was mixed concerning the purpose and effects of bombing strikes. The Joint Chiefs of Staff emphasized that a serious US effort would close North Vietnamese infiltration routes to the South and eventually break the will of the North to support the Viet Cong. Civilians from State and Defense, many of them influenced by intelligence reports that minimized effects of bombing North Vietnam on the insurgents in the South, were not as sanguine; still, they hoped that at the very least the bombing would boost government morale in Saigon, affording it a "breathing spell and opportunity to improve."[39]

Members of the Working Group were also split over the scope, timing, and intensity of American air strikes. Reflecting its differences, the group developed three alternative proposals for American action: Option A called for the continuation of current US policy, including "tit-for-tat" reprisals in response to specific North Vietnamese provocation. Option B offered a systematic program of rapidly escalated military pressure on the North until its leaders ceased to support the insurgents—a plan otherwise known as the "fast/full squeeze." Option C, or "progressive squeeze-and-talk," consisted of gradually escalating attacks accompanied by diplomatic moves aimed at enticing Hanoi into negotiating a withdrawal.

✳ ✳ ✳

Group Chairman Bundy, although an advocate of Option C, tempered his endorsement with lessons he drew from US experience in the Korean War. He cautioned his colleagues that limited escalation might not be sufficient to achieve Washington's objectives in South Vietnam, especially if it caused the Chinese communists to intervene in defense of their neighbor.

> We cannot guarantee to maintain a non-Communist South Vietnam short of committing ourselves to whatever degree of military action would be required to defeat North Vietnam and probably Communist China militarily. Such a commitment would involve high risks of a major conflict in Asia, which could not be confined to air and naval action but would almost inevitably involve a Korean-scale ground action and possibly even the use of nuclear weapons at some point.[40]

William Bundy's use of the Korean War as a source of lessons for US involvement in South Vietnam was not exceptional. Drawing analogies between the two conflicts was so pervasive that the Defense Department representative, Assistant Secretary John T. McNaughton, referred to a "Korea syndrome" among policy planners.[41] For Bundy, the Korean example counseled against entering into another ground war in Asia. It also reminded him that a graduated program could expose the administration to charges of prolonging the war. He wrote,

This course of action is inherently likely to stretch out and be subject to major pressures both within the U.S. and internationally. As we saw in Korea, an "in-between" course of action will always arouse a school of thought that believes things should be tackled quickly and conclusively. On the other side, the continuation of military action and a reasonably firm posture will arouse sharp criticism in other political quarters.[42]

In a concurrent memorandum to Rusk, McNamara, and other presidential advisers, Bundy wondered whether the "slow squeeze" could be carried out "under the klieg lights of democracy." He commented, "This is a key point. . . . The parallel to Korea in 1951–53 is forbidding."[43]

The Joint Chiefs of Staff found the Korean War analogy no more compelling than that of the French-Indochina War. The latter they dismissed out of hand. Americans were not colonialists (and besides had beaten Hitler, and also built the Panama Canal). As advocates of "fast/full squeeze," the JCS were impatient with arguments about alternatives. Rebutting Bundy's assertion that the war might eventually call for Korean-scale ground action, a JCS critic noted,

> Our first objective is to cause the DRV [North Vietnam] to terminate support of the SEA [Southeast Asian] insurgencies. . . . To achieve this objective does not necessarily require that we "defeat North Vietnam," and it almost certainly does not require that we defeat Communist China. Hence our commitment to SVN does not involve a high probability . . . of a major conflict in Southeast Asia. . . . Certainly, no responsible person proposes to go about such a war, if it should occur on a basis remotely resembling Korea. "Possibly even the use of nuclear weapons at some point" is of course why we spend billions to have them.[44]

The disagreement between William Bundy and the JCS illustrates but one of several ways in which Korea, the most recent American war, was invoked during policy debates in 1964. While many members of the administration recalled prosecution of the Korean War with trepidation, they had great admiration for President Truman's decision to send American troops to South Korea in 1950. Truman had acted resolutely to meet a communist challenge, moving without hesitation to oppose aggression. Johnson administration men felt keenly a responsibility to do the same. During the summer of 1964 President Johnson declared, "The challenge that we face in southeast Asia today is the same challenge that we faced with courage and that we have met with strength in Greece and Turkey, in Berlin and Korea."[45] * * *

* * *

Some weeks earlier in a memorandum to Rusk, McNamara, and National Security Adviser McGeorge Bundy (William's brother), Under Secretary of State George Ball had explicitly attacked Korea as an analogue. "South Vietnam is not Korea," Ball wrote "and in making fundamental decisions it would be a mistake for us to rely too heavily on the Korean analogy."[46] Ball included an outline of points distinguishing South Vietnam from Korea, and argued that the *lack* of similarity sharpened risks of *failure* in Vietnam.[47] But Ball had become a leading critic of American involvement in Vietnam. His strictures on Korea simply reinforced his criticism. It was not welcomed by his colleagues and his memorandum did not reach Johnson until January. By then Ball had been labeled "devil's advocate" and was treated accordingly.

As a participant in the post-election discussions of late 1964 Ball was heavily outnumbered. Of the three alternatives proposed by the Working Group, he favored Option A, or the continuation of present US policy— not a strong position under the circumstances. (In private talks with the President, Ball forbore to press the logic of his argument to the point of withdrawal.) Option B, the "fast/full squeeze" was urged by the new chairman of the Joint Chiefs of Staff, General Earle Wheeler. Option C, the "progressive squeeze and talk," found support from McNamara, McNaughton, Rusk, and both Bundys. McNamara and McGeorge Bundy advocated a "firm C" whereas the other three wanted a more restrained, incremental approach.[48]

Among these options Johnson himself indicated on December 1, 1964, that he preferred a compromise between the two Option C approaches. This consisted of a two-phase plan of gradually escalating bombing attacks. Phase One, designed to last thirty days, consisted of limited air raids on Laotian infiltration routes, with a contingency for reprisals against North Vietnam in the event of any major Viet Cong action in the South.[49] It was hoped that this period of limited bombing would encourage the government of South Vietnam to increase efforts toward self-improvement, as well as serve as a foreshadow of things to come if Hanoi did not relent. Once Saigon had overcome its internal disarray the United States would embark on Phase Two, a large-scale air offensive that would

> at first be limited to infiltration targets south of the 19th Parallel, but would gradually work northward, and could eventually encompass all major military-related targets, aerial mining of ports, and a naval blockade, with the weight and tempo of the action being adjusted to the situation as it developed.[50]

Johnson, in short, even after his election, preferred to do as little, and to move as slowly, as he could. (Choosing to do nothing was for him a non-starter.) Having made that preference known he stalled final decisions for two months.

The delay had much—or maybe everything—to do with the chaotic state of the Saigon regime. In an early December 1964 meeting with key advisers including Ambassador Taylor, Johnson gave conditional approval to Phase One operations, but he forbade execution until there was a government in South Vietnam sufficiently stable to withstand the pressure if Hanoi should unleash its regular troops. A Viet Cong attack on an American officers' post in Saigon on Christmas Eve, killing two and wounding thirty-eight, did not persuade Johnson to order reprisals. Taylor was instructed to return to Saigon and convince the civilian leadership to "pull itself together."⁵¹ But in late January 1965 his efforts were defeated: the Vietnam Armed Forces Council, led by Vice Air Marshall Nguyen Cao Ky and General Nguyen Chanh Thieu, ousted the civilian leadership and re-established military control.

Taylor was outraged, as were many South Vietnamese citizens who took to the streets in opposition to the military takeover. Buddhist leaders, cool toward the war and suspicious of American complicity in the coup, refused to acknowledge the new government and initiated a new round of protests. In late January, 5,000 South Vietnamese students attacked the United States Information Service Library in Hué. Meanwhile, the South Vietnamese Army suffered a pair of disastrous defeats at the hands of the Viet Cong, losing two battalions in late December and early January. More ominously, intelligence reports brought evidence that North Vietnamese regulars were on their way South. As rumors spread that a main-force offensive against South Vietnam was imminent, Taylor warned Washington, "To take no positive action now is to accept defeat in the fairly near future."⁵²

Rolling Thunder

The rumblings from the North stirred Johnson from his hedged position. Taylor and McGeorge Bundy feared that the new South Vietnamese government, faced with an invasion from the North, might consider secret, unilateral negotiations with Hanoi, resulting in the neutralization of the South and then the communization of all Vietnam, distressingly soon.⁵³ Bundy prepared a paper for Rusk and Johnson in which he argued that although limited American bombing might have neglible effect on the outcome of the war, it would have "at least a faint hope of really improving the [South] Vietnamese situation." Continuation of current policies could "only lead to disastrous defeat."⁵⁴ McNaughton agreed, pointing out that the United States could make the best of a bad situation and salvage its international prestige, but only if it "kept slugging away" and did not concede to the communists.⁵⁵

On January 27, 1965, McNaughton and McNamara recommended that the United States seize the next opportunity for reprisals and take prompt and firm action against the North Vietnamese. McGeorge Bundy then joined McNamara in a very private paper warning LBJ that present policy could not endure, that the time had come to look hard at the alternatives of moving either up or down. They promised staff-work on both alternatives. (They never delivered on the latter.) Thereupon LBJ sent McGeorge Bundy to South Vietnam for a personal look, his first. McNaughton went with him.⁵⁶

While they were there, on February 6, two Viet Cong units struck a US

Army barracks at Pleiku, killing nine Americans and destroying five aircraft. McGeorge Bundy and McNaughton flew home, urging retaliatory action.

Johnson then acted with the same speed and determination he had shown six months earlier on the Tonkin resolution. After a seventy-five minute meeting at the White House, which included Senate Majority Leader Mike Mansfield and House Speaker John McCormack, the President ordered immediate implementation of Flaming Dart, a plan prepared by the Joint Chiefs of Staff the previous month for reprisal air strikes against North Vietnamese military bases. Of those present, only Mansfield opposed the decision, protesting that the reprisal could provoke Chinese intervention. To that Johnson responded, "We have kept our guns over the mantel and our shells in the cupboard for a long time now. I can't ask our American soliders out there to continue to fight with one hand behind their backs."[57] On February 10 when the Viet Cong staged another dramatic attack, this time on American enlisted men's quarters in Qui Nhon, Johnson quickly authorized Flaming Dart II, the largest retaliatory air strike of the war up to that time.[58]

Flaming Dart II signaled a subtle change in the administration's orientation toward bombing. The strike was not justified as a reprisal for a specific incident, but explained as a general response to "continued acts of aggression."[59] The Johnson administration was moving rapidly toward an endorsement of a graduated, systematic air war against the North. Plans for a strategy of "graduated and sustained reprisals" were presented to Johnson by McGeorge Bundy only days after the Pleiku attack. Bundy and McNaughton had returned to Washington insisting that "the stakes in Vietnam are extremely high" and that "without new U.S. action defeat appears inevitable"; Bundy recommended reprisals for the "overriding reason" that

> There is one grave weakness in our posture in Vietnam which is within our power to fix—and that is the widespread belief that we do not have the will and force and patience and determination to take the necessary action and stay the course.[60]

On February 13, 1965, without substantial debate, Johnson made the formal decision to proceed with the Bundy plan of "sustained reprisals," given the name of Rolling Thunder. In effect, the President had telescoped Phase I of Option C and now faced concrete choices on Phase II—not because Saigon's disarray had been overcome but rather because it persisted.

Immediately after the initiation of Rolling Thunder raids members of the administration began to push for increases in scope and intensity. Johnson had originally intended to determine targets solely on the basis of their psychological or political impact, consistent with a reprisal strategy. To that end he had personally reviewed all targets. But Saigon and the JCS soon warned that the raids were achieving meager results. This led to a new orientation: interdicting North Vietnamese lines of communication and a relaxation of the strict control of bombing operations from the White House.[61] In April American and South Vietnamese pilots flew a total of 3,600 missions against North Vietnamese targets.[62]

As Rolling Thunder started, General Westmoreland asked for deployment of two Marine landing-teams to protect the US air base at Danang from possible Viet Cong reprisals. The base was a center for raids on the North. Ambassador Taylor formally supported Westmoreland's recommendation, but with serious reservations. Taylor questioned the usefulness of American ground troops against Viet Cong guerrillas and was concerned least the deployment of Americans lead the ARVN to rely too heavily upon them. Moreover, Taylor believed that the introduction of Marines would remove an important barrier against the involvement of US troops in another Asian war.[63] Once the first step was taken, he wrote, it would be "very difficult to hold the line."[64]

Taylor's warning went unheeded in Washington. Enthusiasm for Rolling Thunder was gathering momentum, and Westmoreland's request for a limited number of troops for a limited mission seemed a small price to pay for the bombing program. Johnson approved the recommendation after only four days of apparently perfunctory debate, and on March 8 two battalions of Marines ceremoniously landed on a beach near Danang. Although their deployment was justified as a one-time response to a particular security need, it was soon followed by additional requests for American troops with combat missions.

In mid-March 1965 Westmoreland asked for immediate commitment of two US Army divisions to support the ARVN in the Central Highlands. The Viet Cong remained relatively inactive but Westmoreland feared that they were preparing for a major offensive by early summer. Rolling Thunder, still in its initial stages, had not yet produced a conciliatory response from Hanoi, and it appeared as though the North Vietnamese were preparing to endure a strong bombing campaign from the United States. Impatient with the slow pace of American involvement, the Joint Chiefs joined Westmoreland in urging that three divisions of US forces be released for offensive action against the enemy.

By April, then, Johnson and his advisers found themselves on what McNaughton called "the horns of a trilemma." Although there was no sign as yet that Saigon's perilous situation was improving, Washington had so far rejected all three courses of additional remedial action: unlimited bombing of the North, large troop deployment, or withdrawal.[65] At a Honolulu conference in mid-April McNamara and others tried to resolve the "trilemma" by compromise. The ambitious proposals of Westmoreland and the JCS were set aside for the time being. The current bombing campaign would remain the preeminent military operation. But McNamara conceded that "bombing would not do the job alone."[66] It was therefore decided to send an additional 40,000 troops to be used in what Ambassador Taylor called an "enclave strategy." Operating within fifty miles of US bases on the coast, they would harass the enemy just enough to buy time for the build-up of ARVN forces and for the air strikes to take their toll on the North Vietnamese. The aim of the program was to "break the will of the DRV/VC by depriving them of victory."[67]

Public Opposition: Government Response

The decisions of February, March, and April 1965 were veiled from the American public. The air strikes after Pleiku had been billed originally as reprisals. The shift to "sustained reprisals" was never acknowledged as such. In April, when the President acceded to "enclave strategy" involving US troops in offensive action, he ordered his advisers not to tell the press. Only on June 9, when a State Department spokesman released the news by mistake, did it become public knowledge that Marines were being used in ways beyond airbase security details. By then they already had suffered some 200 casualties in offensive action.[68]

Still, beginning in mid-March and continuing through April, the administration's enlargement of the war, as evidenced by bombing in the North, stirred opposition both within the United States and from abroad. The *New York Times* warned of the cost of "lives lost, blood spilt and treasure wasted, of fighting a war on a jungle front 7,000 miles from the coast of California."[69] Faculty members at Harvard, Syracuse, and the University of Michigan staged all-night "teach-ins" on Vietnam. Students at scattered colleges across the country distributed petitions against the bombing and organized small protest rallies. In April, 12,000 students marched in Washington to demonstrate their opposition. Criticism also came from sources closer to the administration. Prominent Democratic senators, among them Mike Mansfield again, recommended that the President pursue a negotiated settlement with North Vietnam. Vice President Hubert Humphrey had earlier urged caution on the President so strongly that he was no longer even consulted. Voices like these were joined by others farther off, such as United Nations Secretary-General U Thant of Burma, Canadian Prime Minister Lester Pearson, and assorted friendly Londoners who urged an end to bombing and a start to negotiations.[70]

Meanwhile, in the Caribbean, Johnson astonished his critics and gave new grounds for criticism by intervening massively in the Dominican Republic to suppress a communist-infiltrated coup. Restoring order and arranging for a moderate succession there took three months and preoccupied several key advisers, notably McGeorge Bundy.

The President himself turned quickly back to Vietnam and moved swiftly to smother his domestic opposition. He met with newspaper editors and members of Congress, vigorously defending his policies in a concerted effort to win converts. On April 7, 1965, he delivered a dramatic and well-publicized address at Johns Hopkins University, in which he proclaimed willingness to join the North Vietnamese in negotiations as soon as possible "without posing any preconditions." In the same speech Johnson tried to placate those who criticized his policy as being "all stick and no carrot." A settlement, he promised, would be followed by a billion-dollar American investment in an economic development program for the Mekong River valley, North and South, a program "on a scale even to dwarf our TVA." In early May the President reluctantly approved a five-day bombing pause, coordinated with a private message to Hanoi. The suggestion was that reduced military pressure on Saigon could bring a corresponding fall-off in the bombing.[71] There was no immediate response—which is what Johnson had predicted. Ho Chi Minh, he felt, must look at Saigon and feel close to victory; too close to deal on any terms Americans could buy, not even with a billion dollars. Pain would have to be inflicted first to take Ho's mind off victory. Then could come settlement and Ho would find that LBJ made generous deals.

In this spirit the administration soon returned to coercive tactics. Except for the five days in May, the number of US bombing runs over Northern targets increased steadily. The Hanoi regime stiffened under pressure and refused to cease what it was doing in the South. It termed the bombing pause a "worn-out trick of deceit and threat."[72] On April 8, however, it had tested Johnson's statement of American readiness to enter "unconditional discussions" by offering a four-point program for a settlement. Some American officials had considered this a hopeful sign and urged its exploration.[73] Rusk and LBJ at once refused, since Hanoi specified approval by the Viet Cong's civil arm, "The National Liberation Front for South Vietnam." This was seen as a communist puppet; two such Vietnams would be tantamount to one—in short a virtual surrender.[74] Instead, Johnson used the lull in criticism that the pause provided him to strengthen his congressional position. On May 4 he asked Congress on short notice for $400 million to support his stepped-up operations in Vietnam, and made it, in effect, a vote of confidence. Reassured by his Johns Hopkins stance and asked to fund troops already in the field, Congress quickly approved.[75]

Going All the Way

In mid-May 1965 the situation in South Vietnam began a precipitious decline from what already was a low point. Premier Phan Huy Quat, who had emerged from coups and countercoups in February, was suddenly forced to resign by the government's military leaders. Air Marshall Ky and General Thieu now took direct charge as they had not done in January and installed themselves as joint heads of government. This was the fifth regime since Diem's assassination. Although they, or at least Thieu, would last eight years until the final fall of Saigon, officials in Washington had no reason to expect this longevity. In 1965, as William Bundy later said, the Thieu-Ky coalition "seemed to all of us the bottom of the barrel, the absolute bottom of the barrel."[76]

More disturbing was the confirmation in early May that the Viet Cong and North Vietnamese were preparing a major offensive. As Westmoreland had predicted, the relative quiescence of enemy forces that spring had been the lull before the storm. In the second week of May Viet Cong units rained down on the South Vietnamese Army, wiping out entire battalions and inflicting the heaviest casualties yet.[77] At the start of July Westmoreland requested immediate deployment of American reinforcements to fight alongside the crippled ARVN in offensive action.

Anticipation of Westmoreland's request set off one more debate in Washington. The general was supported by the Joint Chiefs of Staff. The Chiefs recommended that 179,000 American troops (including those already there) be committed to South Vietnam for offensive operations, on the grounds that "enclave strategy" was already outmoded. Still more troops might be needed later, up to another 200,000, which should suffice to secure South Vietnam in not more than another two and a half years. "You must take the fight to the enemy," insisted JCS Chairman Wheeler. "No one ever won a battle sitting on his ass."[78] Even Ambassador Taylor had come around by the summer of 1965. He later recalled, "the strength of the enemy offensive had completely overcome my former reluctance to use American ground troops in general combat."[79]

In direct opposition to Westmoreland and the JCS stood the Under Secretary of State. Ball was not quite alone; Johnson apparently heard comparable views from Clark M. Clifford, then a private citizen and personal adviser and, had he been willing, could have heard them also from Vice President Humphrey or from Senate Leader Mansfield. Ball, for his part, doubted that American troops could cope successfully with a guerrilla war regardless of their numbers. He thought Westmoreland was inviting protracted war with an "open-ended commitment of US forces, mounting US casualties, no assurances of a satisfactory solution, and a serious danger of escalation at the end of the road."[80] On July 1, Ball sent the President a personal memorandum in which he urged that the administration cut its losses and withdraw peacefully from the conflict. Precisely how, he did not say. He granted that the move would damage American international prestige in the short run, but believed the United States would emerge from the difficult period a "wiser and more mature nation."[81] Clifford's private arguments are said to have been more political—as would befit a man who had been Truman's counsel—but his conclusion, evidently, was about the same."[82]

Also on July 1, McNamara sent a memorandum to the President generally endorsing the JCS call for troops. The day before, McGeorge Bundy had criticized this position in devastating fashion, for the moment joining the "doves." But either because LBJ's mind was already set, or because McNamara had become unstoppable, Bundy soon abandoned his critique, trying instead to promote a proposal of his brother's for a much more limited increase of troops to test their usefulness and South Vietnam's responsiveness while blunting communist attacks until October's rainy season.[83] McNamara could not be convinced. Neither, it seems, could Johnson.

Returning from another of his tours to South Vietnam in mid-July, the Secretary of Defense confirmed his earlier advice in still another paper. He wrote the President that he saw three alternatives for US policy at this juncture:

a. Cut our losses and withdraw under the best conditions that can be arranged—almost certainly conditions humiliating the U.S. . . .

b. Continue at about the present level . . . [while] our position would grow weaker. . . .

c. Expand promptly and substantially the U.S. military pressure against the VC in the South and maintain the military pressure against the NVNese in the North while . . . clarifying our objective [for eventual negotiation].

Despite acknowledged shortcomings, McNamara recommended the third alternative as "the course of action involving the best odds of the best outcome with the most acceptable cost to the U.S."[84] (How he calculated odds he did not state.) He urged the gradual deployment of another hundred thousand American troops—and probably more later. McGeorge Bundy kept William Bundy's alternatives alive a little longer, seeking to put off until at least the fall a full Americanization of the war, but to no avail.

In late July, after a week of formal discussion with his NSC advisers, Johnson embarked upon the wider war. Rejecting unlimited bombing, lest a full-scale assault on North Vietnam bring Chinese intervention as in Korea, he chose saturation bombing in South Vietnam and gradually intensified air raids throughout the North. He would continue to maintain close personal supervision of target selection. To augment the air effort, Johnson ordered immediate deployment of 50,000 additional troops to South Vietnam, with the private promise that another 50,000 would follow before the end of the year, and the implicit guarantee that he would continue to sent Westmoreland additional men as needed. There was talk about a total of 300,000 men for two and a half years. (In that time he would actually provide 575,000 before he balked at 210,000 more.) Last, Johnson authorized Westmoreland to abandon "enclave strategy" and to "commit U.S. troops to combat independent of or in conjunction with CVN forces in any situation . . . when . . . their use is necessary to strengthen the relative position of CVN forces."[85] It was now an American war, and it would soon be "Johnson's war" as Korea became Truman's.

McNamara and the Joint Chiefs had advised that Johnson go to Congress to inform it of the weight of his decisions and to obtain support—both Houses and both parties would be bound to go along. For this there were good reasons, constitutional and practical—among them that he then could call up the reserves, which as a separate action would create still more alarm than in this context. But Johnson feared all sorts of consequences from a formal approach to Congress. If it responded by declaring war, Peking and Moscow might take fright; besides he would be hampered then in limiting hostilities and in ultimately doing that negotiated deal. Truman in 1950 had had comparable thoughts. Moreover, what would happen to domestic programs if opponents could take refuge in priorities for war? Johnson knew what had become of HST's "Fair Deal." He did not want that fate to overwhelm his Great Society program in its first legislative year after election. So he told associates to carry out his orders in a "low key manner . . . (a) to avoid an abrupt challenge to the Communists, and (b) to avoid undue concern and excitement in the Congress and in domestic public opinion."[86]

Johnson himself announced with no fanfare a 50,000-troop contingent for Westmoreland at a televised news conference on July 28. The President denied that there had been a basic change in American policy, and he forbore to say he had already promised additional reinforcements. He took refuge instead in generalities:

> We did not choose to be guardians of the gate, but there is no one else.

> Nor would surrender in Vietnam bring peace, because we learned from Hitler at Munich that success only feeds the appetite of aggression. The battle would be renewed in one country and then another country . . . as we have learned from the lessons of history.

> Moreover, we are in Vietnam to fulfill one of the most solemn pledges of the American Nation. Three Presidents . . . over 11 years have committed themselves and have promised to help defend this small and valiant nation.

> . . . This, then, my fellow Americans, is why we are in Vietnam.[87]

* * *

Why did Johnson do it? Doris Kearns, one of his biographers, theorizes that by temperament he could not bear to make a choice between such deeply felt objectives as assuring his domestic legislation and avoiding Saigon's fall. Others argue that he could not face up to his moral duty as a leader, enlightening the public and avowing both needs as he saw them, because he knew the country's probable response; war comes first.[88] But every month for innovative social legislation may have been a gain worth purchasing, in his eyes, for the country's sake, even if it later cost him dearly in credibility—which means that covertness was a necessity to wring out every month he could before the war caught up with him. Perhaps so. Is that not also "leadership"? Or one can argue that he made a quite straightforward choice between his short-run and long-run risks and simply misjudged both, overstating the short, understating the long—a classic mistake from which his closest associates did little to try to save him.

NOTES

1. US Department of Defense, *The Pentagon Papers: The Defense Department History of United States Decisionmaking on Vietnam*, Senator Gravel edition, vol. 3 (Boston: Beacon Press, 1971), pp. 494–96 [hereafter referred to as *The Pentagon Papers*].
2. George C. Herring, *America's Longest War: The United States and Vietnam, 1950–1975* (New York: John Wiley and Sons, 1979), p. 45.
3. Ibid., p. 56.
4. Ibid., p. 67.
5. Ernest R. May, *"Lessons" of the Past: The Use and Misuse of History in American Foreign Policy* (New York: Oxford University Press, 1973), p. 88.
6. Ibid., p. 92.
7. Herring, pp. 82–85.
8. Ibid., p. 112.
9. May, p. 102.
10. Lyndon B. Johnson, *The Vantage Point* (New York: Holt, 1971), p. 20.
11. David Halberstam, *The Best and the Brightest* (New York: Fawcett Crest, 1972), p. 424.
12. Herring, pp. 114–15.
13. May, pp. 103–04.
14. Ibid., p. 104.
15. Herring, p. 115.
16. *The Pentagon Papers*, vol. 3, pp. 499–500.
17. Ibid., p. 500.
18. Ibid., pp. 500, 504.
19. Ibid., p. 56.
20. Ibid., p. 497.
21. Herring, pp. 115–16.
22. *The Pentagon Papers*, vol. 3, pp. 2–5.
23. Herring, p. 116.
24. *The Pentagon Papers*, vol. 3, pp. 56–58.
25. Herring, p. 116.
26. Ibid.
27. By midsummer the US government had raised its estimates of VC active strength from 28,000 to 34,000. *The Pentagon Papers*, vol. 3, p. 80.
28. Ibid., p. 82.
29. Herring, p. 119.
30. *The Pentagon Papers*, vol. 3, p. 511.
31. Ibid., p. 77.
32. Herring, p. 122.
33. Ibid.

34. Eugene G. Windchy, *Tonkin Gulf* (Garden City, NY: Doubleday, 1971), p. 16.
35. Ibid., p. 25.
36. Herring, p. 124.
37. *The Pentagon Papers*, vol. 3, p. 723.
38. Ibid., p. 216.
39. Herring, p. 126.
40. Ibid., p. 623.
41. May, p. 107.
42. *The Pentagon Papers*, vol. 3, p. 617.
43. May, p. 106.
44. *The Pentagon Papers*, vol. 3, p. 623.
45. May, p. 108.
46. Ibid., p. 109.
47. Ibid., pp. 109–10. For more on Ball's argument see his October 5, 1964 memorandum in *Vietnam Documents* (C94-80-271S).
48. *The Pentagon Papers*, vol. 3, p. 239.
49. Herring, p. 127.
50. *The Pentagon Papers*, vol. 3, p. 289.
51. Ibid., p. 290.
52. Herring, p. 128.
53. *The Pentagon Papers*, vol. 3, pp. 295–96.
54. Herring, p. 128.
55. Ibid., p. 129.
56. For McNaughton paper see *The Pentagon Papers*, vol. 3, p. 686. An excerpt of Bundy's January 27, 1965, memorandum is in *Vietnam Documents* (C94-80-271S).
57. Herring, p. 129.
58. *The Pentagon Papers*, vol. 3, p. 306.
59. Ibid.
60. Ibid., pp. 309, 311.
61. Herring, p. 131.
62. Ibid.
63. *The Pentagon Papers*, vol. 3, p. 389.
64. Herring, p. 131.
65. *The Pentagon Papers*, vol. 3, p. 694.
66. Herring, p. 133.
67. Ibid.
68. *The Pentagon Papers*, vol. 3, p. 460.
69. Herring, p. 134.
70. Ibid.
71. Ibid., pp. 135–36.
72. Ibid., p. 136.
73. Ibid.

74. Ibid.
75. Ibid., p. 137.
76. Ibid., p. 138.
77. *The Pentagon Papers*, vol. 3, p. 438.
78. Herring, p. 139.
79. Ibid.
80. Ibid.
81. *The Pentagon Papers*, vol. 3, p. 472.
82. See May 17, 1965, memorandum to the President from Clark Clifford in *Vietnam Documents* (C94-80-271S).
83. See July 1, 1965, memorandum from Wiliam Bundy, "A 'Middle Way' course of Action . . ." in *Vietnam Documents* (C94-80-271S).
84. *The Pentagon Papers*, vol. 4, pp. 620–21.
85. Herring, p. 141.
86. Ibid., p. 142.
87. *The Pentagon Papers*, vol. 3, pp. 476–77.
88. For further perspective see Larry Berman, *Planning a Tragedy* (New York: Norton, 1982).

Foreign Policy Politics: Diplomacy Begins at Home

Foreign policy politics in the post–Cold War era are a mix of continuity and change. This duality is evident for all five major sets of domestic actors. The readings in this chapter focus on three of those political actors: interest groups, the news media, and public opinion.

The rise of non-governmental organizations (NGOs)—unofficial issue-oriented groups engaged in both advocacy and direct action on foreign policy issues—is one of the most important developments in foreign policy politics. While NGOs have been around for a long time, their number and influence have been increasing dramatically. They are "activists beyond borders," as Margaret Keck and Kathryn Sikkink call them, both because they are often members of transnational networks of groups that influence the policies of governments and international organizations, and because they go beyond lobbying, taking direct action on the front lines by providing humanitarian assistance, monitoring human rights, helping with economic development, and taking on countless other global responsibilities. The first reading in this chapter is drawn from the first chapter of the Keck and Sikkink book.

Warren Strobel's article on "the CNN effect" takes a careful look at the news media's influence in this age of the telecommunications revolution. Conventional wisdom attributes enormous sway over public opinion to "real time" television, bringing crises into the living rooms of America and precipitating military intervention or other major action on the one hand (the CNN curve's up slope), and on the other setting off a run to the exits when American soldiers get killed or some other trauma or dramatic setback is flashed on TV screens day and night (the curve's down slope). While affirming the important role television and other news media do have, Strobel challenges this conventional wisdom as exaggerated and simplistic. His focus is Somalia 1993, the very case on which the CNN-effect theory was based.

In his article, Ole Holsti, a leading scholar on public opinion and foreign policy, surveys and assesses major theories and research findings. Here too there is a conventional wisdom, which is a view of the American public as largely ignorant about and having little influence over public opinion. And here too the conventional wisdom needs challenging, as it increasingly has been by studies that show that while the public does pay limited attention and has limited knowledge about foreign policy, there nevertheless still is a rationality, a consistency, a soundness of judgment in its collective view. This is an interesting and important perspective given other indications that, as Holsti concludes, "we may be moving into a period in which the relationship between public opinion and foreign policy takes on added rather than diminished significance."

6.1 *Interest Groups*

MARGARET E. KECK AND KATHRYN SIKKINK

Transnational Networks in International Politics: An Introduction

World politics at the end of the twentieth century involves, alongside states, many nonstate actors that interact with each other, with states, and with international organizations. These interactions are structured in terms of networks, and transnational networks are increasingly visible in international politics. Some involve economic actors and firms. Some are networks of scientists and experts whose professional ties and shared causal ideas underpin their efforts to influence policy.[1] Others are networks of activists, distinguishable largely by the centrality of principled ideas or values in motivating their formation.[2] We will call these *transnational advocacy networks*.

Advocacy networks are significant transnationally and domestically. By building new links among actors in civil societies, states, and international organizations, they multiply the channels of access to the international system. In such issue areas as the environment and human rights, they also make international resources available to new actors in domestic political and social struggles. By thus blurring the boundaries between a state's relations with its own nationals and the recourse both citizens and states have to the international system, advocacy networks are helping to transform the practice of national sovereignty.

* * *

Major actors in advocacy networks may include the following: (1) international and domestic nongovernmental research and advocacy organizations; (2) local social movements; (3) foundations; (4) the media; (5) churches, trade unions, consumer organizations, and intellectuals; (6) parts of regional and international intergovernmental organizations; and (7) parts of the executive and/or parliamentary branches of governments. Not all these will be present in each advocacy network. Initial research suggests,

From *Activists Beyond Borders: Advocacy Networks in International Politics* (Ithaca, N.Y.: Cornell University Press, 1998), chapter 1.

however, that international and domestic NGOs play a central role in all advocacy networks, usually initiating actions and pressuring more powerful actors to take positions. NGOs introduce new ideas, provide information, and lobby for policy changes.

Groups in a network share values and frequently exchange information and services. The flow of information among actors in the network reveals a dense web of connections among these groups, both formal and informal. The movement of funds and services is especially notable between foundations and NGOs, and some NGOs provide services such as training for other NGOs in the same and sometimes other advocacy networks. Personnel also circulate within and among networks, as relevant players move from one to another in a version of the "revolving door."

Relationships among networks, both within and between issue areas, are similar to what scholars of social movements have found for domestic activism.[3] Individuals and foundation funding have moved back and forth among them. Environmentalists and women's groups have looked at the history of human rights campaigns for models of effective international institution building. Refugee resettlement and indigenous people's rights are increasingly central components of international environmental activity, and vice versa; mainstream human rights organizations have joined the campaign for women's rights. Some activists consider themselves part of an "NGO community."

∗ ∗ ∗

Advocacy networks are not new. We can find examples as far back as the nineteenth-century campaign for the abolition of slavery. But their number, size, and professionalism, and the speed, density, and complexity of international linkages among them has grown dramatically in the last three decades. As Hugh Heclo remarks about domestic issue networks, "If the current situation is a mere outgrowth of old tendencies, it is so in the same sense that a 16-lane spaghetti interchange is the mere elaboration of a country crossroads."[4]

We cannot accurately count transnational advocacy networks to measure their growth over time, but one proxy is the increase in the number of international NGOs committed to social change. Because international NGOs are key components of any advocacy network, this increase suggests broader trends in the number, size, and density of advocacy networks generally.

∗ ∗ ∗

Transnational advocacy networks appear most likely to emerge around those issues where (1) channels between domestic groups and their governments are blocked or hampered or where such channels are ineffective for resolving a conflict, setting into motion the "boomerang" pattern of influence characteristic of these networks; (2) activists or "political entrepreneurs" believe that networking will further their missions and campaigns, and actively promote networks; and (3) conferences and other forms of international contact create arenas for forming and strengthening networks. Where channels of participation are blocked, the international arena may be the only means that domestic activists have to gain attention to their issues. Boomerang strategies are most common in campaigns where the target is a state's domestic policies or behavior; where a campaign seeks broad procedural change involving dispersed actors, strategies are more diffuse.

Political Entrepreneurs

Just as oppression and injustice do not themselves produce movements or revolutions, claims around issues amenable to international action do not produce transnational networks. Activists—"people who care enough about some issue that they are prepared to incur significant costs and act to achieve their goals"[5]—do. They create them when they believe that transnational networking will further their organizational missions—by sharing information, attaining greater visibility, gaining access to wider publics, multiplying channels of institutional access, and so forth. For example, in the campaign to stop the promotion of infant formula to poor women in developing countries, organizers settled on a boycott of Nestlé, the largest producer, as its main tactic. Because Nestlé was a transnational actor, activists believed a transnational network was necessary to bring pressure on corporations and governments.[6] Over time, in such issue areas, participation in transnational networks has become an essential component of the collective identities of the activists involved, and networking a part of their common repertoire. The political entrepreneurs who become the core networkers for a new campaign have often gained experience in earlier ones.

The Growth of International Contact

Opportunities for network activities have increased over the last two decades. In addition to the efforts of pioneers, a proliferation of international organizations and conferences has provided foci for connections. Cheaper air travel and new electronic communication technologies speed information flows and simplify personal contact among activists.[7]

Underlying these trends is a broader cultural shift. The new networks have depended on the creation of a new kind of global public (or civil society), which grew as a cultural legacy of the 1960s.[8] Both the activism that swept Western Europe, the United States, and many parts of the third world during that decade, and the vastly increased opportunities for international contact, contributed to this shift. With a significant decline in air fares, foreign travel ceased to be the exclusive privilege of the wealthy. Students participated in exchange programs. The Peace Corps and lay missionary programs sent thousands of young people to live and work in the developing world. Political exiles from Latin America taught in U.S. and European universities. Churches opened their doors to refugees, and to new ideas and commitments.

Obviously, internationalism was not invented in the sixties. Religious and political traditions including missionary outreach, the solidarity traditions of labor and the left, and liberal internationalism have long stirred action by individuals or groups beyond the borders of their own state. While many activists working in advocacy networks come out of these traditions, they tend no longer to define themselves in terms of these traditions or the organizations that carried them. This is most true for activists on the left who suffered disillusionment from their groups' refusal to address seriously the concerns of women, the environment, or human rights violations in eastern bloc countries. Absent a range of options that in earlier decades would have competed for their commitments, advocacy and activism through either NGOs or grassroots movements became the most likely alternative for those seeking to "make a difference."

* * *

How Do Transnational Advocacy Networks Work?

Transnational advocacy networks seek influence in many of the same ways that other political groups or social movements do. Since they are not powerful in a traditional sense of the word, they must use the power of their information, ideas, and strategies to alter the information and value contexts within which states make policies. The bulk of what networks do might be termed persuasion or socialization, but neither process is devoid of conflict. Persuasion and socialization often involve not just reasoning with opponents, but also bringing pressure, arm-twisting, encouraging sanctions, and shaming. * * *

* * *

Our typology of tactics that networks use in their efforts at persuasion, socialization, and pressure includes (1) *information politics*, or the ability to quickly and credibly generate politically usable information and move it to where it will have the most impact; (2) *symbolic politics*, or the ability to call upon symbols, actions, or stories that make sense of a situation for an audience that is frequently far away;[9] (3) *leverage politics*, or the ability to call upon powerful actors to affect a situation where weaker members of a network are unlikely to have influence; and (4) *accountability politics*, or the effort to hold powerful actors to their previously stated policies or principles.

* * *

Information Politics

Information binds network members together and is essential for network effectiveness. Many information exchanges are informal—telephone calls, E-mail and fax communications, and the circulation of newsletters, pamphlets and bulletins. They provide information that would not otherwise be available, from sources that might not otherwise be heard, and they must make this information comprehensible and useful to activists and publics who may be geographically and/or socially distant.[10]

* * *

Nonstate actors gain influence by serving as alternate sources of information. Information flows in advocacy networks provide not only facts but testimony—stories told by people whose lives have been affected. Moreover, activists interpret facts and testimony, usually framing issues simply, in terms of right and wrong because their purpose is to persuade people and stimulate them to act. How does this process of persuasion occur? An effective frame must show that a given state of affairs is neither natural nor accidental, identify the responsible party or parties, and propose credible solutions. These aims require clear, powerful messages that appeal to shared principles, which often have more impact on state policy than advice of technical experts. An important part of the political struggle over information is precisely whether an issue is defined primarily as technical—and thus subject to consideration by "qualified" experts—or as something, that concerns a broader global constituency.

* * *

Networks strive to uncover and investigate problems, and alert the press and policymakers. One activist described this as the "human rights methodology"—"promoting change by reporting facts."[11] To be credible, the information produced by networks must be reliable and well documented. To gain attention, the information must be timely and dramatic. Sometimes these multiple goals of information politics conflict, but both credibility and drama seem to be essential components of a strategy aimed at persuading publics and policymakers to change their minds.

* * *

Symbolic Politics

Activists frame issues by identifying and providing convincing explanations for powerful symbolic events, which in turn become catalysts for the growth of networks. Symbolic interpretation is part of the process of persuasion by which networks create awareness and expand their constituencies. Awarding the 1992 Nobel Peace Prize to Maya activist Rigoberta Menchú and the UN's designation of 1993 as the Year of Indigenous Peoples heightened public awareness of the situation of indigenous peoples in the Americas. Indigenous people's use of 1992, the 500th anniversary of the voyage of Columbus to the Americas, to raise a host of issues well illustrates the use of symbolic events to reshape understandings.[12]

* * *

Leverage Politics

Activists in advocacy networks are concerned with political effectiveness. Their definition of effectiveness often includes some policy change by "target actors" such as governments, international financial institutions like the World Bank, or private actors like transnational corporations. In order to bring about policy change, networks need to pressure and persuade more powerful actors. To gain influence the networks seek leverage (the word appears often in the discourse of advocacy organizations) over more powerful actors. By leveraging more powerful institutions, weak groups gain influence far beyond their ability to influence state practices directly. The identification of material or moral leverage is a crucial strategic step in network campaigns.

Material leverage usually links the issue to money or goods (but potentially also to votes in international organizations, prestigious offices, or other benefits). * * *

* * *

Although NGO influence often depends on securing powerful allies, their credibility still depends in part on their ability to mobilize their own members and affect public opinion via the media. In democracies the potential to influence votes gives large membership organizations an advantage over nonmembership organizations in lobbying for policy change; environmental organizations, several of whose memberships number in the millions, are more likely to have this added clout than are human rights organizations.

Moral leverage involves what some commentators have called the "mobilization of shame," where the behavior of target actors is held up to the light of international scrutiny. Network activists exert moral leverage on the assumption that governments value the good opinion of others; insofar as networks can demonstrate that a state is violating international obligations or is not living up to its own claims, they hope to jeopardize its credit enough to motivate a change in policy or behavior. The degree to which states are vulnerable to this kind of pressure varies, and will be discussed further below.

Accountability Politics

Networks devote considerable energy to convincing governments and other actors to publicly change their positions on issues. This is often dismissed as inconsequential change, since talk is cheap and governments sometimes change discursive positions hoping to divert network and public attention. Network activists, however, try to make such statements into opportunities for accountability politics. Once a government has publicly committed itself to a principle—for example, in favor of human rights or democracy—networks can use those positions, and their command of information, to expose the distance between discourse and practice. This is embarrassing to many governments, which may try to save face by closing that distance.

* * *

Domestic structures through which states and private actors can be held accountable to their pronouncements, to the law, or to contracts vary considerably from one nation to another, even among democracies. The centrality of the courts in U.S. politics creates a venue for the representation of diffuse interests that is not available in most European democracies.[13] It also explains the large number of U.S. advocacy organizations that specialize in litigation. * * *

Under What Conditions Do Advocacy Networks Have Influence?

To assess the influence of advocacy networks we must look at goal achievement at several different levels. We identify the following types or stages of network influence: (1) issue creation and agenda setting; (2) influence on discursive positions of states and international organizations; (3) influence on institutional procedures; (4) influence on policy change in "target actors" which may be states, international organizations like the World Bank, or private actors like the Nestlé Corporation; and (5) influence on state behavior.

Networks generate attention to new issues and help set agendas when they provoke media attention, debates, hearings, and meetings on issues that previously had not been a matter of public debate. Because values are the essence of advocacy networks, this stage of influence may require a modification of the "value context" in which policy debates takes place. The UN's theme years and decades, such as International Women's Decade and the

Year of Indigenous Peoples, were international events promoted by networks that heightened awareness of issues.

Networks influence discursive positions when they help persuade states and international organizations to support international declarations or to change stated domestic policy positions. The role environmental networks played in shaping state positions and conference declarations at the 1992 "Earth Summit" in Rio de Janeiro is an example of this kind of impact. They may also pressure states to make more binding commitments by signing conventions and codes of conduct.

The targets of network campaigns frequently respond to demands for policy change with changes in procedures (which may affect policies in the future). The multilateral bank campaign is largely responsible for a number of changes in internal bank directives mandating greater NGO and local participation in discussions of projects. It also opened access to formerly restricted information, and led to the establishment of an independent inspection panel for World Bank projects. Procedural changes can greatly increase the opportunity for advocacy organizations to develop regular contact with other key players on an issue, and they sometimes offer the opportunity to move from outside to inside pressure strategies.

A network's activities may produce changes in policies, not only of the target states, but also of other states and/or international institutions. Explicit policy shifts seem to denote success, but even here both their causes and meanings may be elusive. We can point with some confidence to network impact where human rights network pressures have achieved cut-offs of military aid to repressive regimes, or a curtailment of repressive practices. Sometimes human rights activity even affects regime stability. But we must take care to distinguish between policy change and change in behavior; official policies regarding timber extraction in Sarawak, Malaysia, for example, may say little about how timber companies behave on the ground in the absence of enforcement.

We speak of stages of impact, and not merely types of impact, because we believe that increased attention, followed by changes in discursive positions, make governments more vulnerable to the claims that networks raise. (Discursive changes can also have a powerfully divisive effect on networks themselves, splitting insiders from outsiders, reformers from radicals.) A government that claims to be protecting indigenous areas or ecological reserves is potentially more vulnerable to charges that such areas are endangered than one that makes no such claim. At that point the effort is not to make governments change their position but to hold them to their word. Meaningful policy change is thus more likely when the first three types or stages of impact have occurred.

* * *

Issue Characteristics

Issues that involve ideas about right and wrong are amenable to advocacy networking because they arouse strong feelings, allow networks to recruit volunteers and activists, and infuse meaning into these volunteer activities. However, not all principled ideas lead to network formation, and some issues can be framed more easily than others so as to resonate with policymakers and publics.* * *

* * *

As we look at the issues around which transnational advocacy networks have organized most effectively, we find two issue characteristics that appear most frequently: (1) issues involving bodily harm to vulnerable individuals, especially when there is a short and clear causal chain (or story) assigning responsibility; and (2) issues involving legal equality of opportunity. The first respond to a normative logic, and the second to a juridical and institutional one.

* * *

Actor Characteristics

However amenable particular issues may be to strong transnational and transcultural messages, there must be actors capable of transmitting those messages and targets who are vulnerable to persuasion or leverage. * * *

Target actors must be vulnerable either to material incentives or to sanctions from outside actors, or they must be sensitive to pressure because of gaps between stated commitments and practice. Vulnerability arises both from the availability of leverage and the target's sensitivity to leverage; if either is missing, a campaign may fail.

* * *

NOTES

1. Peter Haas has called these "knowledge-based" or "epistemic communities." See Peter Haas, "Introduction: Epistemic Communities and International Policy Coordination," *Knowledge, Power and International Policy Coordination*, special issue, *International Organization* 46 (Winter 1992), pp. 1–36.
2. Ideas that specify criteria for determining whether actions are right and wrong and whether outcomes are just or unjust are shared prin-

cipled beliefs or values, Beliefs about cause-effect relationships are shared casual beliefs, Judith Goldstein and Robert Keohane, eds., *Ideas and Foreign Policy: Beliefs, Institutions, and Political Change* (Ithaca: Cornell University Press, 1993), pp. 8–10.

3. See John D. McCarthy and Mayer N. Zald, "Resource Mobilization and Social Movements: A Partial Theory," *American Journal of Sociology* 82:6 (1977): 1212–41. Myra Marx Feree and Frederick D. Miller, "Mobilization and Meaning: Toward an Integration of Social Psychological and Resource Perspectives on Social Movements," *Sociological Inquiry* 55 (1985): 49–50; and David S. Meyer and Nancy Whittier, "Social Movement Spillover," *Social Problems* 41:2 (May 1994): 277–98.

4. Hugh Heclo, "Issue Networks and the Executive Establishment," in *The New American Political System*, ed. Anthony King (Washington, D.C.: American Enterprise Institute, 1978). p. 97.

5. Pamela E. Oliver and Gerald Marwell, "Mobilizing Technologies for Collective Action," in *Frontiers in Social Movement Theory*, ed. Aldon D. Morris and Carol McClurg Mueller (New Haven: Yale University Press, 1992), p. 252.

6. See Kathryn Sikkink, "Codes of Conduct for Transnational Corporations: The Case of the WHO/UNICEF Code," *International Organization* 40 (Autumn 1986): 815–40.

7. The constant dollar yield of airline tickets in 1995 was one half of what it was in 1966, while the number of international passengers enplaned increased more than four times during the same period. Air Transport Association home page, June 1997, http://www.airtransport.org/data/traffic.htm. See James Rosenau, *Turbulence in World Politics* (Princeton: Princeton University Press, 1990), pp. 12, 25.

8. See Sidney Tarrow, "Mentalities, Political Cultures, and Collective Action Frames: Constructing Meanings through Action," in *Frontiers in Social Movement Theory*, p. 184.

9. Alison Brysk uses the categories "information politics" and "symbolic politics" to discuss strategies of transnational actors, especially networks around Indian rights. See "Acting Globally: Indian Rights and International Politics in Latin America," in *Indigenous Peoples and Democracy in Latin America*, ed. Donna Lee Van Cott (New York: St. Martin's Press/Inter-American Dialogue, 1994), pp. 29–51; and "Hearts and Minds: Bringing Symbolic Politics Back In," *Polity* 27 (Summer 1995): 559–85.

10. Rosenau, *Turbulence*, p. 199, argues that "as the adequacy of information and the very nature of knowledge have emerged as central issues, what were once regarded as the petty quarrels of scholars over the adequacy of evidence and the metaphysics of proof have become prominent activities in international relations."

11. Dorothy Q. Thomas, "Holding Governments Accountable by Public

Pressure," In *Ours by Right: Women's Rights as Human Rights*, ed. Joanna Kerr (London: Zed Books, 1993), p. 83. This methodology is not new. See, for example David H. Lumsdaine, *Moral Vision, in International Politics: The Foreign Aid Regime* (Princeton: Princeton University Press, 1993), pp. 187–88, 211–13.

12. Brysk, "Acting Globally."

13. On access to the courts and citizen oversight of environmental policy in the U.S. and Germany, see Susan Rose Ackerman, *Controlling Environmental Policy: The Limits of Public Law in Germany and the United States* (Hew Haven: Yale University Press, 1995).

WARREN P. STROBEL

The Media and U.S. Policies Toward Intervention: A Closer Look at the "CNN Effect"

With the rise of "real-time" television in the 1980s, the growth of Ted Turner's 24-hour-a-day Cable News Network (CNN), and the deployment of news media technologies that can transmit video signals to and from virtually anywhere on the planet, government officials, legislators, media professionals, and scholars have voiced growing concern that journalists are exercising an irresistible control over western foreign policy.[1] It is said that dramatic images of starving masses, shelled populations, or dead American soldiers spark ill-considered public demands for action from elected officials. These temporary emotional responses may conflict with the more considered judgment of foreign policy officials, forcing them to take action that will soon have to be reversed or modified.

While the term "CNN effect" has numerous definitions and includes a range of phenomena, at heart it is understood to be a loss of policy control on the part of government policymakers.[2] CNN, it is said, makes, or at least exercises inordinate influence on, policy. * * *

This essay argues that these concerns, while understandable in the light of recent international changes, are misplaced. The CNN effect is grossly exaggerated, operating in few, if any, of the cases where it is most commonly cited. The media's effect on foreign policy is far more complex than the CNN-effect label would suggest, and far more dependent on the policy actions of government officials themselves than is seen to be the case. It is true that U.S. government policies and actions regarding international conflict are subject to more open public review than previously in history. But policymakers retain great power to frame events and solicit public support —indeed, CNN at times increases this power. Put another way, if officials

From *Managing Global Chaos: Sources of and Responses to International Conflict*, Chester A. Crocker and Fen Osler Hampson with Pamela Aall, eds. (Washington, D.C.: U.S. Institute of Peace Press, 1996), pp. 357–76.

do not have a firm and well-considered policy or have failed to communicate their views in such a way as to garner the support of the American people, the news media will fill this vacuum (often by giving greater time and attention to the criticisms or policy preferences of its opponents). In this regard, little has changed since Daniel Hallin, studying the reporting of the Vietnam War, an era of much less sophisticated media technology, concluded that the news media's impact is intimately related to the consensus of society as a whole.[3] What *has* changed is the speed with which the news media can expose such gaps.

This analysis will examine the CNN effect as it applies to prospective or actual U.S. interventions in what are now called peace operations or operations other than war.[4] My conclusions are based on more than 100 interviews conducted during 1994–1995 with four main groups: senior policy makers from the Bush and Clinton administrations; military spokespersons and other U.S. officers (primarily from the Army and Marine Corps); print, radio, and television journalists, primarily from U.S. news organizations; and personnel from the United Nations, other international governmental organizations (IGOs), and nongovernmental organizations (NGOs). The findings can be summarized as follows:

- Graphic televised images hold no power to force U.S. policymakers to intervene in a civil conflict where there is no clear national interest.
- There seems to be an inverse relationship between the power of images on policymakers and the presumed costs of intervention. (At the time of the decision, the costs of U.S. action in Somalia appeared to be low.)
- Images do add to the pressures on policymakers to address humanitarian aspects of a crisis, but the news media are not the agenda-setters they are often portrayed to be. Government relief officials, other relief agencies, and U.S. lawmakers play key roles in drawing news media attention to such suffering.
- Because public and media pressures are not specific, policymakers often react with what might be called a minimalist response, attempting to signal more of a policy change than has actually taken place.
- There is evidence that the power of televised images to provoke emotional responses is diminishing as conflict and humanitarian need become ubiquitous features of the post–Cold War era, at least as portrayed on television.
- Media reports have a greater impact when executive branch policy is in flux or is poorly articulated.
- The prevalence of real-time media reports often contracts the policymaking process, giving officials less time before they must respond publicly. But this does not mean the media automatically determine policy outcomes.

In short, the CNN effect does not exist in many places where it is said to be found, and even where its traces can be detected, they are exaggerated, working only in combination with other factors.

* * *

Stepping Back

* * *

The overarching U.S.-Soviet struggle provided a context within which administration officials could explain their policies to the news media and, in turn, helped the news media explain to readers and viewers the significance of complex and far-off events. The news media were more supportive than is usually remembered of U.S. foreign policy aims during the Cold War. Until the 1968 Tet offensive, the television networks and prestige newspapers such as the *New York Times* largely agreed with the White House's claim of the strategic importance of South Vietnam. Journalists such as the *Times'* David Halberstam criticized the means, not the ends.[5]

The end of the Cold War has deprived American administrations of a ready context in which to explain their policies and created a sort of meta-vacuum. This, the media have filled, using their own professional ideology, which puts a high premium on crisis, drama, and unfilled humanitarian needs.[6]

* * *

Somalia: Who Set the Agenda?

Because it is widely accepted that television images of starving civilians, especially children, forced President Bush to dispatch U.S. military forces to Somalia in the fall of 1992, this is a good place to begin a more detailed examination of the news media's impact on U.S. intervention policy. This analysis challenges that widely held belief on three counts. First, the levels of television coverage were incompatible with the types of pressure usually associated with the CNN effect: Sharp increases in the levels of television reporting tended to *follow* administration actions, rather than precede them. Second, the television coverage (and other media attention) that did take place was almost always a result, not of media initiative and agenda-setting, but of deliberate and successful attempts by others to stir up media interest in Somalia in order to move policy. These "others" were a loose coalition of U.S. government relief officials, interested members of Congress, and representatives of NGOs and IGOs. Their efforts highlight the growing role in particular of nongovernmental or supragovernmental bodies in international relations.[7] Finally, interviews with numerous Bush administration officials made it clear that they intervened in Somalia largely because they expected it to be an exercise with low costs and high political benefit. Simultaneously, President Bush was wrestling with the question of a potential U.S. intervention in the former Yugoslavia, which senior officials agreed would require tens of thousands of U.S. ground troops. Somalia was chosen partly because it was easier and would relieve pressure for action in the Balkans.

Even a cursory look at patterns of coverage of Somalia by the three U.S. broadcast television networks and by CNN raises questions about the impact of these media on the decision to intervene in Somalia. President Bush's first major decision regarding Somalia, one that "created an activist consensus in the national security bureaucracy where none had existed earlier,"[8] was to begin an airlift of emergency food supplies to drought-affected areas in Somalia and northern Kenya. This decision was announced August 14, 1992, although it had been made two days earlier. Prior to August 14, there were only fifteen network evening news stories in 1992 that mentioned Somalia; six of them were merely fleeting glimpses of Somalia's plight as part of one-minute or forty-second "round-ups" of news from around the world. CNN coverage patterns were roughly similar, with the exception of a burst of coverage in May stemming from a single correspondent's ten-day visit to Somalia. Once the airlift decision was announced, television coverage jumped to unprecedented levels, remaining relatively high in September, and then almost vanishing in October, no doubt overshadowed by the upcoming 1992 presidential election. Rather than television bringing U.S. troops and airplanes to Somalia in the first place, it was Bush's policy action that attracted increased media attention, with dozens of journalists descending on the country to report on the airlift. Of course, once there, they sent back more reports about the horrible conditions in the countryside. This pattern was repeated in November, prior to Bush's November 25 decision to launch Operation Restore Hope, the dispatch of nearly 30,000 U.S. troops to guard relief supplies. Somalia returned to television's agenda in mid-November, but it was Bush's decision that sparked the most intense media coverage.

* * * Nonetheless, once the images of starvation appeared on American television screens, they did have some further effect. Secretary of State James A. Baker III asked the rhetorical question of whether Bush would have dispatched troops to Somalia in December 1992 absent those images: "We probably wouldn't have," he concluded.[9] The next question is why they had an impact. The answer seems to be that senior Bush administration officials all believed that the Somalia intervention would be low in costs, especially casualties, and high in benefit. One of those benefits was to ease the simultaneous pressure the administration was feeling in the fall of 1992 to engage in a potentially much more costly intervention: the former Yugoslavia. Baker; his successor, Eagleburger; and Scowcroft all used virtually the same words: There was an easy consensus within the administration on doing something about Somalia.[10] In other words, the images from Somalia op-

erated only on a narrow portion of the spectrum of national security concerns: a humanitarian crisis that seemed to be an "easy fix."

* * *

In summary, the case most often held up as an example of the CNN
effect—Somalia—falls apart under close examination. It was not the media
that set the agenda in the fall of 1992, but the Bush administration itself,
the Congress, and relief officials in and out of government. The horrible
images did have an effect, but a narrow one. Reflecting on the experience,
[Assistant Secretary of State Robert] Gallucci said that pictures "don't come
anywhere near" forcing an introduction of U.S. ground troops when it is
known they will be in harm's way.

"When you're short of that, then the pictures are very useful in getting
people to focus on it as a basis for humanitarian support." For anything
more than that, "it's gotta answer the question, Why us?" It is to these limits
of media power that we now turn our attention.

Bosnia and Rwanda: The Limits of Images' Power

* * *

* * * [T]here were two points at which news media pressures for intervention [in Yugoslavia] were at their most intense. The first was in August
1992, with the revelations, first by Gutman in *Newsday* and then on Britain's
Independent Television Network (ITN), of the murder and gross mistreat-
ment of Bosnian Muslims in Serb-run concentration camps. The second,
the televised bloody aftermath of the February 1994 "marketplace massacre"
in Sarajevo, will be examined in a moment.

Gutman's Pulitzer Prize–winning reports in *Newsday* and the vivid ITN
images of emaciated men behind barbed wire, recalling as they did the Ho-
locaust, caused an emotional reaction around the world. In the United
States, journalists, lawmakers, and other politicians—including presidential
candidate Bill Clinton—demanded action to stop the abuses. Yet by this
time, the Bush administration had looked at the question of intervention in
the former Yugoslavia, and determined it was an abyss that would draw in
thousands of U.S. ground troops for an indefinite period (Clinton would
later come to this same conclusion). Two factors about this policy decision
are important in determining why the media had so little effect: The decision
was firmly held, and it was shared by all the senior members of Bush's
national security team. As Warren Zimmermann, the last U.S. ambassador
to Yugoslavia, put it: "It wouldn't have mattered if television was going 24
hours around the clock with Serb atrocities. Bush wasn't going to get in."[11]
Eagleburger used virtually identical language, saying: "Through all the time

we were there, you have to understand that we had largely made a decision we were not going to get militarily involved. And nothing, including those stories, pushed us into it. . . . I hated it. Because this was condoning—I won't say genocide—but condoning a hell of a lot of murder. . . . It made us damn uncomfortable. But this was a policy that wasn't going to get changed no matter what the press said."[12]

In other words, while it was difficult for policymakers not to respond to the news media reports and the outcry that they engendered, they decided it would be even more costly to respond. Politically, however, the Bush administration could not afford to be seen as doing nothing or as uncaring. On August 6, 1992, the day the ITN videotape aired, Bush demanded that the Serbs open the camps to international access. A week later, with U.S. support, the UN Security Council passed Resolution 770, demanding outside access to the camps and authorizing member states to use "all measures necessary" (that is, force) to ensure humanitarian relief supplies were delivered. The news media reports also played a role in the establishment of the first war crimes tribunals in Europe since World War II. While some things had changed on the surface, U.S. policy remained largely the same, defined by Bush's August 7 statement that the United States would not intervene with force. Bush recalled Vietnam, saying, "I do not want to see the United States bogged down in any way into some guerilla warfare. We lived through that once." Resolution 770 never was fully implemented.

This lack of real policy change was further confirmed in interviews with officials and reporters. Scowcroft said, "We did some marginal things, but there was a real consensus—and I think probably an unshakable consensus—to make a real difference . . . would require an American or NATO intervention that we did not see justified." Foreign Service officer George Kenney, who on August 25 publicly resigned to protest the lack of substantive U.S. action, said that government concern with the media "only extended to the appearance of maintaining we were behaving responsibly," while in reality refusing further entanglement in the Balkans. I asked journalist Roy Gutman, who actively tried to raise the alarm within the U.S. government once he had confirmed atrocities were taking place, for his assessment of his reports' impact. He curled two fingers in the symbol for a zero. "Really," he said. "What you had is a lot of reaction to reports, but never any policy change."[13] This is the minimalist response.

The U.S. policy response to the wholesale slaughter of ethnic Tutsis and politically moderate Hutus in Rwanda in 1994 provides an even starker example of the limits of images' power to affect U.S. intervention policy when the proposed intervention involves potentially large costs. By this time, the Clinton administration had learned, in Somalia, that interventions undertaken for the best of reasons and involving seemingly low costs can become expensive in terms of lives, money, and prestige. Whether the administration learned the correct lesson from Somalia or whether a small show of force would have halted the slaughter in Rwanda, as administration critics contend, is beside the point here. What is significant, rather, is that in officials' minds, the Somalia experience far outweighed the media pressures to intervene in Rwanda with force while warfare was underway.

Yet, under traditional CNN-effect theory, the pressures were greater in Rwanda than they were in Somalia. On April 6, 1994, the Hutu presidents of Rwanda and Burundi were killed in a mysterious plane crash, which sparked the subsequent slaughter by extremist Hutus. * * * [There] was more coverage than the networks gave Somalia at any time during 1992, with the exception of December, when U.S. troops already had been dispatched. Nonetheless, these higher coverage levels did not prompt a significant intervention by the Clinton administration. * * * "None of those provoked or provided the kind of catalyst for a U.S. military intervention. . . . The [later scenes of refugee] camps were a different matter. . . . The mind-numbingness of it all was almost a made-to-order operation for what the U.S. can do and do very quickly. But it was into a basically benign environment."[14]

It was only after the fighting largely had ceased (the Tutsi-led Rwandan Patriotic Front seized control of Kigali in early July), that the administration felt any desire or pressure to intervene. It was at this point that hundreds of thousands of Rwandans, most of them Hutus fearing Tutsi reprisals, fled to and beyond the nation's borders. There was now a clear, quick task that could be performed, one requiring logistics available only to the U.S. military. " 'Exit strategy' was the mantra," said a senior Pentagon official. "Everyone felt comfortable enough that that was a specific job that we could perform." Before, during the slaughter, "we didn't see that clear picture."[15]

On July 22, 1994, President Clinton announced a massive U.S. logistics effort in support of the UNHCR and other relief agencies in Rwanda, Operation Support Hope. News media reports, especially television images, contributed to Clinton's decision, officials said. But the actual situation on the ground in Rwanda and the recent history of U.S. intervention in Somalia played a major role in the U.S. response. The media's impact was limited to the humanitarian arena. And the policy response itself was minimalist, inasmuch as Operation Support Hope was tightly circumscribed in its size, duration and scope of activities. Interestingly, the public response to Rwanda—first civil war and then humanitarian tragedy—paralleled that of government policymakers. According to a senior NGO representative, when television was broadcasting images of Rwandans who had been hacked to death, private relief groups "got virtually no money whatsoever" from the viewing public. That did not change until the refugees flooded into Zaire and there were "pictures of women and children . . . innocents in need."[16]

* * *

Real-Time Intervention: The Sarajevo Market Massacres

Another facet of the loss of policy control associated with the idea of a CNN effect is the ability of modern news media to transmit graphic images almost instantaneously. This speed, it is said, overwhelms the traditional policy-making structures, forcing decisions that might not otherwise be made, perhaps before all the facts are in.

A good example of the impact of real-time media reports on intervention decisions is the gruesome footage of the February 5, 1994, "marketplace massacre," in which a mortar shell fired by an unknown party (but almost certainly Bosnian Serbs) landed in a crowded marketplace in Sarajevo, killing 68 people and horribly wounding nearly 200 others. In the aftermath of the attack and the public outcry, the United States abandoned its hands-off policy toward the Balkan conflict. It led NATO in issuing an ultimatum to the Bosnian Serbs to remove their heavy weapons from around Bosnia's capital (an extension of this threat would lead to NATO's first use of offensive force in Europe in its history) and established the five-nation "Contact Group," giving new momentum to the search for a diplomatic solution to the conflict. Sarajevens enjoyed a bit of normalcy after nearly two years of siege.

This clearly seems to be a case where videotaped images led the United States into, or at least toward, intervention. But while the images did have an impact, it was not the simple cause-effect one that this glance at events would indicate. At the time of the shelling, the United States already was moving toward a more active role in the Balkans, for reasons that included intense pressure from France and U.S. concern that the inability to affect the conflict was eroding the Atlantic alliance and American leadership. On February 4, the day *before* the shelling, Secretary of State Warren Christopher proposed that the United States lead a new diplomatic effort, combined with the threat of using force.[17] "I am acutely uncomfortable with the passive position we are now in, and believe that now is the time to undertake a new initiative," he wrote in a letter to Defense Secretary William Perry and National Security Adviser Anthony Lake.[18] "We had a real sense that we didn't have a Bosnia policy that was going anywhere," said a senior State Department official. Before the shelling, "We had already made the psychological determination [about] the direction we wanted to go." This official was in a series of meetings on fashioning a new policy toward Bosnia when the mortar attack occurred—and recalled worrying that the new policy would be seen, incorrectly, as an instant response to the massacre.[19]

This is not to say that the bloody images had no impact; media reports actually had three effects. First, according to White House spokesperson Michael McCurry, they galvanized and accelerated the decision-making process. "The impact of the marketplace bombing . . . was to force there to be a response much quicker than the U.S. government" routinely produces one, McCurry said.[20] Second, it provided ammunition for those, such as Christopher, who had been arguing in administration councils for action. Third, it provided a moment of increased public attention to Bosnia that made it easier for the administration to explain a more robust policy. "It was a short window. We took advantage of it. We moved the policy forward. And it was successful," said McCurry's predecessor, Dee Dee Myers.[21]

In summary, rather than forcing the Clinton administration into doing something (undertaking an intervention) that it did not want to do, the images from Sarajevo helped the administration take a step that some of its senior members were arguing for. The images had an impact because the structure they affected—Clinton Administration foreign policy—was itself in flux.

* * *

Conclusion

This essay has examined the news media's impact on one portion of foreign policy and national security concerns—the decision about whether or not to intervene (in the form of a peace operation) with U.S. military might. There are many other scenarios where the media might have a potential impact. One is an international crisis of great importance to the United States, but where U.S. military intervention is not feasible or realistic. Examples include China's brutal crackdown on student demonstrators in Tiananmen Square in 1989 and the coup attempts in Moscow in 1991 and 1993. Another is when U.S. troops already have intervened and face some setback or change in their mission, as happened with the deaths of eighteen soldiers in Somalia in October 1993. As noted above and expanded upon by this author elsewhere, the news media's potential impact is greater after an intervention is underway. This seems to be true because an intervention elicits the highest levels of media attention, puts U.S. lives and prestige on the line, and prompts significant public attention.

* * *

Perhaps the clearest lesson here is that, in an age of instant, 'round-the-clock television news, foreign policy leadership remains both possible and necessary—perhaps even more necessary than before.* * * There seems little doubt that CNN and its brethren have made leadership more difficult. Numerous officials spoke of the temptation to respond to dramatic video images and the intense public outcry that often can accompany them. These calls can be resisted, but at a political price. If policy is not well anchored, the temptation to respond to the calculation of the moment can be overwhelming. CNN, in particular, gives opponents of policy—whether in the U.S. Congress or in the streets of Mogadishu—a platform to make their views known instantly, thus complicating the life of today's policymaker. Television feeds on conflict, whether political or physical, emphasizing the challenge to policy. * * *

* * *

Nonetheless, while it is neither possible nor advisable to suppress all challenges to policy, this paper has found a clear inverse relationship between leadership and news media impact. When policy is well grounded, it is less likely that the media will be able to shift officials' focus. When policy is clear, reasonably constant, and well communicated, the news media follow officials rather than lead them—by the rules of "objectivity," they can do nothing else.[22] The case of the first Sarajevo market massacre shows how television can be used to advance new policies. Indeed, in the hands of those who understand the role of information in modern governance, CNN can be an extraordinarily powerful—to some, even frightening—tool. It must be noted that each of the cases examined here involved peace operations, where national interests may have been at stake, but these interests were not seen by officials or the public as vital. It seems reasonable to suggest that the power of the executive to frame the debate and present policy options —in short, to use the media, rather than be used by them—increases when the threat to the nation's physical or economic security grows. This, in fact, is what happened during the Persian Gulf War.

Clearly, one area of particular sensitivity for leaders is the media's power to force them to at least focus on cases of humanitarian tragedy. Sometimes, this results in action to address the crisis—if such action is deemed not to involve overly high risks. But many other times, policy makers moved to heal the overt wounds while shying away the much more risky surgery involved in finding a political solution. This finding raises several troublesome questions. Does the public's long-term confidence in U.S. leadership suffer when policymakers, engaging in a minimalist response, promise or suggest more than they can deliver? Are top policymakers and the public spending an inordinate amount of time focused on dramatic crises at the expense of problems that are harder to portray on television? Numerous officials whom I interviewed expressed frustration that more important, but less dramatic problems—the General Agreement on Tariffs and Trade, the future of Russia's reforms, U.S. policy in Asia, to name a few—rarely make the nightly news. Yet this problem may to some extent be self-correcting. Unfortunately for its victims, violence and tragedy, when shown on television, seem to bring diminishing returns in public sympathy and official anxiety. For better or worse, the rude surprise the United States received after intervening in Somalia hastened this self-correction. Whether it is temporary or permanent will become clear over the next few years.

In sum, the awesome powers of communication technology at the news media's disposal have not had as dramatic an impact on this critical aspect of foreign policy as it might seem at first glance. Each of the cases revealed how other, abiding factors played a central role in the decision about whether or not to intervene. These factors included the real potential costs in U.S. blood and treasure; the credibility of the United States on the international scene; the future of important alliances; and the goals and benefits of the proposed mission itself. Journalists have had an impact on the decision about whether or not the United States will send its men and women into combat for a long time, as the case of the Yellow Press, McKinley, and the Spanish-American War shows. They still have an impact—and for the same reasons. What technology per se has changed is the pressures of time. If government officials allow others to dominate the debate, if they fail to communicate their policies and build support, if those policies fail, the news media will reflect all this, and officials will soon find that the impact of the media can be very real—and blindingly swift—indeed.

While the news media have made modern governance more difficult and more risky, Kennan's fears about the obsolescence of official prerogatives are exaggerated at best. Policymakers retain the power to set the agenda, to make policy choices and to lead. To do so, they need a sophisticated understanding, not simplistic descriptions, of the news media's complex role.

NOTES

1. For our purposes, "real-time" means not only images that are broadcast as they are occurring (that is, live) but also those that reach policymakers and other audiences within twenty-four hours of the event. See Nik Gowing, *Real-Time Television Coverage of Armed Conflicts and Diplomatic Crises: Does it Pressure or Distort Foreign Policy Decisions?* Working Paper 94-1, Joan Shorenstein Barone Center on the Press, Politics, and Public Policy, Harvard University, Cambridge, Mass., June 1994.
2. Steven Livingston and Todd Eachus, "Humanitarian Crises and U.S. Foreign Policy: Somalia and the CNN Effect Reconsidered," *Political Communication* 12, no. 4 (October–December 1995): 415–416.
3. Daniel Hallin, *The "Uncensored War": The Media and Vietnam* (Berkeley: University of California Press, 1986).
4. "Peace operations" is the term employed by the Clinton administration in its May 1994 policy declaration, where it was defined as "the entire spectrum of activities from traditional peacekeeping to peace enforcement aimed at defusing and resolving international conflicts." "Operations other than war" (OOTWs), as used by the U.S. military, is somewhat broader, encompassing such activities as drug interdiction and relief missions such as those conducted in Bangladesh (Operation Sea Angel) or south Florida (Hurricane Andrew).
5. Hallin, *The "Uncensored War."*

6. *The Media and Foreign Policy in the Post–Cold War World* (New York: Freedom Forum Media Studies Center, 1993).

7. Livingston and Eachus, "Humanitarian Crises"; and Eric V. Larson, *U.S. Casualties in Somalia: The Media Response and the Myth of the "CNN Effect"* (draft), RAND, Santa Monica, Calif., March 1995, p. 69.

8. Herman J. Cohen, "Intervention in Somalia," *The Diplomatic Record 1992–1993* (Boulder, Colo.: Westview Press, 1994), pp. 62–63.

9. Telephone interview with Baker, September 11, 1995.

10. Interviews: Baker, September 11, 1995; Eagleburger, February 1, 1995; and Scowcroft, February 27, 1995.

11. Interview with Zimmermann, June 8, 1995.

12. Eagleburger interview.

13. Scowcroft interview; interview with Kenney, January 26, 1995; and interview with Gutman, January 31, 1995.

14. Background interview, November 17, 1994.

15. Background interview, July 10, 1994.

16. Background remarks of senior NGO representative at conference on "Media, Military, and the Humanitarian Crises: New Relations for New Challenges," George Washington University, Washington, D.C., May 5, 1995.

17. Elizabeth Drew, *On The Edge: The Clinton Presidency* (New York: Simon and Schuster, 1994).

18. Elaine Sciolino and Douglas Jehl, "As U.S. Sought a Bosnia Policy, the French Offered a Good Idea," *New York Times*, February 14, 1994, p. A1.

19. Background interview, February 3, 1995.

20. Interview with McCurry, May 15, 1995 (at the time of the event, McCurry was State Department spokesperson).

21. Interview with Myers, February 27, 1995.

22. Hallin, *The "Uncensored War."*

6.3 Public Opinion

OLE R. HOLSTI

Public Opinion and Foreign Policy: Challenges to the Almond-Lippmann Consensus

Introduction

Many questions about the role of public opinion in foreign policy are at the center of persisting debates between the liberal-democratic and realist approaches to foreign affairs. Is public opinion a force for enlightenment—indeed, a necessary if not sufficient condition for sound foreign policy—as celebrated by the Wilsonians and other liberals? There is a long, liberal-democratic tradition, dating back at least to Kant and Bentham, that foreign policies of democracies are more peaceful, at least in part because the public can play a constructive role in constraining policy makers; only accountability to the public can restrain the war-making proctivities of leaders.[1]

Alternatively, are Hans Morgenthau and others of the realist school correct in describing public opinion as a barrier to thoughtful and coherent diplomacy, hindering efforts to promote national interests that transcend the moods and passions of the moment? The realist tradition is intensely skeptical of the public's contribution to effective foreign policy. At the very minimum, most realists would distinguish between foreign policy and other public policy issues; the public might be sufficiently informed to deal with local issues that impinge on their daily lives, but foreign affairs are too remote from their experience, and in any case they have little inclination to become more informed about such complex and remote issues. Finally, the effective conduct of diplomacy requires secrecy, flexibility, and other qualities that would be seriously jeopardized were the public to have a significant impact on foreign policy. Thus, to permit the public a strong voice in policy would be to place the democracies, if not the stability of the international system itself, at a distinct disadvantage. Moreover, it would permit the emotional to govern the rational. Hans Morgenthau summarized the case against an active role for public opinion in words that would gain the support of most if not all realists: "The rational requirements of good foreign policy

From *International Studies Quarterly* 36.4 (December 1992).

cannot from the outset count upon the support of a public opinion whose preferences are emotional rather than rational" (Morgenthau, 1978:558).

* * *

The Post–World War II Consensus

The availability after World War II of growing sets of polling data and the institution of systematic studies of voting behavior, combined with the assumption of a leadership role in world affairs by the United States, served to stimulate a growth industry in analyses of public opinion. The consensus view that developed during this period of some fifteen or twenty years after the end of World War II and just prior to the Vietnam escalation centered on three major propositions:

- Public opinion is highly volatile and thus it provides very dubious foundations for a sound foreign policy.
- Public attitudes on foreign affairs are so lacking in structure and coherence that they might best be described as "non-attitudes."
- At the end of the day, however, public opinion has a very limited impact on the conduct of foreign policy.

Public Opinion Is Volatile

As noted earlier, Walter Lippmann's books of the interwar period described the mass public as neither sufficiently interested nor informed to play the pivotal role assigned to it by classical democratic theory. At the height of the Cold War thirty years later, Lippmann had become even more alarmed, depicting the mass public as not merely uninterested and uninformed, but as a powerful force that was so out of synch with reality as to constitute a massive and potentially fatal threat to effective government and policies.

> The unhappy truth is that the prevailing public opinion has been destructively wrong at the critical junctures. The people have impressed a critical veto upon the judgments of informed and responsible officials. They have compelled the government, which usually knew what would have been wiser, or was necessary, or what was more expedient, to be too late with too little, or too long with too much, too pacifist in peace and too bellicose in war, too neutralist or appeasing in negotiations or too intransigent. Mass opinion has acquired mounting power in this country. It has shown itself to be a dangerous master of decision when the stakes are life and death. (Lippmann, 1955:20)

Similarly pessimistic conclusions and dire warnings were emerging from disparate other quarters as well. Drawing on a growing body of polling data and fearing that the American public might relapse into a mindless isolationism, because only a thin veneer of postwar internationalism covered a thick bedrock of indifference to the world, Gabriel Almond depicted public opinion as a volatile and mood-driven constraint upon foreign policy: "The undertow of withdrawal is still very powerful. Deeply ingrained habits do not die easy deaths. The world outside is still very remote for most Americans; and the tragic lessons of the last decades have not been fully digested" (Almond, 1950:85). Consequently, "Perhaps the gravest general problem confronting policy-makers is that of the instability of mass moods, the cyclical fluctuations which stand in the way of policy stability" (Almond, 1950: 239).[2]

*   *   *

Further support for the critics and skeptics emerged from the growing body of polling data which yielded ample evidence of the public's limited store of factual knowledge about foreign affairs. Innumerable surveys revealed such stunning gaps in information as: X percent of the American public are unaware that there is a communist government in China, Y percent believe that the Soviet Union is a member of NATO, or Z percent cannot identify a single nation bordering on the Pacific Ocean. Such data reinforced the case of the critics and led some of them to propose measures to reduce the influence of the public. Thus, Lippmann (1955) called for stronger executive prerogatives in foreign affairs, and Bailey (1948:13) wondered whether the requirements of an effective foreign policy might make it necessary for the executive deliberately to mislead the public.

Public Opinion Lacks Structure and Coherence

A growing volume of data on public opinion and voting behavior, as well as increasingly sophisticated methodologies, enabled analysts not only to describe aggregate results and trends, but also to delve into the structure of political beliefs. Owing to immediate policy concerns about the U.S. role in the postwar era, many of the early studies were largely descriptive, focusing on such issues as participation in international organizations and alliances, the deployment of troops abroad, security commitments, foreign aid, trade and protectionism, and the like. The underlying premise was that a single internationalist-isolationist dimension would serve to structure foreign policy beliefs, much in the way that a liberal-conservative dimension was assumed to provide coherence to preferences on domestic issues.

In a classic study based on data from the late 1950s and early 1960s, Philip Converse (1964) concluded that the political beliefs of the mass public lack a real structure or coherence. Comparing responses across several domestic and foreign policy issues, he found little if any "constraint" or underlying ideological structure that might provide some coherence to political thinking. In contrast, his analyses of elites—congressional candidates—revealed substantially higher correlations among responses to various issues.

Moreover, Converse found that both mass and elite attitudes on a given issue had a short half-life. Responses in 1956 only modestly predicted responses two years later, much less in 1960. These findings led him to conclude that mass political beliefs are best described as "non-attitudes." Although Converse's findings were later to become the center of an active debate, it should be emphasized that his was not a lone voice in the wilderness. His data were drawn from the National Election Studies at the University of Michigan, and his findings were only the most widely quoted of a series of studies from the NES that came to essentially the same conclusion about the absence of structure, coherence, or persistence in the political beliefs of the mass public—especially on foreign affairs (Campbell, Converse, Miller, and Stokes, 1964).

Public Opinion Has Limited Impact on Foreign Policy

* * * The driving force behind much of the post-World War II attention to public opinion on foreign policy issues was the fear that an ill-informed and emotional mass public would serve as a powerful constraint on the conduct of American diplomacy, establishing unwise limits on policy makers, creating unrealistic expectations about what was feasible in foreign affairs, otherwise doing serious mischief to American diplomacy and, given the American role in the world, perhaps even to international stability. As Bernard Cohen (1973) demonstrated in a critical survey of the literature, however, the constraining role of public opinion was often asserted but rarely demonstrated—or even put to a systematic test.

By the middle of the 1960s a consensus in fact seemed to emerge on a third point: Public opinion has little if any real impact on policy. Or, as the point was made most pithily by one State Department official: "To hell with public opinion. . . . We should lead, and not follow" (quoted in Cohen, 1973:62). The weight of research evidence cast doubt on the potency of public opinion as a driving force behind, or even a significant constraint upon, foreign policy-making. For example, a classic study of the public-legislator relationship revealed that constituents' attitudes on foreign policy had less impact on members of the House of Representatives than did their views on domestic issues (Miller and Stokes, 1963). Cohen's research on the foreign policy bureaucracy indicated that State Department officials had a rather modest interest in public opinion, and to the extent that they even thought about the public, it was as an entity to be "educated" rather than a lodestar by which to be guided (Cohen, 1973). The proposition that the president has "almost a free hand" in the conduct of foreign affairs received support from other analysis, including Lipset (1966), LaFeber (1977), Levering (1978), Paterson (1979), and Graebner (1983).

* * *

The Renaissance of Interest in Public Opinion and Foreign Policy

Just as World War II and fears of postwar isolationism among the mass public gave rise to concern about public opinion and its impact on foreign policy, the war in Vietnam was the impetus for a renewed interest in the subject. It was a major catalyst in stimulating a reexamination of the consensus that had emerged during the two decades after World War II. * * * [D]uring the past two decades analysts have begun to challenge important aspects of the consensus described above.

* * *

Mueller's (1973) study of public opinion toward the Korean and Vietnam wars posed [a] challenge to the thesis of mindless changes in public attitudes. To be sure, public support for the U.S. war effort in both conflicts eventually changed, but in ways that seemed explicable and rational, rather than random and mindless. More specifically, he found that increasing public opposition to the conflicts traced out a pattern that fit a curve of rising battle deaths, suggesting that the public used an understandable, if simple, heuristic to assess American policy.[3]

The most comprehensive challenge to the Almond-Lippmann thesis has emerged from studies conducted by Benjamin Page and Robert Shapiro. Their evidence includes all questions that have been posed by major polling organizations since the inception of systematic surveys in the 1930s. Of the more than 6000 questions, almost 20 percent have been asked at least twice, providing Page and Shapiro with a large data set to assess the degree of stability and change in mass public attitudes. Employing a cutoff point of a difference of 6 percent from one survey to another to distinguish between continuity and change, they found that mass opinion in the aggregate is in fact characterized by a good deal of stability and that this is no less true of foreign policy than on domestic issues (Page and Shapiro, 1988). More important, when attitude shifts take place, they seem to be neither random nor 180 degrees removed from the true state of world affairs. Rather, changes appear to be "reasonable, event driven" reactions to the real world, even if the information upon which they are based is marginally adequate at best. They concluded that

> virtually all the rapid shifts [in public opinion] we found were related to political and economic circumstances or to significant events which sensible citizens would take into account. In particular, most abrupt foreign policy changes took place in connection with wars, confrontations, or crises in which major changes in the actions of the United States or other nations quite naturally affect preferences about what policies to pursue.[4]

* * *

Similar conclusions, supporting Page and Shapiro and casting doubt on the Almond-Lippmann thesis, have also emerged from other studies. Jentleson (1992) found that during the post-Vietnam era, variations in public support for the use of force are best explained by differences between force to coerce foreign policy restraint by others, and force to influence or impose internal political changes within another state; the former goal has received much stronger support than the latter.[5]

An interesting variant of the "rational public" thesis stipulates that the public attempts to moderate American behavior toward the USSR by expressing preferences for a conciliatory stance from hawkish administrations while supporting more assertive policies from dovish ones (Nincic, 1988). To the extent that one can generalize from this study focusing on the Carter and Reagan administrations to other periods or other aspects of foreign policy, it further challenges the Almond-Lippmann thesis—indeed, it turns that proposition on its head—for it identifies the public as a source of moderation and continuity rather than of instability and unpredictability.

It is important to emphasize that none of these challenges to the Almond-Lippmann thesis is based on some newly found evidence that the public is in fact well informed about foreign affairs. Not only do polls repeatedly reveal that the mass public has a very thin veneer of factual knowledge about politics, economics, and geography; they also reveal that it is poorly informed about the specifics of conflicts, treaties, negotiations with other nations, characteristics of weapons systems, foreign leaders, and the like. Because the modest factual basis upon which the mass public reacts to international affairs remains an unchallenged—and unchallengeable—fact, we are faced with a puzzle: If a generally poorly informed mass public does indeed react to international affairs in an events-driven, rational manner, what are the means that permit it to do so? Recall that a not-insignificant body of research evidence indicated that mass public attitudes lack the kind of ideological structure that would provide some coherence across specific issues and persistence through time.

* * *

Challenge #2: Do Public Attitudes Lack Structure and Coherence?

* * *

Although the more recent research literature has yet to create a consensus on all aspects of the question, there does appear to be a considerable convergence of findings on two general points relating to belief structures:

1. Even though the general public may be rather poorly informed, attitudes about foreign affairs are in fact structured in at least moderately coherent ways. Indeed, low information and an ambiguous foreign

policy environment are actually likely to motivate rather than preclude some type of attitude structure.
2. A single isolationist-to-internationalist dimension inadequately describes the main dimensions of public opinion on international affairs.

An early study, based on the first of the quadrennial Chicago Council on Foreign Relations (CCFR) surveys, employed factor analysis and other methods to uncover three foreign policy outlooks: "liberal internationalism," "conservative internationalism," and "non-internationalism" (Mandelbaum and Schneider, 1979). A comparable trichotomy ("three-headed eagle") emerged from early analyses of the data on opinion leaders generated by the Foreign Policy Leadership Project (FPLP) (Holsti, 1979; Holsti and Rosenau, 1979, 1984).

Others have questioned the division of foreign policy attitudes into three *types* rather than *dimensions*, and they have offered compelling evidence in support of their critiques. Chittick and Billingsley (1989) have undertaken both original and secondary analyses which indicated the need for three *dimensions*, including one that taps unilateralist-multilateralist sentiments, not three *types*, to describe adequately the foreign policy beliefs of both the mass public and leaders. (See also Bardes and Oldendick, 1978; Chittick, Billingsley, and Travis, 1990).

A major set of contributions to the debate about how best to describe foreign policy attitudes has come from Wittkopf's exemplary secondary analyses of the CCFR surveys of both the general public and leaders (Wittkopf, 1986, 1990). His results, developed inductively from the first four CCFR surveys, revealed that with a single exception, two dimensions are necessary to describe foreign policy attitudes: "support-oppose militant internationalism" (MI) and "support-oppose cooperative internationalism" (CI). Dichotomizing and crossing these dimensions yields four types, with the quadrants labeled as *hard-liners* (support MI, oppose CI), *internationalists* (support MI, support CI), *isolationists* (oppose MI, oppose CI), and *accommodationists* (oppose MI, support CI).

Support for Wittkopf's MI/CI scheme also emerges from a reanalysis of the FPLP data on American opinion leaders (Holsti and Rosenau, 1990). That study put the MI/CI scheme to a demanding test because of three major differences in the data sets: (1) The CCFR surveys were undertaken in 1974, 1978, 1982, and 1986, whereas the four FPLP studies followed two years later in each case; (2) the two sets of surveys have only a few questionnaire items in common; and (3) the MI/CI scheme was developed largely from data on the mass public, whereas the FPLP surveys focused solely on opinion leaders.

It may be worth noting that although the origins of the MI/CI scheme are strictly inductive, the militant internationalism and cooperative internationalism dimensions correspond closely to the most venerable approaches to international relations: realism and liberalism. Realism views conflict between nations as a natural state of affairs rather than an aberration that is subject to permanent amelioration. Such realist concepts as security dilemma, relative capabilities, and "zero sum" view of conflict are also basic to the MI dimension. There are similarly intimate links between liberalism and the cooperative internationalism dimension. Liberalism denies that conflict is an immutable element of relations between nations. It defines security in terms that are broader than the geopolitical-military dimensions, and it emphasizes the cooperative aspects of relations between nations. Institution building, improved international education and communication, and trade are but a few of the ways in which nations may jointly gain and thus mitigate, if not eliminate, the harshest features of international relations in an anarchic system. In short, the CI dimension shares important elements with the liberal school of international relations theory. * * *

Challenge #3: Is Public Opinion Really Impotent?

* * *

Several recent quantitative studies have challenged some important foundations of the theory that, at least on foreign and defense issues, the public is virtually impotent. One element of that thesis is that policy makers are relatively free agents on foreign policy questions because these issues pose few dangers of electoral retribution by voters: elections are said to be decided by domestic questions, especially those sometimes described as "pocketbook" or "bread and butter" issues. However, a systematic study of presidential campaigns between 1952 and 1984 revealed that in five of the nine elections during the period, foreign policy issues had "large effects." Or, as the authors put it, when presidential candidates devote campaign time and other resources to foreign policy issues, they are not merely "waltzing before a blind audience" (Aldrich, Sullivan, and Borgida, 1989).

Recent research on voting behavior has also emphasized the importance of retrospective evaluations on performance on voter choice among candidates, especially when one of them is an incumbent (Fiorina, 1981; Abramson, Aldrich, and Rhode, 1990). Because voters are perceived as punishing incumbent candidates or parties for foreign policy failures (for example, the Iran hostage episode) or rewarding them for successes (for example, the invasion of Panama to capture General Noriega), decisions by foreign policy leaders may be made in anticipation of public reactions and the probabilities of success or failure.

* * *

Finally, two major studies have measured the congruence between changes in public preferences and a broad range of policies over extended periods. The first, a study of public opinion and policy outcomes spanning the years 1960–1974, revealed that in almost two thirds of 222 cases, policy outcomes corresponded to public preferences. The consistency was especially high (92%) on foreign policy issues. Monroe (1979:11) offers three possible explanations for his findings: Foreign policy issues permit more decision-making by the executive, are likely to be the object of relatively less interest and influence by organized interest groups, and are especially susceptible to elite manipulation. The second study covered an even longer span—1935 to 1979—which included 357 significant changes of public preferences (Page and Shapiro, 1983). Of the 231 instances of subsequent policy changes, 153 (66%) were congruent with changes in public preferences. There was little difference in the level of congruence for domestic (70%) and foreign policy (62%) issues.

* * *

Among the more difficult cases are those dealing with public opinion as a possible constraint on action. During the 1980s, the Reagan administration undertook a massive public relations campaign of dubious legality to generate public support for assistance to the "contra" rebels in Nicaragua (Parry and Kornbluh, 1988), but a careful analysis of surveys on the issue revealed that a majority of the public opposed American military involvement in Central America (Sobel, 1989; see also Hinckley, 1992). Would the Reagan administration have intervened more directly or massively in Nicaragua or El Salvador in the absence of such attitudes? Solid evidence about contemporary non-events is, to understate the case, rather hard to come by. Case studies seem to be the only way to address such questions, although even this approach is not wholly free of potential problems. Does an absence of documentary references to public opinion indicate a lack of interest by decision-makers? Alternatively, was attention to public attitudes so deeply ingrained in their working habits that it was unnecessary to make constant references to it? Are frequent references to public opinion an indication of a significant impact on decisions—or of a desire on the part of officials to be "on record" as having paid attention to public sentiments?

* * *

Conclusion

The consensus of the mid-1960s on the nature, structure, and impact of public opinion has clearly come under vigorous challenge during the past quarter century. The Vietnam War, while not the sole causal factor in the reexamination of the conventional wisdom, was certainly a catalyst. If a new consensus has yet to emerge on all of the issues discussed above, at least it seems safe to state that the field is marked by innovative research and active debates on the implications of the results.

* * *

At the broadest level, if we are indeed entering into a period of fewer major power confrontations, and greater attention to such nonmilitary issues as trade, immigration, the environment, and the like—there is ample survey data that much of the American public believes this to be the case—it may also be an era in which public opinion plays a more autonomous role. Even those who do not fully accept the "manipulated public" thesis would acknowledge that crises and confrontations abroad provide a setting in which opportunities and temptations for manipulating the public are far greater than on nonstrategic issues. Not only are the latter typically resolved over a longer time period—providing greater opportunities for the public, pressure groups, the media, and Congress to play a significant role—but they also tend to be more resistant to claims that the needs for secrecy, flexibility, and speed of action make it both necessary and legitimate for the executive to have a relatively free hand.

In short, we may be moving into a period in which the relationship between public opinion and foreign policy takes on added rather than diminished significance, but we should also be wary of assumptions that the theories, evidence, and linkages emerging from research during the Cold War era will necessarily travel intact into an era of strikingly different circumstances.

NOTES

1. Recent research has found that the foreign policies of democracies are indeed different from those of other polities and, further, that democracies do not engage in war against each other.
2. Almond's use of the term "mood" differs from that of Frank Klingberg. Almond refers to sudden shifts of interest and preferences, whereas Klingberg has used the term to explain American foreign policy in terms of generation-long societal swings between introversion and extraversion. For the latter usage, see Klingberg (1952, 1979, 1983) and Holmes (1985).
3. During the summer of 1965, as the Johnson Administration was moving toward fateful decisions regarding Vietnam, George Ball warned: 'We can't win,' he said, his deep voice dominating the Cabinet Room. 'The war will be long and protracted, with heavy casualties. The most we can hope for is a messy conclusion. We must measure this long-term price against the short-term loss that will result from withdrawal.' Producing a chart that correlated public opinion with American casualties in Korea, Ball predicted that the American public would not support a long and inconclusive war (Clifford, 1991:412).
4. Page and Shapiro (1982:34); see also Page and Shapiro (1983, 1984, 1988, 1992): Page, Shapiro, and Dempsey (1987); Shapiro and Page (1988).

5. For additional evidence about the "rational public," the stability of policy preferences, and issue voting, see Bennett (1972:742), Free and Watts (1980:50), Wittkopf (1986, 1990), Graham (1986, 1988, 1989), Krosnick (1988a, 1988b, 1990, 1991), Russett (1990), and Peffley and Hurwitz (1992a, 1992b).

REFERENCES

ABRAMSON, P., J. H. ALDRICH, AND J. RHODE (1990) *Change and Continuity in the 1988 Election.* Washington, DC: Congressional Quarterly.

ALDRICH, J. H., J. I. SULLIVAN, AND E. BORGIDA (1989) Foreign Affairs and Issue Voting: Do Presidential Candidates "Waltz before a Blind Audience?" *American Political Science Review* 83:123–141.

ALMOND, G. (1950) *The American People and Foreign Policy.* New York: Praeger. Reprinted in 1960 with a new introduction.

BAILEY, T. A. (1948) *The Man in the Street: The Impact of American Public Opinion on Foreign Policy.* New York: Macmillan.

BARDES, B. A., AND R. OLDENDICK (1978) Beyond Internationalism: The Case for Multiple Dimensions in Foreign Policy Attitudes. *Social Science Quarterly* 59:496–508.

BENNETT, S. E. (1972) Attitude Structures and Foreign Policy Opinions. *Social Science Quarterly* 55:732–742.

CAMPBELL, A., P. E. CONVERSE, W. E. MILLER, AND D. E. STOKES (1964) *The American Voter.* New York: Wiley.

CHITTICK, W., AND K. R. BILLINGSLEY (1989) The Structure of Elite Foreign Policy Beliefs. *Western Political Quarterly* 42:201–224.

CHITTICK, W., K. R. BILLINGSLEY, AND R. TRAVIS (1990) Persistence and Change in Elite and Mass Attitudes toward U.S. Foreign Policy. *Political Psychology* 11:385–402.

CLIFFORD, C., WITH R. HOLBROOK (1991) *Counsel to the President: A Memoir.* New York: Random House.

COHEN, B. C. (1973) *The Public's Impact on Foreign Policy.* Boston: Little, Brown.

CONVERSE, P. E. (1964) "The Nature of Belief Systems in Mass Publics." In *Ideology and Discontent,* edited by D. E. Apter. New York: Free Press.

FIORINA, M. (1981) *Retrospective Voting in American National Elections.* New Haven, CT: Yale University Press.

FREE, I., AND W. WATES (1980) Internationalism Comes of Age . . . Again. *Public Opinion* 3 (April–May): 46–50.

GRAEBNER, N. A. (1983) "Public Opinion and Foreign Policy: A Pragmatic View." In *Interaction: Foreign Policy and Public Policy,* edited by D. C. Piper and R. J. Terchek. Washington, DC: American Enterprise Institute.

GRAHAM, T. W. (1986) *Public Attitudes toward Active Defense: ABM and Star Wars, 1945–1985.* Cambridge MA: Center for International Studies, M.I.T.

GRAHAM, T. W. (1988) The Pattern and Importance of Public Knowledge in the Nuclear Age. *Journal of Conflict Resolution* 32:319–334.

GRAHAM, T. W. (1989) The Politics of Failure: Strategic Nuclear Arms Control, Public Opinion, and Domestic Politics in the United States—1945–1980. Ph.D. dissertation, M.I.T., Cambridge, MA.

HINCKLEY, R. H. (1992) *People, Polls, and Policy-Makers.* New York: Lexington Books.

HOLMES, J. E. (1985) *The Mood/Interest Theory of American Foreign Policy.* Lexington: University Press of Kentucky.

HOLSTI, O. R. (1979) The Three-Headed Eagle: The United States and System Change. *International Studies Quarterly* 23:339–359.

HOLSTI, O. R., AND J. N. ROSENAU (1979) Vietnam, Consensus, and the Belief Systems of American Leaders. *World Politics* 32:1–56.

HOLSTI, O. R., AND J. N. ROSENAU (1984) *American Leadership in World Affairs: Vietnam and the Breakdown of Consensus.* London: Allen and Unwin.

HOLSTI, O. R., AND J. N. ROSENAU (1990) The Structure of Foreign Policy Attitudes among American Leaders. *Journal of Politics* 52:94–125.

JENTLESON, B. W. (1992) The Pretty Prudent Public: Post–Post Vietnam American Opinion on the Use of Military Force. *International Studies Quarterly* 36:49–73.

KLINGBERG, F. L. (1952) The Historical Alternation of Moods in American Foreign Policy. *World Politics* 4:239–273.

KLINGBERG, F. L. (1979) "Cyclical Trends in American Foreign Policy Moods and Their Policy Implications." In *Challenges to America: United States Foreign Policy in the 1980s* edited by C. W. Kegley, Jr., and P. J. McGowan. Beverly Hills, CA: Sage.

KLINGBERG, F. L. (1983) *Cyclical Trends in American Foreign Policy Moods: The Unfolding of America's World Role.* Lanham, MD: University Press of America.

KROSNICK, J. A. (1988a) Attitude Importance and Attitude Change. *Journal of Experimental Social Psychology* 24:240–255.

KROSNICK, J. A. (1988b) The Role of Attitude Importance in Social Evaluation: A Study of Policy Preferences. Presidential Candidate Evaluations, and Voting Behavior. *Journal of Personality and Social Psychology* 55:196–210.

KROSNICK, J. A. (1990) Americans' Perceptions of Presidential Candidates: A Test of the Projection Hypothesis. *Journal of Social Issues* 46:159–182.

KROSNICK, J. A. (1991) The Stability of Political Preferences: Comparisons of Symbolic and Nonsymbolic Attitudes. *American Journal of Political Science* 35:547–576.

LAFEBER, W. (1977) "American Policy-Makers, Public Opinion and the Outbreak of the Cold War, 1945–1950." In *The Origins of the Cold War in Asia,* edited by Y. Nagai and A. Iriye. New York: Columbia University Press.

LEVERING, R. B. (1978) *The Public and American Foreign Policy, 1918–1978.* New York: Morrow.

LIPPMANN, W. (1955) *Essays in the Public Philosophy.* Boston: Little, Brown.

LIPSET, S. M. (1966) The President, the Polls and Vietnam. *Transaction* (September/October):19–24.

MANDELBAUM, M., AND W. SCHNEIDER (1979) "The New Internationalisms." In *Eagle Entangled: U.S. Foreign Policy in a Complex World,* edited by K. A. Oye *et al.* New York: Longman.

MILLER, W. E., AND D. E. STOKES (1963) Constituency Influence in Congress. *American Political Science Review* 57:45–46.

MONROE, A. D. (1979) Consistency between Public Preferences and National Policy Decision. *American Politics Quarterly* 7:3–19.

MORGENTHAU, H. J. (1978) *Politics among Nations,* 5th ed., rev. New York: Knopf.

MUELLER, J. E. (1973) *War, Presidents and Public Opinion.* New York: Wiley.

NINCIC, M. (1988) The United States, The Soviet Union, and the Politics of Opposites. *World Politics* 40:452–475.

PAGE, B. I., AND R. Y. SHAPIRO (1982) Changes in Americans' Policy Preferences, 1935–1979. *Public Opinion Quarterly* 46:24–42.

PAGE, B. I., AND R. Y. SHAPIRO (1983) Effects of Public Opinion on Policy. *American Political Science Review* 77:175–190.

PAGE, B. I., AND R. Y. SHAPIRO (1984) Presidents as Opinion Leaders: Some New Evidence. *Policy Studies Journal* 12:649–661.

PAGE, B. I., AND R. Y. SHAPIRO (1988) Foreign Policy and the Rational Public. *Journal of Conflict Resolution* 32:211–247.

PAGE, B. I., AND R. Y. SHAPIRO (1992) *The Rational Public: Fifty Years of Trends in Americans' Policy Preferences.* Chicago: University of Chicago Press.

PAGE, B. I., R. Y. SHAPIRO, AND G. R. DEMPSEY (1987) What Moves Public Opinion? *American Political Science Review* 81:23–43.

PARRY, R., AND P. KORNBLUH (1988) Iran-Contra's Untold Story. *Foreign Policy* 72:3–30.

PATERSON, T. G. (1979) Presidential Foreign Policy, Public Opinion, and Congress: The Truman Years. *Diplomatic History* 3:1–18.

PEHLEY, M., AND J. HURWITZ (1922a) International Events and Foreign Policy Beliefs: Public Responses to Changing Soviet-American Relations. *American Journal of Political Science* 36:431–461.

PEHLEY, M., AND J. HURWITZ (1922b) Models of Attitude Constraint in Foreign Affairs. *Political Behavior.*

RUSSETT, B. (1990) *Controlling the Sword.* Cambridge, MA: Harvard University Press.

SHAPIRO, R. Y., AND B. I. PAGE (1988) Foreign Policy and the Rational Public. *Journal of Conflict Resolution* 32:211–247.

SOBEL, R. (1989) Public Opinion about United States Intervention in El Salvador and Nicaragua. *Public Opinion Quarterly* 53:114–128.

WITTKOPF, E. R. (1986) On the Foreign Policy Beliefs of the American People: A Critique and Some Evidence. *International Studies Quarterly* 30: 425–445.

WITTKOPF, E. R. (1990) *Faces of Internationalism: Public Opinion and Foreign Policy.* Durham, NC: Duke University Press.

Peace: Building a Post–Cold War World Order?

Liberal Internationalist theories stress two main roles for the United States in seeking to promote peace—providing leadership in building and strengthening international institutions such as the United Nations, and playing a direct peace broker role in helping to resolve major international conflicts. This chapter's case study, *Getting to Dayton: Negotiating an End to the War in Bosnia*, focuses on one of the major recent cases of U.S. peace brokering.

This case study builds on the discussion of Bosnia and the Dayton Accords in the main text, providing greater depth and more extensive detail on this extremely important case. It also is more generally illustrative of how and why the United States takes on a peace broker role, and what the key factors are affecting the likelihood of success.

The Former Yugoslavia, 1992

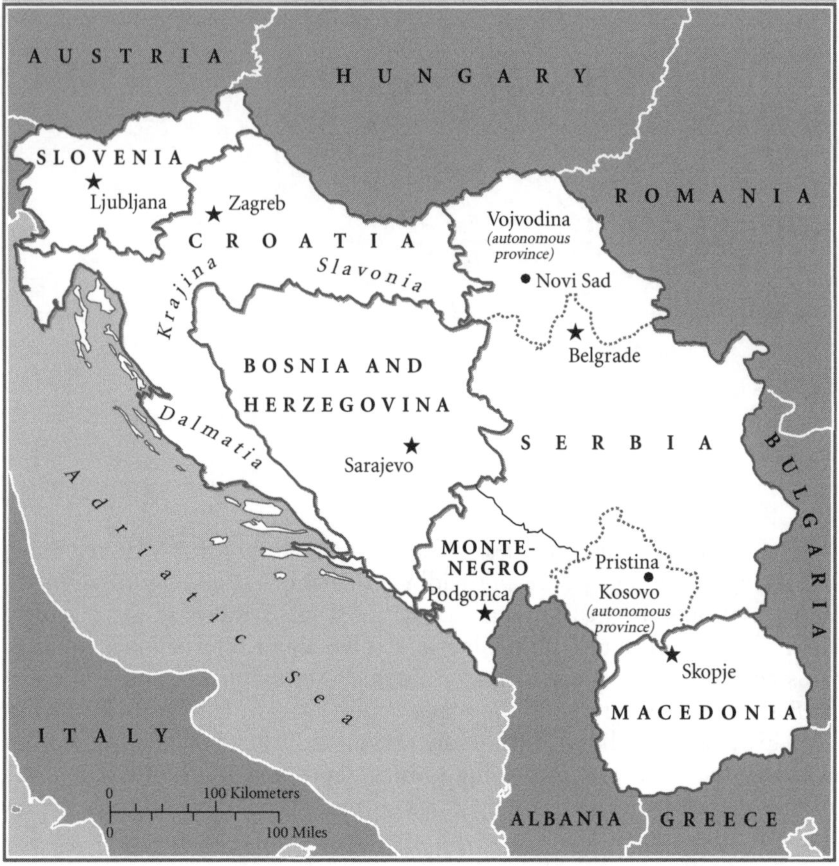

★★★ KEY PLAYERS

United States
Richard C. Holbrooke, U.S. Assistant Secretary of State for European Affairs
Robert C. Frasure, State Department official and key Holbrooke aide
Lt. General Wesley Clark, representative of the Joint Chiefs of Staff
Warren Christopher, Secretary of State
Anthony Lake, National Security Adviser

Former Yugoslavia
Slobodan Milosevic, President of Serbia
Alija Izetbegovic, President of Bosnia and Herzegovina
Franco Tudjman, President of Croatia
Radovan Karadzic, leader of Bosnian Serbs
General Ratko Mladic, commander of Bosnian Serb forces

1980	President Josip Broz Tito, communist party leader and president of Yugoslavia since 1945, dies.
1987	Slobodan Milosevic, longtime communist party official, becomes President of Serbia.
1989	In latest move towards vision of a "greater Serbia," Milosevic suspends autonomy for Kosovo, a province of Serbia with a heavily Albanian population.
1989	Year of the anti-communist revolutions throughout Eastern Europe
1990	Yugoslav federal communist party collapses and forty-five years of a communist regime crumble. Multiparty elections held in most of the republics; among the winners are Franco Tudjman as president of Croatia and Alija Izetbegovic, a Muslim, elected president of Bosnia.
June 25, 1991	Slovenia and Croatia declare independence. Serb-controlled Yugoslav National Army (JNA) seeks to crush Slovenian independence but quickly retreats; Slovenia's lack of a significant ethnic Serb population is a key factor. Serbian-Croatian war breaks out, initially over Krajina, a heavily Serb populated area, with JNA supporting the Krajina Serbs.
September 1991	UN imposes arms embargo on Yugoslavia and former Yugoslav republics. European Community (EC) attempts mediation and peace proposals led by former British Foreign Secretary Lord Peter Carrington.
November 1991	EC imposes fuller economic sanctions against Serbia.
December 1991	Dissolution of the Soviet Union
January 1992	UN negotiates cease-fire in Croatia; United Nations Protection Force (UNPROFOR) deployed as peacekeepers; troops include British and French but not American.
January 1992	EC grants diplomatic recognition to independent Slovenia and Croatia.

March 3, 1992	Bosnians vote in referendum for independence. Bosnian Serbs boycott and threaten that diplomatic recognition of an independent Bosnia would set off a war.
April 1992	United States and the European Union (EU, formerly the EC) grant diplomatic recognition to Bosnia. Radovan Karadzic declares himself president of an independent Bosnian Serb republic, and his forces lay siege to Sarajevo.
May 1992	UN imposes economic sanctions on Serbia.
Summer 1992	First press reports of "ethnic cleansing," including Bosnian Serb concentration camps, mass killings, rapes, and other torture. Tens of thousands of Bosnian Muslims killed, and 750,000 left as refugees.
August 1992	UNPROFOR mandate extended to Bosnia to deliver humanitarian aid.
October 1992	Main diplomatic initiative is the Vance-Owen plan, led by former U.S. Secretary of State Cyrus Vance and former British Foreign Secretary David Owen, and combining the UN and the EU.
Late 1992	Serbs have captured 70 percent of Bosnia; Muslims hold only about 10 percent, Croats the rest.
January–April 1993	Bosnian Muslim–Bosnian Croat conflicts escalate to war.
February 1993	UN establishes Hague International War Crimes Tribunal.
Spring 1993	UNPROFOR establishes six "safe havens" for Muslim refugees: Srebenica, Sarajevo, Zepa, Gorazde, Bihac, and Tuzla. Problems from the start, though, with limited size of UNPROFOR forces and inadequacy of their mandate.
April 1993	NATO declares no-fly zone to protect civilian areas from Serbian bombing.
August 1993	First NATO threat of air strikes against Bosnian Serbs over siege of Sarajevo, but with shared authority ("dual key" arrangement) with UN.
February 1994	Market massacre in Sarajevo inflicted by Bosnian Serbs, killing 68 and wounding over 200, and shown worldwide via CNN. NATO issues ultimatum that leads to cease-fire for Sarajevo, although soon thereafter Bosnian Serbs attack Gorazde safe haven. Bosnian-Croatian cease-fire.

April 1994	First actual NATO air strikes, precipitated by Bosnian Serb attacks on Gorazde. Limited in severity and derided by some as "pinpricks."
March 1, 1994	Muslim-Croat Federation brokered by the United States.
	Contact Group established including the United States, Britain, France, Germany, and Russia as principal coordinating mechanism for international negotiations.
January 1995	Temporary cease-fire negotiated with Karadzic by former President Jimmy Carter; it lasts four months but breaks down and Serbs resume shelling of Sarajevo and other safe havens.
May 1995	NATO air strikes. Bosnian Serbs retaliate by taking UN peacekeepers hostage. UN pressures NATO to stop air strikes.
	Jacques Chirac elected president of France, pushes harder for more decisive policy. In the United States, National Security Advisor Tony Lake and UN Ambassador Madeleine Albright press for new approach.
July 1995	Bosnian Serbs seize Srebenica safe haven, and then Zepa, with massive killings. UN refuses NATO air strikes. NATO issues further threat if Goradze attacked.
August 1995	Croatian forces launch surprise offensive and defeat Serbs and take back Krajina; Serbian army flees and 100,000–150,000 Serbs are left as refugees.
	New peace initiative launched by U.S. Assistant Secretary of State Richard Holbrooke.

**Ethnic Composition of the Former Yugoslavia
(% of total population, pre-war, 1991)**

Bosnia-Herzegovina

Muslim	43.7%
Serb	31.4%
Croat	17.3%

Croatia

Croats	78.1%
Serbs	12.2%

Serbia

Serbs	65.8%
Albanians	17.2% (mostly in Kosovo)

Slovenia

Slovemes	87.6%
Croats	2.7%
Serbs	2.4%

Source: Susan L, Woodward, *Balkan Tragedy: Chaos and Dissolution after the Cold War* (Washington, D.C.: Brookings Institution Press, 1995).

Peace / World Order Case Study

Getting to Dayton: Negotiating an End to the War in Bosnia

In August 1995, Richard Holbrooke, Assistant Secretary of State for Canadian and European Affairs, flew to the Balkan Peninsula with the charge of trying to end the war in Bosnia—the bloodiest conflict in Europe since World War II. Since Bosnia had declared its independence in early 1992, nationalist uprisings backed and aided by covetous neighbors Serbia and Croatia had torn apart the former Yugoslavia's most multi-ethnic republic, resulting in deaths estimated at more than 100,000. But despite Bosnian President Alija Izetbegovich's repeated pleas for Western intervention, as well as regular reports of atrocities such as concentration camp tortures, civilian murders, and systematic rape, both Europe and the US had refused to fight in the grisly war, opting instead to send United Nations peacekeeping forces and to seek a settlement through diplomacy. These efforts at a negotiated agreement, however, including numerous internationally brokered ceasefires, had remained fruitless, spurring intense criticism of Balkan policies in the US and Europe, and calling into question the responsibilities of the world's great powers to resolve regional conflicts in the immediate post–Cold War era. Now, a combination of changed circumstances on the ground and fresh reports of a massacre of Muslim civilians had finally convinced the United States to take the lead with a new diplomatic plan. It would be up to Richard Holbrooke to convince the many parties to the conflict that peace—even one requiring the abdication of long-held goals—was a better option than war.

* * *

This case was written by Susan Rosegrant in collaboration with Michael D. Watkins, Associate Professor, Harvard Business School, for use by the National Security Program, at the John F. Kennedy School of Government, Harvard University.

Holbrooke Steps In

Not everyone saw Richard Holbrooke—known for having one of the most assertive personalities in Washington—as the ideal negotiator to insert into the Balkan morass. No one denied that the assistant secretary had the requisite experience. His lengthy government record included serving as a member of the US delegation to the Paris peace talks in 1968 to negotiate with the Vietcong, as well as conducting sensitive negotiations with the Chinese and with former Filipino President Ferdinand Marcos in the 1970s as former President Jimmy Carter's Assistant Secretary of State for East Asian and Pacific Affairs.[1]

Yet some top officials had reservations, including National Security Adviser [Anthony] Lake. Holbrooke and Lake had been close when both served as foreign service officers in Vietnam in the early 1960s, a posting that led to Holbrooke's later experience as part of the Paris delegation. But their relationship had cooled over the years, and Lake reportedly viewed Holbrooke as a showman—unpredictable and often difficult. In addition, Holbrooke had been both privately and publicly critical of the US's failure to intervene earlier as the Bosnian war worsened, and there were questions about whether he would toe the party line. Holbrooke, himself, had become frustrated by his inability to shape Bosnian policy, and during deliberations in early August had taken a long-planned vacation, leaving behind rumors that he was contemplating a return to Wall Street.

Still, many felt Holbrooke—as the assistant secretary responsible for the region—was simply the logical choice once the US decided to launch a serious negotiation. The more significant decision, Holbrooke insists, had been putting him in charge of the European Bureau back in September 1994, a post that, according to him, "meant the Bosnian negotiations." He adds: "Frasure [Robert C., the State Department's chief Bosnia negotiator] and I had always agreed that when the time was right he would call me, and I would be in Belgrade within 48 hours."[2] In addition, even Holbrooke's critics conceded that his very drawbacks might make him the perfect choice for the job. "Holbrooke was probably the most forceful personality we could possibly find for this kind of negotiating effort," states one top NSC official. "He's both brilliant and has a bullying personality, but that was seen as the combination we needed." With Holbrooke as the negotiator, one State Department official adds wryly, the new diplomatic initiative was assured high visibility.

Accompanied by Frasure, who after the initial round of talks was slated to return to the US to back up the negotiations from Washington, Holbrooke and a small inter-agency team began crisscrossing the Balkans, making preliminary contacts and laying the groundwork for the negotiations. In just a few days, Holbrooke visited Serbian President Slobodan Milosevic in Belgrade twice and Croatian President Franco Tudjman in Zagreb once. But despite an early attempt, Holbrooke was unable to secure a safe route into the surrounded city of Sarajevo to see Bosnian President Alija Izetbegovic, instead meeting with Muslim officials in the Croatian cities of Split and Zagreb. Although the US negotiator asked Milosevic to intervene on his behalf, Bosnian Serb Gen. Ratko Mladic would not give Holbrooke a guarantee of safe passage.

On August 19, Holbrooke and his team made their second effort to reach Sarajevo by the only route available, the precarious Mt. Igman road. Holbrooke and military representative Lieut. Gen. Wesley Clark rode in a Humvee—a squat and stable all-terrain Army jeep—while the rest of the team traveled in a French armored personnel carrier. But part way down the mountain, a tragic accident occurred. As the personnel carrier tried to pass a French convoy, it tumbled off the rain-soaked road, plummeting into a steep ravine and erupting into flames. Three key members of the Bosnian negotiating team died in the crash—Frasure, Deputy Assistant Secretary of Defense Joseph Kruzel, and Col. S. Nelson Drew of the National Security Council. The accident, which Holbrooke still describes as "unbelievable," devastated officials who had been involved in the Balkan conflict—many of whom had been close friends of the three who died. It also dealt a profound blow to the nascent diplomatic effort. "We lost our historical continuity with Bob Frasure," observes Lieut. Gen. Clark.[3]

President Bill Clinton, however, was determined that the negotiating effort not lose momentum. After a sober memorial service August 23 in Fort Myer, Virginia, Clinton met with senior officials and a new Bosnia team that had been hastily assembled. * * *

On August 27, the new team took off for Paris, where they planned to meet Bosnian President Izetbegovic and the Contact Group, an entity formed to address the Balkan crisis including representatives from the US, France, Britain, Germany, and Russia. "If this peace initiative does not get moving, dramatically moving, in the next week or two, the consequences will be very adverse to the Serbian goals," Holbrooke declared that morning on NBC's "Meet the Press." "One way or another, NATO will be heavily involved, and the Serbs don't want that." In truth, Holbrooke did not foresee NATO playing a direct role any time soon, although he hoped the alliance's recent threats of punishing air strikes had shaken the Bosnian Serbs and readied them for negotiation. But the next day, a new challenge made Holbrooke's words appear eerily prescient. Just as the flight landed in Paris, the Bosnian Serbs lobbed a mortar into a marketplace in Sarajevo, killing 37 and wounding more than 80. As in February 1994, the UN sought to confirm the origin of the mortar. This time, though, there was no lingering controversy. International investigators quickly announced that available evidence pointed to its being a Bosnian Serb attack. "With the new rules of engagement that were then in place, the decks were cleared for action," says Holbrooke. "We instantly recommended massive NATO retaliation."

Pinpricks No More

The mortar attack on August 28 in the face of the firmly stated NATO threats surprised and perplexed observers. Most who fathomed a guess about the Serbs' thinking, however, speculated that it was a kind of calling card, testing both the new diplomatic initiative and NATO's trumpeted shift in resolve. After all, NATO's warnings had been meaningless in the past. There was no proof things would be different now." * * *

There were significant changes, though, that made it possible for NATO to stand by its word. Not only were the NATO allies agreed that the deadly bombing of Sarajevo could not go unpunished, the fall of the safe areas the month before had created conditions on the ground conducive to a forceful military response. With Srebrenica and Zepa already in the hands of the Serbs, the UN had only to quietly pull some 80 peacekeepers from the safe area of Gorazde to have almost all its troops out of risk of attack or hostage taking.

On August 30, two days after the attack, the NATO bombing began, concentrating at first on Bosnian Serb positions near Sarajevo, such as artillery sites, radar and communications centers, and ammunition depots, then gradually expanding to include targets near Gorazde and Tuzla. While there was some debate among the allies as to what exactly the Bosnian Serbs had to do to end the bombing, it was generally agreed that they must move some 300 heavy artillery pieces at least 12.5 miles from Sarajevo, open the Sarajevo airport, and allow safe access by road to the Bosnian capital. With no immediate sign of capitulation, however, speculation increased about what the bombing's impact would be. Although the US had been pushing for strategic air strikes for years, not everyone in the Clinton administration believed bombing would achieve its desired—if largely unspoken—goal: not only to push the Bosnian Serbs back from Sarajevo, but to convince the Pale leadership to engage in serious peace negotiations. "There was a huge argument inside our country as to how much effect bombing would have," says one team member, "because of the experience in Vietnam where we just bombed the hell out of them for months on end, only to have very little effect at the negotiating table."

Holbrooke's team members, however, were of a mind. The bombing campaign was not only essential, it was an unexpected gift—dramatic proof that things were not going to be business as usual. The biggest concern, they say, was what reception they would get from Milosevic, whom they would be meeting as a team for the first time one day after the bombing began. Milosevic, Holbrooke had become convinced, was the key to influencing the Bosnian Serbs. But if the Serbian president was enraged by the NATO action, or found it politically untenable to meet with the Americans while the bombing was in progress, it could mean days or even weeks before the negotiations would pick up speed. Nevertheless, it was a risk they were eager to take. "I always believed that it was necessary to back diplomacy with military power," reflects Lieut. Gen. Clark. "Whether it scuttled the negotiations was a tactical issue, not a strategic issue."

Holbrooke's team arrived in Belgrade August 31 fearing the worst. Their reception, however, was almost warm. Milosevic began by expressing sympathy over the deaths of the three diplomats. Then, Holbrooke recounts, Milosevic announced, "I've been very busy while you've been gone," and pulled a paper written in Serbian from his breast pocket. The one-page letter, signed by Milosevic, Bosnian Serb leader Radoran Karadzic, Mladic, and other Yugoslav and Bosnian Serb leaders, and witnessed by the Serbian Orthodox Patriarch, announced that in future negotiations, the interests of Serbia and the Bosnian Serbs would be represented by a six-person delegation, with three of the six members handpicked by Milosevic. In the event of a deadlock, Milosevic would step in to cast the deciding vote.

Holbrooke, who describes himself as "stunned" by the unexpected document, soon dubbed the "Patriarch Paper," says it's difficult to overstate the importance of Milosevic's masterstroke. "We had spent sixteen months arguing over who spoke for the Bosnian Serbs, and here we had the answer in writing . . . the answer to who will speak for the Pale Serbs was Slobodan Milosevic." Adds Holbrooke aide Christopher Hill: "That was an absolute breakthrough. It was the rock upon which every other negotiation had been shipwrecked."

* * *

The Shuttle Picks Up Speed

That the negotiations were underway was driven home over the next week as Holbrooke and his team flew from city to city, announced new developments, and worked behind the scenes to ensure a continued robust international response. Even as the NATO bombing first began, Holbrooke had been wondering how to make the negotiating process more efficient. "I had come to the conclusion that you had to approach this negotiation piecemeal, step by step, locking in your gains," he recalls. "But you couldn't lock in your gains simply by shuttling, because whenever you were in City A, whatever you agreed to, City B wouldn't agree to." The solution, Holbrooke concluded, was to bring representatives of the Balkan countries together to produce some sort of an agreement. Lieut. Gen. Clark remembers the idea coming to Holbrooke in a flash a few days into the trip. "Dick called us aside and he said, 'Let's set up a two-day negotiation in Geneva,'" Clark says. "'We'll come up with an agreement. We'll agree on principles. We'll call it basic principles! We'll get something and we'll make them agree to it!'"

* * *

* * * On Friday, Sept. 1, the Clinton administration announced there would be a meeting of the Balkan foreign ministers in one week, the first such talk in two years.

Meanwhile, officials at NATO and the UN were trying to gauge the early response to the NATO air strikes, both within Bosnia and the broader international community. On that same Friday, its third day of bombing, NATO declared a pause in the air strikes over the Labor Day weekend to allow Bosnian Serb Gen. Mladic and UN Commander Gen. Bernard Janvier to talk, and to give Mladic a chance to comply with NATO's demands. As originally conceived, the pause was to last just 72 hours. If the Bosnian Serbs refused to cooperate, NATO would resume and intensify its assault.

But as the weekend progressed and Mladic showed no sign of caving in to NATO's demands, Holbrooke says, some members of the UN command tried to prevent the bombing's resumption. The primary fear, team members say, was that the UN and NATO would be accused of going too far, of siding with the Bosnian Muslim government and essentially declaring war on the Bosnian Serbs. The question was also being debated in Washington, with some officials arguing that NATO had already proven its resolve, and that further bombing would be unnecessarily punitive.[4] After Holbrooke pleaded by phone with US officials to intervene, however, NATO bombing resumed.

As Holbrooke and his team pursued diplomatic opportunities around the region, reporters took notice. "Everyone knew there was something incredible going on," Hill says. "We'd be sitting in Sarajevo and Holbrooke would lean over to me and say, 'I think we ought to go back to Belgrade tonight.' I'd say, 'Dick, we were just there yesterday.' He'd say, 'Trust me, I know what I'm doing. We ought to go back to Belgrade.' So off we'd go, back to Belgrade, we'd have one more conversation with Milosevic, there may be some little nugget there that we didn't have before." He adds: "Could it have been done on the phone? I don't know. The point is, the journalists were simply dazzled by this energy and it showed that this American team was going to get this thing done."

In fact, some journalists began to suggest a superhuman quality to the effort that perhaps exceeded the demands of the situation. Holbrooke, however, who says the "whole charge about publicity seeking was at its core wrong," insists that the team's brutal pace—which often involved flights to several cities in one day—had nothing to do with grandstanding and everything to do with successful diplomacy. "The plane was our great secret weapon," he insists, dismissing the possibility that some of the trips could have been replaced by phone calls. "These people are intensely suspicious of each other. Even in more civilized negotiations, no one negotiates by telephone." Distances among the key cities were short, Holbrooke notes, with most flights taking just 45 minutes to an hour. Only Sarajevo proved difficult to reach, he says, because of safety restrictions forcing the team to change to a US Air Force transport plane in Italy. "The Bosnians kept complaining that we weren't coming to Sarajevo enough," he admits, "and they had a point."

The Foreign Ministers' Meeting

As NATO resumed its air strikes, Holbrooke and his team shaped the ideas to be presented to the foreign ministers on Friday, September 8. In early discussions with the Balkan leaders, the team broached the different issues to be resolved, ranging from the constitution to the map. But while none was simple, territorial issues invariably froze the discussion. "We learned that the map was going to be very hard, very specific, very concrete," Clark recalls. "You can't dodge problems. You can't draw a ten-kilometer zone and say, 'We will generally divide it this way.' " Roberts Owen, Washington lawyer and team member recruited for his Balkan arbitration experience, agrees. "We knew the map was going to be a horror when we got to it, and we didn't think we could make much progress on the map until we had other things straightened out, so we worked on these basic principles first." Despite resistance, Clark says, they continued to pull the map out during discussions and to broach difficult issues, both to get a better understanding of what obstacles they faced, and to "make the ideas more acceptable to the parties by constant repetition and familiarity."

Under Holbrooke's direction, Owen built on concepts already put forward by the Contact Group—and by Lake and Under Secretary of State for Political Affairs Peter Tarnoff during an earlier European tour—to draft a single page of relatively uncontroversial principles. It was important that the document represent real progress, yet not be so bold that the ministers would not sign. Holbrooke's attention to detail, however, went beyond the actual document, his team members say. In what Hill calls "the trick of the table," for example, Holbrooke dictated the actual physical dimensions of the negotiating table to guarantee it would only accommodate the five Contact Group representatives, European Union special negotiator Carl Bildt, and the foreign ministers of Bosnia, Serbia, and Croatia.[5] Any Bosnian Serb representatives would have to sit on the periphery. "He did not want any delegation to feel they had room to bring a second person to the table," explains Hill. "He wanted Milosevic to speak for the Serbs, in that case Milosevic's foreign minister."

The meeting itself was a tense affair, with hostile officials clustered tightly around the custom-built table. The Muslims, Hill says, objected strenuously to the concept of giving the Bosnian Serbs their own semi-autonomous entity within Bosnia. The Serbs, for their part, opposed all provisions that buttressed Bosnia's powers as a state. And the subject of eastern Slavonia, a sliver of land that was the last area of Croatia still occupied by Serbs, provoked so much dissension that it was dropped altogether. Nevertheless, at the end of the day, Holbrooke was able to present a page of Agreed Basic Principles. "It was a very risky thing to do," because of the possibility of a complete stalemate, Holbrooke says, "and it came very close to a disaster, but we got out of it with an agreement which was word for word what Roberts Owen had drafted."

The basic principles agreed to by the foreign ministers did the following:

- recognized Bosnia's existing external borders
- created two entities within Bosnia—the Federation of Bosnia and Herzegovina and a Bosnian Serb region to be known as the Republika Srpska—relying on the Contact Group split of 51/49 as "the basis for a settlement"
- allowed each entity the right to establish "parallel special relationships" with neighboring countries
- and asserted a commitment to basic human rights standards (see Exhibit 4 for the complete agreement).

According to Hill, the meeting, which capped off the first shuttle trip, was most significant for jump-starting the process and producing a tangible agreement. Holbrooke, however, says, "At the time, the most important thing was the momentum. But of course, in retrospect, it's the words in the agreement."

Not everyone approved of how far those words went. Some critics, for example, complained that this first set of principles omitted the "connective tissue" that would unite Bosnia's two entities, doing more to partition than to unite the beleaguered nation. Moreover, some administration officials professed their disappointment that Holbrooke had failed to quickly negotiate a ceasefire. Holbrooke, however, insists that the basic principles went as far as any first agreement could go. Nor did he have an interest in seeking a ceasefire that early in the process, a serious challenge in itself that could complicate the ultimate goal of securing a lasting peace in Bosnia.

* * *

The Hunting Lodge

On September 10, two days after the meeting in Geneva, NATO expanded its air strikes, using Navy cruiser-based Tomahawk cruise missiles and precision-guided bombs against Serb radar and surface-to-air missile sites in northwest Bosnia near the Serb stronghold of Banja Luka. Gen. Mladic still hadn't indicated he was ready to comply with international demands. Nevertheless, the initial allied skepticism over whether the bombing would bite was gradually being replaced by gratified surprise at how effective it appeared to be. "Those air strikes were amazing," exclaims Owen. "The United States just looked like not only the strongest kid on the block, but the brightest, most democratically minded, and well-intentioned, and I was terribly impressed."

Although US defense officials insist that NATO had not destroyed the Bosnian Serbs' warmaking capability, the Bosnian Serbs—while still publicly defiant—seemed desperate to bring the bombing to a halt. "It was heavily, heavily psychological," says one team member.[6] Milosevic, who wanted not only the lifting of economic sanctions but also a return to international respectability, was similarly distressed.[7] "One night he was talking about the bombs falling and I said, 'You do understand that sixteen of the most powerful nations in the world—the sixteen nations of NATO, the heart of Europe—are at war with you right now?' " recalls one team member. "And he said, 'Yeah, unfortunately I know that all too well.' "

Despite its apparent effectiveness in getting the Serbs' attention, however, many NATO and UN officials were growing increasingly anxious to stop the air campaign—with or without concessions. Primary among their concerns was the fact that NATO was running out of so-called Level One and Level Two targets, classic military hits such as ammunition depots and command and control centers. If NATO expanded to Level Three, including targets such as power plants, airports, roads, and railways, it would put more civilians at risk; possibly alter the military balance between the Federation and the Bosnian Serbs to the extent that NATO would appear to have entered the war on the side of the Muslims; and almost certainly break the fragile alliance with Russia, whose pro-Serbian officials were already condemning the military action.

For Holbrooke, who did not want the bombing to end without Bosnian Serb compliance, the stakes were growing higher. He did not believe that the British or the French would support an expansion of NATO targets. In addition, he says, the team was "under some pressure from Washington to produce some movement." In a September 12 interview, as he prepared to fly back to the Balkans, Holbrooke painted a gloomy picture, declaring, "Nothing is agreed upon until everything is agreed upon."[8] At the same time, Holbrooke pointedly raised the prospect of future incentives, speaking of the billions of dollars of international economic aid that would likely flow into the region in the event of a settlement.

One day later, Holbrooke and his team met Milosevic at a hunting lodge outside of Belgrade. According to Hill, the Serbian president got right to the point: "Milosevic said, 'The bombing has got to be stopped,' and Holbrooke said, 'The terms are very clear.' " Although Holbrooke insisted he didn't control the bombing—that the decision was in the hands of the UN and NATO—Milosevic clearly believed otherwise. Holbrooke, meanwhile, though an advocate of further bombing, was convinced NATO was going to halt the attacks shortly. As a result, he had a strong incentive to push Milosevic for an immediate settlement. "We knew when we were sitting in that villa," he says, "that the bombing would stop within hours of us telling NATO it should stop."

For a second time, Milosevic seized the moment with a surprise announcement. He asked if Holbrooke would be willing to meet with the

Bosnian Serb leaders, adding that Mladic, Karadzic, and other members of the Pale leadership [Pale was the small city that served as headquarters for the Bosnian Serbs] were waiting in a villa about 200 meters away. One team member, who describes the night at the hunting lodge as "one of Holbrooke's finest hours," says, "I can just see Holbrooke collecting his thoughts and seeing how he was going to proceed here."[9] While Milosevic's request was a bombshell, however, Holbrooke says he had expected the Bosnian Serb leaders would be produced at some point in the process. "We all knew it was going to come," he says. "We were totally prepared for it. It was the moment we were unprepared for."

* * *

With little ado, Clark began drafting a withdrawal offer that would satisfy NATO demands. In a scene that one negotiator describes as "bizarre," Clark then stood in the glow of the outdoor patio lights, while the Bosnian Serb leaders gathered around him and Holbrooke and Milosevic sat to the side under a tree. As Clark read the paper aloud, however, Karadzic began to shake his head. When Clark finished, Karadzic immediately denounced the agreement as unacceptable, and Mladic launched into a diatribe about how the Bosnian Serbs would not allow themselves to be so humiliated. One team member recalls thinking they should simply bolt from the ugly scene. Instead, Holbrooke laid out the choices in stark terms. "Holbrooke, who had been sitting down, got out of his chair and rose to his full six-feet-one and said, 'That's enough,' " recalls Owen. " 'Either you agree to negotiate on the basis of this document or we are going home and the NATO bombing will continue.' " After a dead silence, Owen says, Karadzic agreed to work with the draft.

Over the next several hours, Karadzic sat between Clark and Pardew refining the language and terms of the agreement.[10] The main sticking points, Owen says, were which roads into the capital to open, which military units to move, and what weight of weapon to ban from the 12.5-mile Sarajevo exclusion zone. At about two in the morning, the Bosnian Serbs finally approved and signed a withdrawal agreement that would end the siege of Sarajevo. "What the bombing campaign proved beyond a reasonable doubt," says Ivo Daalder, National Security Council director for Global Affairs," is that Milosevic controlled the Serbs."

For the US negotiators, the deliverance of Sarajevo from the shelling and sniper fire estimated to have killed 10,000 over three years was a great step forward. Ironically, Izetbegovic and his government saw it differently. When Holbrooke's team met with the Bosnian Muslim leaders the following day in Mostar, they were greeted not with praise but with angry criticism. "From their perspective, they had been suffering in that city for a long time, and a little bit more suffering was not nearly as big a deal as watching those NATO planes go over and bomb the hell out of the Pale Serbs," says one negotiator.

"This was something they'd been waiting for for a long, long time."[11] Izetbegovic's mood was not improved by the discovery of a mistake in the agreement's wording regarding the caliber of weapons to be removed, a careless error the US negotiators attribute to the haste of the drafting and the lateness of the hour. Once the slip-up was discovered, however, Milosevic quickly agreed to its correction.

Holbrooke's meeting with Mladic and Karadzic also stirred up some criticism back in the US about the wisdom and morality of dealing with indicted war criminals. According to some observers, the US had no business meeting with or negotiating with such people, even as members of Milosevic's delegation. Owen, however, insists direct contact was the unfortunate cost of making progress. The alternative, he says, a labored shuttling of conditions back and forth, would have been at best time-consuming and at worst a failure. "It would have taken weeks," Owen exclaims, "and we got it all done in one night." With the siege of Sarajevo lifting at last, Owen says, the negotiators began to talk about the possibility of a presidential peace conference to negotiate an end to the Bosnian war.

Discouraging the Muslim-Croat Advance

As Holbrooke made advances at the negotiating table, the Muslim-Croat Federation was making unexpected advances on the battlefield. Back in July, Izetbegovic had met with Croatian president Tudjman and given him permission to send Croatian troops into Bosnia in aid of a united effort to take land back from the Bosnian Serbs. On September 9, Croatian troops entered western Bosnia in the Bihac area and joined Bosnian Croat forces, mostly retaking towns with majority Croat populations, but also capturing villages that had been primarily Serb or Muslim. At the same time, Bosnian Muslim forces intensified their own efforts to reclaim land from the Bosnian Serbs' Republika Srpska, sometimes fighting alone, and sometimes fighting alongside Croat troops.

To the astonishment of most observers, the Muslims and Croats battled to great effect. The NATO bombing attacks coming on the heels of the collapse of the Krajina Serbs, as well as the ever more apparent fact that Milosevic would not step forward to intervene, appeared to have seriously demoralized the once dreaded Bosnian Serb forces. "The whole myth about them was they were ten feet tall," says Hill. "They were not ten feet tall after that campaign." In fact, Federation forces in many areas met with so little resistance that some observers speculated that the fleeing Serbs, believing the war to be coming to an end, had concluded they would rather lose towns on the battlefield than have to face the political backlash of relinquishing them in an eventual negotiation.

* * *

Those closely monitoring the military advance had an even bigger fear, however: that further fighting could destroy the shaky Muslim-Croat Federation. It was unclear whether the Muslim forces approaching Banja Luka were capable of capturing and holding the city. According to Hill, the commander of the operation had a reputation for launching an attack, not covering his flanks, and later losing the ground he had taken. If this happened, it was likely Croat forces would intervene, an occurrence that had become all too common. Already, Croatian troops were dominating the offensive, and most of the important victories were Croat or combined Croat-Bosnian Croat victories, not Muslim victories. Hill, who describes the dynamics within the Federation as "dangerous," says, "The gains that they seemed able to consolidate were all Croat gains. At some point, when you have so much Croatian success and so little Muslim success, you create futher tensions within the Muslim-Croat alliance."[12] The NSC's Daalder puts it more bluntly: "I think Tudjman was trying to take over half the country." Indeed, Holbrooke notes a "very disturbing" episode during the advance when Bosnian and Croat forces turned on each other. "Sometimes they worked together, sometimes they worked separately, and sometimes they fought each other," he says. "That's the Balkan way."

On September 19, Holbrooke says, he held a "very dramatic meeting" with Tudjman and Izetbegovic in Zagreb, telling them he did not want them to take Banja Luka. While he offered no concrete incentives for backing off, the negotiator says, he made it clear that further fighting would be against the wishes of the US. After a good deal of yelling, mostly at each other, the two leaders finally turned to Holbrooke and asked him to announce the decision on their behalf. "The parties didn't dare get in the way of Holbrooke," says Hill. "He'd run them over. And the parties could make concessions to Holbrooke that they would not make to each other."

* * *

The US negotiating team was still operating under the auspices of the Contact Group. "Unless the United States wishes to pay all the bills itself, which we no longer can do as we did in the '40s and '50s, we have to involve the Europeans as partners," notes Holbrooke. But tensions were arising on both sides of this "partnership." Holbrooke says he chafed at the time demands of Contact Group meetings, particularly since the European representatives typically would not meet him in the Balkans, but insisted he come to them. Moreover, despite "constant briefings," Holbrooke says, some conducted by him and some by Senior Deputy Assistant Secretary John Komblum, the Europeans were not satisfied. "It wasn't their show," he notes. "They were being humiliated." For their part, the Contact Group representatives often didn't agree either with Holbrooke's high-powered tactics or his goals. Nor did they like the fact that despite regular briefings, the chief US negotiator frequently neglected to tell them what he planned to do next.

Holbrooke admits there were times he kept the Contact Group in the dark. Indeed, he says, it was often necessary to exclude the Europeans until the last moment due to internal divisions among the group and possible news leaks. Arranging the foreign ministers' meeting in Geneva, he says, was a perfect example of the dilemma of dealing with the Europeans. After getting commitments from the Balkan leaders on September 1 and 2, Holbrooke called Deputy Secretary of State Strobe Talbott and Kornblum, urging that they first have the US announce the meeting from Washington in four hours, and then work to clear the event with the Contact Group members, who would need to send their own representatives. "They came on board very fast," Holbrooke recalls. "But if we had asked in advance should we do it, they would have leaked it before we had it arranged, and then we might not have been able to arrange it. Or, alternatively, they would have said, 'Well, yes, but with the following provisions. . .'" Having to accommodate extraneous demands was something Holbrooke was anxious to avoid.

The Foreign Ministers Meet Again

Ever since the foreign ministers' meeting September 8, Owen and other members of the team had been trying to build on the initial page of basic principles to more fully describe what Bosnia would look like after a peace settlement. The first set of principles had shown, in a sense, how Bosnia would be divided, Hill says. The second set would show how it would be made whole by defining the governmental superstructure to bind the two entities together. With these key constitutional arrangements in place, Hill says, it would be time to turn to the map.

As the end of September approached, and as the team wrestled a very circumscribed set of principles through the approval process, Holbrooke scheduled a second meeting of the Balkan foreign ministers for Sept. 26 at the US Mission to the UN in New York. While Holbrooke flew back to prepare, Owen, Hill, and James Pardew, director of the Defense Department's Balkan Task Force, shepherded a draft of the principles through its final stops, first getting Sarajevo's approval, then taking the draft to Belgrade to show the Bosnian Serbs. After a few minor changes, the Americans faxed the altered draft to Sarajevo and began their flight back to the US.

Bosnian Prime Minister Haris Silajdzic, however, who had objected to the principles from the start, took this opportunity to reject the new draft, declaring that Bosnia's foreign minister would not attend the New York meeting. * * *

The Bosnian Muslims threatened to boycott the session almost to the end, and both Holbrooke and Secretary of State Warren Christopher deliberated with the various foreign ministers late into the night on the eve of the meeting. But despite uncertainties as to what the day would accomplish—an anxiety reflected by the fact that the State Department prepared two statements in advance, one announcing the accord and the other con-ceding failure—the meeting, chaired by Holbrooke and European Union envoy Carl Bildt, produced a next round of principles to build on those agreed on two-and-a-half weeks earlier. Of particular importance in the two-page statement were principles defining the unifying structures to govern all of Bosnia, such as a parliament, a presidency, and a constitutional court; a commitment to free democratic elections under international supervision in both parts of Bosnia "as soon as social conditions permit;" and a pledge to allow the international community to monitor compliance with the agreement.

The meeting did not, however, achieve everything the US team had wanted. Concrete details as to how the new Bosnian government would actually function, and how the Federation and Republika Srpska entities would interact, had proven too divisive to pursue. A joint statement accom-panying the principles, issued by the Contact Group and Bildt, cited the "significant, if incomplete, achievements, which must be fleshed out in much greater detail in the next round of negotiations." Among the many issues still not confronted, the statement noted, was the ever-looming issue of the map, as well as such key federal matters as the handling of foreign trade, currency, citizenship and passports, and protection of borders.

In fact, Holbrooke, once again, hadn't tried to tackle the map with the foreign ministers. But the time for that was rapidly approaching. The idea of bringing the Balkan leaders together for a peace summit had been gaining momentum since the team first discussed it in mid-September. After the agreement in New York, Owen says, "it was clear that there was going to be a peace conference somewhere." Where, however, was not at all apparent. The team was becoming increasingly convinced that the US would be the only effective location for such a conference. In Washington, though, offi-cials were shying away from linking the Clinton administration too directly with the difficult negotiations. "There were still people who were concerned that this thing wasn't really going to gel, and that therefore we should not do a US venue," recalls Hill. "We felt that it would only work if there was a US venue."

In any event, the debate was still academic. First, Holbrooke would have to end the fighting. "We did not feel we could announce a peace confer-ence," Hill says, "while people were still shooting at each other."

Locking in a Ceasefire

Two days after the meeting in New York, the US team headed back to Sarajevo to try to negotiate a ceasefire. At Holbrooke's insistence, Federation forces had backed off from Banja Luka the previous week. Elsewhere in the country, however, Muslim and Croat forces were still advancing. Although there were signs that the Bosnian Serb line was stiffening, and Federation troops were declaring fewer victories, Bosnian President Izetbegovic insisted that his troops were not ready to lay down their arms. "It was clear that Izetbegovic was the biggest obstacle to peace," says the NSC's Ivo Daalder. "He had the most to lose. The fact that the war was going well made it even more difficult to get him on our side—on the side of negotiations."

* * *

* * * On October 4, Holbrooke sat down with Izetbegovic to persuade him that the time to seek a military solution had passed. * * *

But, convincing Izetbegovic wasn't easy. Holbrooke didn't offer economic aid or other incentives, both because he wanted to save those for an eventual peace conference, and because, he insists, such carrots weren't the point in this kind of negotiation. "You couldn't trade peace for aid," he says. "It just doesn't fly."[13] What ultimately won the Muslim leader over, suggests Defense Under Secretary Walter Slocombe, was the fear of his country being abandoned to a questionable fate. "They understood that if they were responsible for there not being a peace, they would forfeit the support that they'd gotten from the US and from the Europeans," Slocombe explains. "They were also genuinely concerned that with Croatia, they were allied with a tiger, and it was very much in their interest to get a peace agreement which—while far short of what they, in some sense rightly, think they deserve—stabilized the situation and got them a deal." If the Muslims had continued fighting, Slocombe insists, "it would not have been their military solution, it would have been Tudjman's military solution."

That afternoon, Izetbegovic and his government negotiated terms for a ceasefire that Tudjman also found acceptable. While Hill and Pardew stayed in Sarajevo, Holbrooke and Owen took the two-page agreement to Belgrade, and the negotiators traded demands by phone until Milosevic signed late that night. The eight-point ceasefire—to begin five days from its signing— not only ended the 42 months of fighting, it included such conditions as the restoration of all utilities to Sarajevo, and the opening of a road to the eastern safe area of Gorazde, a town that while not as isolated as Srebrenica and Zepa had been, was nevertheless a Muslim island in the middle of Serb-held land. As part of the agreement, the Balkan presidents also consented to attend a peace conference. "We could not go to the map without the guys being in the room together," says Hill. "You couldn't do shuttle diplomacy with a map. It was just not practical."

* * *

Free-Flying Shuttle

By mid-October, Holbrooke and the members of his team began feeling cautiously optimistic—though by no means sure—that they might achieve a settlement in Bosnia. In just six weeks they had lifted the siege of Sarajevo;

negotiated two sets of basic principles in Geneva and New York establishing ground rules for a settlement in Bosnia; mediated a countrywide ceasefire; scheduled an international peace conference; and gotten demonstrated proof that Milosevic could negotiate on behalf of the Bosnian Serbs.

* * *

During the early weeks of the mission, Holbrooke had kept reporters off the plane, leaving it up to officials in Washington to dole out stories to the press.[14] But after the White House got tired of being barraged with questions, the State Department asked the negotiators to begin handling the press themselves. According to Holbrooke, this offered an unusual opportunity to shape news coverage of the developing negotiation. Each day, he says, the team would agree on a key phrase that would capture the shuttle's latest accomplishment, or communicate a particular message. "We began to decide, OK, today's headline is going to be 'Important Procedural Breakthrough,' or 'We Come on a Mission of Peace at a Moment of War,'" Holbrooke says. "I remember saying that one day and getting on every network in the world."

Holbrooke's high level of control was not limited to the press. Both critics and supporters agree that Holbrooke operated with an unusual degree of freedom for a government negotiator. "There are very, very few traditional foreign service officers who would have dared to go off the reservation the way he did," says one team member. "They would have felt they couldn't make any decision without checking back, because if the decision was wrong, then they would have to take the blame."

Even so, Holbrooke checked in with Washington every day, primarily talking with Peter Tarnoff, John Kornblum, Strobe Talbott, or Christopher's chief of staff, Thomas Donilon. In addition, he flew back to Washington every few weeks to bring officials up to date and argue specific points of policy. For the most part, however, the lead negotiator was not contacting Washington for advice or approval, but to provide an overview of progress. "They gave me parameters," he says, "but left the details to us." This free rein was particularly important at the negotiating table, says Hill, where to take time out to call Washington would have destroyed Holbrooke's momentum. "When you're trying to bring this thing to a halt, this terrible war," Hill asserts, "you had to be empowered to make decisions on the spot, to move very quickly, and to assess the mood of people and the feel for the situation." Holbrooke vehemently agrees. "You cannot run a negotiation long distance," he declares. "Tactical considerations for negotiation must be left to the negotiator."

* * *

Preparing for Peace Talks

Getting the parties to the Bosnian conflict to agree to talks in the US was unquestionably one of Holbrooke's greatest shuttle achievements. Indeed, the fact that the Balkan presidents who had so recently been at war could have signed a ceasefire and agreed to attend an international peace conference seemed almost unbelievable to some observers. Those in regular contact with the leaders, though, say they were all deeply war-weary. In addition, each had an incentive to settle.

* * *

Managing these difficult relationships remained a challenge. Yet the pace for the negotiators slowed considerably in mid-October. "The first eight weeks we flew more than 100,000 miles," says Owen. "After that we slowed down." With the ceasefire in place, much of the focus shifted to Washington, where the State Department was overseeing the crafting of a massive draft agreement that the Clinton administration intended to present to the Balkan leaders on their arrival for talks in the US. In addition to the Framework Peace Agreement, State Department teams were churning out annexes covering such issues as military responsibilities, regional stabilization, elections, the constitution, arbitration, human rights, refugees and displaced persons, and the international police task force. "The idea was to present people with a complete package," says Hill, "and that took a lot of work." At the same time, the US was refining its plan for what the international military force expected to enter Bosnia soon after a peace agreement should do, with input from the British, French, and other major contributors. By the time talks began, US officials hoped, NATO would already have accepted the military concept.

As work on the draft agreement progressed, OSD asked the Air Force to identify appropriate locales for the talks. Finding the right setting, Holbrooke believed, would be critical. The site should be secluded and secure; easy to close off from the press—both to control news leaks and to limit opportunities for the Balkan leaders to hold mini press conferences; able to provide equivalent accommodations for all the presidents; and not too convenient to Washington and its top officials. "We didn't want to have them continually saying, 'Bring the President and the Secretary of State in here and we can talk about it,' " notes Owen.[15]

On October 18, administration officials announced their choice—the Wright-Patterson Air Force Base near Dayton. While Wright-Patterson lacked the intimacy and cachet of a Camp David, it was ideal in its own way, says Daalder, being "sufficiently remote so that you could actually imprison them in this place, but sufficiently large that they didn't feel imprisoned." Milosevic apparently felt differently. "You want to lock me up in Dayton, Ohio?" *The New York Times* reported him as protesting. "I'm not a priest, you know."

* * *

The Dayton Accord

On November 1, the Dayton talks began. Despite earlier threats, all three presidents, including Tudjman, had arrived with a pledge to get results. "Holbrooke got them to agree to come and stay for as long as it took to reach an agreement," says Owen. "Now that's an amazing concept. Because they knew there were going to be some terrible disagreements." Milosevic, who as the representative of the Bosnian Serbs seemed blithely ready to deal on their behalf, continued to charm those around him. "He took over the Officers' Club at Dayton," one team member recalls. "It was his place. He'd be sitting at this big table saying, 'Bring more wine. Bring, please, for my friends. Bring lobster.' It's the Godfather. He's the perfect Godfather."

For most of the participants, however, the Dayton negotiations were a grim process. Those who were there scoff at news reports that organizers achieved a convivial atmosphere that brought the different sides together. "There was no collegiality amongst the delegations," declares Paul Williams, director of a London-based legal aid nonprofit, who served as part of the Bosnian government's negotiating team at Dayton. Meetings were tense and often stalemated, stretching long into the early morning hours. The three presidents did not meet together at first, but huddled with their own delegations while US negotiators shuttled with drafts and revisions from group to group.

* * *

In spite of this steady resistance, Holbrooke continued to hammer away at the delegations, arguing that Dayton was their last chance to resolve the war with the help of the US and the international community. "He browbeats people," attests one NSC official. "He talks until they're tired. Everything was geared to getting this agreement, and he was working 21 . . . 22 hours a day on this stuff." After two weeks of haggling, some of the obstacles finally gave way. Milosevic approved an adequate corridor to link the eastern enclave of Gorazde with Sarajevo, satisfying a key Muslim concern. In addition, the Serb president agreed that the Bosnian Muslims had "earned" Sarajevo after their years of hardship under siege, and gave the city away, along with four Sarajevan suburbs that the Bosnian Serbs had held since the beginning of the war. Another crisis arose, though, when the Serbs discovered that the last-minute dealmaking had left them with only 45 percent of Bosnia, rather than the 49 percent promised in the principles. Most of the land needed to make up the difference came from the Croats, who only relented after Clinton called Tudjman to plead for his cooperation.[16]

After all these hard-won deals, however, a final snag threatened to kill the entire settlement. On November 20, almost three weeks into the talks, Izetbegovic raised the ante, demanding that Brcko—a Serb-held town in the Posavina Corridor connecting Serbia with the Republika Srpska—be returned to Bosnia's control. Faced with this new demand and the unlikelihood of resolving it, Christopher and Holbrooke distributed a "failure statement" to all the Balkan leaders at midnight. According to the statement, crafted by Holbrooke, the Dayton peace talks would end at 10 the following morning, at which time the US would turn the negotiations back to the Europeans. The announcement, Holbrooke says, was no bluff. President Clinton had authorized the shutdown. Still, Holbrooke was not quite ready to give up. At half past midnight he sent Komblum, Hill, and Pardew to meet with Milosevic one last time and to tell him that unless he could think of a solution, the negotiations were over.[17]

Early the next morning, after first talking to Tudjman, Milosevic went to Holbrooke's room with an offer to break the deadlock. "In the interests of peace, I will walk the last mile," the Serbian president announced, says Holbrooke. "I will agree to arbitration for Brcko. I won't give it away, but I'll agree to arbitration." With Tudjman's endorsement, Christopher and Holbrooke took the offer to Izetbegovic, who listened grimly with Bosnian Foreign Minister Muhamed Sacirbey and Prime Minister Haris Silajdzic at his side. "There was this long pause," Holbrooke recounts, "and Izetbegovic said, 'This is not a just peace,' Another long pause. 'But my people need peace. Let's go ahead.'" Holbrooke and Christopher hurried from the room, anxious to avoid further debate and to notify Clinton as quickly as possible. Once the President had announced the breakthrough, they reasoned, it would be harder for the Bosnian government to back down from its grudging commitment.

Late that morning, as President Clinton was declaring the talk's success on national television, Christopher and Holbrooke called for Owen, who rushed down the hall to a computer and with a young lawyer pieced together an arbitration provision for Brcko. The provision, Owen says, was then hustled around to all the participants, signed, and slapped into the Dayton accord. "The initialing ceremony was half-an-hour late and we got it in," he says. "Now that was not done the way it is supposed to be done. But if we hadn't gotten it done, the whole thing would have fallen apart and we had 30 minutes to do it, so we did it in 30 minutes."

At the end of 21 days, the General Framework Agreement for Peace in Bosnia and Herzegovina was finally initialed by representatives of the Republic of Bosnia and Herzegovina, the Republic of Croatia, and the Federal Republic of Yugoslavia, and witnessed by representatives of the Contact Group nations and Bildt.[18] Izetbegovic and the rest of his delegation remained angry and reluctant to the end. "It was very hard for them to accept this," says one team member. "Izetbegovic described this as a bitter and unjust peace, even in the signing ceremony." The Bosnian Serbs, who reportedly only saw the final document minutes before the signing, refused even to come. For Holbrooke's team, all of whom admit the accord was an imperfect solution, the initialing ceremony marked a moment of profound relief. "Holbrooke is a closer, and that's what it takes," says one member. "Sometimes that's a brutal process. You can have people come up with the greatest negotiating scheme in the world, but if you can't bring it to closure, it doesn't go anywhere."

The 10 articles and 11 annexes of the agreement included the following key provisions: Sarajevo would remain united as the capital city of Bosnia; there would be free elections under international supervision; Bosnia's estimated 2.2 million refugees would have the right of return or to obtain just compensation; and entities within Bosnia would have the right to establish parallel links with neighboring countries, namely the Bosnian Serbs with Serbia and the Bosnian Croats with Croatia. NATO's implementation force, or IFOR, would keep the peace for one year, overseeing the withdrawal of troops behind ceasefire lines, and the enforcement of a 2.5-mile wide zone of separation between the two entities of Bosnia and Republika Srpska. Other international groups, including the Organization for Security and Cooperation in Europe and the UN High Refugee Command, would monitor human rights and the return of refugees. Mladic, Karadzic, and other indicted war criminals would not be allowed to run for, or hold, any public office, and all signers of the agreement agreed to cooperate fully with the War Crimes Tribunal. On December 1, NATO authorized IFOR's implementation, and soon after the peace agreement was signed, 20,000 US troops began arriving in Bosnia to take part in the 60,000-member NATO force.

In many respects, the Dayton agreement, bringing a settlement to the 42-month Bosnian war, was a much needed foreign policy coup for the Clinton administration. Holbrooke and his team had ended the terrible and intractable Balkan conflict, allowing the long process of refugee return, reconstruction, and reconciliation to begin. But even Holbrooke would not venture a prediction as to whether the accord could satisfy the second part of his challenge—to craft a sustainable peace incorporating Muslims, Croats, and Serbs within Bosnia's existing borders. "I feel like this is the best anyone could do," says one of Holbrooke's team members. "I'm not ashamed of it. It's probably the most important thing I've ever worked on in my life."

* * *

NOTES

1. Holbrooke left government for a stint on Wall Street when Ronald Reagan became president.
2. Richard Holbrooke interviews with writer, June 5 and July 1, 1996.

Unless otherwise specified, subsequent quotes attributed to Holbrooke are drawn from these interviews.

3. Lieut. Gen. Wesley Clark interview with writer. May 2, 1996. Unless otherwise specified, subsequent quotes attributed to Clark are drawn from this interview.

4. Some news reports claimed the Pentagon was considering a proposal that the Bosnian Serbs merely silence their artillery but be allowed to keep them in place.

5. Bildt had replaced envoy Lord David Owen in the spring of 1995.

6. One US negotiator recalls an incident at the eventual peace talks when a cooling system kicked in with a boom and Momcilo Krajisnik, a Bosnian Serb leader known for his toughness, winced, then leaned back and said in halting English, "NATO." "For Krajisnik to be flinching with air conditioning units going on," says the negotiator, "told me that there was a significant personal psychological impact."

7. Milosevic would press for sanctions relief throughout the shuttle, but Holbrooke wanted to save that incentive for an eventual peace conference. "I kept saying, 'Well, that isn't my authority, that's Washington's,'" Holbrooke says, "but I was playing a game."

8. Elaine Sciolino, "U.S. Envoy Highlights Fine Print on Bosnia," *The New York Times*, September 13, 1995.

9. As Holbrooke quickly mulled his options, one team member recalls thinking. "I'm glad I'm the junior partner in this deal. The negotiating consequences of that kind of meeting were absolutely unclear to me."

10. The team did not even have a typewriter available, and had to request a computer be sent to the lodge from Belgrade.

11. Although the Bosnian government may not have been pleased, one team member recalls "a very touching moment" a few days later when a group of Sarajevans across from the presidency building recognized Holbrooke as he spoke to the press and began applauding.

12. In fact, after a year-and-a-half, the Federation was still an alliance in name more than in practice. Federation towns such as Mostar remained divided into Muslim and Croat sections, for example, and cars in many towns with a Bosnian Croat majority sported Croatian license plates.

13. The Balkan leaders were undoubtedly aware, however, that back in Washington, Clinton administration officials were estimating a possible infusion of $1 billion in regional aid over a three-year period in the event of a settlement, with perhaps $500 million of it slated for Bosnia.

14. Two reporters, Joe Klein and Roger Cohen, were allowed on briefly under tight guidelines.

15. In fact, it had already been decided that Clinton would not put in an appearance, largely because of the risk of putting his personal impri-

matur on a negotiation that might fail. If the talks succeeded, Clinton would attend the eventual signing ceremony.

16. Largely as a result of the Croatian military successes in Bosnia during the September advance, the Bosnian Croats still ended up with 21 percent of Bosnia, 4 percent more than they had originally been offered under the Contact Group plan. "The Bosnians kept saying to us, 'You've got to get the Croatians back down to 17 percent,'" says Holbrooke. "And we said, 'That's not our business. These percentages are between the two of you.'"

17. Bosnian Foreign Minister Muhamed Sacirbey went overnight to the Holiday Inn where most journalists covering the Dayton talks were staying to announce that the negotiations were about to end, news that the press quickly disseminated.

18. The formal signing ceremony would be held December 14 in Paris as a reward to French President Chirac for his ongoing support for a tougher military and political stance in Bosnia.

8 Power: Still the Name of the Game?

There is no question that the United States enters the twenty-first century as the world's most powerful nation. It is number one in military might. Its nuclear arsenal is second to none. Its armed forces are the best trained and have the best military technology available. It also has the most active diplomacy, drawing on a broad range of strategies of statecraft.

But to what extent can this massive power be converted to actual influence, either over other countries or over other forces that affect U.S. interests?

The Gulf Crisis: Building a Coalition for War case study focuses on the U.S.–led response to the 1990 Iraqi invasion of Kuwait. It covers the diplomatic strategy for gaining broad multilateral support and the politics of mobilizing and sustaining U.S. domestic support, as well as the military strategy of Operations Desert Shield and Desert Storm. As with other cases, the *Gulf Crisis* case has both unique aspects and broader implications with regard to the scope and also the limits of American power.

The Gulf Crisis: Map of the Region

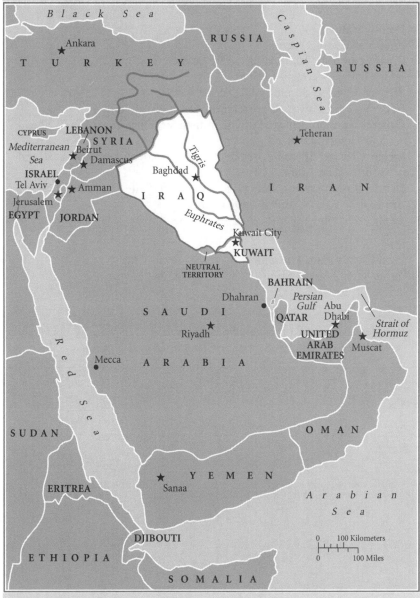

Source: Lawrence Freedman and Efraim Karsh, *The Gulf Conflict 1990–1991: Diplomacy and War in the New World Order* (Princeton: Princeton University Press, 1993), p. xix.

★★★ **KEY PLAYERS**

United States
President George Bush
Brent Scowcroft, National Security Adviser
James Baker, Secretary of State
Richard Cheney, Secretary of Defense
General Colin Powell, Chairman, Joint Chiefs of Staff
General Norman Schwarzkopf, Commander, Operations Desert Shield and Desert Storm
Richard Haass, Special Assistant to the President for Near East and South Asian Affairs
Dennis Ross, Director, Policy Planning Staff, State Department
April Glaspie, U.S. Ambassador to Iraq

Iraq
President Saddam Hussein
Tariq Aziz, Foreign Minister

Others
President Mikhail Gorbachev, Soviet Union
Javier Perez de Cuellar, Secretary-General, United Nations

1920	Iraq established as a League of Nations mandate under Great Britain.
1932	Iraq gains independence from Britain.
1955	Baghdad Pact created under U.S. and British auspices as a pro-Western regional defense organization with Iraq as key member.
1958	Following leftist military coup, Iraq withdraws from Baghdad Pact.
1961	Kuwait gains independence from Britain.
1972	Iraq signs Treaty of Friendship and Cooperation with the Soviet Union.
January 1979	Shah of Iran falls, Ayatollah Khomeini comes to power.
July 1979	Saddam Hussein, for many years the power behind the scenes, becomes president of Iraq.
November 1979	Seventy-six Americans taken hostage at the American embassy in Teheran, Iran.
September 1980	Iran-Iraq War begins with Iraqi attack on Iran.
1982	Reagan administration begins opening to Iraq, following the logic of "the enemy of my enemy is my friend."
1984	Full U.S.-Iraqi diplomatic relations restored.
1987–88	U.S. provides military protection for Kuwaiti oil tankers and pledges to maintain freedom of the seas in the Persian Gulf, in a move that further tilts toward Iraq and leads to numerous military clashes with Iran in the Gulf.
July 1988	Iran-Iraq War ends.
August 1988	Saddam uses chemical weapons against the Iraqi Kurds, but Reagan administration opposes economic sanctions.
1989	Bush administration policy review supports continuation of strategy of seeking accommodation with Iraq.
August 1, 1990	Iraq invades Kuwait.
August 2	United States imposes initial sanctions; UN Security Council passes first resolution condemning Iraq.
August 8	President Bush announces Operation Desert Shield.
October 30	Bush decides to double U.S. military forces deployed against Iraq.

November 29	UN Security Council passes Resolution 678, setting January 15 deadline for Iraqi withdrawal from Kuwait, and authorizing the use of "all necessary means" if the deadline is not met.
January 9	Last-ditch diplomacy by Secretary of State James Baker fails as Iraqi Foreign Minister Aziz refuses to accept letter from President Bush.
January 12	U.S. Congress passes joint resolution supporting use of force against Iraq.
January 16	Operation Desert Storm launched as U.S.-led allied forces begin bombing Baghdad.
February 28	President Bush declares victory.

 *Power Case Study*

The Gulf Crisis: Building a Coalition for War

On August 2, 1990, Iraqi President Saddam Hussein jolted the world by launching a crushing invasion of tiny neighboring Kuwait. Although Iraqi troops had been massed at the border for weeks, most military and intelligence experts had dismissed the buildup as a scare tactic, or the prelude to a limited land grab, at worst. Within hours, denunciations began to pour forth from around the world. In Washington, D.C., the initial reaction to the invasion was firm, though restrained. Saddam had done wrong, but it was not immediately clear what stake the US had in redressing it.

But within days, the US response became urgent and purposeful. President George Bush had seized on the far-away conflict as a flagrant challenge to "the new world order"—the greater harmony between nations that many hoped would follow the end of the Cold War. The Saddams of the world had a lesson to learn, particularly if they sat on major oil reserves and threatened to seize more, and the US was determined to teach them. Over the next several months, the Bush administration labored toward its objective: to piece together an international coalition with the political and military muscle to drive Saddam out of Kuwait, and—equally key—to support the President's goals.

* * *

The Bush Administration Responds

* * * When word of the invasion reached Washington, D.C. at 7 p.m., August 1, the reaction of officials—already well seasoned by conflicts such as the invasion of Panama in 1989—was swift. The Deputies Committee— a crisis management group made up of sub-Cabinet level representatives from State, Defense, and other agencies—quickly convened to set in motion a series of diplomatic responses to Saddam's aggression. At 11:20, with

This case was written by Susan Rosegrant in collaboration with Michael D. Watkins, Associate Professor, Harvard Business School, for use by the National Security Program, at the John F. Kennedy School of Government, Harvard University.

Bush's approval, the White House released a public response calling for "the immediate and unconditional withdrawal of all Iraqi forces."

In New York, meanwhile, US Ambassador to the United Nations Thomas Pickering had received an urgent call from the State Department directing him to convene a special session of the United Nations Security Council to consider a resolution condemning Iraq. The Security Council, whose members in 1990 included the Soviet Union, Cuba, and Yemen, was in many respects an unlikely vehicle for speedy diplomatic action, particularly for a US-led resolution. Nevertheless, after meeting through the night, the Council quickly passed a draft that had been largely written by the State Department in Washington, D.C. Resolution 660, condemning the invasion of Kuwait and calling for Iraq to withdraw its forces "immediately and unconditionally," was approved without dissent, with only Yemen abstaining. Pickering attributes the swiftness of the response and its unanimity to the "outrageous" nature of the Kuwaiti invasion, which he describes as "very much contrary to what people had come to expect the end of the Cold War might mean."[1] By the time Bush met with the National Security Council the morning after the invasion, the UN resolution was in place, and the US had already frozen Kuwaiti as well as Iraqi assets—to keep Iraq from plundering Kuwait's substantial foreign accounts—and begun to look at the question of US deployment.

For the US, as for many other countries, these initial acts of condemnation had occurred almost without debate. Bush and his key advisers—a group dubbed the "Gang of Eight," consisting of Bush, Vice President Dan Quayle, National Security Adviser General Brent Scowcroft, Secretary of State James Baker, Defense Secretary Richard Cheney, Chief of Staff John Sununu, Chairman of the Joint Chiefs of Staff Colin Powell, and Deputy National Security Adviser Robert Gates—had also begun to call leaders in Europe and the Middle East, both to gauge and to help coordinate the growing international response.

But what to do next was not so obvious. The US had maintained its right to intercede militarily against threats to the Persian Gulf since 1980, when President Jimmy Carter declared the oil-rich region a "vital" American interest. Clearly, the invasion of Kuwait was just such a threat. Saddam had already taken control of 20 percent of the world's known oil reserves, and his troops were poised at the Saudi Arabian border. If Iraqi forces marched on to capture the Saudi capital of Riyadh, just 275 miles to the south, Saddam would double his reserves and his power over the economically critical market.

Yet Saddam's actual intentions regarding Saudi Arabia were impossible to discern. Moreover, Saudi Arabia's King Fahd might not even allow US troops to defend his country. Finally, it was unclear what support the Bush administration could muster in the US for military involvement in a faraway conflict that posed no immediate threat to the nation other than higher oil prices. The meeting on August 2, which National Security Adviser Brent

Scowcroft criticizes as "lackadaisical," concluded with these questions un-answered.[2]

Later that same day, however, Bush's resolve began to harden. Accompanied by Scowcroft, the President flew to Aspen, Colorado, to attend a long-planned session with British Prime Minister, Margaret Thatcher. Thatcher, known as a hawk on international conflicts, was the only Western leader from the start to be as outspoken about the invasion as Bush, and their discussion that day was far-ranging. Some commentators later claimed it was this meeting that put real fire in the President's blood. But British and American officials present insist the Aspen session merely provided a meeting of like minds, and gave both Bush and Thatcher a chance to shape their emerging ideas.

Both because of the Thatcher encounter, and because of careful preparation on Scowcroft's part, the second National Security Council meeting the next morning achieved the sense of urgency the first had lacked. Scowcroft had met earlier with Defense Secretary Richard Cheney and Deputy Secretary of State Lawrence Eagleburger to enlist their aid in pushing things to a head. Now all three urged a hard look at US options, arguing that far more was at stake than just the independence of a tiny Gulf emirate. There was the possible disruption of vital oil supplies, and the resultant repercussions through world markets; the growing imbalance of power in the region, particularly if Saddam marched on into Saudi Arabia; the danger to the more than 3,000 Americans, and the thousands of other foreigners, caught behind the closed borders of Iraq and Kuwait; and the threat that Israel might be drawn into the conflict by a direct Iraqi attack. All three advisers spoke out in support of sending forces to Saudi Arabia. "The first meeting was, 'Well, it's a fait accompli, and how do we adjust to it?'" Scowcroft recalls. "The second was, 'This is an event that affects vital American interests. What are we going to do about it?'"[3]

✶ ✶ ✶

An Unforeseen Link with the Soviets

When Iraq invaded Kuwait, Secretary of State James Baker was off meeting with Soviet Foreign Minister Eduard Shevardnadze in Siberia. Iraq was not on the agenda, and, in fact, Shevardnadze had reassured Baker that despite the Iraqi troop buildup at Kuwait's border, an invasion was highly unlikely.

Just hours after the invasion was launched, Baker decided to go ahead with a long-scheduled and politically sensitive stopoff in Mongolia. Dennis Ross, director of the State Department's policy planning staff, went quickly on to Moscow with the returning Soviets. Ross was sent with no instructions. But when an aide suggested the idea of a joint US-Soviet statement condemning the invasion, Ross immediately seized on the idea. "I was very concerned that if we and the Soviets were not together right away that there would be potential for Saddam to create a difference between us and then exploit that within the Middle East," Ross recalls. "If he had a sense that the Superpowers weren't together, it would create a great degree of ambiguity about whether in fact the international community was aligned against him."[4]

* * *

Ross and his Soviet counterpart, Sergei Tarasenko went back and forth on drafts, with the American rejecting the "emasculated" Soviet rewrites. Because of communications problems, Ross was unable to warn Baker about the ongoing stalemate. But to pressure the Soviets, he told Tarasenko that if he reached Baker, he would tell him not to bother to come, a warning Ross now admits he used as a device. "I was arguing with Tarasenko that either we're going to have a partnership or we aren't. If we can't cooperate and engage as partners on something like this, then all this is a charade." Ross's hard line worked. With Shevardnadze's approval, the joint draft he finally handed Baker on his arrival August 3 condemned the invasion and called on the international community to join in an arms embargo of Iraq. The only significant deletion from his original, Ross recalls, was a threat to resort to additional steps, including the possible use of military force, a threat Ross concedes he was "in no position to deliver on our side at that point."[5]

Looking back on this seminal moment of cooperation, one top State Department official not only marvels that it came about so quickly, but that it happened at all. "Had Baker not been in a position to stand up there in Moscow within 24 hours after the invasion happened with Shevardnadze and have the foreign minister of the Soviet Union and the American secretary of state condemning the action of a Soviet client state, it could have been different," he muses. "We still had substantial work to do, but it certainly locked the Soviets into condemnation of the action." National Security Adviser Scowcroft saw the joint statement more simply. "That's when I first thought the Cold War might be over," he recalls.[6]

Assembling the Arab Coalition

* * *

Although they felt angry and betrayed, and in the case of Saudi Arabia, directly threatened, most Arab nations were anxious to avoid outside interference. Foreign intervention in the area, typically on the part of the Soviet Union or the US, had often exacerbated regional tensions instead of relieving them. Moreover, some Arab leaders believed that Saddam would be more likely to consider a negotiated withdrawal if not confronted with a direct demand to get out of Kuwait. Saddam confirmed this belief when he told Jordan's King Hussein the day of the invasion that he planned to begin withdrawing troops within days, but at the same time asked King Hussein to "do whatever you can with the Arabs to persuade them that condemnation and threats don't work with us."[7] The UN Security Council resolution demanding Iraq's unconditional withdrawal had already complicated efforts at achieving a regional solution. But most Arab nations felt the resolution was redeemed by its specific call for Iraq and Kuwait to begin "intensive negotiations," supported by the League of Arab States.

* * *

The afternoon of the second National Security Council meeting, Brent Scowcroft invited Saudi Arabia's ambassador to Washington, Prince Bandar Ibn Sultan, to the White House to review classified US intelligence photos showing Iraqi troops massing at the Saudi Arabian border. Bandar, known to be a powerful emissary to the king, agreed to lobby for the US deployment. The next day, President Bush called King Fahd directly to impress on him both the real danger of an invasion, and the US's willingness to help. At Fahd's invitation, Bush agreed to send a team to Jeddah the following day to discuss the proposed deployment. Fahd originally requested a mere technical team, but Bush feared that a low-level group would be too easily disregarded. Instead, on August 6, the king accepted a group led by Defense Secretary Richard Cheney and including Deputy National Security Adviser Robert Gates and General Schwarzkopf, commander of Central Command, the Joint Command responsible for the Middle East.

* * *

Once Cheney showed the Saudi king US intelligence photos, and gave proof of President Bush's resolve by promising at least 200,000 troops, Fahd quickly accepted the offer of American forces. Less than 40 hours after he approved the deployment, the US had F-15s on the ground in Saudi Arabia. Only following the acceptance of US forces did King Fahd risk Saddam's wrath by agreeing to shut down the Iraqi oil pipeline that ran through Saudi Arabia.

* * *

Many Arab League members—including Jordan, Libya, Yemen, and Tunisia—denounced the acceptance of outside intervention and continued to argue for an Arab solution. When the League met for an emergency summit meeting August 10, only a slim majority of heads of state voted to endorse the arrival of foreign forces. But at the same meeting, Egypt, Morocco, and Syria all agreed to contribute troops to defend Saudi Arabia and the Gulf, a commitment that gave the US critical proof of regional support for the deployment. Arab efforts at mediation continued, but their likelihood of bearing fruit was low. The arrival of US and other foreign troops had signalled a change of stakes and the "internationalization" of the Gulf crisis.

Desert Shield Begins

At 9 a.m. on August 8, President Bush appeared on national television from the Oval Office to announce Desert Shield, the deployment of US troops to protect Saudi Arabia. "At my direction," he declared, "elements of the 82d Airborne Division as well as key units of the United States Air Force are arriving today to take up defensive positions in Saudi Arabia." The mission was "wholly defensive," Bush emphasized. "No one commits America's armed forces to a dangerous mission lightly," he said. "But after perhaps unparalleled international consultation and exhausting every alternative, it became necessary to take this action." At a Pentagon press conference later that day, Cheney and Powell declined to discuss the size of the deployment, but within a few days, the actual figure of up to 250,000 was leaked to the press.

The first days of the deployment were tense. For one thing, it would take a couple of weeks before enough troops and equipment would arrive to resist an Iraqi attack. "There was nothing to stop Saddam," asserts Richard Clarke, the State Department's assistant secretary for military and political affairs. "Even after the 82d Airborne deployed at Dhahran, they essentially deployed with the bullets in the rifles that they carried, and they didn't have anything much beyond that for days."[8] In addition, except for the ever-enthusiastic British and a couple of Arab nations, it was not clear how significant participation in the international military coalition would be, particularly when it came to supplying ground troops. "So far," one columnist wrote August 11, "[the] multinational label is largely a gleam in America's eye."[9]

In truth, the US expected and was fully prepared to handle the lion's share of the defensive operation itself. In terms of actual military effectiveness, once Saudi Arabia made its bases available, the US wanted only time to pull together a sufficient defense. Moreover, the Arab League vote of August 10 condemning Iraq and committing troops had been critical in casting the conflict as an international response, rather than a US vendetta against an Arab country. But from a political standpoint, the US still needed the legitimacy that would come from a broad-based, multinational operation. President Bush, who was on a first name basis with many foreign leaders after his years in government as vice president, director of the CIA, and ambassador to the UN, stepped up the "telephone diplomacy" that had characterized his early response to the crisis. Indeed, the President's penchant for calling his counterparts in capitals around the world earned him the nickname among State Department foreign service officers of "the mad dialer." "Bush's personal relationships with a lot of people really helped," asserts Richard Haass, special assistant to the President for Near East and South Asian Affairs. "You don't want to make your first call to someone be the time you need them."[10]

Within days, the nascent military coalition began to grow, aided not only by pressure from Bush, but also by Iraq's decision August 11 to retain as hostages the thousands of Western and Soviet nationals who had not escaped before the Iraqi and Kuwaiti borders were sealed.[11] Belgium, Greece, Spain, the Netherlands, and Italy—all members of the Western European Union —announced on August 22 that they would contribute naval units to the operation. Egypt, which was evolving into a key coalition ally, had sent 5,000 troops by late August. By mid-September, Britain had expanded its commitments of naval and air forces to include an armoured brigade. And France—which had originally distanced itself from the coalition, preferring to respond independently—had committed to sending 4,200 ground troops.

In these early efforts to stitch together a military coalition, Cheney says, the focus was strictly on defending Saudi Arabia. "It wasn't in our interest to talk publicly about offensive military action," he explains. "We didn't have enough forces over there to defend Saudi Arabia at the outset. If Saddam had figured out that we were going to get after him, he might have been smart enough to go ahead and move another 250 or 300 miles and take the Saudi airfields and the ports that we needed to get in there."[12]

In fact, the President still had not revealed his hand on liberating Kuwait, even to his closest "Gang of Eight" advisers. Partly as a result, most Americans still viewed the sending of US troops to launch an attack as a far-off and unlikely prospect. But by the end of August, Cheney says, he and many others had begun to think in terms of offensive action. * * *

* * * "Did we think at that time that we would have to mount a military operation?" asks Brent Scowcroft. "Not necessarily. But by then we'd decided it was basically up to Saddam how he got out."[13]

The UN Security Council: Advocate or Adversary

Although the administration had turned to the UN Security Council as one of its initial diplomatic moves, US Ambassador to the UN Thomas Pickering describes the first resolution that was passed as "a box that had to be checked" rather than as a centerpiece of US strategy. In the weeks after the invasion, however, the US continued to push through resolutions, helped by Saddam's blatant acts of aggression and his inability—or unwillingness —to turn world opinion in his favor (see Exhibit 4 for a summary of UN Security Council resolutions responding to the Iraqi invasion). On August 6 the Council easily approved Resolution 661 imposing full economic sanctions against Iraq.[14] And when Saddam announced a new Kuwaiti "provisional government" whose ministers all happened to be Iraqi, even Cuba and Yemen joined the vote on Resolution 662, declaring the annexation "null and void."

That the Security Council would continue to support the US position and take such a strong role in the dispute was by no means a given. During its 45-year history, the Council's rules and operating procedures, as well as the differing political agendas of its members, had made it difficult for any one country to lead a sustained response to an international crisis. For a resolution to pass, nine of the 15 members had to approve it, and the five permanent members—all with veto power—had to either approve or abstain. Thus, for the United States to win passage of a resolution, it needed not only nine votes but the support of the other four permanent members —China, France, Great Britain, and the Soviet Union.

In the past, the Soviets could be counted on to reject US-led resolutions, with the Chinese usually following their lead. But with relations between the US and the Soviets thawing daily, and the joint condemnation of Iraq in hand, UN Ambassador Pickering says there was an almost unprecedented opportunity for cooperation among the permanent five. "Those traditional recalcitrants on the Council who were normally galvanized by the Soviets were left to drift by the fact that the Soviets were immediately with us," he explains. "Without the Soviets, we had no successful strategy."[15]

* * *

But despite Pickering's success with the first three resolutions, some in the administration began to question the wisdom of allowing the UN to become the implementing agent and the de facto final arbiter in the crisis. Haass, while acknowledging the advantage of having the Security Council's "Good Housekeeping seal of approval," recalls fretting over the precedent being set. "The idea that before you could ever do anything you have to go to the Council was not an approach to international relations that filled me with great confidence," he says.[16] The Pentagon, in particular, was concerned that the US might eventually find itself shackled if the Council voted to oppose the use of force.

The question of whether to continue with the Security Council came to a head less than two weeks into the crisis. When the Council voted August 6 to impose full economic sanctions ending all trade with Iraq, the question of enforcement was not addressed. According to President Bush, however, and to the even more adamant Margaret Thatcher, the US and Britain had the authority to enforce the embargo and to stop Iraqi ships— using military force if necessary—under Article 51 of the UN Charter. This article, affirming "the inherent right of individual or collective self-defense," could be invoked once the Kuwaiti emir asked for help, and the US, Britain, and France had all received such formal requests for assistance.

But when Bush—invoking Article 51—declared on August 11 that the

US had the right to take unilateral action against Iraqi tankers, he set off a firestorm of criticism among allies and the Security Council. Two days later, angry Council members meeting in a closed door session claimed such a unilateral move on Bush's part would amount to an act of war. And UN Secretary General Perez de Cuellar claimed that "only the UN, through Security Council resolutions, can really bring about a blockade."[17] Thatcher and some administration officials, including Scowcroft and Cheney, discounted the critics and continued to push for decisive action. "Inside the US government there were people who said, 'Haven't we run the UN string out?' " recalls Robert Kimmitt, under secretary of state for political affairs. " 'Isn't now the time just to take matters into our own hands?' "[18]

* * *

By August 22, the permanent five—with the exception of China—were generally comfortable adding the threat of force to give more bite to the embargo. But Gorbachev, who continued to exchange envoys with Saddam, and who had sensed some mellowing on the Iraqi leader's part, argued for a few more days in which to try to persuade Iraq to withdraw.[19] Although Bush feared this was just more stalling on Saddam's part, with or without Soviet complicity, he granted Gorbachev three more days before putting a resolution allowing use of force to a vote.

* * *

On August 25, after the Soviets admitted no progress with Saddam, the Security Council approved what amounted to a naval blockade against Iraq, with only Cuba and Yemen voting against it. Resolution 665 allowed member states cooperating with Kuwait, and with maritime forces in the area, "to use such measures commensurate to the specific circumstances as may be necessary" to enforce the embargo. The resolution's purposeful ambiguity not only discouraged anti-war rhetoric in the US, but was critical in avoiding a Chinese veto. As Pickering explains, "The Chinese finally abstained on the thesis that the resolution text didn't authorize the use of force in their view, a statement they made in public at the end of the debate, which we had agreed we would not try to counter."[20] Even Colombia and Malaysia voted in favor, claiming that despite their objections to the text, they did not want to send the wrong message to Saddam.

* * *

* * * Bush administration officials had reason to be pleased with what they had accomplished. Less than a month into the crisis, an American-run military operation was taking shape in Saudi Arabia with unprecedented Arab backing; the Soviets were escalating their criticisms of Iraq, almost hand-in-hand with the US; and an international embargo—backed by a UN sanctioned threat of military force—had isolated Iraq both economically and militarily. A multinational coalition was coming together against Iraq, just as the US had planned.

The "Tin Cup" Trips: Cash and Favors

When President Bush first decided to send forces to Saudi Arabia, the support his administration sought was political, not economic. The US was going to do all it could to build a powerful international alliance against Saddam. But by the end of August, when the cost of the deployment reached an average of $28.9 million a day, raising money—or, as Baker carefully phrased it, "responsibility sharing"—became both a practical and a political necessity. Belt tightening was a major concern domestically, where a weak economy promised to make the upcoming budget debate more acrimonious than usual. Moreover, Congress, which had remained relatively passive about the deployment decision itself, was unreservedly vocal about the need to share the burden on cost. "The Hill at that point was just hammering the administration about, 'Well, what are the Germans putting up? What are the Japanese putting up?' " recalls an aide to Baker. "In order to get domestic support, you needed to make sure other people were putting up money."

* * *

Around Labor Day, Baker set out for the Middle East, while Treasury Secretary Nicholas Brady flew to Europe and Asia for the first of what came to be known as the "tin cup" trips, trips that one Baker aide describes as "laying the political-economic basis for the coalition." The Kuwaiti government in exile, not surprisingly, was already bankrolling the US effort. Now the administration targeted Saudi Arabia and the other Gulf countries that were reaping the benefits of inflated oil prices and that also stood to gain most directly from US efforts to check Saddam's aggression. The US also sought major financial aid from Germany and Japan, countries with strong stakes in a stabilized oil supply and a subdued Iraq, but whose national constitutions made it difficult or impossible to participate militarily in the Gulf.

The two-pronged fundraising effort, which continued as the crisis escalated, was highly successful. By November, an ad hoc group created by the Deputies Committee to manage the collection and disbursal of funds to other countries—the Gulf Crisis Financial Coordination Group—had arranged a $13 billion aid package. Moreover, the administration could legitimately claim that America had not shouldered the financial burden of the Gulf response alone. According to the Defense Department, the US eventually collected $53.7 billion from allies, leaving $7.4 billion to absorb from its military involvement in the Gulf.[21]

* * *

The multinational coalition assembled against Saddam served US interests well. The geopolitical diversity as well as the sheer number of countries included in the alliance served as constant proof of a world united in outrage. But this same diversity made for a lot of work. "One of the real challenges was creating and holding together the coalition over a multi-month period," admits Robert Gates, the President's deputy national security adviser. "It was a very diverse coalition and people were in it for very different reasons."[22]

* * *

Both the Soviet Union and France continued to search for some common ground with Saddam, even while cooperating with the coalition. On September 24, for example, in a speech to the UN General Assembly, French President Francois Mitterrand shocked US officials and some other allies by bluntly proposing a comprehensive regional peace conference to follow an Iraqi pullout from Kuwait. The Soviet Union, for its part, continued to set up meetings between Saddam and Yevgeny Primakov, an Arabist and special envoy for Gorbachev, who often opposed US tactics, and who believed that the promise of a Middle East peace conference might help induce Saddam to withdraw.

UN Secretary General Perez de Cuellar was also known to be sympathetic both to the idea of seeking a negotiated settlement with Iraq and addressing the broader Arab-Israeli conflict, and specifically the Palestinian issue, which Iraq wanted to link to any discussion of Kuwait. But administration officials in Washington and Pickering at the UN made clear their distaste for such proposals. There could be no hedging, they declared, on the "unconditional withdrawal" demanded in the first Security Council resolution. "This was not a traditional negotiation," asserts a White House official. "I was not looking to save Saddam from himself, I was simply looking to get him out —bottom line." He adds: "He was going to choose the method of his leaving Kuwait. That was the choice we gave him."

Doubling of Forces: The Offensive Option

* * *

Throughout October, as Saddam continued to snub the few overtures at negotiation being made, the Bush administration began planning more seriously for war. Briefings with Schwarzkopf, Powell, and other military advisers produced the rudiments of a plan. An offensive option would require twice the number of troops currently deployed; conveniently, with the end of the Cold War, many of those troops could be pulled directly from Germany and moved to the Saudi Arabian front. Ideal timing for the conflict would be after January 1—when sufficient troops and equipment would be in place—and before February 15—when the onset of bad weather and a series of Muslim religious holidays would complicate logistics. In a strictly military sense, only Saudi Arabia's cooperation was vital, and that was for its bases. "The bottom line," one senior Pentagon official asserts, "was that the war was going to be run by the United States and was going to involve primarily US forces."

On October 30, Bush met with his top advisers to reach a decision on preparing an offensive to retake Kuwait. The Security Council had just passed a tenth resolution condemning Iraq, and overall, the coalition still looked solid. But the administration was alarmed by the ongoing French and Soviet attempts to reach a negotiated settlement with Iraq, possibly in violation of Security Council resolutions. Gorbachev, just the day before at a Paris press conference, had seemed to withdraw his support for a future military course. In addition, there were rumors that Saudi Arabia was considering striking a deal with Saddam.

Concerned by such evidence that the coalition might break down; impressed by the argument made by Baker and some others that the threat of military action might be the only way to convince Iraq to withdraw; and buoyed by predictions that if it came to war, the US would win handily, the President approved the buildup the next day. There was disagreement within the administration as to when to announce the increase, but Bush decided to hold the news for at least a week, to avoid influencing the upcoming Congressional elections.

* * *

Baker set off on a round-the-world trip, hoping to solidify the support of key allies before the troop buildup was made public. Congress and the American people, he believed, had not been adequately prepared to accept such an escalation. But as news of the increase began to leak out, Bush went ahead with a news conference on November 8, Veteran's Day. "After consultation with King Fahd and our other allies, I have today directed the secretary of defense to increase the size of US forces committed to Desert Shield to insure that the coalition has an adequate offensive military option should that be necessary to achieve our common goals," the President announced, in part. "Iraq's aggression is not just a challenge to the security of Kuwait and other Gulf nations, but to the better world that we all have hoped to build in the wake of the Cold War."

Challenges Back Home

Without question, the doubling of forces caught Congress by surprise, a surprise made particularly galling by the fact that the President had met with key leaders a little more than a week before he made the troop increase public, but had not indicated such a decision was imminent. "There were two times we did not consult closely with Congress," reflects one White House official. "One was the doubling of force. The other was in August when we made the basic decision that we were going to resist."

More troubling than the surprise, though, was the message itself. For many Bush administration officials, the troop increase was simply the next logical step in a chain of events begun in August. "The White House position had been absolutely consistent from day one," asserts Philip Zelikow, the National Security Council's director for European security affairs.[23] But for many in Congress, and for a significant percentage of the American public, neither the timing nor the need for a military buildup was obvious. Senator Sam Nunn, chairman of the Senate Armed Services Committee, appearing on CBS, described the increase as a "fundamental change" in US policy. No longer, it seemed, was the Bush administration willing to give sanctions a chance. No longer was the international pressure of the carefully assembled coalition considered adequate. Suddenly, a US-led war had become a real possibility. Faced with this new development, both the Senate and the House announced they would hold public hearings at the end of the month on the nation's Gulf policy.

* * *

The start of Congressional hearings in late November presented a new challenge to the momentum of the administration's buildup. While those who testified included ardent advocates of the President's policies, there were also harsh critics, including individuals Bush found difficult to ignore. On November 28, for example, Admiral William J. Crowe, Jr., who had served as chairman of the Joint Chiefs of Staff under both Ronald Reagan and Bush, made a strong plea for restraint:

> In my view, the critical foreign policy questions we must ask are not whether Saddam Hussein is a brutal, deceitful, or as Barbara Bush would put it, a dreadful man—he is all of those things. Whether initiating conflict against Iraq will moderate the larger difficulties in the Gulf region and will put Washington in a better position to work with the Arab world in the future, is in my estimation, the more important question. . . . It would be a sad commentary if Saddam Hussein, a two-bit tyrant who sits on seventeen million people and possesses a gross national product of $40 billion, proved to be more patient than the United States, the world's most affluent and powerful nation.[24]

* * *

As surveys showed faltering public support for the President's Gulf policies, Bush began working with his pollster, Robert Teeter, to develop a new, more coherent message that would communicate the gravity necessary to justify a military escalation. Their solution: to portray Saddam as a significant nuclear threat. Bush introduced the idea in a Thanksgiving Day speech to US troops in Saudi Arabia, declaring that "every day that passes brings Saddam Hussein one step closer to realizing his goal of a nuclear weapons arsenal—and that's another reason, frankly, why our mission is marked by a real sense of urgency." In fact, ongoing intelligence scrutiny of Iraq had produced warnings that Saddam might be closer to producing a nuclear bomb than previously believed. Nevertheless, Bush's warning—repeated often in coming weeks—aroused a fair amount of cynicism in government circles, even among some White House staff who believed there was no evidence to support the claim. As recently as August, after all, government estimates had indicated Iraq wouldn't have a nuclear capability for at least five years.[25]

Nevertheless, the President kept returning to Saddam's potential to initiate a nuclear confrontation. Bush's pollster had found that containing this threat was one issue the American public really cared about.

Back to the Security Council: Gambling on the Coalition

In early November, Baker had left on a multi-nation trip to begin drumming up support for a UN resolution authorizing force. But not everyone in the administration was convinced this was a good political move. Scowcroft and Cheney, in particular, were afraid that in the event of a Security Council veto, the US would either be hobbled, or would be subject to potentially paralyzing international and domestic criticism if it went ahead with a unilateral attack. "The key risk was that we might fail" to get the UN vote, Ambassador Pickering states bluntly. "Once having failed, the entire structure on which our activity was based would have become insufficient, at least in the minds of many people."[26]

Complicating the decision was the conviction on the part of many within the administration that Security Council authorization was largely a political gesture. The US, they believed, had the legal right under Article 51 to move forward unilaterally to liberate Kuwait. Not only that, defense officials predicted that while some of the more skittish Arab states, such as Syria, might back down without the UN umbrella, the allies that mattered most militarily, such as Saudi Arabia and Britain, would stick with the US under Article 51. "We did not need Security Council action," Cheney declares. "Partly what made the coalition successful was the fact that it became clear over time that we would do it whether we had anybody else on board or not."[27]

* * *

The draft resolution finally put before the Council on November 29 was jointly sponsored by the US, the Soviet Union, Canada, and Great Britain. Resolution 678 called on Iraq to take advantage of this "one final opportunity, as a pause of goodwill," to comply with all eleven preceding UN resolutions by January 15, 1991. If it did not, "all necessary means" could be used to enforce the resolutions and "to restore international peace and security in the area." As the Bush administration had wished, the resolution did not give the UN jurisdiction over any prospective offensive operation, but granted the right to take military action—rather ambiguously—to "Member States cooperating with the Government of Kuwait." In effect, this left military coordination in the hands of the US.

Baker's month of travelling diplomacy paid off: The final vote on Resolution 678 was twelve in favor, with Cuba and Yemen voting against, and China abstaining.[28] "What is probably the single most important Security Council resolution in history was negotiated everywhere except New York," Bolton declares.[29] But while the gamble on the UN had succeeded, the hard work was not over. The Bush administration still had to prove to Congress and the American public that if it came to war, the US would not be fighting alone. In the wake of the Security Council vote, for example, Representative Les Aspin, chairman of the House Armed Services Committee, expressed his fears that the allies wouldn't pull their weight in an armed confrontation, asserting, "The vote for the UN resolution is, in effect, a vote by the members of the Security Council to let the United States fight Iraq."[30]

* * *

War: The Preferred Alternative

One day after the Security Council approved the use of force, President Bush—with Baker's strong support—made a controversial televised offer. To "go the extra mile for peace," Bush said, he was inviting Iraqi Foreign Minister Tariq Aziz to Washington. Baker, he hoped, would be able to return the visit and meet with Saddam in Baghdad sometime before January 15.

In the US, the diplomatic overture was a coup. Although the Congressional hearings on Gulf policy launched in late November continued to provide a forum for anti-administration views, Bush's approval rating began to rebound amidst this new evidence that the President was not rushing precipitously toward war. Moreover, an early movement among some legislative critics for a Congressional vote on Bush's right to use force against

Iraq lost momentum in the face of this gesture. "We were saved from ourselves," jokes one administration official who opposed the Bush offer. "It looked like we were going the extra mile."

But many coalition members, and Arab allies, in particular, heard the invitation for high-level contact with astonishment and dismay. The message Saddam would take from this, they were convinced, was that the US was not serious about its ability or willingness to use force. Brent Scowcroft, who had counseled against making the offer, had his own fear: that Aziz would use his visit to strengthen the case against war. "I was concerned about Tariq Aziz coming to Washington and being able to mobilize," he admits. "We talked about whether we could just let him go to the UN and then leave, but we decided he would have to be allowed to go and meet the press."[31]

That Baker and Scowcroft should be on opposite sides of this issue was no surprise. During the fall, an important split had developed in the administration. Baker and General Colin Powell were still anxious to work sanctions and diplomacy to the full. But Cheney, Scowcroft, and—for the most part—Bush had gradually become convinced not only that offensive force might be necessary, but that war was actually the preferred alternative. "Saddam had demonstrated that he had strong intentions about Kuwait," asserts Scowcroft. "If he pulled back intact, we would be in a very awkward situation because he would be there as a constant threat, and we couldn't keep forces over there forever." He adds: "The best way to do it was to deal with it now."[32]

* * *

Saddam, however, did not take advantage of the opportunity Bush had handed him, even though he appeared to have interpreted the invitation much in the vein that some allies feared—as evidence of last-minute American capitulation and openness to negotiation. Iraqi newspapers ran gloating stories, claiming that the US had submitted to Saddam's demands to resolve the Palestinian issue before addressing Kuwait. And one week after Bush's announcement, Saddam released all foreign hostages, perhaps in an attempt to solidify the US's apparent move toward peace. But the likelihood that substantive talks would occur began to fade almost as soon as they were offered, as the two sides bickered over timing and other logistical issues.

As Baker had hoped, however, the standing US offer served to discourage other countries from seizing the waiting period before the UN deadline to put forward their own efforts at diplomacy. In the meantime, there was no concrete proposal out of Baghdad for a partial withdrawal—a proposal that could have hamstrung the US move to war. "Rarely," says Gates, "has anyone been so fortunate in the clumsiness and stupidity and incompetence of the enemy."[33]

With the UN vote authorizing use of force in place, planning for war began in earnest. General Schwarzkopf, commander of allied forces for the US-led operation, continued the daunting task of coordinating the international military effort, a job made even more difficult by Baker's enthusiasm for coalition-building. While the State Department vigorously enlisted participants for the political legitimacy they would lend the military coalition, the Defense Department scrambled to find space, supplies, and food for the onslaught of incoming—and often ill-prepared—foreign troops. As Richard Clarke puts it: "There was not an easy fit between our State Department's desire to get a lot of countries involved and the Defense Department's desire not to."[34]

* * *

As the military coalition congealed, the State Department paid particular attention to Arab representation. With the switch to an overt offensive mission, membership in the US-led alliance had become politically sensitive for many Arab nations, especially less moderate countries like Syria. "Putting troops in the field against another Arab was really a big bump for all these guys, especially under the umbrella of the United States," Gates says. "They might kill each other to a fare thee well, but partnering with us was a big problem, and even the Egyptians had to play it very carefully."[35]

But Baker was determined that Arab troops play a visible role in any military action. A lack of Arab involvement would feed into Saddam's attempts to rally regional support by claiming that the international coalition represented a Western-led vendetta against the Arab world. There were domestic considerations, too. From the conflict's start, some critics had questioned why the US had to play cop for the world and resolve a far-away Gulf dispute. Now, with the prospect of war and major casualties looming, the charge that US troops had been reduced to mercenaries for the oil-rich Gulf states was one the administration particularly wanted to avoid.

* * *

The final allied force included units from 36 countries * * * . Even with this broad-based involvement, though, US troops still represented 85 percent of the force in the Gulf. States one Pentagon official: "It was primarily a US show from beginning to end."

Baker and Aziz Meet at Last

By the end of December, after weeks of haggling, the US and Iraq still had not agreed on a time for Baker to go to Baghdad or for Aziz to come to Washington. The US refused dates too close to the January 15 deadline, protesting they would allow Saddam to deadlock the resolution. Saddam, for his part, refused to have dates dictated to him by the Americans. Finally, on January 3, the President made a new offer, mindful of the fact that Congress was returning from its break that day, and might soon call a vote on whether to authorize Bush to use military force against Iraq. Instead of traveling to each others' capitals, Bush proposed, Baker and Aziz could meet in Geneva sometime between January 7 and 9. This narrow range of dates would give both sides time to prepare, while allowing Congress to process the results of the meeting before considering its own resolution.

* * *

With Saddam's acceptance, Baker and Aziz arranged to meet in Geneva January 9. Although there was no evidence either side had fresh offers to bring to the table, Scowcroft viewed the exercise with alarm. "I personally was concerned that it might work," he confides.[36] But he needn't have worried. After almost seven hours at the table, during which the Iraqi foreign minister continued to try to link the Kuwaiti invasion to other regional disputes, Aziz did not even accept the eight-page letter Bush had written to Saddam, declaring that it was "full of threats and it has a language which is not normally used in dialogue between heads of state."[37] Despite Baker's reiteration of the seriousness and the technological superiority of the forces united against Iraq, Aziz insisted that Iraq would win if it came to war. Of perhaps equal significance, he also asserted that "never has an Arab regime entered into a war with Israel or the United States and lost politically."[38]

"Ultimately, Saddam was his own worst enemy," declares Kimmitt. "If Aziz had walked in and said, 'We screwed up, we will be out by the deadline,' or 'We'll have started full withdrawal by the deadline,' maybe that would have disappointed some people. But that is an offer that we would have had to accept."[39]

According to Cheney, he personally gave up on any thought of avoiding war when he and the President, watching TV in a room off the Oval Office, saw Baker emerge—grim-faced—from the meeting with Aziz. "I heard nothing today that suggested to me any Iraqi flexibility whatsoever on complying with the United Nations Security Council resolutions," Baker declared. ". . . The choice is Iraq's. If it should choose to continue its brutal occupation of Kuwait, Iraq will be choosing a military confrontation which it cannot win, and which will have devastating consequences for Iraq." The President, for his part, professed himself "discouraged," and described the Iraqi response as, "a total stiff-arm, this was a total rebuff." At a post-meeting press conference, Bush asserted, "The conclusion is clear. Saddam Hussein continues to reject a diplomatic solution." For all his harsh words, though, Bush insisted he had "not given up on a peaceful outcome."

The Baker-Aziz meeting provided an ideal prelude to the Congressional vote on use of force. According to one Democrat, Baker's press conference alone was worth 20 votes for the administration.[40] From Geneva, Baker flew to Saudi Arabia to get King Fahd's permission for a military operation based on Saudi territory. The next day, Congress began considering a resolution that would, in their minds, give the President permission to go to war.

Courting Congress

Just a week earlier, it had been unclear whether Bush would ask Congress for authorization to use force. It was also unclear whether Capitol Hill would call a vote unilaterally. Since the doubling of forces in November, Congress had been muttering about taking matters into its own hands. Indeed, some Democrats regretted that they had not acted sooner, when support for the President's policies was low. But the issue's potential explosiveness had discouraged Congressional action. "Congress doesn't want to have to vote on any military endeavor," concludes one top official grimly. "They want to sit back there and if it works, they say, 'Terrific, Mr. President. Wonderful for the nation and God bless America.' But if it doesn't work, they want to dump all over him."

As Baker left for Geneva, though, the issue came to a head. The UN deadline for Iraqi withdrawal was less than two weeks away. Moreover, it now looked likely that Congress would take up authorization on its own, right after the Baker-Aziz session. But within the administration, the question of going to Congress remained, in Scowcroft's words, a "strong, sharp debate."[41] Cheney advised against involving Congress because he believed the President already had the constitutional authority to go to war. By asking for a vote, Bush would appear to be relinquishing that authority. Scowcroft and Lawrence Eagleburger also opposed a vote, mainly because they feared Bush wouldn't win. According to Eagleburger, if the US attacked Iraq after Congress had refused authorization, it would be "disastrous" for the President. "I can see impeachment resolutions," he says.[42] Adds Scowcroft: "It would have been a firestorm in the United States."[43]

* * *

In the end, however, Bush was persuaded that the risks involved in ignoring Congress were greater than the risk of losing the vote. Vice President Dan Quayle had insisted on the importance of involving Congress, and even some stalwart Republican supporters on the Hill had confided they would oppose a war on constitutional grounds unless Bush sought Congressional authorization. In addition, Bush was swayed by an account he was reading about the Vietnam War, and the ultimately debilitating erosion of public support that Lyndon Johnson suffered during that conflict, in part due to Congressional opposition to the war. On the day Baker met with Aziz, Bush sent Congress a letter requesting support to use "all necessary means" to remove Iraq from Kuwait, the same language that appeared in the UN resolution on use of force.

* * *

The Congressional debate that began January 10 lasted three days, including an overnight session the night before the vote. On January 12, both houses approved the Joint Congressional Resolution, effectively giving Bush the authority to go to war. The Senate vote was close, with 52 in favor and 47 opposed, but the resolution passed easily in the House, 250 to 183. The resolution, which called directly for "the use of United States Armed Forces pursuant to United Nations Security Council Resolution 678," relied almost exclusively for its justification on the Security Council actions that had preceded it. "We couldn't have gotten the Congress earlier, I don't think," says Scowcroft, "and if there had been no coalition and no UN vote, we would never have gotten Congress."[44]

* * *

The Congressional authorization was yet another stamp of approval for the President's policies. But according to Gates, even had Congress voted no, the outcome would have been the same. "As long as Saddam was adamant (about staying), there was going to be a war, with or without the UN sanction, with or without Congressional sanction," he declares. "George Bush was going to throw the son of a bitch out of Kuwait and there was never any doubt about it."[45]

The Last Proposals for Peace

* * *

The US was almost ready to go to war. But for the allies that had doggedly pursued a negotiated resolution, it was the last chance to seek peace. Moscow was still in regular contact with Baghdad, and on January 12, Saddam told Gorbachev's envoy Yevgeny Primakov that Iraq was prepared to relinquish Kuwait. The Soviets feverishly pressed for the promised withdrawal over the next two days before finally beginning to abandon hope. "The Soviets wanted to find a way to have their cake and eat it, too," Gates concludes. "To be supportive of the coalition, but at the same time to get credit with Saddam for having prevented the conflict."[46]

UN Secretary General Perez de Cuellar, whose negotiating efforts the US had discouraged during the conflict, made a final trip to Baghdad January 12, this time with the administration's blessing. The mission was destined to failure, the Bush administration believed, but would underscore once again the multilateral alliance against Saddam. According to one report,

Perez de Cuellar left for Baghdad "with wretched misgivings about his mission: damned if he went, damned if he stayed."[47] After meeting with Saddam, he announced simply, "I don't see any reason for hope."[48]

French President Mitterrand also made repeated appeals to Baghdad, but to no avail. Undeterred, on January 14, French diplomats drafted a new UN resolution and presented it to the Security Council's permanent five members for discussion. The draft not only failed to mention the UN deadline, it also harked back to the dreaded "linkage," promising UN participation in resolving other regional differences once Iraq's withdrawal was procured. The British countered with their own resolution the next day and the French abandoned their move. "Keeping the coalition together against the natural inclination of all of these countries to want to see a war avoided was not easy," one State Department official says. "But we were of the view that we really didn't have any room to negotiate down from the UN resolutions we had sponsored." Adds a top aide: "That was an added benefit of going the multilateral route, in that the resolutions became a baseline that made it hard for members of the coalition to defect backwards from us."

On January 15, the day of the deadline, Perez de Cuellar delivered a final appeal at the United Nations, urging Saddam to withdraw, and adding, "I have every assurance, once again from the highest levels of government, that with the resolution of the present crisis, every effort will be made to address, in a comprehensive manner, the Arab-Israeli conflict, including the Palestinian question. I pledge my every effort to this end."

It Comes to War

Up to the deadline, Bush and his top advisers held their breath, wondering if Saddam would surprise them all with a last-minute parry. "There was no way we could have launched anything if it looked like he was finally fulfilling the resolutions," Haass explains. "We could never appear not willing to accept 'Yes' for an answer." He adds: "Saddam never gave us anything but 'No.' "[49]

On January 16, one day after the deadline, administration officials began notifying allies and Congressional leaders that the war would begin that night; Israel was one of the first to be called. At 7 p.m. Washington time, 3 a.m. in the Gulf, White House spokesman Marlin Fitzwater announced that "The liberation of Kuwait has begun." Two hours later, President Bush delivered a speech from the Oval Office. After describing the rudiments of the air war, Bush continued, "Some may ask, why act now? Why not wait? The answer is clear. The world could wait no longer. . . . We have before us the opportunity to forge for ourselves and for future generations a new world order, a world where the rule of law, not the law of the jungle, governs the conduct of nations."

The war lasted just 42 days. Allied losses were low, with only 240 troops killed, including 148 Americans. Iraqi casualties, however, were high. Estimates of the number killed in the brief war ranged from 35,000 to 100,000. "I think Saddam never thought we would do it," muses Gates. "I think right until the very end he never thought that this would actually happen."[50]

NOTES

1. Thomas Pickering interview with writer, May 17, 1994.
2. General Brent Scowcroft interview with writer, May 24, 1994.
3. Ibid.
4. Dennis Ross interview with writer, July 7, 1994.
5. Ibid.
6. Scowcroft interview.
7. Pierre Salinger and Eric Laurent, *Secret Dossier: The Hidden Agenda Behind the Gulf War* (New York: Penguin Books, 1991), pp. 96–7.
8. Richard Clarks interview with writer, June 13, 1994.
9. *The Economist*, "Aggressors, Go Home," August 11, 1990.
10. Richard Haass interview with writer, June 13, 1994.
11. Saddam released Arab and Third World citizens as part of his campaign to present Iraq as a crusader against Western imperialism.
12. Richard Cheney interview with writer, June 29, 1994.
13. Scowcroft interview.
14. The value of UN action was driven home when Turkish President Turgut Ozal agreed to close the Iraqi pipeline running through Turkey within hours of the vote.
15. Pickering interview.
16. Haass interview.
17. Lawrence Freedman and Efraim Karsh, *The Gulf Conflict 1990–1991: Diplomacy and War in the New World Order* (Princeton, N.J.: Princeton University Press, 1993), p. 145.
18. Robert Kimmitt interview with writer, June 1, 1994.
19. Since the early joint US-Soviet statement condemning the Iraqi invasion, the Soviet Union had reverted to a more cautious stance. "Soviet foot-dragging was a constant source of heartburn, and it was rarely clear at any given time that the hard-liners might not stage a comeback," declares Assistant Secretary of State Bolton. "There were any number of occasions when we wanted to move a resolution or take some other action, only for Baker to hear from Shevardnadze that he needed a few more hours or days to reconcile positions within the Soviet government."
20. Pickering interview.
21. Both Japan and Germany, whose initial response to the Gulf conflict was described as sluggish at best, ultimately came through as major donors. Japan's nearly $10 billion donation made it the largest donor outside the Gulf, while Germany managed to contribute $6.5 billion despite the financial demands of its own reunification.

22. Robert Gates interview with writer, June 29, 1994.
23. Philip Zelikow interview with writer, May 2, 1994.
24. Micah L. Sifry and Christopher Cerf. ed., *The Gulf War Reader: History, Documents, Opinions* (New York: Times Books, 1991), pp. 236–7.
25. Ironically, internal Iraqi documents uncovered later suggested Iraq may only have been 18–24 months away from having a bomb. "So what Bush had done largely for propaganda turned out to have some truth," one official grins.
26. Pickering interview.
27. Chency interview.
28. Yemen's vote was costly: The US immediately cancelled its aid to the Arab nation—worth $70 million—and encouraged other allies to do the same.
29. Bolton interview.
30. *U.S. News & World Report.* "Counting on New Friends," December 10, 1990.
31. Scowcroft interview.
32. Ibid.
33. Gates interview.
34. Clarke interview.
35. Gates interview.
36. Scowcroft interview.
37. Freedman and Karsh, p. 256. The US promptly made the letter available to world newspapers to make sure Saddam would have an opportunity to read it himself.
38. Ibid., p. 258.
39. Kimmitt interview, June 1, 1994.
40. Freedman and Karsh, p. 292.
41. Scowcroft interview.
42. Eagleburger interview.
43. Scowcroft interview.
44. Scowcroft interview.
45. Gates interview.
46. Gates interview.
47. *The Economist,* "Iraq puts out the light," January 12, 1991.
48. US News & World Report, *Triumph Without Victory*, p. 208.
49. Haass interview.
50. Gates interview.

CHAPTER

9

Prosperity: Foreign Economic and Social Policy in an Age of Globalization

The profound changes in the international political economy stand with the end of Cold War bipolarity and the spread of democracy as the driving forces of this new era. Globalization is a complex phenomenon, posing new challenges and defining crucial foreign policy choices for the United States and for the international community.

One key major debate is free trade versus protectionism. While hardly a new debate, the contemporary version has been quite contentious. It is being driven in part by "globaphobia," as Gary Burtless and his Brooking Institution colleagues call it, a fear of globalization and related forces that points to imports and other aspects of the international economy as the principal causes of the economic problems that continue to trouble at least some sectors of the American economy and some segments of the American workforce. This reading, taken from their book *Globaphobia: Confronting Fears about Open Trade*, acknowledges that there are losers as well as winners from globalization, but it sees in protectionism a cure worse than the disease.

On a global scale the worsening of inequality is a more profound problem. Any number of statistical indicators show poverty, hunger, disease, and other problems not only still plaguing much of the world, but growing worse. Globalization cannot be just about booming financial markets, it also needs "a human face," as it is put in the United Nations Development Program's *Human Development Report 1999*. This "social stewardship" of course is not just a problem for U.S. foreign policy, but the United States is looked to for leadership on this as on other problems.

One of those other problems is the global environment. While progress has been made in recent years in this area, many see the pace as too slow and the scope as too limited. This is cause for concern in a number of respects, including as an economic issue, as a quality of life issue, and as a source of political and even international instability. Thomas Homer-Dixon's book *Environment, Scarcity and Violence* is a leading analysis of these issues; we include a portion of the "Overview" chapter.

9.1 Free Trade vs. Protectionism

Gary Burtless, Robert Z. Lawrence, Robert E. Litan, and Robert J. Shapiro

Globaphobia

To some, the performance of the U.S. economy since 1992 has been the best in a generation. In the summer of 1997, when the economy had expanded for more than five years, Federal Reserve Board chairman Alan Greenspan called this performance extraordinary. A few years earlier, then secretary of Labor Robert Reich had coined the label "Goldilocks economy"—neither too hot (with accelerating inflation) nor too cold (with rising unemployment).

Reich's term accurately describes the country's economic performance in recent years. Figure 1-1 sums up the good news of the 1990s: an unemployment rate falling steadily to its lowest level in more than twenty-five years; low and stable inflation; and stock prices far higher than at the beginning of the decade (despite some nervous jitters toward the end of 1997).

To others, however, the economy looks quite different: very kind to a few at the top, but barely rewarding for many in the middle, and a continuing nightmare for those at the bottom. Figure 1-2 illustrates the economic bad news:

- Notwithstanding the expansion in the 1990s, the wages (excluding fringe benefits) of the typical worker have barely grown since 1973, after steadily advancing about 2¼ percent a year over the previous twenty-five years.
- Men at the very bottom of the income distribution have actually suffered a sizable *drop* in their wages, while wage growth has disappeared for women at the bottom.
- The fact that well-paid Americans have continued to do well alongside

From *Globaphobia: Confronting Fears about Open Trade* (Washington, D.C.: Brookings Institution, 1998), chapter 1.

FIGURE 1–1. U.S. Economic Indicators: The Positive Picture

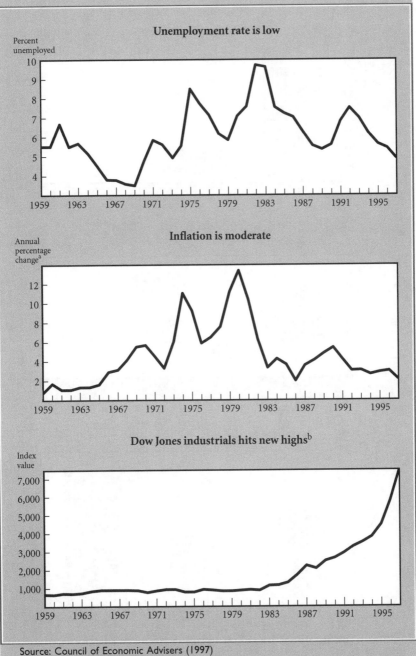

Source: Council of Economic Advisers (1997)
a. U.S. Consumer Price Index.
b. Annual average of daily closing prices.

FIGURE 1–2. U.S. Economic Indicators: The Negative Picture

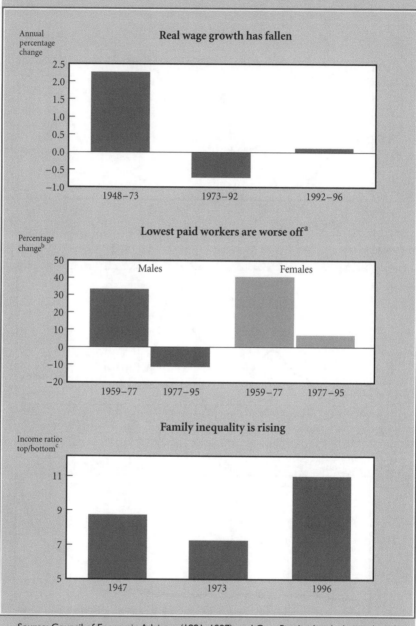

Source: Council of Economic Advisers (1991, 1997); and Gary Burtless's calculations based on decennial census and Current Population Surveys (March files).

a. Workers in bottom quintile of earnings distribution of 25–58-year-old, full-time, year-round workers.

b. Real annual earnings.

c. Average income in top quintile / Average income in bottom quintile.

the economic stagnation or deterioration of those not so fortunate has generated resentment over growing inequality.

- And, not shown in the figure but widely recognized is the anxiety of many middle class workers, who face the threat of being "downsized" or "reengineered." Watching their friends or neighbors lose jobs, they fear that they will be next.

The Dr. Jekyll–Mr. Hyde character of the U.S. economy cries out for explanation. One answer heard with increasing frequency in the halls of Congress, on talk shows, and perhaps also at dinner tables in homes across the country, is that "globalization"—the increasing economic linkage between the United States and other nations—is the main reason for the bad economic news just described. The logic behind this explanation is seductive. Figure 1-3 identifies three measures of globalization that have increased significantly since the early 1970s, when the adverse trends shown in figure 1-2 began. Imports have increased, not just absolutely, but in relation to the size of the economy, arguably placing strong pressure on the wages and jobs of U.S. workers. At the same time, American companies have significantly increased their investments abroad, which some critics believe has led to the export of American jobs and downward pressure on the wages of workers left behind. Moreover, the share of the U.S. population that consists of immigrants has nearly doubled during the past twenty-five years, further weakening the bargaining power of less-skilled Americans.

The fate of the U.S. economy has become increasingly linked with the economies of other nations for two reasons. One is well known and is, in fact, the result of deliberate policy. Since the end of the World War II, nations around the world, led by the United States, have been steadily lowering trade barriers—in recent cases, unilaterally. Average tariffs imposed by high-income countries like the United States have dropped from over 40 percent to just 6 percent, while barriers to services trade have come down. Many countries have negotiated free trade agreements with their neighbors.

The other force behind globalization is one over which politicians have little or no control: the continuing progress of technology. Faster and bigger airplanes move people and goods more quickly and cheaply. The cost of communication, fueled by a revolution in computer and materials technologies, continues to plummet. Although most investment stays at home, large pools of liquid capital nonetheless flow around the world at a quickening pace in search of the best returns, as the Asian currency crisis of late 1997 vividly demonstrated.

Whatever the reasons behind it, globalization has aroused concern and outright hostility among some in the United States. Both were much in evidence in the fall of 1997, during the tense debate in Congress over the extension of "fast-track" trade negotiating authority for the president and in the ultimate decision to postpone a vote on the issue until some time in 1998. Critics of globalization are not limited to well-known figures in the

FIGURE 1–3. Common Measures of Globalization

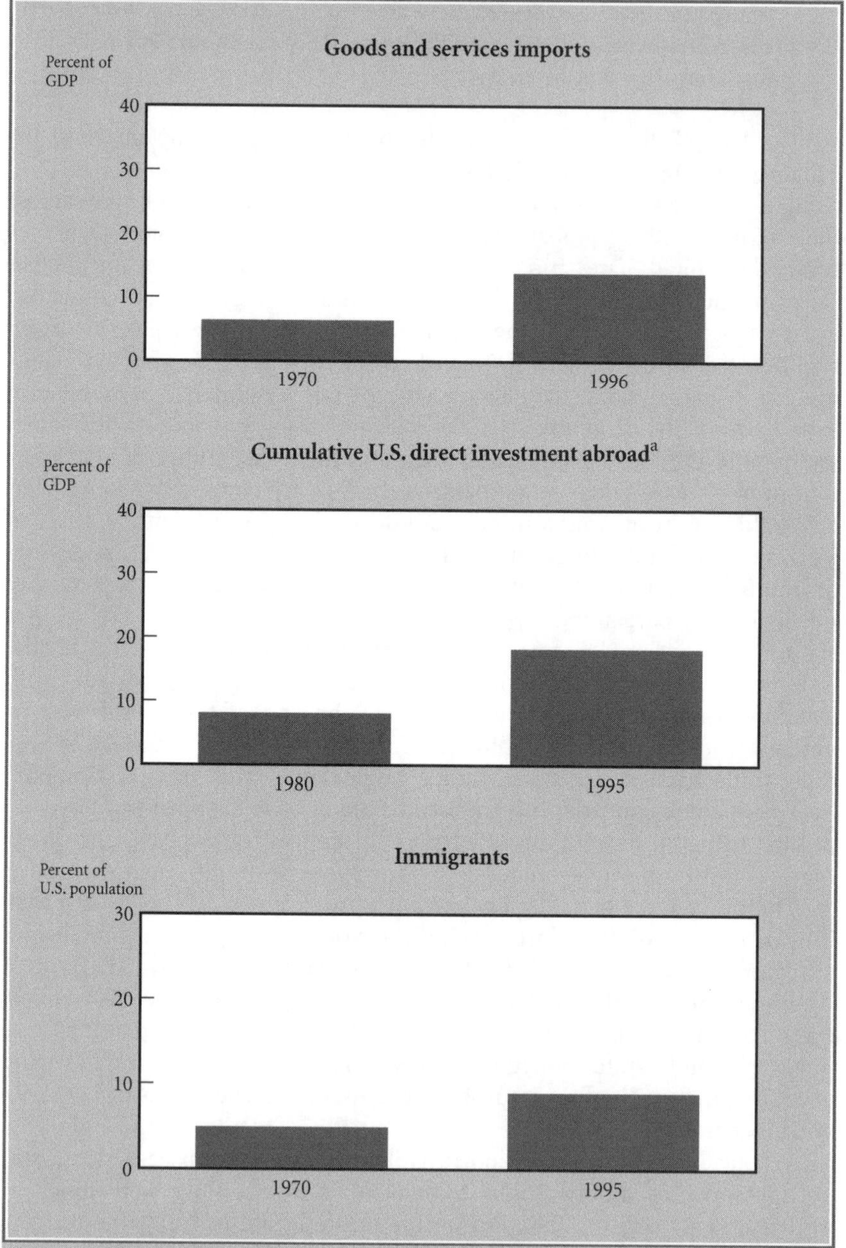
Goods and services imports
Percent of GDP
40
30
20
10
0
1970
1996
Cumulative U.S. direct investment abroad[a]
Percent of GDP
40
30
20
10
0
1980
1995
Immigrants
Percent of U.S. population
30
20
10
0
1970
1995

Source: Council of Economic Adviser (1987, 1997); *Statistical Analysis of the United States*, 1984, 1988, 1997.

a. Historical cost basis.

three major political parties—Patrick Buchanan, Richard Gephardt, and Ross Perot. Opinion surveys show that at least half of the American population believes that "globalization"—whatever people assume the term means—does more harm than good and that expanded trade will lead to lower wages for American workers. These views no doubt help to explain why many polls show most Americans opposed to new free trade agreements. A similar, if not greater, degree of hostility to world economic integration is common in Europe.

We have written this book to demonstrate that the fear of globalization—or "globaphobia"—rests on very weak foundations. We do not dispute that the American economy, in particular, has a half full-half empty character. This is plain from figures 1–1 and 1–2. In the pages that follow, we argue that the surface appeal of globaphobia has nonetheless led many American voters and policymakers astray in a number of respects.

First, the United States globalized rapidly during the golden years before 1973, when productivity and wages were growing briskly and inequality was shrinking, demonstrating that living standards can advance at a healthy rate while the United States increases its links with the rest of the world. In any event, it is useful to keep in mind that the U.S. economy is no more globalized today—measured by the share of trade in its total output—than it was *before World War I.*

Second, even though globalization harms some American workers, the protectionist remedies suggested by some trade critics are, at best, short-term palliatives and, at worst, harmful to the interests of the broad class of workers that they are designed to help. Sheltering U.S. firms from imports may grant some workers a short reprieve from wage cuts or downsizing. But protection dulls the incentives of workers and firms to innovate and stay abreast of market developments. As a result, its benefits for individual workers and firms are often temporary. Indeed, protection invites foreign exporters to leap trade barriers by building plants in this country—as foreign manufacturers of automobiles, automobile parts, film, and other products have done. We are not criticizing this result: the United States has a strong national interest in attracting foreign investors, who typically bring technologies and management practices that ultimately yield higher wages and living standards for U.S. workers. But the movement to the United States of foreign companies and their plants simply underscores how erecting barriers to imports is often fools' gold for those who believe that protection will permanently shelter jobs or the profits of employers.

Third, erecting new barriers to imports also has an unseen boomerang effect in depressing exports. This is one of the most important, but least understood, propositions that we discuss in this book. While higher barriers to imports can temporarily improve the trade balance, this improvement would cause the value of the dollar on world exchange markets to rise, undercutting the competitive position of U.S. exports and curtailing job opportunities for Americans in export industries. Moreover, by increasing the costs of inputs (whether imported or domestic) that producers use to generate goods and services, protection further damages the competitive position of U.S. exporters. This is especially true in high-tech industries, where many American firms rely on foreign-made parts or capital equipment. The dangers of protection are further compounded to the extent it provokes retaliation by other countries. In that event, some Americans who work in exporting industries would lose their jobs, both directly and because higher barriers abroad would induce some of our exporting firms to move their plants (and jobs) overseas. In short, protection is not a zero-sum policy for the United States: it is a *negative sum* policy.

Fourth, globaphobia distracts policymakers and voters from implementing policies that would directly address the major causes of the stagnation or deterioration in the wages of less-skilled Americans. *The most significant problem faced by underpaid workers in the United States is not foreign competition. It is the mismatch between the skills that employers increasingly demand and the skills that many young adults bring to the labor market.* For the next generation of workers, the problem can be addressed by improvements in schooling and public and private training. The more difficult challenge is faced by today's unskilled adults, who find themselves unable to respond to the help wanted ads in daily newspapers, which often call for highly technical skills. It is easy to blame foreign imports for low wages, but doing so will not equip these workers with the new skills that employers need. The role of government is to help those who want to help themselves; most important, by maintaining a high-pressure economy that continues to generate new jobs, and secondarily, by facilitating training and providing effective inducements to displaced workers to find new jobs as rapidly as possible.

Fifth, Americans in fact have a vested interest in negotiating additional reductions of overseas barriers that limit the market for U.S. goods and services. These barriers typically harm the very industries in which America leads the world, including agriculture, financial services, pharmaceuticals, aircraft, and telecommunications. The failure of Congress to grant the president fast-track negotiating authority sends an odd and perverse message to the rest of the world. The United States, which once led the crusade for trade liberalization, now seems to have lost faith in the benefits of trade. Over time, this loss of faith may give ammunition to opponents of free trade in other countries, not only in resisting further trade liberalization but in imposing new barriers.

Sixth, it cannot be stressed too heavily that open trade benefits consumers. Each barrier to trade raises prices not only on the affected imports but also on the domestically produced goods or services with which they compete. Those who would nonetheless have the United States erect barriers to foreign goods—whether in the name of "fair trade," "national security," or some other claimed objective—must face the fact that they are asking the government to tax consumers in order to achieve these goals. And Americans must decide how willing they are to pay that tax. By contrast, lowering barriers to foreign goods delivers the equivalent of a tax cut to American consumers, while encouraging U.S. firms to innovate. The net result is higher living standards for Americans at home.

Finally, to ensure support for free trade, political leaders must abandon the argument traditionally used to advance the cause of trade liberalization: that it will generate *more* jobs. Proponents of freer trade should instead stick with the truth. Total employment depends on the overall macroeconomic environment (the willingness and capacity of Americans to buy goods and services) not on the trade balance (which depends on the difference between the amounts that Americans save and invest). We trade with foreigners for the same reasons that we trade among ourselves: to get better deals. Lower trade barriers in other countries mean *better* jobs for Americans. Firms in industries that are major exporters pay anywhere from 5 to 15 percent more than the average national wage. The "price" for gaining those trade opportunities—reducing our own trade barriers—is one that Americans should be glad to pay.

In spite of the enormous benefits of openness to trade and capital flows from the rest of the world and notwithstanding the additional benefits that Americans would derive from further liberalization, it is important to recognize that open borders create losers as well as winners. Openness exposes workers and company owners to the risk of major losses when new foreign competitors enter the U.S. market. Workers can lose their jobs. This has certainly occurred in a wide range of industries exposed to intense foreign competition—autos, steel, textiles, apparel, and footwear. Indeed, the whole point of engaging in trade is to shift resources—capital and labor—toward their most productive uses, a process that inevitably causes pain to those required to shift. In some cases, workers are forced to accept permanent reductions in pay, either in the jobs they continue to hold in a trade-affected industry or in new jobs they must take after suffering displacement. Other workers, including mainly the unskilled and semiskilled, may be forced to accept small pay reductions as an indirect effect of liberalization. Indeed, the job losses of thousands of similar workers in traded goods industries may tend to push down the wages of *all* workers—even those in the service sector—in a particular skill category.

We acknowledge that these losses occur, though their size is vastly exaggerated in media accounts and the popular imagination. Nonetheless, we believe the nation has both a political and a moral responsibility to offer better compensation to the workers who suffer sizable losses as a result of trade liberalization. In the final chapter we spell out a detailed program for doing so. Decent compensation for the workers who suffer losses is easily affordable in view of the substantial benefits the country enjoys as a result of open trade. Liberal trade, like technological progress, mainly creates winners, not losers. Among the big winners are the stockholders, executives, and workers of exporting firms such as Boeing, Microsoft, and General Electric, as well as Hollywood (whose movies and television shows are seen around the world). There are many millions of more modest winners as well, including the workers, retirees, and nonworking poor, who benefit from lower prices and a far wider and better selection of products.

One problem in making the case for open borders is that few of the winners recognize the extent of the gains they enjoy as a result of free trade. The losses suffered by displaced workers in the auto, apparel, or shoemaking industries are vividly portrayed on the nightly news, but few Americans realize that cars, clothes, and shoes are cheaper, better made, or more varied as a result of their country's openness to the rest of the world. Workers who make products sold outside the United States often fail to recognize how much their jobs and wages depend on America's willingness to import as well as its capacity to export. People contributing to a pension fund seldom realize that their returns (and future pensions) are boosted by the fund's ability to invest overseas, and almost no borrower understands that the cost of a mortgage or car loan is lower because of America's attractiveness to foreigners as a place to invest their money. All of these benefits help improve the standard of living of typical Americans, and they can be directly or indirectly traced to our openness. They are nearly invisible to most citizens, however; certainly far less visible than the painful losses suffered by workers who lose their jobs when a factory is shut down.

* * *

9.2 Social Stewardship: Globalization and Global Inequality

UNITED NATIONS DEVELOPMENT PROGRAM

Globalization with a Human Face

"The real wealth of a nation is its people. And the purpose of development is to create an enabling environment for people to enjoy long, healthy and creative lives. This simple but powerful truth is too often forgotten in the pursuit of material and financial wealth." Those are the opening lines of the first *Human Development Report*, published in 1990. This tenth *Human Development Report*—like the first and all the others—is about people. It is about the growing interdependence of people in today's globalizing world.

Globalization is not new, but the present era has distinctive features. Shrinking space, shrinking time and disappearing borders are linking people's lives more deeply, more intensely, more immediately than ever before.

More than $1.5 trillion is now exchanged in the world's currency markets each day, and nearly a fifth of the goods and services produced each year are traded. But globalization is more than the flow of money and commodities—it is the growing interdependence of the world's people. And globalization is a process integrating not just the economy but culture, technology and governance. People everywhere are becoming connected—affected by events in far corners of the world. The collapse of the Thai baht not only threw millions into unemployment in South-East Asia—the ensuing decline in global demand meant slow-downs in social investment in Latin America and a sudden rise in the cost of imported medicines in Africa.

Globalization is not new. Recall the early sixteenth century and the late nineteenth. But this era is different:

- *New markets*—foreign exchange and capital markets linked globally, operating 24 hours a day, with dealings at a distance in real time.

From *Human Development Report 1999*, United Nations Development Program (New York: Oxford University Press, 1999).

- *New tools*—Internet links, cellular phones, media networks.
- *New actors*—the World Trade Organization (WTO) with authority over national governments, the multinational corporations with more economic power than many states, the global networks of non-governmental organizations (NGOs) and other groups that transcend national boundaries.
- *New rules*—multilateral agreements on trade, services and intellectual property, backed by strong enforcement mechanisms and more binding for national governments, reducing the scope for national policy.

Globalization offers great opportunities for human advance—but only with stronger governance.

This era of globalization is opening many opportunities for millions of people around the world. Increased trade, new technologies, foreign investments, expanding media and Internet connections are fuelling economic growth and human advance. All this offers enormous potential to eradicate poverty in the 21st century—to continue the unprecedented progress in the 20th century. We have more wealth and technology—and more commitment to a global community—than ever before.

Global markets, global technology, global ideas and global solidarity can enrich the lives of people everywhere, greatly expanding their choices. The growing interdependence of people's lives calls for shared values and a shared commitment to the human development of all people.

The post–cold war world of the 1990s has sped progress in defining such values—in adopting human rights and in setting development goals in the United Nations conferences on environment, population, social development, women and human settlements.

But today's globalization is being driven by market expansion—opening national borders to trade, capital, information—outpacing governance of these markets and their repercussions for people. More progress has been made in norms, standards, policies and institutions for open global markets than for people and their rights. And a new commitment is needed to the ethics of universalism set out in the Universal Declaration of Human Rights.

Competitive markets may be the best guarantee of efficiency, but not necessarily of equity. Liberalization and privatization can be a step to competitive markets—but not a guarantee of them. And markets are neither the first nor the last word in human development. Many activities and goods that are critical to human development are provided outside the market—but these are being squeezed by the pressures of global competition. There is a fiscal squeeze on public goods, a time squeeze on care activities and an incentive squeeze on the environment.

When the market goes too far in dominating social and political outcomes, the opportunities and rewards of globalization spread unequally and inequitably—concentrating power and wealth in a select group of people, nations and corporations, marginalizing the others. When the market gets out of hand, the instabilities show up in boom and bust economies, as in the financial crisis in East Asia and its worldwide repercussions, cutting global output by an estimated $2 trillion in 1998–2000. When the profit motives of market players get out of hand, they challenge people's ethics—and sacrifice respect for justice and human rights.

The challenge of globalization in the new century is not to stop the expansion of global markets. The challenge is to find the rules and institutions for stronger governance—local, national, regional and global—to preserve the advantages of global markets and competition, but also to provide enough space for human, community and environmental resources to ensure that globalization works for people—not just for profits. Globalization with:

- *Ethics*—less violation of human rights, not more.
- *Equity*—less disparity within and between nations, not more.
- *Inclusion*—less marginalization of people and countries, not more.
- *Human security*—less instability of societies and less vulnerability of people, not more.
- *Sustainability*—less environmental destruction, not more.
- *Development*—less poverty and deprivation, not more.

The opportunities and benefits of globalization need to be shared much more widely.

Since the 1980s many countries have seized the opportunities of economic and technological globalization. Beyond the industrial countries, the newly industrializing East Asian tigers are joined by Chile, the Dominican Republic, India, Mauritius, Poland, Turkey and many others linking into global markets, attracting foreign investment and taking advantage of technological advance. Their export growth has averaged more than 5% a year, diversifying into manufactures.

At the other extreme are the many countries benefiting little from expanding markets and advancing technology—Madagascar, Niger, the Russian Federation, Tajikistan and Venezuela among them.

These countries are becoming even more marginal—ironic, since many of them are highly "integrated", with exports nearly 30% of GDP for Sub-Saharan Africa and only 19% for the OECD. But these countries hang on the vagaries of global markets, with the prices of primary commodities having fallen to their lowest in a century and a half. They have shown little growth in exports and attracted virtually no foreign investment. In sum, today, global opportunities are unevenly distributed—between countries and people (see figure).

If global opportunities are not shared better, the failed growth of the last decades will continue. More than 80 countries still have per capita incomes lower than they were a decade or more ago. While 40 countries have sustained average per capita income growth of more than 3% a year since 1990,

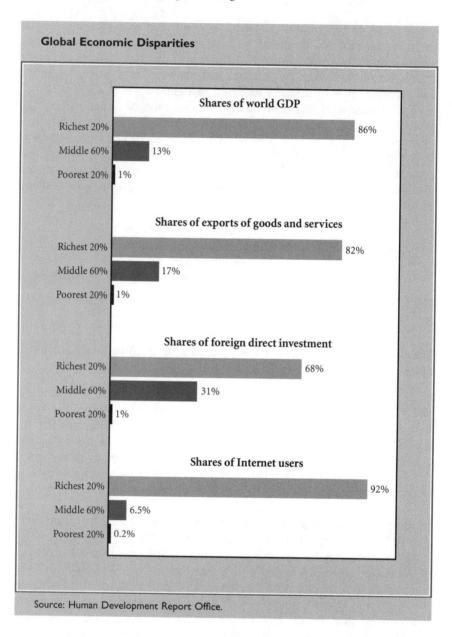

Global Economic Disparities

Shares of world GDP

Richest 20% — 86%
Middle 60% — 13%
Poorest 20% — 1%

Shares of exports of goods and services

Richest 20% — 82%
Middle 60% — 17%
Poorest 20% — 1%

Shares of foreign direct investment

Richest 20% — 68%
Middle 60% — 31%
Poorest 20% — 1%

Shares of Internet users

Richest 20% — 92%
Middle 60% — 6.5%
Poorest 20% — 0.2%

Source: Human Development Report Office.

55 countries, mostly in Sub-Saharan Africa and Eastern Europe and the Commonwealth of Independent States (CIS), have had declining per capita incomes.

Many people are also missing out on employment opportunities. The global labour market is increasingly integrated for the highly skilled—corporate executives, scientists, entertainers and the many others who form the global professional elite—with high mobility and wages. But the market for unskilled labour is highly restricted by national barriers.

Inequality has been rising in many countries since the early 1980s. In China disparities are widening between the export-oriented regions of the coast and the interior: the human poverty index is just under 20% in coastal provinces, but more than 50% in inland Guizhou. The countries of Eastern Europe and the CIS have registered some of the largest increases ever in the Gini coefficient, a measure of income inequality. OECD countries also registered big increases in inequality after the 1980s—especially Sweden, the United Kingdom and the United States.

Inequality between countries has also increased. The income gap between the fifth of the world's people living in the richest countries and the fifth in the poorest was 74 to 1 in 1997, up from 60 to 1 in 1990 and 30 to 1 in 1960. In the nineteenth century, too, inequality grew rapidly during the last three decades, in an era of rapid global integration: the income gap between the top and bottom countries increased from 3 to 1 in 1820 to 7 to 1 in 1870 and 11 to 1 in 1913.

By the late 1990s the fifth of the world's people living in the highest-income countries had:

- 86% of world GDP—the bottom fifth just 1%.
- 82% of world export markets—the bottom fifth just 1%.
- 68% of foreign direct investment—the bottom fifth just 1%.
- 74% of world telephone lines, today's basic means of communication—the bottom fifth just 1.5%.

Some have predicted convergence. Yet the past decade has shown increasing concentration of income, resources and wealth among people, corporations and countries:

- OECD countries, with 19% of the global population, have 71% of global trade in goods and services, 58% of foreign direct investment and 91% of all Internet users.
- The world's 200 richest people more than doubled their net worth in the four years to 1998, to more than $1 trillion. The assets of the top three billionaires are more than the combined GNP of all least developed countries and their 600 million people.
- The recent wave of mergers and acquisitions is concentrating industrial power in megacorporations—at the risk of eroding competition. By 1998 the top 10 companies in pesticides controlled 85% of a $31 billion global market—and the top 10 in telecommunications, 86% of a $262 billion market.
- In 1993 just 10 countries accounted for 84% of global research and development expenditures and controlled 95% of the US patents of the past two decades. Moreover, more than 80% of patents granted in developing countries belong to residents of industrial countries.

All these trends are not the inevitable consequences of global economic integration—but they have run ahead of global governance to share the benefits.

Globalization is creating new threats to human security—in rich countries and poor.

One achievement of recent decades has been greater security for people in many countries—more political freedom and stability in Chile, peace in Central America, safer streets in the United States. But in the globalizing world of shrinking time, shrinking space and disappearing borders, people are confronting new threats to human security—sudden and hurtful disruptions in the pattern of daily life.

Financial volatility and economic insecurity. The financial turmoil in East Asia in 1997–99 demonstrates the risks of global financial markets. Net capital flows to Indonesia, the Republic of Korea, Malaysia, the Philippines and Thailand rocketed in the 1990s, reaching $93 billion in 1996. As turmoil hit market after market, these flows reversed overnight—with an outflow of $12 billion in 1997. The swing amounted to 11% of the precrisis GDPs of these countries. Two important lessons come out of this experience.

First, the human impacts are severe and are likely to persist long after economic recovery.

Bankruptcies spread. Education and health budgets came under pressure. More than 13 million people lost their jobs. As prices of essentials rose sharply, real wages fell sharply, down some 40–60% in Indonesia. The consequences go deeper—all countries report erosion of their social fabric, with social unrest, more crime, more violence in the home.

Recovery seems to be on the way, most evidently in Korea and least in Indonesia. But while output growth, payment balances, interest rates and inflation may be returning to normal, human lives take longer to recover. A review of financial crises in 80 countries over the past few decades shows that real wages take an average of three years to pick up again, and that employment growth does not regain precrisis levels for several years after that.

Second, far from being isolated incidents, financial crises have become increasingly common with the spread and growth of global capital flows. They result from rapid buildups and reversals of short-term capital flows and are likely to recur. More likely when national institutions regulating financial markets are not well developed, they are now recognized as systemic features of global capital markets. No single country can withstand their whims, and global action is needed to prevent and manage them.

Job and income insecurity. In both poor and rich countries dislocations from economic and corporate restructuring, and from dismantling the institutions of social protection, have meant greater insecurity in jobs and incomes. The pressures of global competition have led countries and employers to adopt more flexible labour policies with more precarious work arrangements. Workers without contracts or with new, less secure contracts make up 30% of the total in Chile, 39% in Colombia.

France, Germany, the United Kingdom and other countries have weakened worker dismissal laws. Mergers and acquisitions have come with corporate restructuring and massive layoffs. Sustained economic growth has not reduced unemployment in Europe—leaving it at 11% for a decade, affecting 35 million. In Latin America growth has created jobs, but 85% of them are in the informal sector.

Health insecurity. Growing travel and migration have helped spread HIV/AIDS. More than 33 million people were living with HIV/AIDS in 1998, with almost 6 million new infections in that year. And the epidemic is now spreading rapidly to new locations, such as rural India and Eastern Europe and the CIS. With 95% of the 16,000 infected each day living in developing countries. AIDS has become a poor person's disease, taking a heavy toll on life expectancy, reversing the gains of recent decades. For nine countries in Africa, a loss of 17 years in life expectancy is projected by 2010, back to the levels of the 1960s.

Cultural insecurity. Globalization opens people's lives to culture and all its creativity—and to the flow of ideas and knowledge. But the new culture carried by expanding global markets is disquieting. As Mahatma Gandhi expressed so eloquently earlier in the century, "I do not want my house to be walled in on all sides and my windows to be stuffed. I want the cultures of all the lands to be blown about my house as freely as possible. But I refuse to be blown off my feet by any." Today's flow of culture is unbalanced, heavily weighted in one direction, from rich countries to poor.

Weightless goods—with high knowledge content rather than material content—now make for some of the most dynamic sectors in today's most advanced economies. The single largest export industry for the United States is not aircraft or automobiles, it is entertainment—Hollywood films grossed more than $30 billion worldwide in 1997.

The expansion of global media networks and satellite communications technologies gives rise to a powerful new medium with a global reach. These networks bring Hollywood to remote villages—the number of television sets per 1,000 people almost doubled between 1980 and 1995, from 121 to 235. And the spread of global brands—Nike, Sony—is setting new social standards from Delhi to Warsaw to Rio de Janeiro. Such onslaughts of foreign culture can put cultural diversity at risk, and make people fear losing their cultural identity. What is needed is support to indigenous and national cultures—to let them flourish alongside foreign cultures.

Personal insecurity. Criminals are reaping the benefits of globalization. Deregulated capital markets, advances in information and communications technology and cheaper transport make flows easier, faster and less restricted not just for medical knowledge but for heroin—not just for books and seeds but for dirty money and weapons.

Illicit trade—in drugs, women, weapons and laundered money—is contributing to the violence and crime that threaten neighbourhoods around the world. Drug-related crimes increased from 4 per 100,000 people in Belarus in 1990 to 28 in 1997, and from 1 per 100,000 to 8 in Estonia. The weapons trade feeds street crime as well as civil strife. In South Africa machine guns are pouring in from Angola and Mozambique. The traffic in women and girls for sexual exploitation—500,000 a year to Western Europe alone—is one of the most heinous violations of human rights, estimated to be a $7 billion business.

The Internet is an easy vehicle for trafficking in drugs, arms and women through nearly untraceable networks. In 1995 the illegal drug trade was estimated at 8% of world trade, more than the trade in motor vehicles or in iron and steel. Money laundering—which the International Monetary Fund (IMF) estimates at equivalent to 2–5% of global GDP—hides the traces of crime in split seconds, with the click of a mouse.

At the root of all this is the growing influence of organized crime, estimated to gross $1.5 trillion a year, rivalling multinational corporations as an economic power. Global crime groups have the power to criminalize politics, business and the police, developing efficient networks, extending their reach deep and wide.

Environmental insecurity. Chronic environmental degradation—today's silent emergency—threatens people worldwide and undercuts the livelihoods of at least half a billion people. Poor people themselves, having little choice, put pressure on the environment, but so does the consumption of the rich. The growing export markets for fish, shrimp, paper and many other products mean depleted stocks, less biodiversity and fewer forests. Most of the costs are borne by the poor—though it is the world's rich who benefit most. The fifth of the world's people living in the richest countries consume 84% of the world's paper.

Political and community insecurity. Closely related to many other forms of insecurity is the rise of social tensions that threaten political stability and community cohesion. Of the 61 major armed conflicts fought between 1989 and 1998, only three were between states—the rest were civil.

Globalization has given new characteristics to conflicts. Feeding these conflicts is the global traffic in weapons, involving new actors and blurring political and business interests. In the power vacuum of the post–cold war era, military companies and mercenary armies began offering training to governments—and corporations. Accountable only to those who pay them, these hired military services pose a severe threat to human security.

New information and communications technologies are driving global-ization—but polarizing the world into the connected and the isolated.

With the costs of communications plummeting and innovative tools easier to use, people around the world have burst into conversation using the Internet, mobile phones and fax machines. The fastest-growing communi-cations tool ever, the Internet had more than 140 million users in mid-1998, a number expected to pass 700 million by 2001.

Communications networks can foster great advances in health and ed-ucation. They can also empower small players. The previously unheard voices of NGOs helped halt the secretive OECD negotiations for the Mul-tilateral Agreement on Investment, called for corporate accountability and created support for marginal communities. Barriers of size, time and dis-tance are coming down for small businesses, for governments of poor coun-tries, for remote academics and specialists.

Information and communications technology can also open a fast track to knowledge-based growth—a track followed by India's software exports. Ireland's computing services and the Eastern Caribbean's data processing.

Despite the potential for development, the Internet poses severe prob-lems of access and exclusion. Who was in the loop in 1998?

- *Geography divides.* Thailand has more cellular phones than Africa. South Asia, home to 23% of the world's people, has less than 1% of Internet users.
- *Education is a ticket to the network high society.* Globally, 30% of users had at least one university degree.
- *Income buys access.* To purchase a computer would cost the average Bangladeshi more than eight years' income, the average American, just one month's wage.
- *Men and youth dominate.* Women make up just 17% of the Internet users in Japan, only 7% in China. Most users in China and the United Kingdom are under 30.
- *English talks.* English prevails in almost 80% of all Websites, yet less than one in 10 people worldwide speaks it.

This exclusivity is creating parallel worlds. Those with income, education and—literally—connections have cheap and instantaneous access to infor-mation. The rest are left with uncertain, slow and costly access. When people in these two worlds live and compete side by side, the advantage of being connected will overpower the marginal and impoverished, cutting off their voices and concerns from the global conversation.

This risk of marginalization does not have to be a reason for despair. It should be a call to action for:

- *More connectivity*: setting up telecommunications and computer hardware.

- *More community*: focusing on group access, not just individual ownership.
- *More capacity*: building human skills for the knowledge society.
- *More content*: putting local views, news, culture and commerce on the Web.
- *More creativity*: adapting technology to local needs and opportunities.
- *More collaboration*: developing Internet governance to accommodate diverse national needs.
- *More cash*: finding innovative ways to fund the knowledge society everywhere.

Global technological breakthroughs offer great potential for human advance and for eradicating poverty—but not with today's agendas.

Liberalization, privatization and tighter intellectual property rights are shaping the path for the new technologies, determining how they are used. But the privatization and concentration of technology are going too far. Corporations define research agendas and tightly control their findings with patents, racing to lay claim to intellectual property under the rules set out in the agreement on Trade-Related Aspects of Intellectual Property Rights (TRIPS).

Poor people and poor countries risk being pushed to the margin in this proprietary regime controlling the world's knowledge:

- In defining research agendas, money talks, not need—cosmetic drugs and slow-ripening tomatoes come higher on the priority list than drought-resistant crops or a vaccine against malaria.
- From new drugs to better seeds, the best of the new technologies are priced for those who can pay. For poor people, they remain far out of reach.
- Tighter property rights raise the price of technology transfer, blocking developing countries from the dynamic knowledge sectors. The TRIPS agreement will enable multinationals to dominate the global market even more easily.
- New patent laws pay scant attention to the knowledge of indigenous people. These laws ignore cultural diversity in the way innovations are created and shared—and diversity in views on what can and should be owned, from plant varieties to human life. The result: a silent theft of centuries of knowledge from some of the poorest communities in developing countries.
- Despite the risks of genetic engineering, the rush and push of commercial interests are putting profits before people.

A broader perspective is needed. Intellectual property rights were first raised as a multilateral trade issue in 1986 to crack down on counterfeit goods. The reach of those rights now goes far beyond that—into the ownership of life. As trade, patents and copyright determine the paths of technology—and of nations—questioning today's arrangements is not just about economic flows. It is about preserving biodiversity. Addressing the ethics of patents on life. Ensuring access to health care. Respecting other cultures' forms of ownership. Preventing a growing technological gap between the knowledge-driven global economy and the rest trapped in its shadows.

The relentless pressures of global competition are squeezing out care, the invisible heart of human development.

Caring labour—providing for children, the sick and the elderly, as well as all the rest of us, exhausted from the demands of daily life—is an important input for the development of human capabilities. It is also a capability in itself. And it is special—nurturing human relationships with love, altruism, reciprocity and trust. Without enough care, individuals do not flourish. Without attention and stimulus, babies languish, failing to reach their full potential. And without nurturing from their families, children underperform in school.

Human support to others is essential for social cohesion and a strong community. It is also essential for economic growth. But the market gives few incentives and few rewards for it. Societies everywhere have allocated women much of the responsibility and the burden for care—women spend two-thirds of their work time in unpaid activities, men only a quarter. Women predominate in caring professions and domestic service. Families, nations and corporations have been free-riding on caring labour provided mostly by women, unpaid or underpaid.

But today's competitive global market is putting pressures on the time, resources and incentives for the supply of caring labour. Women's participation in the formal labour market is rising, yet they continue to carry the burden of care—women's hours spent in unpaid work remain high. In Bangladesh women in the garment industry spend 56 hours a week in paid employment on top of 31 hours in unpaid work—a total of 87 hours, compared with 67 by men. Men's share of unpaid care work is increasing slowly in Europe and other OECD countries but not in most developing countries and in Eastern Europe.

Meanwhile, fiscal pressures are cutting back on the supply of state-provided care services. Tax revenue declined in poor countries from 18% of GDP in the early 1980s to 16% in the 1990s. Public services deteriorated markedly—the result of economic stagnation, structural adjustment programmes or the dismantling of state services, especially in the transition economies of Eastern Europe and the CIS.

And global economic competition has put pressure on the wages for caring labour, as the wage gap increases between tradable and non-tradable sectors, and between the skilled and unskilled.

How can societies design new arrangements for care in the global economy? The traditional model of a patriarchal household is no solution—a new approach must build gender equity into sharing the burdens and responsibility for care. New institutional mechanisms, better public policy and a social consensus are needed to provide incentives for rewarding care and increasing its supply and quality:

- Public support for care services—such as care for the elderly, day care for children and protection of social services during crises.
- Labour market policies and employer action to support the care needs of employees.
- More gender balance and equity in carrying the burden of household care services.

Each society needs to find its own arrangements based on its history and conditions. But all societies need to devise a better solution. And all need to make a strong commitment to preserving time and resources for care—and the human bonds that nourish human development.

National and global governance have to be reinvented—with human development and equity at their core.

None of these pernicious trends—growing marginalization, growing human insecurity, growing inequality—is inevitable. With political will and commitment in the global community, they can all be reversed. With stronger governance—local, national, regional and global—the benefits of competitive markets can be preserved with clear rules and boundaries, and stronger action can be taken to meet the needs of human development.

Governance does not mean mere government. It means the framework of rules, institutions and established practices that set limits and give incentives for the behavior of individuals, organizations and firms. Without strong governance, the dangers of global conflicts could be a reality of the 21st century—trade wars promoting national and corporate interests, uncontrolled financial volatility setting off civil conflicts, untamed global crime infecting safe neighbourhoods and criminalizing politics, business and the police.

With the market collapse in East Asia, with the contagion to Brazil, Russia and elsewhere and with the threat of a global recession still looming, global governance is being re-examined. But the current debate is:

- Too narrow, limited to the concerns of economic growth and financial stability and neglecting broader human concerns such as persistent global poverty, growing inequality between and within countries, exclusion of poor people and countries and persisting human rights abuses.
- Too geographically unbalanced, dominated by the largest economies —usually the G-7, sometimes just the G-1, and only occasionally bringing in the large newly industrializing countries. Most small and poor developing countries are excluded, as are people's organizations.

Nor does the debate address the current weaknesses, imbalances and inequities in global governance—which, having developed in an ad hoc way, leaves many gaps.

- Multilateral agreements have helped establish global markets without considering their impacts on human development and poverty.
- The structures and processes for global policy-making are not representative. The key economic structures—the IMF, World Bank. G-7, G-10, G-22, OECD, WTO—are dominated by the large and rich countries, leaving poor countries and poor people with little influence and little voice, either for lack of membership or for lack of capacity for effective representation and participation. There is little transparency in decisions, and there is no structured forum for civil society institutions to express their views.
- There are no mechanisms for making ethical standards and human rights binding for corporations and individuals, not just governments.

In short, stronger national and global governance are needed for human well-being, not for the market.

* * *

THOMAS F. HOMER-DIXON
Environment, Scarcity and Violence

Preliminary research indicates that scarcities of critical environmental resources—especially of cropland, freshwater, and forests—contribute to violence in many parts of the world. These environmental scarcities usually do not cause wars among countries, but they can generate severe social stresses within countries, helping to stimulate subnational insurgencies, ethnic clashes, and urban unrest. Such civil violence particularly affects developing societies, because they are, in general, highly dependent on environmental resources and less able to buffer themselves from the social crises that environmental scarcities cause.

Although this violence affects developing societies most, policymakers and citizens in the industrialized world ignore it at their peril. It can harm rich countries' national interests by threatening their trade and economic relations, entangling them in complex humanitarian emergencies, provoking distress migrations, and destabilizing pivotal countries in the developing world.

In South Africa, for example, severe land, water, and fuelwood scarcities in the former black homelands have helped drive millions of poor blacks into squatter settlements around the major cities. The settlements are often constructed on the worst urban land, in depressions prone to flooding, on hillsides vulnerable to slides, or near heavily polluting industries. Scarcities of land, water, and fuelwood in these settlements help provoke interethnic rivalries and violent feuds among settlement warlords and their followers. This strife jeopardizes the country's transition to democratic stability and prosperity.

In Pakistan, shortages and maldistribution of good land, water, and forests in the countryside have encouraged millions of the rural poor to migrate into major cities, such as Karachi and Hyderabad. The conjunction of this in-migration with high fertility rates is causing city populations to grow at an astonishing 4 to 5 percent a year, producing fierce competition—and

From *Environment, Scarcity and Violence* (Princeton: Princeton University Press, 1999), chapter 2.

often violence—among ethnic groups over land, basic services, and political and economic power. This turmoil exacts a great toll on the national economy.

In Chiapas, Mexico, Zapatista insurgents rose against land scarcity and insecure land tenure caused by ancient inequalities in land distribution, by rapid population growth among groups with the least land, and by changes in laws governing land access. The insurgency rocked Mexico to the core, helped trigger a peso crisis, and reminded the world that Mexico remains —despite the pretenses of the country's economic elites—a poor and profoundly unstable developing country.

The Critical Role of Environmental Resources

It is easy for the billion-odd people living in rich countries to forget that the well-being of about half of the world's population of 6.0 billion remains directly tied to local natural resources. Sixty to seventy percent of the world's poor people live in rural areas, and most depend on agriculture for their main income; a large majority of these people are smallholder farmers, including many who are semisubsistence (which means they survive mainly by eating what they grow). Over 40 percent of people on the planet—some 2.4 billion—use fuelwood, charcoal, straw, or cow dung as their main source of energy; 50 to 60 percent rely on these biomass fuels for at least some of their primary energy needs. Over 1.2 billion people lack access to clean drinking water; many are forced to walk far to get what water they can find.

The cropland, forests, and water supplies that underpin the livelihoods of these billions are renewable. Unlike nonrenewable resources such as oil and iron ore, renewables are replenished over time by natural processes. In most cases, if used prudently, they should sustain an adequate standard of living indefinitely. Unfortunately, in many regions where people rely on renewables, they are being depleted or degraded faster than they are being renewed. From Gaza to the Philippines to Honduras, the evidence is stark: aquifers are being overdrawn and salinized, coastal fisheries are disappearing, and steep uplands have been stripped of their forests leaving their thin soils to erode into the sea.

This environmental scarcity helps generate chronic, diffuse, subnational violence—exactly the kind of violence that bedevils conventional military institutions. Around the world, we see conventional armies pinned down and often utterly impotent in the face of interethnic violence or attacks by ragtag bands of lightly armed guerrillas and insurgents. As yet, environmental scarcity is not a major factor behind most of these conflicts, but we can expect it to become a more important influence in coming decades because of larger populations and higher per capita resource consumption rates.

In 1900, when the world's human population was about 1.65 billion, its annual growth was around 10 million; today, with a base of about 6.0 billion, the annual growth is about 80 million. The fourfold increase in total world population since 1900 has combined with much higher per capita consumption of materials and energy to produce huge jumps in global energy consumption, carbon emissions, water use, fish consumption, land degradation, and deforestation.

Currently, the human population is growing by 1.3 percent a year. This figure peaked at about 2.1 percent between 1965 and 1970 and has fallen since then. In recent years, fertility rates have dropped surprisingly sharply in most poor countries; women are having, on average, significantly fewer children. But it is wildly premature to declare, as some commentators have, that the problem of human population growth is behind us. The largest cohorts of girls ever born have yet to reach their reproductive years, which ensures tremendous momentum behind global population growth. Consequently, even under the most optimistic projections, the planet's population will expand by almost a third, or by about 2 billion people, by 2025.

Real economic product per capita is also currently rising by about 1.0 percent a year. Combined with global population growth, Earth's total economic product is therefore increasing by about 2.3 percent annually. With a doubling time of around thirty years, today's global product of about $30 trillion should exceed $50 trillion in today's dollars by 2025.

A large component of this two-thirds growth will be achieved through yet higher consumption of the planet's natural resources. Already, as the geographers R. Kates, B. L. Turner, and W. C. Clark write, "transformed, managed, and utilized ecosystems constitute about half of the ice-free earth; human mobilized material and energy flows rival those of nature."[1] Such changes are certain to increase, because of the ever-greater scale and intensity of human economic activity. We will see a decline in the total area of high-quality cropland, along with the widespread loss of remaining virgin forests. We will also see continued degradation and depletion of rivers, aquifers, and other water resources, and the further decline of wild fisheries.

Regional scarcities of these renewables are already affecting large populations in poor countries. But during the last decade, global environmental problems, especially climate change and stratospheric ozone depletion, have generally received more attention in the popular media in the industrialized world. The social impacts of these problems, in particular of climate change, may eventually be very large, but these impacts will probably not be decisively clear until well into the next century. Moreover, climate change is most likely to have a major effect on societies, not by acting as an isolated environmental pressure, but by interacting with other long-present resource pressures, such as degraded cropland and stressed water supplies.[2] Although global atmospheric problems are important, policymakers, the media, and the public in rich countries should focus more of their attention on regional environmental scarcities of cropland, water, and forests in the developing world.

Sources of Environmental Scarcity

Environmental scarcities usually have complex causes. The depletion and degradation of a resource are a function of the physical vulnerability of the resource, the size of the resource-consuming population, and the technologies and practices this population uses in its consumption behavior. The size of the population and its technologies and practices are, in turn, a result of a wide array of other variables, from women's status to the availability of human and financial capital.

In addition, resource depletion and degradation are together only one of three sources of environmental scarcity. Depletion and degradation produce a decrease in total resource *supply* or, in other words, a decrease in the size of the total resource "pie." But population growth and changes in consumption behavior can also cause greater scarcity by boosting the *demand* for a resource. Thus, if a rapidly growing population depends on a fixed amount of cropland, the amount of cropland per person—the size of each person's slice of the resource pie—falls inexorably. In many countries, resource availability is being squeezed by both these supply and demand pressures.

Finally, scarcity is often caused by a severe imbalance in the distribution of wealth and power that results in some groups in a society getting disproportionately large slices of the resource pie, whereas, others get slices that are too small to sustain their livelihoods. Such unequal distribution—or what I call *structural* scarcity—is a key factor in virtually every case of scarcity contributing to conflict. Often the imbalance is deeply rooted in institutions and class and ethnic relations inherited from the colonial period. It is frequently sustained and reinforced by international economic relations that trap developing countries into dependence on a few raw material exports. It can also be reinforced by heavy external debts that encourage countries to use their most productive environmental resources—such as their best croplands and forests—to generate hard currency rather than to support the most impoverished segments of their populations.

In the past, analysts and policymakers have usually addressed these three sources of scarcity independently. But research shows that supply, demand, and structural scarcities interact and reinforce each other in extraordinarily pernicious ways.

One type of interaction is *resource capture*. It occurs when powerful groups within a society recognize that a key resource is becoming more scarce (due to both supply and demand pressures) and use their power to shift in their favor the laws and institutions governing resource access. This shift imposes severe structural scarcities on weaker groups. Thus, in Chiapas, worsening land scarcities, partly caused by rapid population growth, encouraged powerful land owners and ranchers to exploit weaknesses in the state's land laws in order to seize lands from campesinos and indigenous farmers. Gradually these peasants were forced deeper into the state's lowland rain forest, farther away from the state's economic heartland, and deeper into poverty.

In the Jordan River basin, Israel's critical dependence on groundwater flowing out of the West Bank—a dependence made acute by an increasing Israeli population and salinization of aquifers along the Mediterranean coast—has encouraged Israel to restrict groundwater withdrawals on the West Bank during the occupation. These restrictions have been far more severe for Palestinians than for Israeli settlers. They have contributed to the rapid decline in Palestinian agriculture in the region, to the dependence of Palestinians on day labor within Israel and, ultimately, to rising frustrations in the Palestinian community.

Another kind of interaction, *ecological marginalization*, occurs when a structural imbalance in resource distribution joins with rapid population growth to drive resource-poor people into ecologically marginal areas, such as upland hillsides, areas at risk of desertification, and tropical rain forests. Higher population densities in these vulnerable areas, along with a lack of the capital and knowledge needed to protect local resources, causes local resource depletion, poverty, and eventually further migration, often to cities.

Ecological marginalization affects hundreds of millions of people around the world, across a wide range of geographies and economic and political systems. We see the same process in the Himalayas, Indonesia, Central America, Brazil, Rajasthan, and the Sahel. For example, in the Philippines, an extreme imbalance in cropland distribution between landowners and peasants has interacted with high population growth rates to force large numbers of the landless poor into interior upland regions of the archipelago. There, the migrants use slash-and-burn agriculture to clear land for crops. As more millions arrive from the lowlands, new land becomes hard to find; and as population densities on the steep slopes increase, erosion, landslides, and flash floods become critical. During the 1970s and 1980s, the resulting poverty helped drive many peasants into the arms of the communist New People's Army insurgency that had a stranglehold on upland regions. Poverty also drove countless others into wretched squatter settlements in cities like Manila.

The Importance of Context

Of course, numerous contextual factors have combined with environmental and demographic stress to produce these outcomes. Environmental scarcity is never a sole or sufficient cause of large migrations, poverty, or violence; it always joins with other economic, political, and social factors to produce its effects. * * *

* * *

Although context is important, analysts should avoid swinging to the opposite extreme, in which the causal role of environmental scarcity is entirely subordinated to that of contextual factors. For example, some skeptics claim that environmental scarcity's contribution to conflict merits little independent attention, because scarcity is wholly a result of political, economic, and social factors, such as failed institutions and policies.[3] Since these factors are the ultimate causes of the conflict, policymakers trying to prevent conflict should focus on them and not on the scarcity. But our research has identified three reasons why such arguments are incomplete at best.

First, environmental scarcity is not only influenced by social factors like institutions and policies, it can itself affect these institutions and policies in harmful ways. In other words, we should not assume that institutions and policies, taken together, are a completely independent and external starting point in the causal chain; it turns out that they can be shaped by environmental scarcity, sometimes negatively. * * *

* * *

Second, the degree of environmental scarcity a society experiences is not, as it turns out, wholly a result of economic, political, and social factors, such as failed institutions and policies; it is also partly a function of the particular physical characteristics of the society's surrounding environment. These characteristics are, in some respects, independent of human activities. For instance, the depth of soils in the Filipino uplands prior to land-clearing and the features that make Israel's aquifers vulnerable to salt intrusion are physical "givens" of these environmental resources. Third, once environmental scarcity becomes irreversible (as, for example, when Haiti's vital topsoil washes into the sea), then the scarcity is, almost by definition, an external influence on society. Even if enlightened reform of institutions and policies removes the underlying political and economic causes of the scarcity, because the scarcity itself is irreversible, it will remain a continuing burden on society.

Policymakers will neither adequately understand nor respond to many important cases of civil violence around the world—cases such as the Filipino insurgency or the chronic instability in Haiti—if they do not take into account the independent causal role of environmental scarcity.

Pivotal Countries

* * *

Close study of such cases shows that severe environmental scarcity can constrain local food production, aggravate poverty of marginal groups, spur large migrations, enrich elites that capture resources, deepen divisions among social groups, and undermine a state's moral authority and capacity to govern. Marginal groups that are highly dependent on increasingly scarce resources find themselves trapped in a vise between rising scarcity on one side and institutional and policy failures on the other. These long-term, tectonic stresses can slowly tear apart a poor society's social fabric, causing chronic popular unrest and violence by boosting grievances and changing the balance of power among contending social groups and the state. (Support for this claim comes not only from close qualitative study of multiple cases: statistical analysis of data from over one hundred countries on land degradation, water pollution, and forest loss shows a significant correlation between environmental degradation and civil strife.[4])

Thus, environmental scarcity is mainly an *indirect* cause of violence, and this violence is mainly *internal* to countries. It is not the type of violence that analysts commonly assume will occur when critical resources are scarce—that is, "resource wars" among countries, in which scarcity directly stimulates one country to try to seize the resources of another.

Although this internal violence may not be as conspicuous or dramatic as wars among countries, it may nonetheless have broad implications. Some of the countries worst affected by internal environmental scarcity are *pivotal*; in other words, their stability and well-being profoundly affect broader regional and world security.[5] These countries include South Africa, Mexico, Pakistan, India, and China. India and China deserve particular attention because of their size and importance; together they make up nearly 40 percent of the world's population. Although neither currently exhibits widespread violence in which environmental factors play a role, in both cases, there are clear reasons to believe that environmentally induced violence may be widespread in the future.

India

Since independence, India has often seemed on the brink of disintegration. But it has endured, despite enormous difficulties, and by many measures the country has made real progress in bettering its citizens' lives. Recent economic liberalization has produced a surge of growth and a booming middle class (often estimated at 150 million strong). However, the country's prospects remain uncertain at best.

Although India has reduced its fertility rates significantly, the rate of population growth in 1998 is still high, at about 1.5 percent a year. India's population in 1998 is 975 million, and it expands by some 15 million people annually, which means it adds the equivalent of Indonesia to its population every 14 years. About 700 million of these people live in the countryside, and one-third still lack the income to buy a nutritionally adequate number of calories.[6] The UN's latest low and medium projections for India's population in 2025 are 1.22 and 1.33 billion, respectively.[7]

Already, water scarcities and cropland fragmentation, erosion, and salinization are widespread. Fuelwood shortages, deforestation, and desertification also affect broad tracts of countryside. * * *

Rural resource scarcities and population growth have combined with an inadequate supply of rural jobs and economic liberalization in cities to widen wealth differentials between countryside and urban areas. These differentials propel waves of rural-urban migration. The growth rates of many of India's cities are nearly twice that of the country's population, which means that cities like Delhi, Mumbai, and Bangalore double in size every twenty years. Their infrastructures are overtaxed: Delhi has among the worst urban air pollution in the world, power and water are regularly unavailable, garbage is left in the streets, and the sewage system can handle only a fraction of the city's wastewater.

* * *

China

Population growth and environmental scarcities are also putting extreme pressure on China's populace and government. Most experts and commentators on China have been distracted by the phenomenal economic boom in the country's coastal areas. They have tended to project these trends onto the rest of the country and to neglect the dangers posed by demographic and environmental stresses.[8] But, as with India, the costs of misreading the Chinese situation could be very high. The country has over a fifth of the world's population, a huge military with growing power-projection capability, and unsettled relations with some of its neighbors. The effects of Chinese civil unrest and internal disruption could spread far beyond its borders.

In recent years, China has embarked on an economic and social transition that is almost unimaginably complicated. Countless urgent problems, some small and some very large, must be addressed immediately as the country develops at breakneck speed. Given China's vast population, this transition will be far harder than that of South Korea or Taiwan, two countries that optimistic commentators often consider exemplars. The management demands on the central, provincial, and local Chinese governments are without precedent in human history.

Chinese leaders recognize that unchecked expansion of the country's already huge population—now around 1.25 billion—will make economic development far more difficult. Fertility rates peaked during the Cultural Revolution between 1969 and 1972. Population growth peaked at about 13 million per year in the mid-1990s, as the babies born during the Cultural Revolution reached their reproductive years.

In the late 1980s and early 1990s, specialists tempered their optimism about Chinese ability to bring population growth down to replacement rate.[9] Market liberalization in the countryside had undermined the one-child policy. In rural areas, state coercion seemed less effective, and peasants enriched by market reforms could more easily pay fines levied for having too many children. In some provinces, therefore, it became common for mothers to bear two or more children. More recent evidence, however, suggests that

Chinese authorities have renewed their commitment to limiting population growth. In response to often extremely coercive measures by low-level officials, fertility rates have fallen below two children per woman for the first time.[10] But experts are not sure that this accomplishment can be sustained for long, and even if it is, China's population will continue to grow well into the next century. The UN's current low and medium projections for China's population in 2025 are 1.37 and 1.48 billion, respectively.

Larger populations and higher per capita resource consumption (resulting from economic growth) aggravate regional scarcities of water and land. Water shortages in much of northern and western China are now critical and constrain development.[11] In 1995, the great Yellow River, still referred to as the "sorrow of China" because of its catastrophic floods in years passed, was dry at its mouth for over one hundred days because of upstream withdrawals. The aquifers under Beijing supply 50 percent of the city's water, but their water levels are falling by a meter a year, causing the ground to sink throughout the region as groundwater is extracted. The central government has responded by announcing plans to build a giant canal to move 15 billion metric tons of water annually from a tributary of the Yangtze River in the south to northern regions, including Beijing, a distance of almost fourteen hundred kilometers. If built, this canal will be one of the great engineering feats of human history, cutting across hundreds of geological formations, streams, and rivers; the current plan is to construct an eight-kilometer siphon to suck the water under and past the Yellow River.[12]

* * *

Water scarcity is only one of a host of evermore tangled resource problems in China.[13] At about a tenth of a hectare per capita, cropland availability is among the lowest in the developing world. Several hundred thousand hectares of farmland are lost every year to erosion, salinization, and urban expansion. Tracts of villas and suburban-style homes are gobbling up rich rice fields around major cities. Near many towns and cities, new Special Economic Zones—industrial parks that offer tax and service advantages to foreign investors—sprawl across good farmland. Each new auto-assembly plant, poultry-processing site, or paint factory takes a further chunk of valuable farmland. When these losses are combined with population growth, the amount of cropland per person is falling steadily by 1.5 percent a year.

* * *

We all have a stake in the success of the grand Chinese experiment with economic liberalization. In a land of scarce environmental resources and a still-expanding population, rapid economic growth is essential to provide capital, jobs, and know-how. But this rapid growth itself often worsens the country's underlying resource scarcities and environmental problems, and these problems, in turn, threaten growth. Whether and how China breaks out of this vicious cycle will shape much of human history for decades, if not centuries, to come.

Ingenuity and Adaptation

Some people reading the preceding accounts of India and China will say "nonsense!" They will argue that market reforms and adequate economic growth will enable these countries to manage their problems of population growth, environmental stress, and poverty relatively easily.

These optimists, who are often economists, generally claim that few if any societies face strict limits to population or consumption. Many intervening factors—physical, technological, economic, and social—permit great resilience, variability, and adaptability in human-environmental systems. In particular, they claim, properly functioning economic institutions, especially markets, can provide incentives to encourage conservation, resource substitution, the development of new sources of scarce resources, and technological innovation. Increased global trade allows resource-rich areas to specialize in production of goods (like grain) that are derived from environmental resources, while other areas specialize in nonresource-intensive production, such as services, and high technology. These economic optimists are commonly opposed by neo-Malthusians—often biologists and ecologists—who claim that finite natural resources place strict limits on the growth of human population and consumption both regionally and globally; if these limits are exceeded, poverty and social breakdown result.

The debate between these two camps is now largely sterile. Nevertheless, although neither camp tells the whole story, each grasps a portion of the truth. The economic optimists are right to stress the extraordinary ability of human beings to surmount scarcity and improve their lot. The dominant trend over the past two centuries, they point out, has not been rising scarcity but increasing aggregate wealth. In other words, most important resources have become *less* scarce, at least in economic terms.

The optimists also provide a key insight that we should focus on the supply of human ingenuity in response to increasing resource scarcity rather than on strict resource limits. Many societies adapt well to scarcity without undue hardship to their populations; in fact, they often end up better off than they were before. In these societies, necessity is the mother of invention; they supply enough ingenuity in the form of new technologies and new and reformed social institutions—like efficient markets, clear and enforced property rights, and effective government—to alleviate the effects of scarcity.

The critical question then is, What determines a society's ability to supply this ingenuity? The answer is complex: different countries—depending on their social, economic, political, and cultural characteristics—will respond to scarcity in different ways and, as a result, they will supply varying amounts and kinds of ingenuity.

In the next decades, growing populations, rising per capita resource consumption, and persistent inequalities in resource access guarantee that scarcities of renewables will affect many poor countries with unprecedented severity, speed, and scale. As a result, resource substitution and conservation tasks will be more urgent, complex, and unpredictable, boosting the need for many kinds of ingenuity. In other words, these societies will have to be smarter—technically and socially—in order to maintain or increase their well-being in the face of rising scarcities.

Optimists often make the mistake of assuming that an adequate supply of the right kinds of ingenuity is always assured. But supply will be constrained by a number of factors, including the brain drain out of many poor societies, limited access to capital, and often incompetent bureaucracies, corrupt judicial systems, and weak states. Moreover, markets in developing countries frequently do not work well: property rights are unclear; prices for water, forests, and other common resources do not adjust accurately to reflect rising scarcity; and thus incentives for entrepreneurs to respond to scarcity are inadequate. Most importantly, however, the supply of ingenuity can be restricted by stresses generated by the very resource crises the ingenuity is needed to solve. Scarcity can engender intense rivalries among interest groups and elite factions that impede the development and delivery of solutions to resource problems. It changes the behavior of subgroups within societies by changing their profit and loss calculations in ways that can exacerbate political conflict.

It turns out that we cannot leave to economists the task of predicting the social consequences of severe environmental scarcity. Politics—the sometimes nasty struggle for relative advantage and power among narrow groups—is a key factor affecting whether or not societies adapt successfully to environmental scarcity.

In Haiti, for example, shortages of forests and soil have inflamed competition among social groups; this competition, in turn, obstructs technical and institutional reform. In some cases, powerful groups that profit from high fuel-wood prices have ripped up the seedlings of reforestation projects to keep the supply of fuelwood limited. In the Indian state of Bihar, which has some of the highest population growth rates and rural densities in the country, land scarcity has deepened divisions between landholding and peasant castes, promoting intransigence on both sides that has helped bring land reform to a halt. In South Africa, scarcity-driven migrations into urban areas, and the resulting conflicts over urban environmental resources (such as land and water), have encouraged communities to segment along lines of ethnicity or residential status. This segmentation has shredded networks of trust and eviscerated local institutions. Powerful warlords, linked to Inkatha or the African National Congress, have taken advantage of these dislocations to manipulate group divisions within communities, often producing horrific violence and further institutional breakdown.

Societies like these face a widening "ingenuity gap" as their requirement for ingenuity to deal with environmental scarcity rises while their supply of ingenuity stagnates or drops. A persistent and serious ingenuity gap raises grievances and erodes the moral and coercive authority of government, which boosts the probability of serious civil turmoil and violence. This violence further undermines the society's ability to supply ingenuity. If these processes continue unchecked, the country may fragment as the government becomes enfeebled and peripheral regions come under the control of renegade authorities. Countries with a critical ingenuity gap therefore risk becoming trapped in a vicious cycle, in which severe scarcity further undermines their capacity to mitigate or adapt to scarcity.

In coming decades, we can expect an increasing division of the world into those societies that can keep the ingenuity gap closed—thus adapting to environmental scarcity and avoiding turmoil—and those that cannot. If several pivotal countries fall on the wrong side of this divide, humanity's overall prospects will dramatically worsen. Such a world will be neither environmentally sustainable nor politically stable. The rich will be unable to fully isolate themselves from the crises of the poor, and there will be little prospect of building the sense of global community needed to address the array of grave problems—economic, political, as well as ecological—that humanity faces.

NOTES

1. B. L. Turner II et al., eds., *The Earth as Transformed by Human Action* (Cambridge: Cambridge University Press, 1990), 13.
2. For example, climate change may interact with long-term soil degradation that produces a loss of rooting depth and increased susceptibility of crops to drought. Together, these changes could cause much greater declines in agricultural yields than either would produce by itself.
3. For an argument that stresses the importance of such factors, see Ronnie Lipschutz, "Environmental Conflict and Environmental Determinism: The Relative Importance of Social and Natural Factors," in *Conflict and the Environment*, ed. Nils Petter Gleditsch (Dordrecht, The Netherlands: Kluer, 1997), 35–50; see also Wenche Hauge and Tanja Ellingsen, "Beyond Environmental Scarcity: The Casual Pathways to Conflict," *Journal of Peace Research* 35, no. 3 (1998):299–317.
4. Hauge and Ellingsen, "Beyond Environmental Scarcity."
5. For a definition, see Robert Chase, Emily Hill, and Paul Kennedy, "Pivotal States and U.S. Strategy," *Foreign Affairs* 75, no. 1 (1996):33–51.
6. Robert Repetto, *The "Second India" Revisited: Population, Poverty, and Environmental Stress over Two Decades* (Washington, D.C.: World Resources Institute, 1994), 5.
7. United Nations Population Division, *World Population Prospects: The*

1996 Revision, Demographic Indicators 1950–2050. Diskettes 1–4 (New York: United Nations, 1996); see also Leela Visaria and Pravin Visaria, *Prospective Population Growth and Policy Options for India, 1991–2101* (New York: Population Council, 1996), 6.

8. See, for example, Barber Conable and David Lampton, "China: The Coming Power," *Foreign Affairs* 72, no. 5 (92/93):133–49. In their assessment of the pressures on contemporary China, the authors devote one-half sentence to these stresses. Even commentators who are skeptical about China's rise neglect ecological issues. See Robert Dujarric, "No Solid Foundations: China's Prospects of Becoming a Great Power," *Internationale Politik und Gesellschaft*, 3 (1997):276–90.

9. Griffith Feeney et al., "Recent Fertility Dynamics in China: Results from the 1987 One Percent Population Survey," *Population and Development Review* 15, no. 2 (1989):297–321; Shanti Conly and Sharon Camp, *China's Family Planning Program: Challenging the Myths*, Country Study Series, No. 1 (Washington, D.C.: Population Crisis Committee, 1992).

10. Nicholas Kristof, "China's Crackdown on Births: A Stunning, and Harsh, Success," *New York Times*, 25 April 1993, p. A1, national edition.

11. Elizabeth Economy, *Reforms and Resources: The Implications for State Capacity in the People's Republic of China*, Occasional Paper of the Project on Environmental Scarcities, State Capacity and Civil Violence (Cambridge, Mass.: American Academy of Arts and Sciences and the University of Toronto, 1997).

12. Patrick Tyler, "Huge Water Project Would Supply Beijing by 800-Mile Aqueduct." *New York Times*, 19 July 1994, p. A8, national edition.

13. Vaclav Smil, *China's Environmental Crisis: An Inquiry into the Limits of National Development* (Armonk, N.Y.: M.E. Sharpe, 1993).

10 *Principles: The Coming of a Democratic Century?*

At the beginning of the 1990s there was near euphoria about the global triumph of democracy. From the crumbling of the Berlin Wall, to the defeat of a pro-communist restorative coup in Russia, to the election of Nelson Mandela as president of a post-apartheid South Africa, to the first free elections in Nicaragua's history, democracy seemed on the march. However, as the 1990s went on, amidst such horrors and setbacks as ethnic cleansing in the former Yugoslavia, genocide in Rwanda, further human rights violations in China, and a very mixed record for Russian democracy, the prospects for global democracy seemed much more uncertain.

The first two articles in this chapter present two contrasting views of these prospects. Indeed, no two articles in the field have attracted more attention and debate in recent years. Francis Fukuyama's "The End of History?" is the quintessential statement of the triumph of democracy, that the 1990s witnessed not just the end of the Cold War but "the universalization of Western liberal democracy as the final form of human government." Samuel Huntington's "The Clash of Civilizations?" is much less bullish, seeing in "the great divisions among humankind," with their deep cultural and historical roots, "the battle lines for the future."

The U.S. interest in global democracy is connected most closely to American principles and the democratic idealist tradition that right should be given priority over might. In addition, as articulated most strongly in "democratic peace" theories, the global spread of democracy makes for a safer and more peaceful world because although democracies fight wars against nondemocracies, democracies do not fight against each other. Michael Doyle is one of the leading proponents of democratic peace theory; one of his articles is included herein. Critics, though, such as Edward Mansfield and Jack Snyder, question the validity of democratic peace theory. This debate is hardly just a theoretical matter given the importance of democracy promotion to U.S. foreign policy.

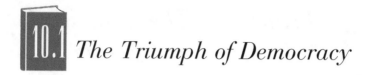

The Triumph of Democracy

Francis Fukuyama

The End of History?

In watching the flow of events over the past decade or so, it is hard to avoid the feeling that something very fundamental has happened in world history. The past year has seen a flood of articles commemorating the end of the Cold War, and the fact that "peace" seems to be breaking out in many regions of the world. Most of these analyses lack any larger conceptual framework for distinguishing between what is essential and what is contingent or accidental in world history, and are predictably superficial. If Mr. Gorbachev were ousted from the Kremlin or a new Ayatollah proclaimed the millennium from a desolate Middle Eastern capital, these same commentators would scramble to announce the rebirth of a new era of conflict.

And yet, all of these people sense dimly that there is some larger process at work, a process that gives coherence and order to the daily headlines. The twentieth century saw the developed world descend into a paroxysm of ideological violence, as liberalism contended first with the remnants of absolutism, then bolshevism and fascism and finally an updated Marxism that threatened to lead to the ultimate apocalypse of nuclear war. But the century that began full of self-confidence in the ultimate triumph of Western liberal democracy seems at its close to be returning full circle to where it started: not to an "end of ideology" or a convergence between capitalism and socialism, as earlier predicted, but to an unabashed victory of economic and political liberalism.

The triumph of the West, of the Western *idea*, is evident first of all in the total exhaustion of viable systematic alternatives to Western liberalism. In the past decade, there have been unmistakable changes in the intellectual climate of the world's two largest communist countries, and the beginnings of significant reform movements in both. But this phenomenon extends beyond high politics and it can be seen also in the ineluctable spread of consumerist Western culture in such diverse contexts as the peasants' markets and color television sets now omnipresent throughout China, the cooperative restaurants and clothing stores opened in the past year in Moscow,

From *National Interest*, no. 16 (summer 1989).

the Beethoven piped into Japanese department stores, and the rock music enjoyed alike in Prague, Rangoon, and Tehran.

What we may be witnessing is not just the end of the Cold War, or the passing of a particular period of postwar history, but the end of history as such: that is, the end point of mankind's ideological evolution and the universalization of Western liberal democracy as the final form of human government. This is not to say that there will no longer be events to fill the pages of *Foreign Affairs*'s yearly summaries of international relations, for the victory of liberalism has occurred primarily in the realm of ideas or consciousness and is as yet incomplete in the real or material world. But there are powerful reasons for believing that it is the ideal that will govern the material world *in the long run*. To understand how this is so, we must first consider some theoretical issues concerning the nature of historical change.

* * *

III

Have we in fact reached the end of history? Are there, in other words, any fundamental "contradictions" in human life that cannot be resolved in the context of modern liberalism, that would be resolvable by an alternative political-economic structure? If we accept the idealist premises laid out above, we must seek an answer to this question in the realm of ideology and consciousness. Our task is not to answer exhaustively the challenges to liberalism promoted by every crackpot messiah around the world, but only those that are embodied in important social or political forces and movements, and which are therefore part of world history. For our purposes, it matters very little what strange thoughts occur to people in Albania or Burkina Faso, for we are interested in what one could in some sense call the common ideological heritage of mankind.

In the past century, there have been two major challenges to liberalism, those of fascism and of communism. The former[1] saw the political weakness, materialism, anomie, and lack of community of the West as fundamental contradictions in liberal societies that could only be resolved by a strong state that forged a new "people" on the basis of national exclusiveness. Fascism was destroyed as a living ideology by World War II. This was a defeat, of course, on a very material level, but it amounted to a defeat of the idea as well. What destroyed fascism as an idea was not universal moral revulsion against it, since plenty of people were willing to endorse the idea as long as it seemed the wave of the future, but its lack of success. After the war, it seemed to most people that German fascism as well as its other European and Asian variants were bound to self-destruct. There was no material reason why new fascist movements could not have sprung up again after the war in other locales, but for the fact that expansionist ultranationalism, with its promise of unending conflict leading to disastrous military defeat, had completely lost its appeal. The ruins of the Reich chancellory as well as the atomic bombs dropped on Hiroshima and Nagasaki killed this ideology on the level of consciousness as well as materially, and all of the proto-fascist movements spawned by the German and Japanese examples like the Peronist movement in Argentina or Subhas Chandra Bose's Indian National Army withered after the war.

The ideological challenge mounted by the other great alternative to liberalism, communism, was far more serious. Marx, speaking Hegel's language, asserted that liberal society contained a fundamental contradiction that could not be resolved within its context, that between capital and labor, and this contradiction has constituted the chief accusation against liberalism ever since. But surely, the class issue has actually been successfully resolved in the West. As Kojève (among others) noted, the egalitarianism of modern America represents the essential achievement of the classless society envisioned by Marx. This is not to say that there are not rich people and poor people in the United States, or that the gap between them has not grown in recent years. But the root causes of economic inequality do not have to do with the underlying legal and social structure of our society, which remains fundamentally egalitarian and moderately redistributionist, so much as with the cultural and social characteristics of the groups that make it up, which are in turn the historical legacy of premodern conditions. Thus black poverty in the United States is not the inherent product of liberalism, but is rather the "legacy of slavery and racism" which persisted long after the formal abolition of slavery.

∗ ∗ ∗

If we admit for the moment that the fascist and communist challenges to liberalism are dead, are there any other ideological competitors left? Or put another way, are there contradictions in liberal society beyond that of class that are not resolvable? Two possibilities suggest themselves, those of religion and nationalism.

The rise of religious fundamentalism in recent years within the Christian, Jewish, and Muslim traditions has been widely noted. One is inclined to say that the revival of religion in some way attests to a broad unhappiness with the impersonality and spiritual vacuity of liberal consumerist societies. Yet while the emptiness at the core of liberalism is most certainly a defect in the ideology—indeed, a flaw that one does not need the perspective of religion to recognize[2]—it is not at all clear that it is remediable through politics. Modern liberalism itself was historically a consequence of the weakness of religiously-based, societies which, failing to agree on the nature of the world's nationalist movements do not have a political program beyond the negative desire of independence *from* some other group or people, and do not offer anything like a comprehensive agenda for socio-economic organization. As such, they are compatible with doctrines and ideologies that do offer such agendas. While they may constitute a source of conflict for liberal societies, this conflict does not arise from liberalism itself so much as from the fact that the liberalism in question is incomplete. Certainly a great deal of the world's ethnic and nationalist tension can be explained in terms of peoples who are forced to live in unrepresentative political systems that they have not chosen.

While it is impossible to rule out the sudden appearance of new ideologies or previously unrecognized contradictions in liberal societies, then, the present world seems to confirm that the fundamental principles of sociopolitical organization have not advanced terribly far since 1806. Many of the wars and revolutions fought since that time have been undertaken in the name of ideologies which claimed to be more advanced than liberalism, but whose pretensions were ultimately unmasked by history. In the meantime, they have helped to spread the universal homogenous state to the point where it could have a significant effect on the overall character of international relations.

*   *   *

V

The passing of Marxism-Leninism first from China and then from the Soviet Union will mean its death as a living ideology of world historical significance. For while there may be some isolated true believers left in places like Managua, Pyongyang, or Cambridge, Massachusetts, the fact that there is not a single large state in which it is a going concern undermines completely its pretensions to being in the vanguard of human history. And the death of this ideology means the growing "Common Marketization" of international relations, and the diminution of the likelihood of large-scale conflict between states.

This does not by any means imply the end of international conflict *per se.* For the world at that point would be divided between a part that was historical and a part that was post-historical. Conflict between states still in history, and between those states and those at the end of history, would still be possible. There would still be a high and perhaps rising level of ethnic and nationalist violence, since those are impulses incompletely played out, even in parts of the post-historical world. Palestinians and Kurds, Sikhs and Tamils, Irish Catholics and Walloons, Armenians and Azeris, will continue to have their unresolved grievances. This implies that terrorism and wars of national liberation will continue to be an important item on the international agenda. But large-scale conflict must involve large states still caught in the grip of history, and they are what appear to be passing from the scene.

The end of history will be a very sad time. The struggle for recognition, the willingness to risk one's life for a purely abstract goal, the worldwide ideological struggle that called forth daring, courage, imagination, and idealism, will be replaced by economic calculation, the endless solving of technical problems, environmental concerns, and the satisfaction of sophisticated consumer demands. In the post-historical period there will be neither art nor philosophy, just the perpetual caretaking of the museum of human history. I can feel in myself, and see in others around me, a powerful nostalgia for the time when history existed. Such nostalgia, in fact, will continue to fuel competition and conflict even in the post-historical world for some time to come. Even though I recognize its inevitability, I have the most ambivalent feelings for the civilization that has been created in Europe since 1945, with its north Atlantic and Asian offshoots. Perhaps this very prospect of centuries of boredom at the end of history will serve to get history started once again.

NOTES

1. I am not using the term "fascism" here in its most precise sense, fully aware of the frequent misuse of this term to denounce anyone to the right of the user. "Fascism" here denotes any organized ultranationalist movement with universalistic pretensions—not universalistic with regard to its nationalism, of course, since the latter is exclusive by definition, but with regard to the movement's belief in its right to rule other people. Hence Imperial Japan would qualify as fascist while former strongman Stoessner's Paraguay or Pinochet's Chile would not. Obviously fascist ideologies cannot be universalistic in the sense of Marxism or liberalism, but the structure of the doctrine can be transferred from country to country.
2. I am thinking particularly of Rousseau and the Western philosophical tradition that flows from him that was highly critical of Lockean or Hobbesian liberalism, though one could criticize liberalism from the standpoint of classical political philosophy as well.

 *Ongoing Threats to Democracy*

SAMUEL P. HUNTINGTON
The Clash of Civilizations?

The Next Pattern of Conflict

World politics is entering a new phase, and intellectuals have not hesitated to proliferate visions of what it will be—the end of history, the return of traditional rivalries between nation states, and the decline of the nation state from the conflicting pulls of tribalism and globalism, among others. Each of these visions catches aspects of the emerging reality. Yet they all miss a crucial, indeed a central, aspect of what global politics is likely to be in the coming years.

It is my hypothesis that the fundamental source of conflict in this new world will not be primarily ideological or primarily economic. The great divisions among humankind and the dominating source of conflict will be cultural. Nation states will remain the most powerful actors in world affairs, but the principal conflicts of global politics will occur between nations and groups of different civilizations. The clash of civilizations will dominate global politics. The fault lines between civilizations will be the battle lines of the future.

* * *

The Nature of Civilizations

During the cold war the world was divided into the First, Second and Third Worlds. Those divisions are no longer relevant. It is far more meaningful now to group countries not in terms of their political or economic systems or in terms of their level of economic development but rather in terms of their culture and civilization.

What do we mean when we talk of a civilization? A civilization is a cultural entity. Villages, regions, ethnic groups, nationalities, religious

From *Foreign Affairs* 72.3 (summer 1993).

groups, all have distinct cultures at different levels of cultural heterogeneity. The culture of a village in southern Italy may be different from that of a village in northern Italy, but both will share in common Italian culture that distinguishes them from German villages. European communities, in turn, will share cultural features that distinguish them from Arab or Chinese communities. Arabs, Chinese and Westerners, however, are not part of any broader cultural entity. They constitute civilizations. A civilization is thus the highest cultural grouping of people and the broadest level of cultural identity people have short of that which distinguishes humans from other species. It is defined both by common objective elements, such as language, history, religion, customs, institutions, and by the subjective self-identification of people. People have levels of identity: a resident of Rome may define himself with varying degrees of intensity as a Roman, an Italian, a Catholic, a Christian, a European, a Westerner. The civilization to which he belongs is the broadest level of identification with which he intensely identifies. People can and do redefine their identities and, as a result, the composition and boundaries of civilizations change.

* * *

Why Civilizations Will Clash

Civilization identity will be increasingly important in the future, and the world will be shaped in large measure by the interactions among seven or eight major civilizations. These include Western, Confucian, Japanese, Islamic, Hindu, Slavic-Orthodox, Latin American and possibly African civilization. The most important conflicts of the future will occur along the cultural fault lines separating these civilizations from one another.

Why will this be the case?

First, differences among civilizations are not only real; they are basic. Civilizations are differentiated from each other by history, language, culture, tradition and, most important, religion. The people of different civilizations have different views on the relations between God and man, the individual and the group, the citizen and the state, parents and children, husband and wife, as well as differing views of the relative importance of rights and responsibilities, liberty and authority, equality and hierarchy. These differences are the product of centuries. They will not soon disappear. They are far more fundamental than differences among political ideologies and political regimes. Differences do not necessarily mean conflict, and conflict does not necessarily mean violence. Over the centuries, however, differences among civilizations have generated the most prolonged and the most violent conflicts.

Second, the world is becoming a smaller place. The interactions between peoples of different civilizations are increasing; these increasing interactions intensify civilization consciousness and awareness of differences between civilizations and commonalities within civilizations. North African immigration to France generates hostility among Frenchmen and at the same time increased receptivity to immigration by "good" European Catholic Poles. * * *

The interactions among peoples of different civilizations enhance the civilization-consciousness of people that, in turn, invigorates differences and animosities stretching or thought to stretch back deep into history.

Third, the processes of economic modernization and social change throughout the world are separating people from longstanding local identities. They also weaken the nation state as a source of identity. In much of the world religion has moved in to fill this gap, often in the form of movements that are labeled "fundamentalist." Such movements are found in Western Christianity, Judaism, Buddhism and Hinduism, as well as in Islam. In most countries and most religions the people active in fundamentalist movements are young, college-educated, middle-class technicians, professionals and business persons. The "unsecularization of the world," George Weigel has remarked, "is one of the dominant social facts of life in the late twentieth century." The revival of religion, "la revanche de Dieu," as Gilles Kepel labeled it, provides a basis for identity and commitment that transcends national boundaries and unites civilizations.

Fourth, the growth of civilization-consciousness is enhanced by the dual role of the West. On the one hand, the West is at a peak of power. At the same time, however, and perhaps as a result, a return to the roots phenomenon is occurring among non-Western civilizations. Increasingly one hears references to trends toward a turning inward and "Asianization" in Japan, the end of the Nehru legacy and the "Hinduization" of India, the failure of Western ideas of socialism and nationalism and hence "re-Islamization" of the Middle East, and now a debate over Westernization versus Russianization in Boris Yeltsin's country. A West at the peak of its power confronts non-Wests that increasingly have the desire, the will and the resources to shape the world in non-Western ways.

* * *

Fifth, cultural characteristics and differences are less mutable and hence less easily compromised and resolved than political and economic ones. In the former Soviet Union, communists can become democrats, the rich can become poor and the poor rich, but Russians cannot become Estonians and Azeris cannot become Armenians. In class and ideological conflicts, the key question was "Which side are you on?" and people could and did choose sides and change sides. In conflicts between civilizations, the question is "What are you?" That is a given that cannot be changed. And as we know, from Bosnia to the Caucasus to the Sudan, the wrong answer to that question can mean a bullet in the head. * * *

Finally, economic regionalism is increasing. The proportions of total trade that were intraregional rose between 1980 and 1989 from 51 percent to 59 percent in Europe, 33 percent to 37 percent in East Asia, and 32 percent to 36 percent in North America. The importance of regional economic blocs is likely to continue to increase in the future. On the one hand, successful economic regionalism will reinforce civilization-consciousness. On the other hand, economic regionalism may succeed only when it is rooted in a common civilization.

* * *

As people define their identity in ethnic and religious terms, they are likely to see an "us" versus "them" relation existing between themselves and people of different ethnicity or religion. The end of ideologically defined states in Eastern Europe and the former Soviet Union permits traditional ethnic identities and animosities to come to the fore. Differences in culture and religion create differences over policy issues, ranging from human rights to immigration to trade and commerce to the environment. Geographical propinquity gives rise to conflicting territorial claims from Bosnia to Mindanao. Most important, the efforts of the West to promote its values of democracy and liberalism as universal values, to maintain its military predominance and to advance its economic interests engender countering responses from other civilizations. Decreasingly able to mobilize support and form coalitions on the basis of ideology, governments and groups will increasingly attempt to mobilize support by appealing to common religion and civilization identity.

The clash of civilizations thus occurs at two levels. At the micro-level, adjacent groups along the fault lines between civilizations struggle, often violently, over the control of territory and each other. At the macro-level, states from different civilizations compete for relative military and economic power, struggle over the control of international institutions and third parties, and competitively promote their particular political and religious values.

* * *

The West Versus the Rest

The West is now at an extraordinary peak of power in relation to other civilizations. Its superpower opponent has disappeared from the map. Military conflict among Western states is unthinkable, and Western military power is unrivaled. Apart from Japan, the West faces no economic challenge. It dominates international political and security institutions and with Japan international economic institutions. Global political and security issues are effectively settled by a directorate of the United States, Britain and France, world economic issues by a directorate of the United States, Germany and Japan, all of which maintain extraordinarily close relations with each other to the exclusion of lesser and largely non-Western countries. Decisions made at the U.N. Security Council or in the International Monetary Fund that reflect the interests of the West are presented to the world as reflecting the desires of the world community. The very phrase "the world community" has become the euphemistic collective noun (replacing "the Free World") to give global legitimacy to actions reflecting the interests of the United States and other Western powers.[1] * * *

Differences in power and struggles for military, economic and institutional power are thus one source of conflict between the West and other civilizations. Differences in culture, that is basic values and beliefs, are a second source of conflict. V. S. Naipaul has argued that Western civilization is the "universal civilization" that "fits all men." At a superficial level much of Western culture has indeed permeated the rest of the world. At a more basic level, however, Western concepts differ fundamentally from those prevalent in other civilizations. Western ideas of individualism, liberalism, constitutionalism, human rights, equality, liberty, the rule of law, democracy, free markets, the separation of church and state, often have little resonance in Islamic, Confucian, Japanese, Hindu, Buddhist or Orthodox cultures. Western efforts to propagate such ideas produce instead a reaction against "human rights imperialism" and a reaffirmation of indigenous values, as can be seen in the support for religious fundamentalism by the younger generation in non-Western cultures. The very notion that there could be a "universal civilization" is a Western idea, directly at odds with the particularism of most Asian societies and their emphasis on what distinguishes one people from another. Indeed, the author of a review of 100 comparative studies of values in different societies concluded that "the values that are most important in the West are least important worldwide."[2] In the political realm, of course, these differences are most manifest in the efforts of the United States and other Western powers to induce other peoples to adopt Western ideas concerning democracy and human rights. Modern democratic government originated in the West. When it has developed in non-Western societies it has usually been the product of Western colonialism or imposition.

The central axis of world politics in the future is likely to be, in Kishore Mahbubani's phrase, the conflict between "the West and the Rest" and the responses of non-Western civilizations to Western power and values.[3] Those responses generally take one or a combination of three forms. At one extreme, non-Western states can, like Burma and North Korea, attempt to pursue a course of isolation, to insulate their societies from penetration or "corruption" by the West, and, in effect, to opt out of participation in the Western-dominated global community. The costs of this course, however, are high, and few states have pursued it exclusively. A second alternative, the equivalent of "band-wagoning" in international relations theory, is to attempt to join the West and accept its values and institutions. The third alternative is to attempt to "balance" the West by developing economic and military power and cooperating with other non-Western societies against the

West, while preserving indigenous values and institutions; in short, to modernize but not to Westernize.

* * *

The Confucian-Islamic Connection

The obstacles to non-Western countries joining the West vary considerably. They are least for Latin American and East European countries. They are greater for the Orthodox countries of the former Soviet Union. They are still greater for Muslim, Confucian, Hindu and Buddhist societies. Japan has established a unique position for itself as an associate member of the West: it is in the West in some respects but clearly not of the West in important dimensions. Those countries that for reason of culture and power do not wish to, or cannot, join the West compete with the West by developing their own economic, military and political power. They do this by promoting their internal development and by cooperating with other non-Western countries. The most prominent form of this cooperation is the Confucian-Islamic connection that has emerged to challenge Western interests, values and power.

* * *

Implications for the West

This article does not argue that civilization identities will replace all other identities, that nation states will disappear, that each civilization will become a single coherent political entity, that groups within a civilization will not conflict with and even fight each other. This paper does set forth the hypotheses that differences between civilizations are real and important; civilization-consciousness is increasing; conflict between civilizations will supplant ideological and other forms of conflict as the dominant global form of conflict; international relations, historically a game played out within Western civilization, will increasingly be de-Westernized and become a game in which non-Western civilizations are actors and not simply objects; successful political, security and economic international institutions are more likely to develop within civilizations than across civilizations; conflicts between groups in different civilizations will be more frequent, more sustained and more violent than conflicts between groups in the same civilization; violent conflicts between groups in different civilizations are the most likely and most dangerous source of escalation that could lead to global wars; the paramount axis of world politics will be the relations between "the West and the Rest"; the elites in some torn non-Western countries will try to make their countries part of the West, but in most cases face major obstacles to accomplishing this; a central focus of conflict for the immediate future will be between the West and several Islamic-Confucian states.

This is not to advocate the desirability of conflicts between civilizations. It is to set forth descriptive hypotheses as to what the future may be like. If these are plausible hypotheses, however, it is necessary to consider their implications for Western policy. These implications should be divided between short-term advantage and long-term accommodation. In the short term it is clearly in the interest of the West to promote greater cooperation and unity within its own civilization, particularly between its European and North American components; to incorporate into the West societies in Eastern Europe and Latin America whose cultures are close to those of the West; to promote and maintain cooperative relations with Russia and Japan; to prevent escalation of local inter-civilization conflicts into major inter-civilization wars; to limit the expansion of the military strength of Confucian and Islamic states; to moderate the reduction of Western military capabilities and maintain military superiority in East and Southwest Asia; to exploit differences and conflicts among Confucian and Islamic states; to support in other civilizations groups sympathetic to Western values and interests; to strengthen international institutions that reflect and legitimate Western interests and values and to promote the involvement of non-Western states in those institutions.

In the longer term other measures would be called for. Western civilization is both Western and modern. Non-Western civilizations have attempted to become modern without becoming Western. To date only Japan has fully succeeded in this quest. Non-Western civilizations will continue to attempt to acquire the wealth, technology, skills, machines and weapons that are part of being modern. They will also attempt to reconcile this modernity with their traditional culture and values. Their economic and military strength relative to the West will increase. Hence the West will increasingly have to accommodate these non-Western modern civilizations whose power approaches that of the West but whose values and interests differ significantly from those of the West. This will require the West to maintain the economic and military power necessary to protect its interests in relation to these civilizations. It will also, however, require the West to develop a more profound understanding of the basic religious and philosophical assumptions underlying other civilizations and the ways in which people in those civilizations see their interests. It will require an effort to identify elements of commonality between Western and other civilizations. For the relevant future, there will be no universal civilization, but instead a world of different civilizations, each of which will have to learn to coexist with the others.

NOTES

1. Almost invariably Western leaders claim they are acting on behalf of "the world community." One minor lapse occurred during the run-up to the Gulf War. In an interview on "Good Morning America," Dec. 21, 1990, British Prime Minister John Major referred to the ac-

tions "the West" was taking against Saddam Hussein. He quickly corrected himself and subsequently referred to "the world community." He was, however, right when he erred.

2. Harry C. Triandis, *The New York Times*, Dec. 25, 1990, p. 41, and "Cross-Cultural Studies of Individualism and Collectivism," Nebraska Symposium on Motivation, vol. 37, 1989, pp. 41–133.

3. Kishore Mahbubani, "The West and the Rest," *The National Interest*, Summer 1992, pp. 3–13.

10.3 *Democratic Peace Theory*

Michael W. Doyle

An International Liberal Community

Americans have always wanted to stand for something in the world. As liberals, we have wanted to stand for freedom, when we could. In recent times, both Republicans and Democrats have joined in this cause.

* * *

Realist skeptics, however, have denounced the pursuit of liberal ideas in foreign affairs as a dangerous illusion that threatens our security. Instead, they say we should focus on employing our national resources to promote our power in a world where nothing but self-help and the balancing of power against power will assure our security.[1] Radical skeptics, on the other hand, have portrayed liberal foreign affairs as little more than a cloak for imperialism.[2] Both sets of critics have identified actual dangers in liberal foreign policy.

What the skeptics miss, however, is the successful establishment of a liberal community of nations, and in missing the liberal community, they miss what appears to be the single best hope for the growth of a stable, just, and secure international order.

* * *

A Liberal Community of Peace

For almost two centuries liberal countries have tended and, now, liberal democratic countries do tend, to maintain peaceful relations with each other. This is the community's first legacy. Other democracies are our natural allies. We tend to respect and accommodate democratic countries. We negotiate rather than escalate disputes.

During the nineteenth century, the United States and Great Britain en-

From *Rethinking America's Security*, Graham Allison and Gregory F. Treverton, eds. (New York: W. W. Norton, 1992), pp. 307–28.

gaged in nearly continual strife. But after the Reform Bill of 1832 defined actual representation as the formal source of the sovereignty of the British Parliament, Britain and the United States negotiated their disputes despite, for example, severe British grievances against the Northern blockade of the South, with which Britain had close economic ties. Despite severe Anglo-French colonial rivalry, liberal France and liberal Britain formed an entente against illiberal Germany before World War I, and in 1914-15, Italy, the liberal member of the Triple Alliance with Germany and Austria, chose not to fulfill its treaty obligations under the Triple Alliance to support its allies. Instead, Italy joined in an alliance with Britain and France that had the effect of preventing it from having to fight other liberal states, and declared war on Germany and Austria. Despite generations of Anglo-American tension and Britain's wartime restrictions on American trade with Germany, the United States leaned toward Britain and France from 1914 to 1917, before entering World War I on their side.

Liberal states thus appear to exercise peaceful restraint, and a separate peace exists among them. This separate peace provides a political foundation that defines common strategic interests for the United States' crucial alliances with the liberal powers—NATO (North Atlantic Treaty Organization), our Japanese alliance, ANZUS (Australia, New Zealand, United States Treaty Alliance). This foundation resists the corrosive effects of the quarrels with our allies that bedeviled the Carter and Reagan administrations. It also offers the promise of a continuing peace among liberal states and, as the number of liberal states increases, it announces the possibility of global peace this side of the grave and short of a single world empire.

* * *

Liberal Imprudence

Liberalism, as the critics note, also carries with it other legacies. Peaceful restraint only seems to work in the liberals' relations with other liberals. Liberal states have fought numerous wars with nonliberal states.

Many of these wars have been defensive, and thus prudent by necessity. Liberal states have been attacked and threatened by nonliberal states that do not exercise any special restraint in their dealings with liberal states. Authoritarian rulers both stimulate and respond to an international political environment in which conflicts of prestige, of interest, and of pure fear of what other states might do all lead states toward war. War and conquest have thus characterized the careers of many authoritarian rulers and ruling parties, from Louis XIV and Napoleon to Mussolini's Fascists, Hitler's Nazis, and Stalin's Communists.

But we cannot simply blame warfare on the authoritarians or totalitarians, as many of our more enthusiastic politicians would have us do.[3] Although most wars arise out of calculations and miscalculations of interest, misunderstandings, and mutual suspicions, such as those that characterized the origins of World War I, aggression by the liberal state has also characterized a large number of wars. Both France and Britain fought expansionist colonial wars throughout the nineteenth century. The United States fought a similar war with Mexico in 1846–48, waged a war of annihilation against the American Indians, and intervened militarily against sovereign states many times before and after World War II. Liberal states invade weak nonliberal states and display striking distrust in dealings with powerful nonliberal states.

We need therefore to remind ourselves that a "freer world" does not automatically mean "a more peaceful world." Trying to make the world safe for democracy does not necessarily make democracies safe for the world.

On the one hand, democracies are prone to being tempted into aggressive crusades to expand overseas the "free world" of mutual security, civil liberties, private property, and democratic rule, and this has led in the past to enormous suffering and only infrequently to successful transplants of democratic rule to previously nondemocratic countries. Furthermore, we distrust nondemocratic countries, sometimes excessively. We regard their domestic oppression as an inherent sign of aggressive intent and downplay the role of error. * * *

On the other hand, democratic majorities sometimes succumb to bouts of isolationism and appeasement, tempting aggressive states to employ strategies of piecemeal conquest (salami tactics). Self-indulgent majorities thus undermine what can be vital collective security interests.

Foundations

*   *   *

Perpetual Peace, an essay by the eighteenth-century German philosopher Immanuel Kant, helps us understand the effects of democratic republicanism on foreign affairs. In that essay, Kant shows how liberal republics lead to dichotomous international politics: peaceful relations—a "pacific union" among similarly liberal states—and a "state of war" between liberals and nonliberals.

First, Kant argues, republican governments tame the aggressive interests of absolutist monarchies by making government decisions subject to the control of majority representation. They also ingrain the habit of respect for individual rights. Wars then appear as the direct charges on the people's welfare that he and the other liberals thought them to be. Yet these domestic republican restraints do not end war. If they did, liberal states would not be warlike, which is far from the case. They do introduce republican caution, Kant's "hesitation," in place of monarchical caprice. Liberal wars are only fought: for popular, liberal purposes. The historical liberal legacy is laden with popular wars fought to promote freedom, protect private property, or support liberal allies against nonliberal enemies.[4]

Second, in order to see how the pacific union removes the occasion of wars among liberal states and not wars between liberal and nonliberal states, we need to shift our attention from constitutional law to international law. Complementing the constitutional guarantee of caution, international law, according to Kant, adds a second source—a guarantee of respect. The separation of nations is reinforced by the development of separate languages and religions. These further guarantee a world of separate states—an essential condition needed to avoid a "global, soul-less despotism." Yet at the same time, they also morally integrate liberal states: "as culture grows and men gradually move towards greater agreement over their principles, they lead to mutual understanding and peace." As republics emerge (the first source) and as culture progresses, an understanding of the legitimate rights of all citizens and of all republics comes into play, and this, now that caution characterizes policy, sets up the moral foundations for the liberal peace.

Correspondingly, international law highlights the importance of Kantian publicity. Domestically, publicity helps ensure that the officials of republics act according to the principles they profess to hold just and according to the interests of the electors they claim to represent. Internationally, free speech and the effective communication of accurate conceptions of the political life of foreign peoples are essential to establish and preserve the understanding on which the guarantee of respect depends.

Domestically just republics, which rest on consent, presume foreign republics to be also consensual, just, and therefore deserving of accommodation. The experience of cooperation helps engender further cooperative behavior when the consequences of state policy are unclear but (potentially) mutually beneficial. At the same time, liberal states assume that nonliberal states, which do not rest on free consent, are not just. Because nonliberal governments are perceived to be in a state of aggression with their own people, their foreign relations become for liberal governments deeply suspect. Wilhelm II of Imperial Germany may or may not have been aggressive (he was certainly idiosyncratic); liberal democracies such as England, France, and the United States, however, assumed that whatever was driving German policy, reliable democratic, constitutional government was not restraining it. They regarded Germany and its actions with severe suspicion—to which the Reich reacted with corresponding distrust. In short, fellow liberals benefit from a presumption of amity; nonliberals suffer from a presumption of enmity. Both presumptions may be accurate. Each, however, may also be self-fulfilling.

Democratic liberals do not need to assume either that public opinion directly rules foreign policy or that the entire governmental elite is liberal. They can also assume a third possibility: that the elite typically manages public affairs but that potentially nonliberal members of the elite have reason to doubt that antiliberal policies would be electorally sustained and endorsed by the majority of the democratic public.

Lastly, "cosmopolitan law" adds material incentives to moral commitments. The cosmopolitan right to hospitality permits the "spirit of commerce" sooner or later to take hold of every nation, thus creating incentives for states to promote peace and to try to avert war. Liberal economic theory holds that these cosmopolitan ties derive from a cooperative international division of labor and free trade according to comparative advantage. Each economy is said to be better off than it would have been under autarky; each thus acquires an incentive to avoid policies that would lead the other to break these economic ties. Since keeping open markets rests upon the assumption that the next set of transactions will also be determined by prices rather than coercion, a sense of mutual security is vital to avoid security motivated searches for economic autarky. Thus, avoiding a challenge to another liberal state's security or even enhancing each other's security by means of alliance naturally follows economic interdependence.

A further cosmopolitan source of liberal peace is that the international market removes difficult decisions of production and distribution from the direct sphere of state policy. A foreign state thus does not appear directly responsible for these outcomes; states can stand aside from, and to some degree above, these inevitably contentious market rivalries and be ready to step in to resolve crises. The interdependence of commerce and the international contacts of state officials also help create crosscutting transnational ties that serve as lobbies for mutual accommodation. According to modern liberal scholars, international financiers and transnational and transgovernmental organizations create interests in favor of accommodation. Moreover, their variety has ensured that no single conflict sours an entire relationship by setting off a spiral of reciprocated retaliation. Conversely, a sense of suspicion, like that characterizing relations between liberal and nonliberal governments, makes transnational contacts appear subversive. Liberal and nonliberal states then mutually restrict the range of contacts between societies, and this can further increase the prospect that a single conflict will determine an entire relationship.

No single constitutional, international, or cosmopolitan source is alone sufficient. Kantian theory is neither solely institutional nor solely ideological, nor solely economic. But together (and only together) the three specific strands of liberal institutions, liberal ideas, and the transnational ties that follow from them, plausibly connect the characteristics of liberal polities and economies with sustained liberal peace.[5] But in their relations with nonliberal states, liberal states have not escaped from the insecurity caused by anarchy in the world political system considered as a whole.[6] Moreover, the very constitutional restraint, international respect for individual rights, and shared commercial interests that establish grounds for peace among liberal states establish grounds for additional conflict in relations between liberal and nonliberal societies.

* * *

Securing and Expanding the Liberal Community

An important alternative to the balancing of enemies is thus the cultivation of friends. If the actual history of the liberal community is reliable, a better strategy for our foreign relations lies in the development of the liberal community.

* * *

Preserving the Community. Above all, liberal policy should strive to preserve the pacific union of similarly liberal societies. It is not only currently of immense strategic value (being the political foundation of both NATO and the Japanese alliance); it is also the single best hope for the evolution of a peaceful world. Liberals should be prepared, therefore, to defend and formally ally with authentically liberal, democratic states that are subject to threats or actual instances of external attack or internal subversion. We must continue to have no liberal enemies and no unconditional alliances with nonliberal states.

* * *

Managing the Community. Much of our success in alliance management has to be achieved on a multilateral basis. The current need to redefine NATO and the increasing importance of the U.S. relationship with Japan offer us an opportunity to broaden the organization of liberal security. Joining all the democratic states together in a single democratic security organization would secure an important forum for the definition and co-ordination of common interests that stretch beyond the regional concerns of Europe and the Far East.

* * *

Protecting the Community. The liberal community needs to be pro-tected. Two models could fit liberal national strategy designed to protect against the international power of nonliberal states.[7]

If faced with severe threats from the nonliberal world, the liberal com-munity might simply balance the power of nonliberal states by playing divide and rule within the nonliberal camp, triangulating, for example, between Russia and China as the United States did during the 1970s.

If, on the other hand, the liberal community becomes increasingly pre-dominant (or collectively unipolar) as it now appears to be becoming, the liberal community could adopt a more ambitious grand strategy. Arms exports, trade, and aid could reflect the relative degrees of liberal principle that nonliberal domestic and foreign policies incorporate. Liberal foreign policy could be designed to create a ladder of rewards and punishments— a set of balanced incentives, rewarding liberalization and punishing oppression, rewarding accommodation and punishing aggression. This strategy would both satisfy liberal demands for publicity—consistent public legitimation—and create incentives for the progressive liberalization of nonliberal states.

Expanding the Community. There are few direct measures that the liberal world can take to foster the stability, development, and spread of liberal democratic regimes. Many direct efforts, including military intervention and overt or covert funding for democratic movements in other countries, discredit those movements as the foreign interference backfires through the force of local nationalism. * * *

Much of the potential success of a policy designed to foster democracy rests therefore on an ability to shape an economic and political environment that indirectly supports democratic governance and creates pressures for the democratic reform of authoritarian rule.

Politically, there are few measures more valuable than an active human rights diplomacy, which enjoys global legitimacy and (if successful) can assure a political environment that tolerates the sort of dissent that can nourish an indigenous democratic movement.

* * *

Choices in Liberal Foreign Policy

In the years ahead we will need to chart our own national strategy as a liberal democracy faced with threats, but now also with opportunities for new thinking. In order to fulfill the promise of liberal internationalism, we must ensure a foreign policy that tries to reconcile our interests with our principles.

We will need to address the hard choices that no government truly committed to the promotion of human rights can avoid. Acknowledging that there may arise circumstances where international action—even force—is needed, we need strategic thinking that curbs the violent moods of the moment.

We will also need to keep our larger purposes in view. Those committed to freedom have made a bargain with their governments. We need only to live up to it. The major costs of a liberal strategy are borne at home. Not merely are its military costs at the taxpayers' expense, but a liberal foreign policy requires adjustment to a less controlled international political environment—a rejection of the status quo in favor of democratic choice. Tolerating more foreign change requires more domestic change. Avoiding an imperial presence in the Persian Gulf may require a move toward energy independence. Allowing for the economic development of the world's poor calls for an acceptance of international trade adjustment. The home front thus becomes the front line of liberal strategy.

The promises of successful liberal internationalism, however, are large and can benefit all. The pursuit of freedom does not guarantee the maintenance of peace. Indeed, the very invocation of "crusade" as a label for President Reagan's democratic initiative of the 1980s warns us otherwise. But the peaceful intent and restraint to which liberal institutions, principles, and interests have led in relations among liberal democracies suggest the possibility of world peace this side of the grave. They offer the promise of a world peace established by the expansion of the separate peace among liberal societies.

NOTES

1. For an eloquent polemic defending this view, see the fine essay by Mearsheimer (1990). For a thoughtful and thorough critique of the position and prescription, see Ullman (1991), chapter 7.
2. An important account of the many ways in which liberal ideology has served as a cloak for imperialism in U.S. foreign policy can be found in Williams (1962).
3. There are, however, serious studies that show that Marxist regimes have higher military spending per capita than non-Marxist regimes. But this should not be interpreted as a sign of the inherent aggressiveness of authoritarian or totalitarian governments or—with even greater enthusiasm—the inherent and global peacefulness of liberal regimes. Marxist regimes, in particular, represent a minority in the current international system; they are strategically encircled, and, due to their lack of domestic legitimacy, they might be said to "suffer" the twin burden of needing defenses against both external and internal enemies.
4. Kant regards these wars as unjust and warns liberals of their susceptibility to them. At the same time, he argues that each nation "can and ought to" demand that its neighboring nations enter into the pacific union of liberal states.
5. For a more extensive description and analysis of the liberal community, see Doyle (1983a). Streat (1939), pp. 88, 90–92, seems to have been the first to point out (in contemporary foreign relations) the empirical tendency of democracies to maintain peace among themselves, and he made this the foundation of his proposal for (non-Kantan) federal union of the fifteen leading democracies of the 1930s. Recent work by Russett, Maoz, Ray, and Modelski has extended this field into consideration of wider strategies of international reform and the evolution of the international system.

6. For evidence, see Doyle (1983b).
7. For a discussion of strategy toward once-enemies now in a transition zone toward potential friends, see Allison (1988).

REFERENCES

MEARSHEIMER, JOHN J. (1990) Back to the Future: Instability in Europe after the Cold War. *International Security* 15:5–57.

ULLMAN, RICHARD. (1991) *Securing Europe.* Princeton: Princeton University Press.

WILLIAMS, WILLIAM APPLEMAN. (1962) *The Tragedy of American Diplomacy.* New York: W. W. Norton & Co.

DOYLE, MICHAEL. (1983a) Kant, Liberal Legacies, and Foreign Affairs: Part I. *Philosophy and Public Affairs* 12:323–353.

STREIT, CLARENCE. (1939) *Union Now.* New York: Harper and Brothers.

DOYLE, MICHAEL. (1983b) Kant, Legacies, and Foreign Affairs: Part II. *Philosophy and Public Affairs* 12:205–235.

ALLISON, GRAHAM. (1988) Testing Gorbachev. *Foreign Affairs* 67:18–33.

10.4 Democratic Peace?

EDWARD D. MANSFIELD AND JACK SNYDER

Democratization and the Danger of War

One of the best-known findings of contemporary social science is that no democracies have ever fought a war against each other, given reasonably restrictive definitions of democracy and of war.[1] This insight is now part of everyday public discourse and serves as a basis for American foreign policymaking. President Bill Clinton's 1994 State of the Union address invoked the absence of war between democracies as a justification for promoting democratization around the globe. In the week following the U.S. military landing in Haiti, National Security Adviser Anthony Lake reiterated that "spreading democracy . . . serves our interests" because democracies "tend not to abuse their citizens' rights or wage war on one another."[2]

It is probably true that a world where more countries were mature, stable democracies would be safer and preferable for the United States. However, countries do not become mature democracies overnight. More typically, they go through a rocky transitional period, where democratic control over foreign policy is partial, where mass politics mixes in a volatile way with authoritarian elite politics, and where democratization suffers reversals. In this transitional phase of democratization, countries become more aggressive and war-prone, not less, and they do fight wars with democratic states.

The contemporary era shows that incipient or partial democratization can be an occasion for the rise of belligerent nationalism and war.[3] Two pairs of states—Serbia and Croatia, and Armenia and Azerbaijan—have found themselves at war while experimenting with varying degrees of partial electoral democracy. Russia's poorly institutionalized, partial democracy has tense relationships with many of its neighbors and has used military force brutally to reassert control in Chechnya; its electorate cast nearly a quarter of its votes for the party of radical nationalist Vladimir Zhirinovsky.

This contemporary connection between democratization and conflict is no coincidence. Using the same databases that are typically used to study the democratic peace, we find considerable statistical evidence that democratizing states are more likely to fight wars than are mature democracies or

From *International Security* 20.1 (summer 1995): 5–38.

stable autocracies. States like contemporary Russia that make the biggest leap in democratization—from total autocracy to extensive mass democracy— are about twice as likely to fight wars in the decade after democratization as are states that remain autocracies. However, reversing the process of democratization, once it has begun, will not reduce this risk. Regimes that are changing toward autocracy, including states that revert to autocracy after failed experiments with democracy, are also more likely to fight wars than are states whose regime is unchanging.

Moreover, virtually every great power has gone on the warpath during the initial phase of its entry into the era of mass politics. Mid-Victorian Britain, poised between the partial democracy of the First Reform Bill of 1832 and the full-fledged democracy of the later Gladstone era, was carried into the Crimean War by a groundswell of belligerent public opinion. Napoleon III's France, drifting from plebiscitary toward parliamentary rule, fought a series of wars designed to establish its credentials as a liberal, popular, nationalist type of empire. The ruling elite of Wilhelmine Germany, facing universal suffrage but limited governmental accountability, was pushed toward World War I by its escalating competition with middle-class mass groups for the mantle of German nationalism. Japan's "Taisho democracy" of the 1920s brought an era of mass politics that led the Japanese army to devise and sell an imperial ideology with broad-based appeal.[4] In each case, the combination of incipient democratization and the material resources of a great power produced nationalism, truculence abroad, and major war.

Why should democratizing states be so belligerent? The pattern of the democratizing great powers suggests that the problem lies in the nature of domestic political competition after the breakup of the autocratic regime. Elite groups left over from the ruling circles of the old regime, many of whom have a particular interest in war and empire, vie for power and survival with each other and with new elites representing rising democratic forces. Both old and new elites use all the resources they can muster to mobilize mass allies, often through nationalist appeals, to defend their threatened positions and to stake out new ones. However, like the sorcerer's apprentice, these elites typically *find* that their mass allies, once mobilized, are difficult to control. When this happens, war can result from nationalist prestige strategies that hard-pressed leaders use to stay astride their unmanageable political coalitions.[5]

The problem is not that mass public opinion in democratizing states demonstrates an unvarnished, persistent preference for military adventure. On the contrary, public opinion often starts off highly averse to war. Rather, elites exploit their power in the imperfect institutions of partial democracies to create *faits accomplis*, control political agendas, and shape the content of information media in ways that promote belligerent pressure-group lobbies or upwellings of militancy in the populace as a whole.

Once this ideological connection between militant elites and their mass constituents is forged, the state may jettison electoral democracy while re-taining nationalistic, populist rhetoric. As in the failure of Weimar and Taisho democracy, the adverse effects of democratization on war-proneness may even heighten after democracy collapses. Thus, the aftershock of failed democratization is at least one of the factors explaining the link between autocratization and war.

* * *

How Democratization Causes War

Why are democratization and autocratization associated with an increased chance of war? What causal mechanism is at work?* Based on case studies of four great powers during their initial phases of democratization, we argue that threatened elites from the collapsing autocratic regime, many of whom have parochial interests in war and empire, use nationalist appeals to com-pete for mass allies with each other and with new elites. In these circum-stances, the likelihood of war increases due to the interests of some of the elite groups, the effectiveness of their propaganda, and the incentive for weak leaders to resort to prestige strategies in foreign affairs in an attempt to enhance their authority over diverse constituencies. Further, we speculate that transitional regimes, including both democratizing and autocratizing states, share some common institutional weaknesses that make war more likely. At least in some cases, the link between autocratization and war re-flects the success of a ruling elite in using nationalist formulas developed during the period of democratization to cloak itself in populist legitimacy, while dismantling the substance of democracy. In explaining the logic behind these arguments, we draw on some standard theories about the conse-quences of different institutional arrangements for political outcomes.

We illustrate these arguments with some contemporary examples and with cases drawn from four great powers at early stages in the expansion of mass political participation: mid-Victorian Britain, the France of Napo-leon III, Bismarckian and Wilhelmine Germany, and Taisho Japan. * * *

Democratic versus Democratizing Institutions

Well-institutionalized democracies that reliably place ultimate authority in the hands of the average voter virtually never fight wars against each other. Moreover, although mature democracies do fight wars about as frequently as other types of states, they seem to be more prudent: they usually win their wars; they are quicker to abandon strategic overcommitments; and they

---

*   Editor's Note: Autocratization is shifting away from democracy toward autocracy or other nondemocratic rule.

do not fight gratuitous "preventive" wars.[6] Explanations for these tendencies focus variously on the self-interest of the average voter who bears the costs of war, the norms of bargaining and conflict resolution inherent in democracy, the moderating impact of constitutional checks and balances, and the free marketplace of ideas.[7]

However, these happy solutions typically emerge only in the very long run. In the initial stages of expanding political participation, strong barriers prevent the emergence of full-fledged democratic processes and the foreign policy outcomes associated with them. The two main barriers are the weakness of democratic institutions and the resistance of social groups who would be the losers in a process of full-fledged democratization.

Popular inputs into the policymaking process can have wildly different effects, depending on the way that political institutions structure and aggregate those inputs.[8] It is a staple of political science that different institutional rules—for example, proportional representation versus single-member districts, or congressional versus executive authority over tariffs—can produce different political outcomes, even holding constant the preferences of individual voters. In newly democratizing states, the institutions that structure political outcomes may allow for popular participation in the policy process, but the way they channel that input is often a parody of full-fledged democracy. As Samuel Huntington has put it, the typical problem of political development is the gap between high levels of political participation and weak integrative institutions to reconcile the multiplicity of contending claims.[9] In newly democratizing states without strong parties, independent courts, a free press, and untainted electoral procedures, there is no reason to expect that mass politics will produce the same impact on foreign policy as it does in mature democracies.

In all of the democratizing great powers, public inputs were shaped and aggregated in ways that differed from those of mature democracies. In mid-Victorian Britain, rural areas had greater representation than urban areas, the ballot was not secret, and only propertied classes could vote.[10] In rural France under Napoleon III, the local prefect, appointed in Paris, stood at the ballot box and exercised control over voters' choices.[11] In Wilhelmine Germany, the parties that won the elections could not name governmental ministers; rather, they had to use their limited powers over the budget to bargain over policy with ministers named by the kaiser.[12] In Taisho Japan, the electoral franchise was widened, but the choice of who would govern was left to the oligarchs who had founded the Meiji state.[13] And in Russia today almost none of the major institutions of representative government work in a reliable way: constitutional rules change to fit the needs of the moment; constitutional courts take sides on transparently political grounds; elections are postponed or announced on short notice; and political parties are transitory elite cliques, not stable organizations for mobilizing a mass coalition. Moreover, in all of these cases, the political press was to some degree bribed or censored by the government or had not yet institutionalized the objectivity, knowledge, and professionalism needed to create a full and fair public debate.[14]

* * *

Both in the nineteenth century cases and in the contemporary post-communist ones, it is striking that many of the groups with an interest in retarding democratization are also those with a parochial interest in war, military preparation, empire, and protectionism. This is not accidental. Most of the benefits of war, military preparations, imperial conquest, and protectionism—e.g., in career advancement or in protection from foreign economic competition—are disproportionately concentrated in specific groups.[15] Any special interest group, including the military, that derives parochial benefits from a public policy has to feel wary about opening up its affairs to the scrutiny and veto of the average voter, who pays for subsidies to special interests. Whenever the costs of a program are distributed widely, but the benefits are concentrated in a few hands, democratization may put the program at risk.

When autocratic states start to democratize, many of the interests threatened by democratization are military in nature. As Charles Tilly says, "war made the state and the state made war."[16] In early modern Europe, military organizations occupied a privileged position in the state, which was built to serve their needs. Moreover, ruling aristocracies were intertwined with military institutions, so democratization inherently challenged the vested social, economic, and bureaucratic interests of an old elite that was at its core a military elite. Joseph Schumpeter constructed a whole theory of imperialism on the atavistic interests of the military-feudal aristocracy.[17] It is true that middle-class reformers sometimes wanted to build up the state's military power: this was a rallying cry of English radicals in the Crimean War, and of German middle-class officers before 1914. However, they wanted to replace aristocratic dead wood with middle-class rationalizers. Democratization led by proponents of military power was thus nearly as much of a threat to the old army as democratization led by pacifists like Richard Cobden.[18]

* * *

COMPETITIVE MASS MOBILIZATION. In a period of democratization, threatened elite groups have an overwhelming incentive to mobilize allies among the mass of people, but only on their own terms, using whatever special resources they still retain. These have included monopolies of information (e.g., the German Navy's unique "expertise" in making strategic assessments); propaganda assets (the Japanese Army's public relations blitz justifying the invasion of Manchuria); patronage (British Foreign Secretary Palmerston's gifts of foreign service postings to the sons of cooperative journalists); wealth (Krupp steel's bankrolling of mass nationalist and militarist leagues); organizational skills and networks (the Japanese army's exploitation of rural reservist organizations to build a social base); and the ability to use the control of traditional political institutions to shape the political agenda and structure the terms of political bargains (the Wilhelmine ruling elite's deal with the Center Party, eliminating anti-Catholic legislation in exchange for support in the Reichstag on the naval budget).[19]

* * *

Ideology takes on particular significance in the competition for mass support. New participants in the political process may be uncertain of where their political interests lie, because they lack established habits and good information, and are thus fertile ground for ideological appeals. Ideology can yield particularly big payoffs, moreover, when there is no efficient free marketplace of ideas to counter false claims with reliable facts. Elites try out all sorts of ideological appeals, depending on the social position that they need to defend, the nature of the mass group that they want to recruit, and the type of appeals that seem plausible in the given political setting. A nearly universal element in these ideological appeals is nationalism, which has the advantage of positing a community of interest that unites elites and masses, thus distracting attention from class cleavages.

Nationalist appeals have often succeeded even though the average voter was not consistently pro-war or pro-empire.

* * *

Implications for Policy

In light of these findings, it would be hard to maintain a naive enthusiasm for spreading peace by promoting democratization. Pushing nuclear-armed great powers like Russia or China toward democratization is like spinning a roulette wheel, where many of the potential outcomes are likely to be undesirable. However, in most cases the initial steps on the road to democratization will not be produced by the conscious policy of the United States, no matter what that policy may be. The roulette wheel is already spinning for Russia, and perhaps China, regardless of what the West does. Moreover, reversals of democratization are nearly as risky as democratization itself. Consequently, the international community needs a strategy not so much for promoting or reversing democratization as for managing the process in ways that minimize its risks and facilitate smooth transitions.

What might be some of these mitigating conditions, and how might they be promoted? The association of democratization with war is probabilistic. Democratization can lead either to war or to peace, depending on a variety of factors, such as the incentives facing the old elites during the transition process, the structure of the marketplace of foreign policy ideas, the speed and thoroughness of the democratic transition, and the character of the international environment in which democratization occurs. Some of these features may be subject to manipulation by astute democratic reformers and their allies in the international community.

One of the major findings of scholarship on democratization in Latin America is that the process goes most smoothly when elites that are threatened by the transition, especially the military, are given a "golden parachute."[20] Above all, they need a guarantee that if they relinquish power they will not wind up in jail. The history of the democratizing great powers broadens this insight. Democratization was least likely to lead to imprudent aggression in cases where the old elites saw a reasonably bright future for themselves in the new social order. British aristocrats, for example, had more of their wealth invested in commerce and industry than they did in agriculture, so they had many interests in common with the rising middle classes. They could face democratization with relative equanimity. In contrast, Prussia's capital-starved, small-scale Junker landholders had no choice but to rely on agricultural protection and military careers.

In today's context, finding benign, productive employment for the erstwhile Communist *nomenklatura*, military officer corps, nuclear scientists, and smoke stack industrialists ought to rank high on the list of priorities. Policies aimed at giving them a stake in the privatization process and subsidizing the conversion of their skills to new, peaceful tasks in a market economy seem like a step in the right direction. According to some interpretations, Russian Defense Minister Pavel Grachev was eager to use force to solve the Chechen confrontation in order to show that Russian military power was still useful and that increased investment in the Russian army would pay big dividends. Instead of pursuing this reckless path, the Russian military elite needs to be convinced that its prestige, housing, pensions, and technical competence will rise if and only if it transforms itself into a western-style military, subordinate to civilian authority and resorting to force only in accordance with prevailing international norms. Moreover, though old elites need to be kept happy, they also need to be kept weak. Pacts should not prop up the remnants of the authoritarian system, but rather create a niche for them in the new system.

A top priority must also be placed on creating a free, competitive, yet responsible marketplace of ideas in the newly democratizing states. Most of the war-prone democratizing great powers had pluralistic public debates, but the terms of these debates were skewed to favor groups with money, privileged access to the media of communication, and proprietary control over information, ranging from historical archives to intelligence about the military balance. Pluralism is not enough. Without an even playing field, pluralism simply creates the incentive and opportunity for privileged groups to propound self-serving myths, which historically have often taken a nationalist turn. One of the rays of hope in the Chechen affair was the alacrity with which Russian journalists exposed the true costs of the fighting and the lies of the government and the military about it. Though elites should get a golden parachute in terms of their pecuniary interests, they should be given no quarter on the battlefield of ideas. Mythmaking should be held up to the utmost scrutiny by aggressive journalists who maintain their credibility by scrupulously distinguishing fact from opinion and tirelessly verifying their sources. Promoting this kind of journalistic infrastructure is probably the most highly leveraged investment that the West can make in a peaceful democratic transition.

Our research offers inconclusive results about the wisdom of speed and thoroughness in transitions to democracy. On the one hand, we found that states making the big jump from autocracy to democracy were much more war-prone than those moving from autocracy to anocracy. This would seem to favor a strategy of limited goals. On the other hand, the experience of the former Communist states suggests that those that have gone farthest and fastest toward full democracy are less nationalistic and less involved in militarized quarrels. This is a question that needs more research.

Finally, what kind of ruling coalition emerges in the course of democratization depends a great deal on the incentives that are created by the international environment. Both Germany and Japan started on the path toward liberal, stable democratization in the mid-1920s, encouraged in part by abundant opportunities for trade and investment from the advanced democracies and by credible security treaties that defused nationalist scaremongering in domestic politics. But when the international supports for free trade and democracy were yanked out in the late 1920s, their liberal coalitions collapsed. Especially for the case of contemporary China, whose democratization may occur in the context of sharply expanding economic ties to the West, the steadiness of the Western commercial partnership and security presence is likely to play a major role in shaping the incentives of proto-democratic coalition politics.

In the long run, the enlargement of the zone of stable democracy will probably enhance the prospects for peace. But in the short run, there is a lot of work to be done to minimize the dangers of the turbulent transition.

NOTES

1. Michael Doyle, "Liberalism and World Politics," *American Political Science Review*, Vol. 80, No. 4 (December 1986), pp. 1151–1169; Bruce Russett, *Grasping the Democratic Peace* (Princeton: Princeton University Press, 1993). For skeptical views, see David E. Spiro, "The Insignificance of the Liberal Peace," *International Security*, Vol. 19, No. 2 (Fall 1994), pp. 50–86; and Christopher Layne, "Kant or Cant: The Myth of the Democratic Peace," *International Security*, Vol. 19, No. 2

(Fall 1994), pp. 5–49. They are rebutted by Bruce Russett, "The Democratic Peace: 'And Yet It Moves'," *International Security*, Vol. 19, No. 4 (Spring 1995), pp. 164–175.

2. "Transcript of Clinton's Address," *New York Times*, January 26, 1994, p. A17; Anthony Lake, "The Reach of Democracy: Tying Power to Diplomacy," *New York Times*, September 23, 1994, p. A35.

3. Zeev Maoz and Bruce Russett, "Normative and Structural Causes of the Democratic Peace, 1956–1986," *American Political Science Review*, Vol. 87, No. 3 (September 1993), pp. 630, 636; they note that newly created democracies, such as those in Eastern Europe today, may experience conflicts, insofar as their democratic rules and norms are not adequately established. See also Russett, *Grasping the Democratic Peace*, p. 134, on post-Soviet Georgia.

4. Asa Briggs, *Victorian People*, rev. ed. (Chicago: University of Chicago, 1970), chaps. 2–3; Geoff Eley, *Reshaping the German Right* (New Haven: Yale University Press, 1980); Alain Plessis, *De la fête impériale au mur des fédérés, 1852–1871* (Paris: Editions du seuil, 1973), translated as *The Rise and Fall of the Second Empire, 1852–1871* (Cambridge: Cambridge University Press, 1985); Jack Snyder, *Myths of Empire: Domestic Politics and International Ambition* (Ithaca: Cornell University Press, 1991), chaps. 3–5.

5. Hans Ulrich Wehler, *The German Empire*, 1871–1918 (Dover, N.H.: Berg, 1985); Jack S. Levy, "The Diversionary Theory of War: A Critique," In Manus Midlarsky, ed., *Handbook of War Studies* (Boston: Unwin-Hyman, 1989), pp. 259–288.

6. David Lake, "Powerful Pacifists," *American Political Science Review*, Vol. 86, No. 1 (March 1992), pp. 24–37; Snyder, *Myths of Empire*, pp. 49–52; Randall Schweller, "Domestic Structure and Preventive War: Are Democracies More Pacific?" *World Politics*, Vol. 44, No. 2 (January 1992), pp. 235–269.

7. Russett, *Grasping the Democratic Peace*; Miles Kahler, "Introduction," in Miles Kahler, ed., *Liberalization and Foreign Policy* (forthcoming); Jack Snyder, "Democratization, War, and Nationalism in the Post-Communist States," in Celeste Wallander, ed., *The Sources of Russian Conduct after the Cold War* (Boulder: Westview, forthcoming).

8. Kenneth Shepsle, "Studying Institutions: Some Lessons from the Rational Choice Approach," *Journal of Theoretical Politics*, Vol. 1, No. 2 (April 1989), pp. 131–147.

9. Samuel Huntington, *Political Order in Changing Societies* (New Haven: Yale University Press, 1968).

10. D.C. Moore, "The Other Face of Reform," *Victorian Studies*, Vol. 5, No. 1 (September 1961), pp. 7–34.

11. Theodore Zeldin, *The Political System of Napoleon III* (New York: Norton, 1958), pp. 84–85, 91–94, 135.

12. Wehler, *German Empire*.

13. Peter Duus, *Party Rivalry and Political Change in Taisho Japan* (Cambridge, Mass.: Harvard University Press, 1968).

14. Lynn M. Case, *French Opinion on War and Diplomacy during the Second Empire* (Philadelphia: University of Pennsylvania Press, 1954), pp. 2–6; Stephen Koss, *The Rise of the Political Press in England* (London: Hamish Hamilton, 1981), pp. 72–80.

15. Snyder, *Myths of Empire*, pp. 32–35, 49–52; Lance Davis and Robert Huttenback, *Mammon and the Pursuit of Empire: The Political Economy of British Imperialism, 1860–1912* (Cambridge: Cambridge University Press, 1986).

16. Charles Tilly, "Reflections on the History of European State-Making," in Charles Tilly, ed., *The Formation of National States in Europe* (Princeton: Princeton University Press, 1975), p. 42.

17. Joseph Schumpeter, *Imperialism and Social Classes* (New York: Kelly, 1950; orig. ed. 1919).

18. Olive Anderson, *A Liberal State at War: English Politics and Economics during the Crimean War* (New York: St. Martin's, 1967).

19. Snyder, *Myths of Empire*, pp. 103, 140–141, 205; Louise Young, "Mobilizing for Empire: Japan and Manchukuo, 1931–1945," Ph.D. dissertation, Columbia University, 1992.

20. On the importance of bargaining with and co-opting old elites (giving them incentives, a "golden parachute," to depart from power), see the literature summarized in Doh Chull Shin, "On the Third Wave of Democratization: A Synthesis and Evaluation of Recent Theory and Research," *World Politics*, Vol. 47, No. 1 (October 1994), pp. 135–170, esp. 161–163.

Credits